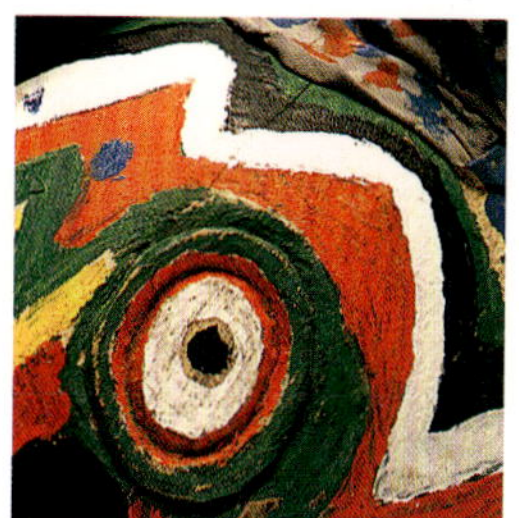

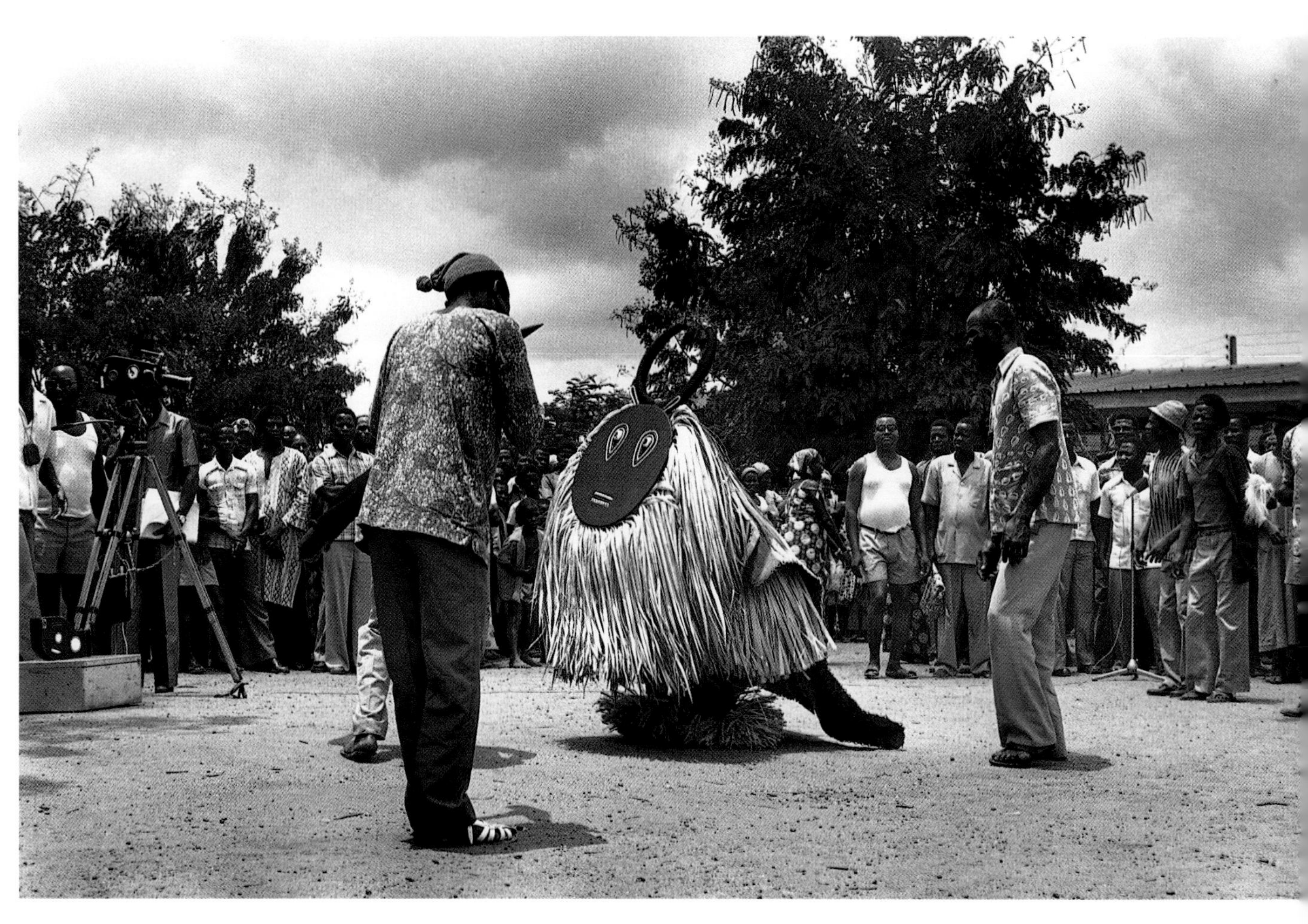

VISIONS OF AFRICA

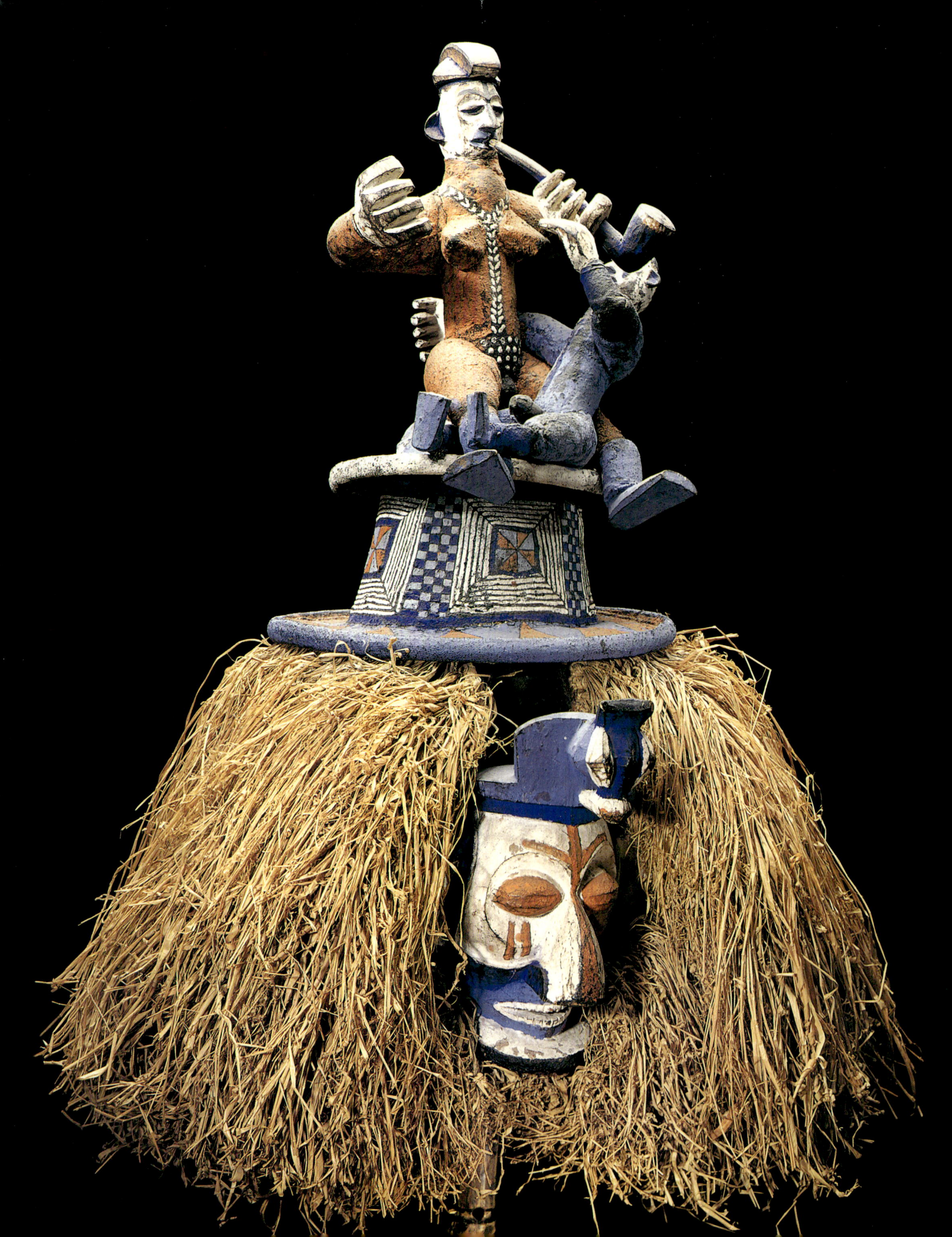

VISIONS OF AFRICA

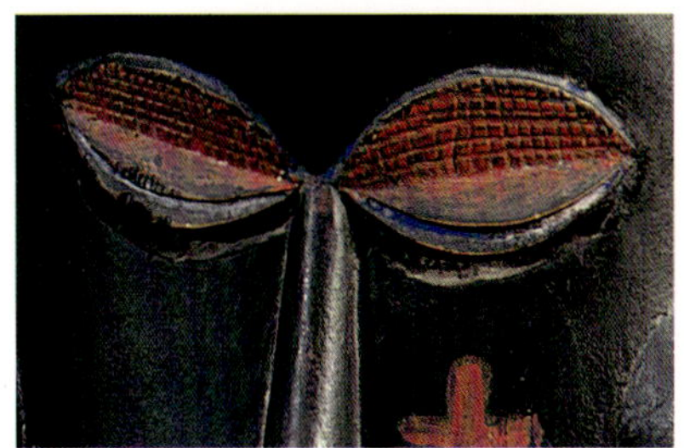

The Jerome L. Joss
Collection of African Art
at UCLA

DORAN H. ROSS, EDITOR

Fowler Museum of Cultural History ▼▲▼ University of California, Los Angeles

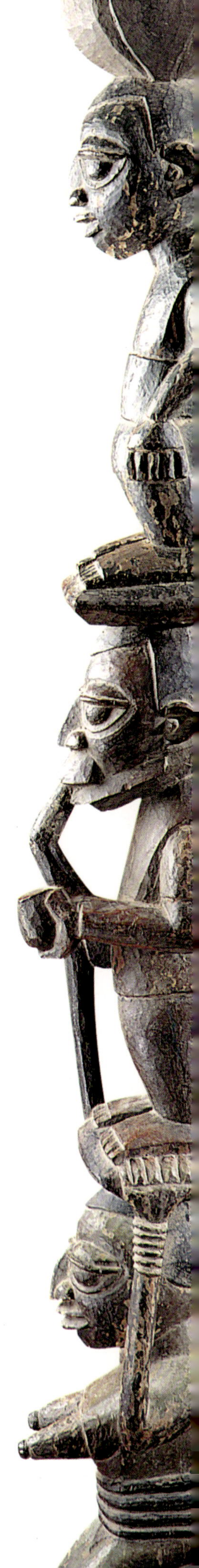

This catalogue and associated exhibition were
supported by funding from the following:

Ahmanson Foundation
National Endowment for the Humanities
    Challenge Grant
Manus, the Support Group of the
    Fowler Museum of Cultural History

FOWLER MUSEUM OF CULTURAL HISTORY
UNIVERSITY OF CALIFORNIA, LOS ANGELES
405 HILGARD AVENUE
LOS ANGELES, CALIFORNIA, USA 90024-1549

Printed and bound in Hong Kong by
Pearl River Printing Company.

ISBN 0-930741-33-1 casebound
ISBN 0-930741-34-X softbound

Library of Congress
Catalog Card Number: 94-070815

COVER: Igbo Ekeleke headdress, Nigeria,
              Cat. 47, page 90.

PAGE 1:   Goli mask performance.
              Photo: P. Ravenhill, 1977.

PAGE 2:   Yaka mask, Zaire,
              Cat. 66, page 118.

TITLE PAGE: Detail, Yorùba housepost, Nigeria,
              Cat. 32, page 71.

PAGE 8:   Detail, beaded stool,
              Fig. 13, page 22.

PAGE 10:   Detail, Swahili Koran, Kenya,
              Cat. 88, page 145.

PAGE 12:   Detail, Yorùba beaded container lid,
              Cat. 36, page 75.

PAGE 160:   Detail, Benin memorial head, Nigeria,
              Cat. 45, page 87.

PAGE 162:   Detail, Object in the style of a reliquary
              guardian, Wumbu and Ndasa peoples,
              People's Republic of the Congo or the
              Republic of Gabon, Cat. 54, page 99.

CONTRIBUTING AUTHORS

RAMONA M. AUSTIN	The Art Institute of Chicago
MARIE-LOUISE BASTIN	Brussels, Belgium
MARLA C. BERNS	University Art Museum, University of California, Santa Barbara
BARBARA W. BLACKMUN	San Diego Mesa College
ARTHUR P. BOURGEOIS	Governors State University, University Park, Illinois
ELISABETH L. CAMERON	University of California, Los Angeles
HERBERT M. COLE	University of California, Santa Barbara
HENRY JOHN DREWAL	University of Wisconsin, Madison
MASSUMEH FARHAD	National Museum of African Art, Washington, D.C.
ANITA J. GLAZE	University of Illinois, Champaign
FRANCES HARDING	School of Oriental and African Studies, University of London
DUNJA HERSAK	Universite Libre de Bruxelles
DELLA JENKINS	University of California, Santa Barbara
SIDNEY KASFIR	Emory University, Atlanta, Georgia
FREDERICK LAMP	The Baltimore Museum of Art
PATRICK McNAUGHTON	Indiana University, Bloomington
NIANGI BATULUKISI	Universite Libre de Bruxelles
MARY H. NOOTER	Museum for African Art, New York
SIMON OTTENBERG	University of Washington, Seattle
PAULETTE PARKER	University of California, Los Angeles
JOHN PICTON	School of Oriental and African Studies, University of London
PHILIP L. RAVENHILL	National Museum of African Art, Washington, D.C.
DORAN H. ROSS	UCLA Fowler Museum of Cultural History
ENID SCHILDKROUT	American Museum of Natural History, New York
WILLIAM SIEGMANN	The Brooklyn Museum, New York
RAYMOND A. SILVERMAN	Michigan State University, East Lansing
LEON SIROTO	Regal Park, New York
ROSLYN A. WALKER	National Museum of African Art, Washington, D.C.
JERI BERNADETTE WILLIAMS	University of California, Los Angeles

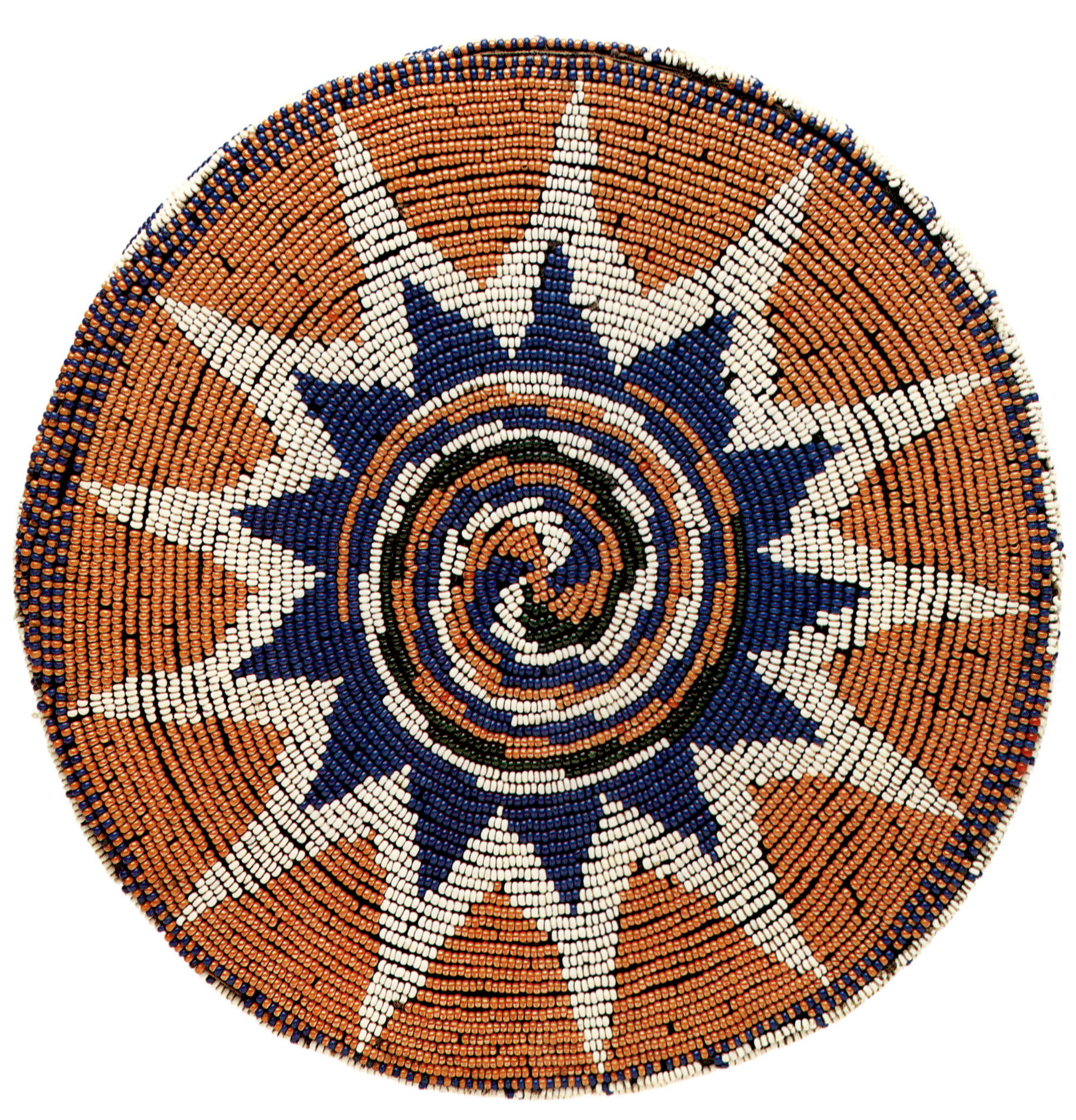

TABLE OF CONTENTS

Acknowledgements	11	
Introduction	13	

THE CATALOGUE		**ALPHABETICAL LISTING**	
Bamana	33	141	Azande
Lobi	36	33	Bamana
Senufo	38	53	Bassa
Djimini/Dyula community	40	54	Baule
Bondoukou region	41	86	Benin Court
Bidjogo	44	58	Bete
Limba	48	44	Bidjogo
Nalu/Baga	49	41	Bondoukou region
Dan	50	136	Chokwe
Sapo	52	95	Dakakari
Bassa	53	50	Dan
Baule	54	40	Djimini/Dyula community
Bete	58	60	Effutu
Grebo	59	97	Ekpari Clan
Effutu	60	84	Esan (Ishan)
Mamprussi	62	100	Fang
Yorùba	64	59	Grebo
Esan (Ishan)	84	116	Holo
Benin Court	86	88	Igbo
Igbo	88	134	Kanyok
Tiv	94	124	Kuba
Dakakari	95	48	Limba
Ekpari Clan	97	108	Loango
Wumbu & Ndasa	99	36	Lobi
Fang	100	126	Luba
Tsogho	102	62	Mamprussi
Ngbandi	106	142	Mangbetu
Loango	108	114	Manyanga
Yombe	110	138	Maravi
Manyanga	114	122	Mbala
Holo	116	49	Nalu/Baga
Yaka	117	106	Ngbandi
Nkanu	120	120	Nkanu
Mbala	122	52	Sapo
Kuba	124	38	Senufo
Luba	126	144	Swahili
Kanyok	134	94	Tiv
Tukongo (Kongo-Dinga)	135	102	Tsogho
Chokwe	136	135	Tukongo (Kongo-Dinga)
Upper Zambezi	136	136	Upper Zambezi
Maravi	138	99	Wumbu & Ndasa
Azande	141	117	Yaka
Mangbetu	142	110	Yombe
Swahili	144	64	Yorùba

Bibliography	154	

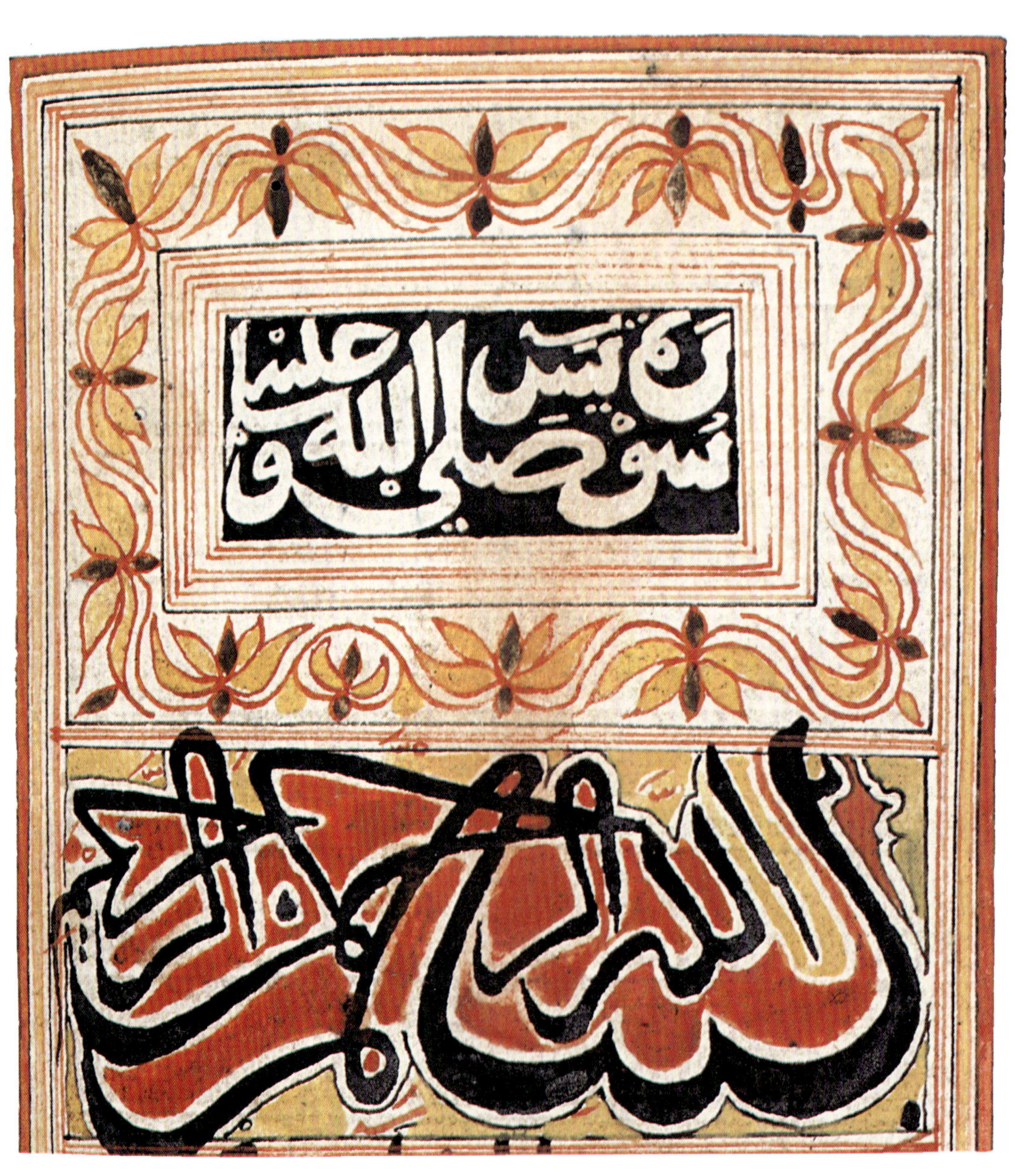

ACKNOWLEDGMENTS

This publication is a companion volume to *Sleeping Beauties: The Jerome L. Joss Collection of African Headrests at UCLA.* Like its predecessor it honors the gift of the Joss collection of African art to the UCLA Fowler Museum of Cultural History. Also like the preceding volume, it highlights the importance of the collection through the learned comments of leading scholars in the field, who elucidate key features/ideas about the objects.

With this publication, we would again like to thank Mr. Joss for committing his collection to a public institution where it will serve as an important resource for present and future generations in the greater Los Angeles community.

I also want to reiterate my profound appreciation for Jerry's friendship. I value highly our many conversations that have roamed over the landscape of African art, including questions of attribution, provenance, function, as well as authenticity and the capriciousness of the museum world and art market, and, of course, the people who participate in them. The staff of the Museum joins me in thanking Jerry for his many courtesies and consistent thoughtfulness. For a brief biography of Jerome Joss, I refer the reader to the essay by Henrietta Cosentino in *Sleeping Beauties.*

On behalf of Mr. Joss and myself, I want to thank the many contributors listed at the beginning of this volume. They brought new information and special insights to the objects included here. Their attentiveness to this project is greatly appreciated. I would like to single out Henry Drewal and Philip Ravenhill for their extra efforts in helping to realize this publication and its associated exhibition.

As with *Sleeping Beauties,* Paulette Parker served a critical role in marshaling and coordinating all the records, correspondence and files related to the Joss collection. Paulette's organizational skills and care for detail set the stage for the successful completion of this work. Her successor, Elisabeth Cameron, carried on with equal enthusiasm and concern. Elisabeth's hard work, intelligent scholarship and good humor were essential to finishing this volume. I am sincerely indebted to them both.

Amy Walsh skillfully handled the complicated task of editing twenty-nine different authors, each with a distinct style and focus. Her consideration of the needs of this project coupled with her sensitivity to the author's ideas is greatly appreciated.

We are also grateful to UCLA Publication Design Services. Barbara Kelly provided the elegant design for this volume and Judy Hale coordinated production with the Museum's Director of Publications Daniel R. Brauer. We are appreciative of their continuing efforts on our behalf.

The exhibition associated with this publication was imaginatively designed by David Mayo, who combined space and color to impressive and vibrant results. Exhibition labels were insightfully developed by Betsy Quick, Judith Herschman and Paulette Parker.

The rest of the Museum staff, listed at the back of this volume, contributed in many crucial ways to tremendous effect. As with all our projects, it is the coordinated efforts of all personnel that ensured the successful conclusion of this project. Again, pride of place is reserved for Jerry Joss who motivated us all.

DORAN H. ROSS
DEPUTY DIRECTOR

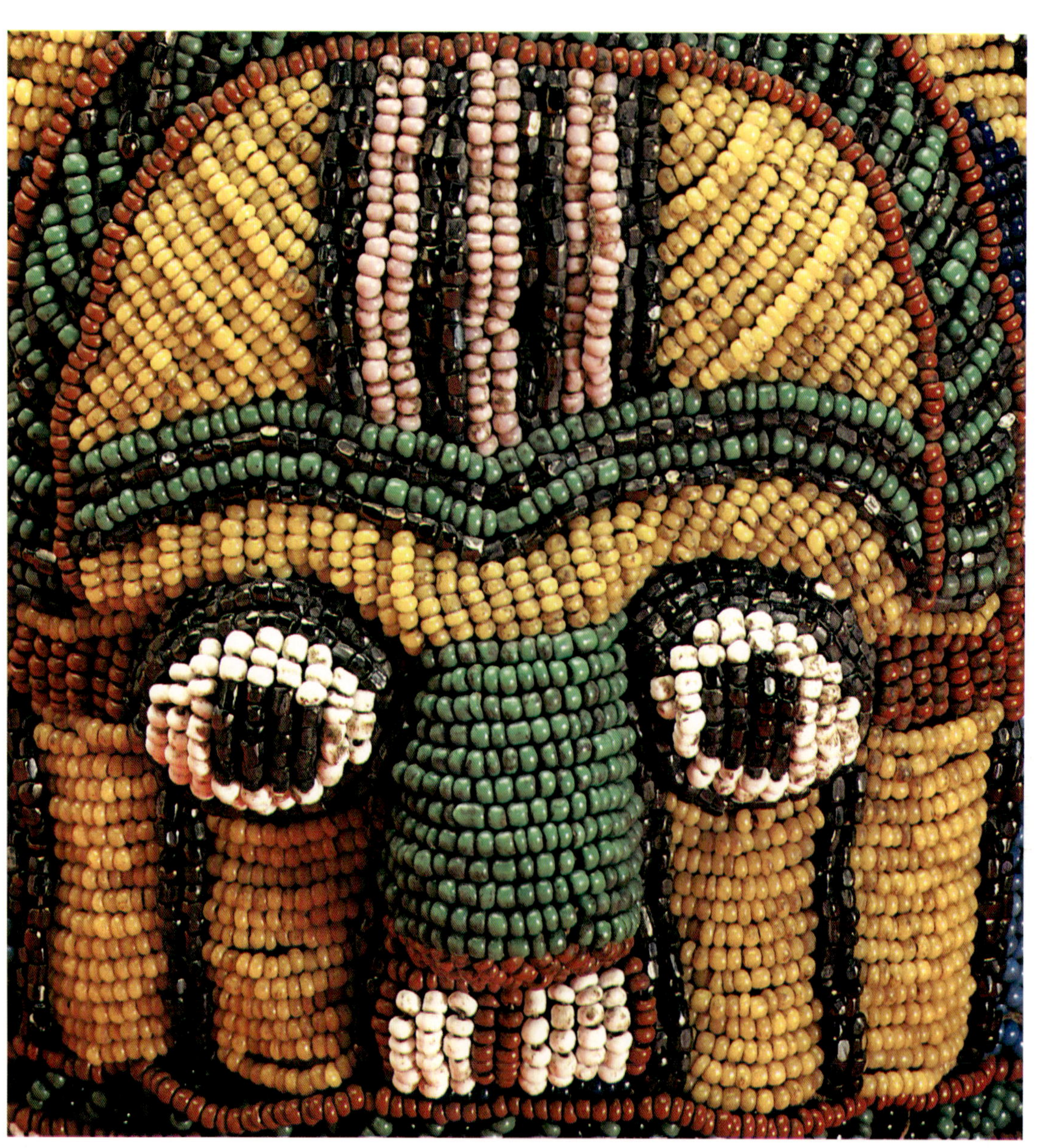

INTRODUCTION

THE JEROME L. JOSS COLLECTION OF AFRICAN ART AND THE FOWLER MUSEUM OF CULTURAL HISTORY

One thing that differentiates the Joss collection of African art from many distinguished gifts to the Fowler Museum is that most of Mr. Joss' acquisitions were made with the Museum's collections specifically in mind. To understand the significance of this, one should first briefly consider the nature of the Museum. Founded in 1963 as the UCLA Museum and Laboratories of Ethnic Arts and Technologies, the Museum's initial mission was:

> "to build and organize collections of objects which exemplify the range of material culture, specifically the arts, of people who lived until recently at the margin or beyond the orbit of the major occidental civilizations; only the 'fine' arts of the western world after the end of classic antiquity are beyond the realm of the collecting activities."

Despite some problematic language, the emphasis on "art" was clearly stated in both the Museum's name and mandate. More recently the Museum has redefined its mission statement to read:

> The UCLA Fowler Museum of Cultural History is organized to collect, preserve, study, interpret, exhibit, and publish art and material culture primarily from Africa, Asia, Oceania, Native and Latin America, past and present. With this focus the museum is committed to presenting highly contextualized interpretive exhibitions, publications, and public programming heavily informed by interdisciplinary approaches and by the perspectives of the cultures being represented. In terms of audience, the museum directs its energies to serving the teaching and research interests of the students, faculty and staff of the university and to providing an accessible educational resource for the diverse communities of greater Los Angeles.

The Joss collection has already helped fulfill significant parts of this mandate by supplying key objects for five exhibition/publication projects developed and carried out by the Museum. These have involved three graduate student seminars at UCLA and one at the University of California, Santa Barbara. Mr. Joss also sponsored a juried art exhibition, organized after the publication of *Sleeping Beauties*, with the challenge "to design a headrest or 'rigid pillow' in any material that is artistically compelling and functions as a support for the head while resting or sleeping." Entrants were encouraged to create "contemporary interpretations which reflect an artist's [the entrant's] personal aesthetic and cultural background." While many of our Museum's educational programs have targeted the enhancement of written and verbal skills, this project was clearly oriented towards students who make things with their hands. The competition attracted 615 entries, 48 of which were displayed in connection with the Sleeping Beauties exhibition. The winners of the four divisions—middle school, high school, college/university, and open—are illustrated here (Figs. 1-4).

Even after the publication of *Sleeping Beauties*, Mr. Joss has continued to build his collection of African headrests for the Fowler Museum. Six exam-

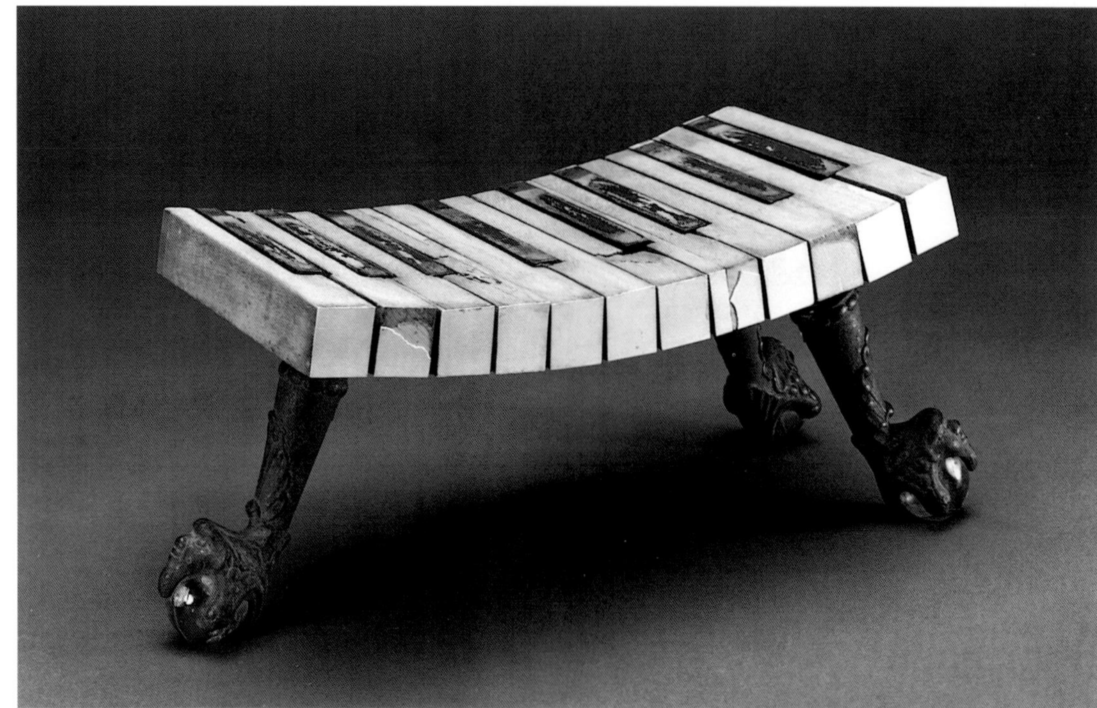

FIG. 1
MR. JOPLIN TAKES FIVE
by
Raphael X. Reichert
1993
Wood, paint,
metal and glass
L. 28.5 cm.
Winner,
Open Division

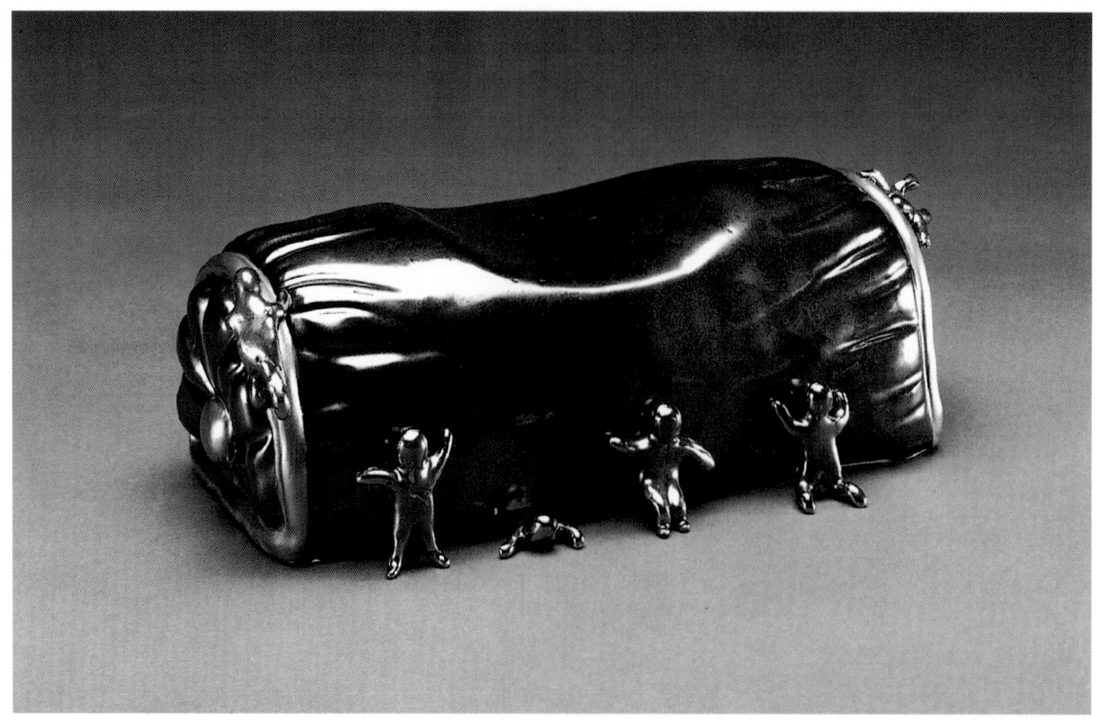

FIG. 2
GULLIVER'S PILLOW
by
Estinen Mailian
1993
Ceramic and
metallic glaze
L. 28 cm.
Winner,
High School Division

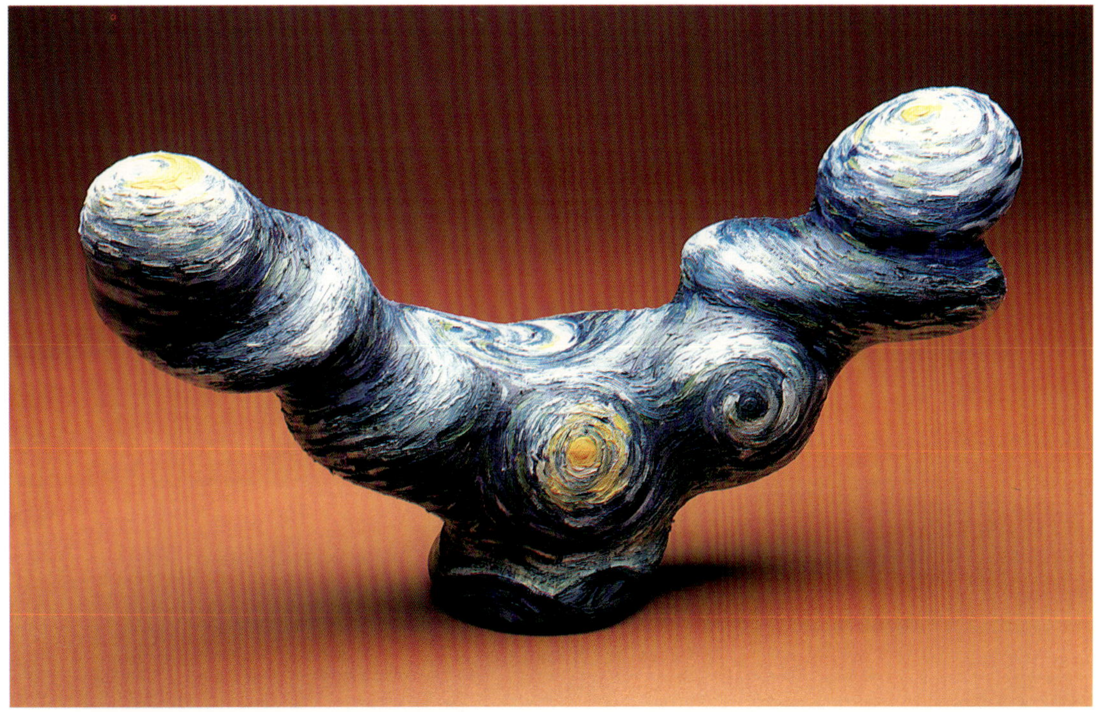

FIG. 3

ALMOST
VINCENT'S PILLOW
by
Todd Feldman
1993
Wood, bondo, latex,
oil and alkyd
L. 39.5 cm.
Winner,
College Division

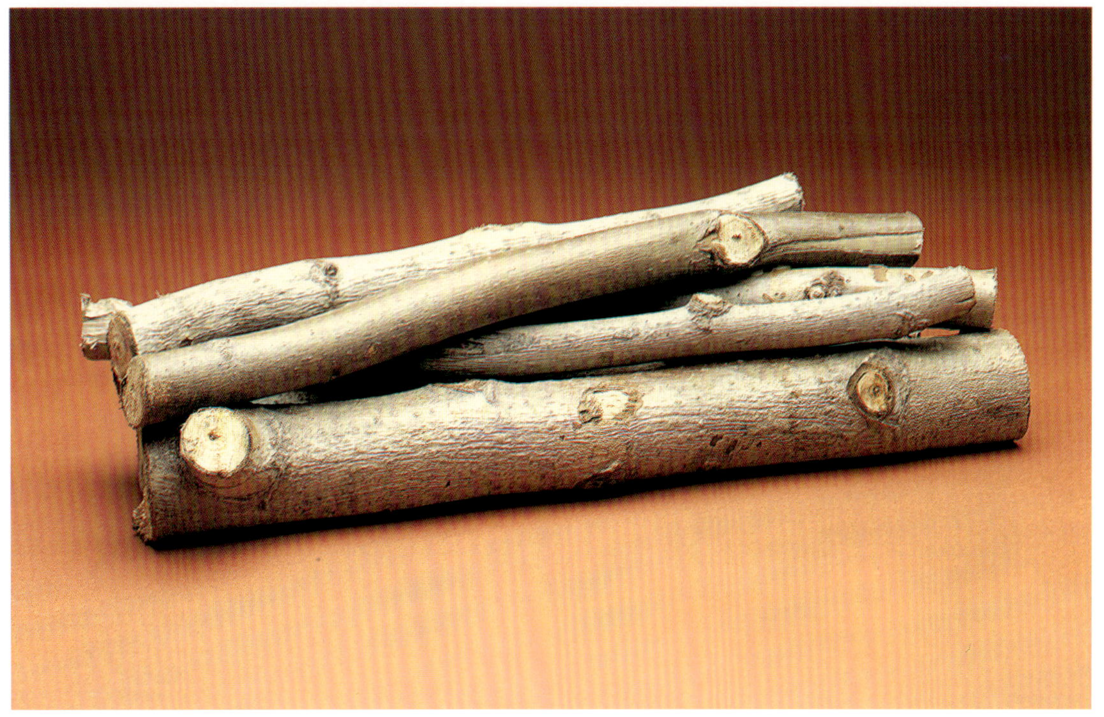

FIG. 4

UNTITLED
by
Michele Aguilar
1993
Walnut branches
and glue
L. 40 cm.
Winner,
Middle School Division

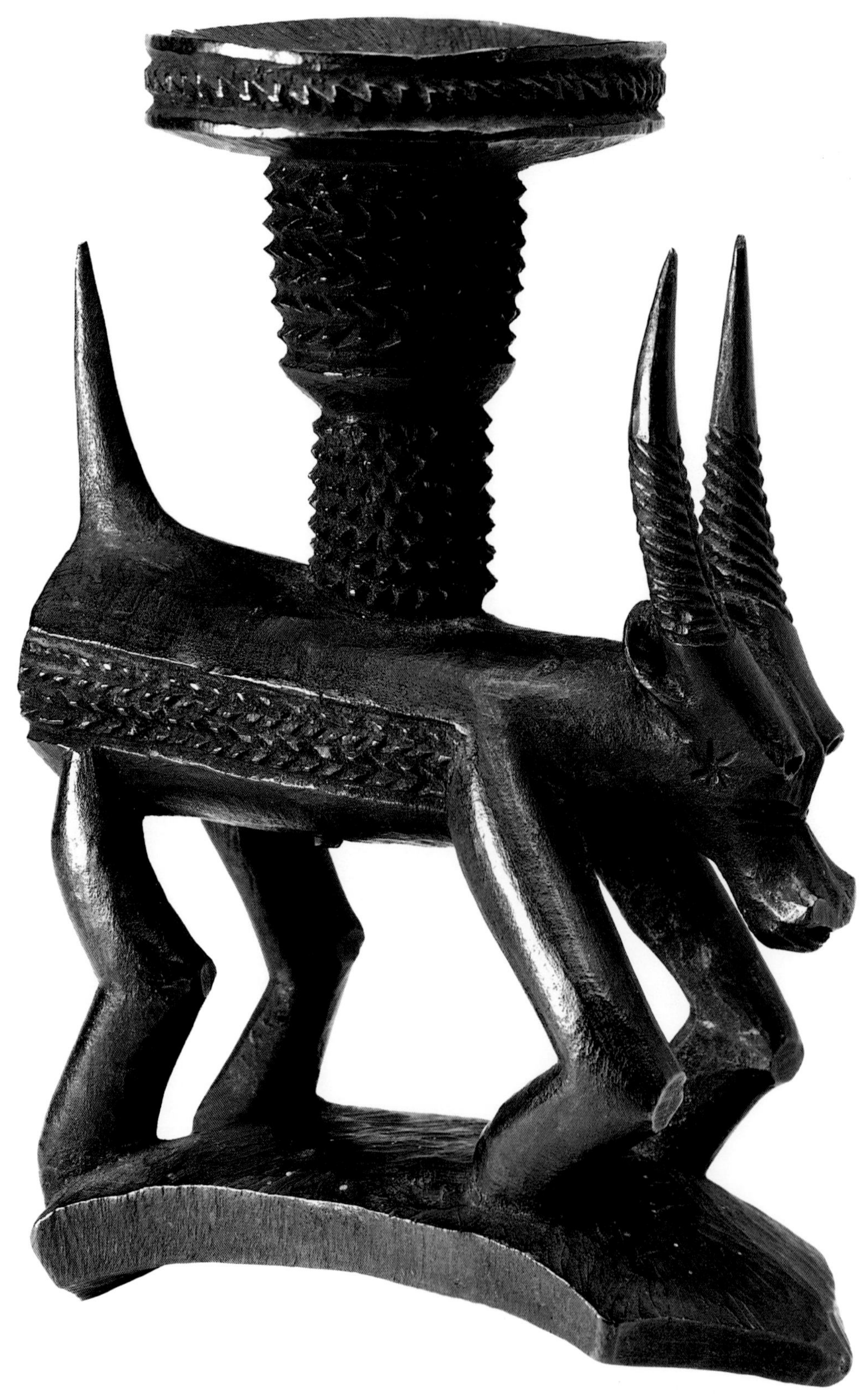

FIG. 5
HEADREST
Chokwe, Zaire
Wood
W. 20 cm.
FMCH 93.8.8

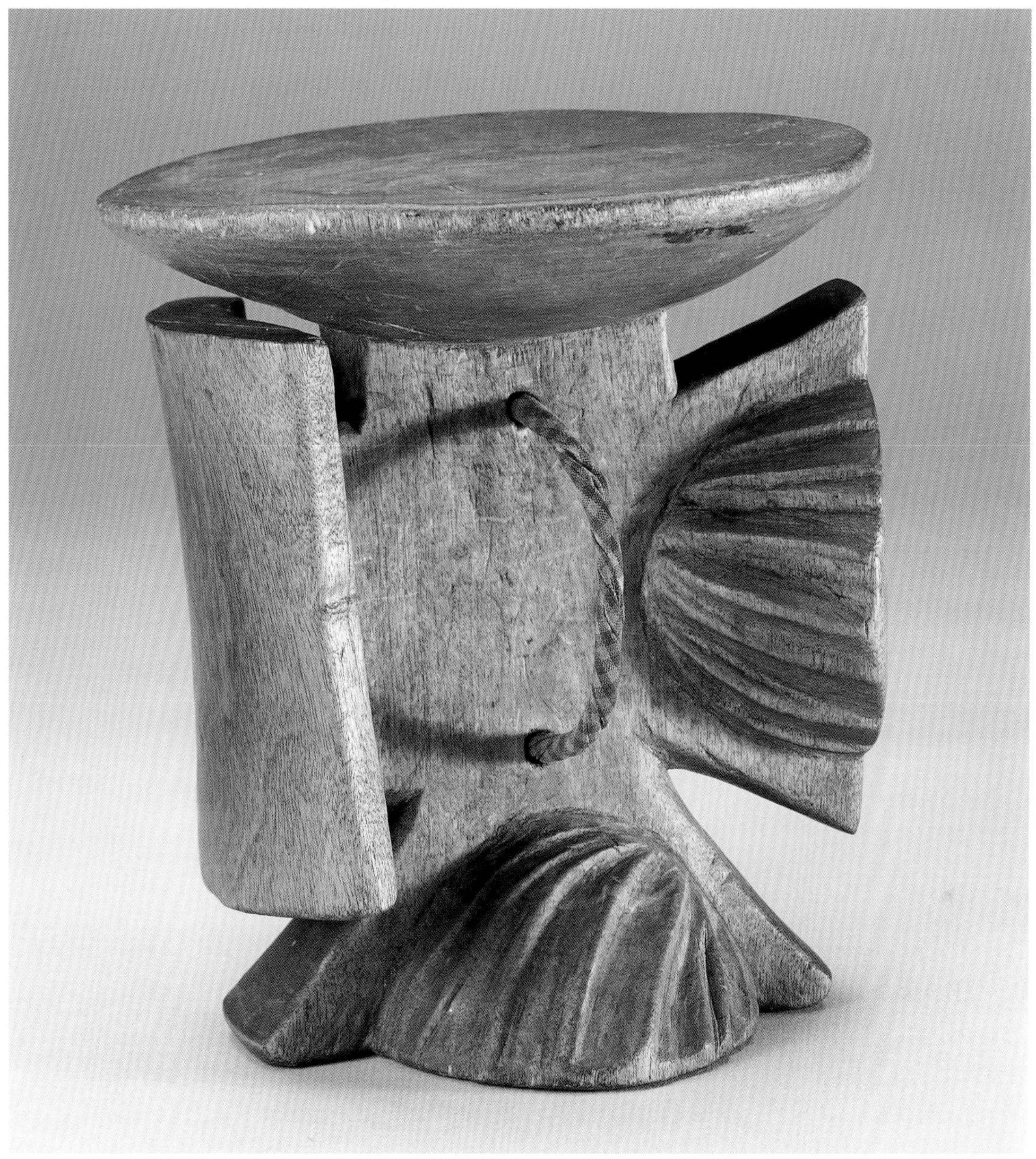

ples are included here. Perhaps the most striking is from the Chokwe peoples of Angola and Zaire. This unique combination of pipe (with missing stem) and headrest features an antelope support (Fig. 5). Equally clever is the Kenyan piece, which combines typical Pokot stool and headrest, set perpendicular to each other and carved from the same piece of wood (Fig. 6). Although impossible to prove, artistic virtuosity rather than any functional or symbolic consid-erations seem to have motivated the production of both the Chokwe and Pokot pieces. A rare iron head-rest (Fig. 7) from the Tellem culture of Mali was apparently a burial item from the caves above one of the present day Dogon villages of the Bandiagara escarpment (see Bedaux 1977:75, Fig. 46-36). An atypical Tsonga headrest (Fig. 9) and two unusual pieces whose provenance still requires refinement (Figs. 8 & 10) round out the new acquisitions.

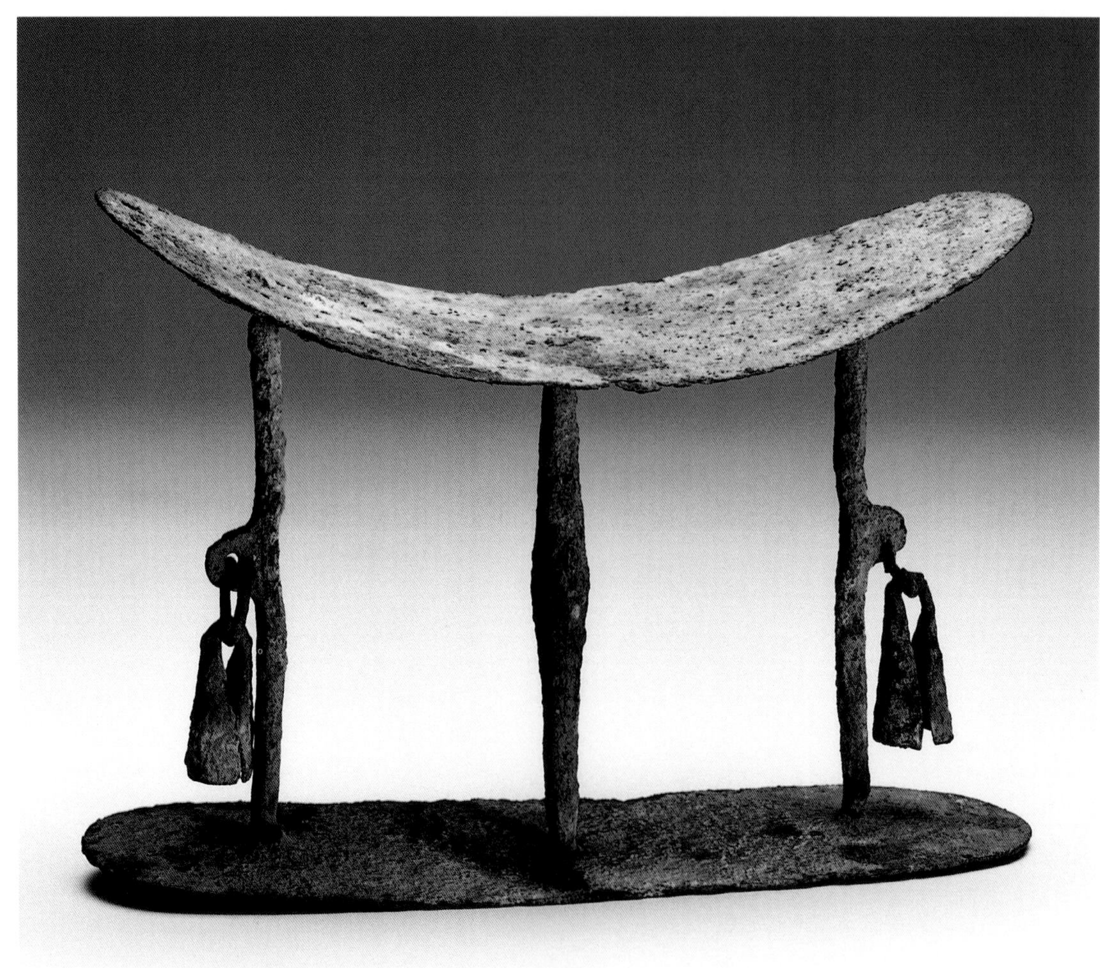

FIG. 7
HEADREST
Tellem culture, Mali
Iron
W. 25 cm.
FMCH 93.37.1

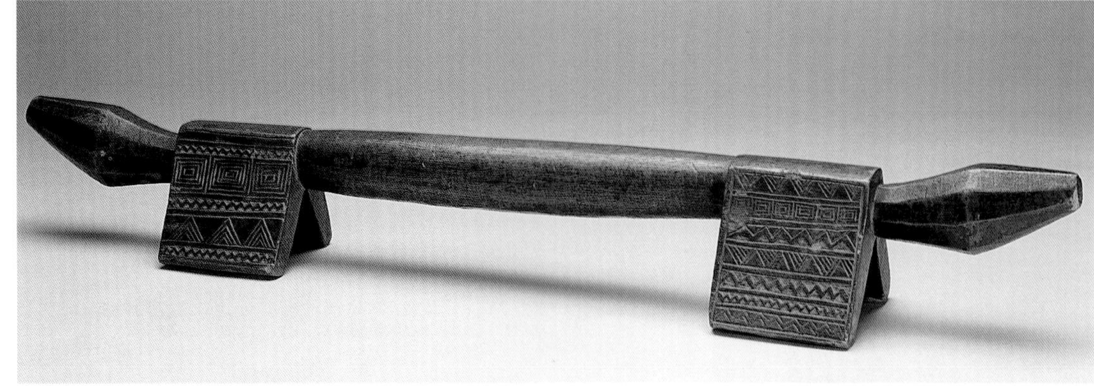

FIG. 8
HEADREST
Wute (?), Cameroon
Wood
L. 59 cm.
FMCH 93.8.5

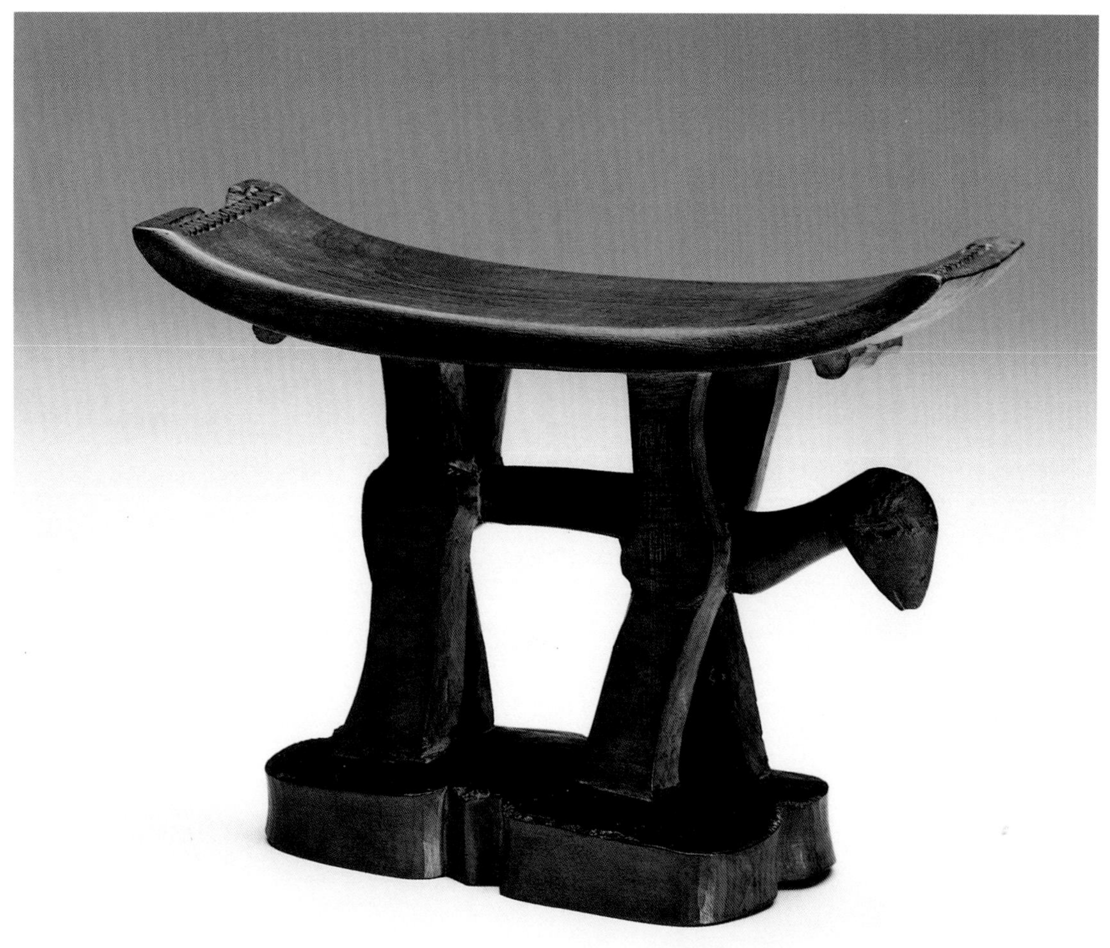

FIG. 9
Headrest
Tsonga (?), Zimbabwe
Wood
L. 20 cm.
FMCH 93.37.2

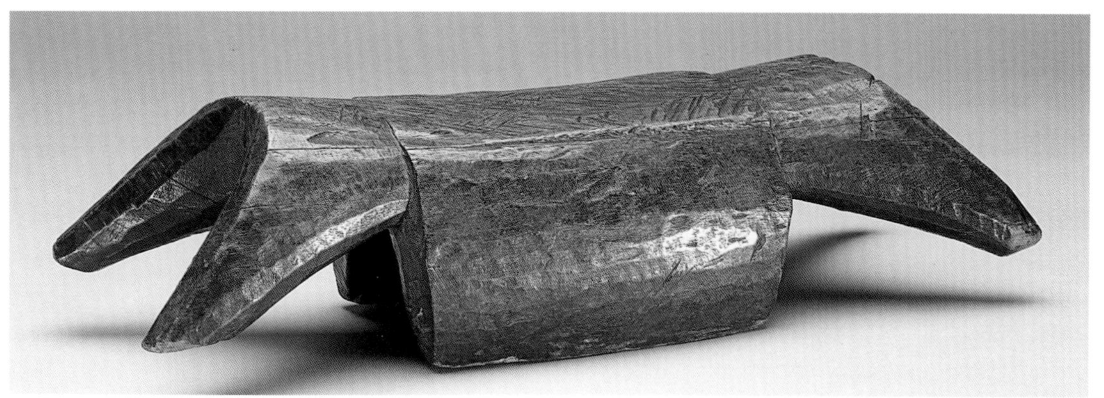

FIG. 10
HEADREST
Northeastern Zaire (?)
Wood
L. 43.5 cm.
FMCH 93.8.6

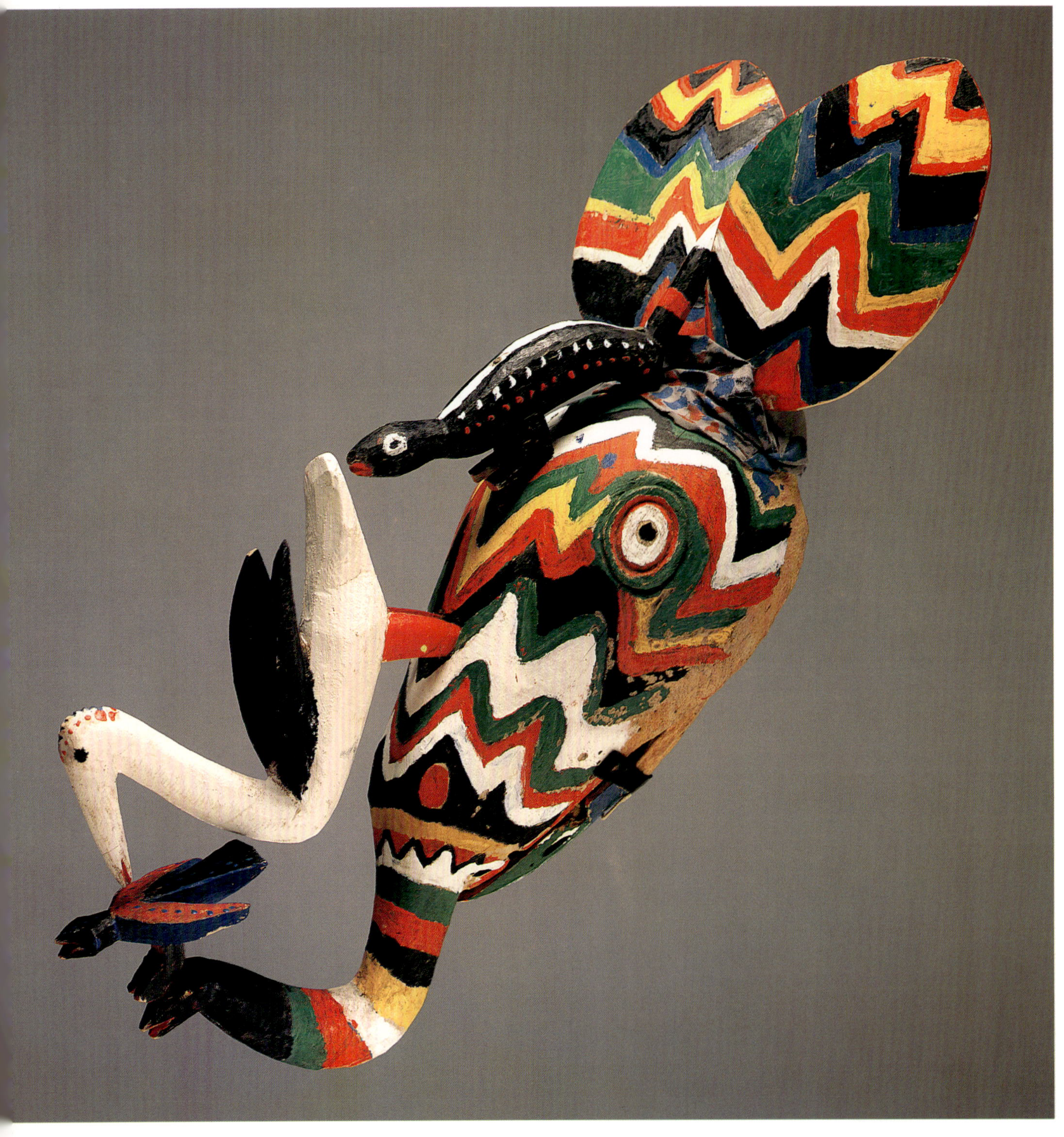

In enlarging the African collections, the Museum has sought to balance a desire to build on existing strengths with the goal of filling significant voids in the collections. The Joss collection fulfills both needs. The art of the Yoruba peoples of southwestern Nigeria has been a strength of the Museum since its inception and the focus of three exhibitions, beginning with *Black Gods and Kings*, and important parts of at least four others. The Joss collection has an especially strong group of Yoruba material. The splendid houseposts by Obembe Alaye (Cat. 32) are major additions to our holdings, which were previously represented by only a few modest examples. Likewise, the monumental Ifa divination tray (Cat. 35) surpasses in scale and complexity any of the trays already in the collection. Other Joss objects fill holes in our Yoruba holdings. The iron tipped wood staff (*òpá òkò*, Cat. 31), the brass and iron staff from Ilé-Ifè (Cat. 40), and the ceremonial sword with beaded sheath (*udámalore*, Cat. 39) are all meaningful acquisitions. Also in this category is the doll (*omolangidi*, Cat. 41) attributed to Olowe of Ise, which joins a well-worn box by this master carver from the Wellcome collection (Fig. 32).

One region that has been severely underrepresented in the Fowler Museum's collection is the Swahili area of east Africa. This was corrected, in part, by a significant purchase by Mr. Joss from the late Swahili scholar James de Vere Allen. In addition to the magnificent Koran discussed by Farhad (Cat. 88) and an unusual *bao* board considered by Walker (Cat. 89), the acquisition included several chair types (Cats. 97-99), architectural elements (Cats. 94-96), a bed, and a few domestic implements. This group has been augmented by the acquisition of five decorated coconut-scrapers (*mbuzi*, Cats. 90-93).

A number of Joss acquisitions were purchased in support of specific projects, especially for the recent exhibition "Elephant: The Animal and Its Ivory in African Culture." Included in this project is the massive Idoma elephant mask discussed by Kasfir (Cat. 53), which joined the Igbo *Ogboni Enyi* already in the collection and addressed here by Cole (Cat. 49). The headpiece of a Bamana puppet masquerade (Fig. 11, see Ezra & Arnoldi 1992:107) and the simple Ijaw "cap-mask" (Fig. 12), presumably worn in one of the festivals addressing water spirits, were also included in this effort. In addition there is a beaded stool from Cameroon (Fig. 13) and a Kuba *itombwa* or friction oracle from Zaire (Fig. 14).

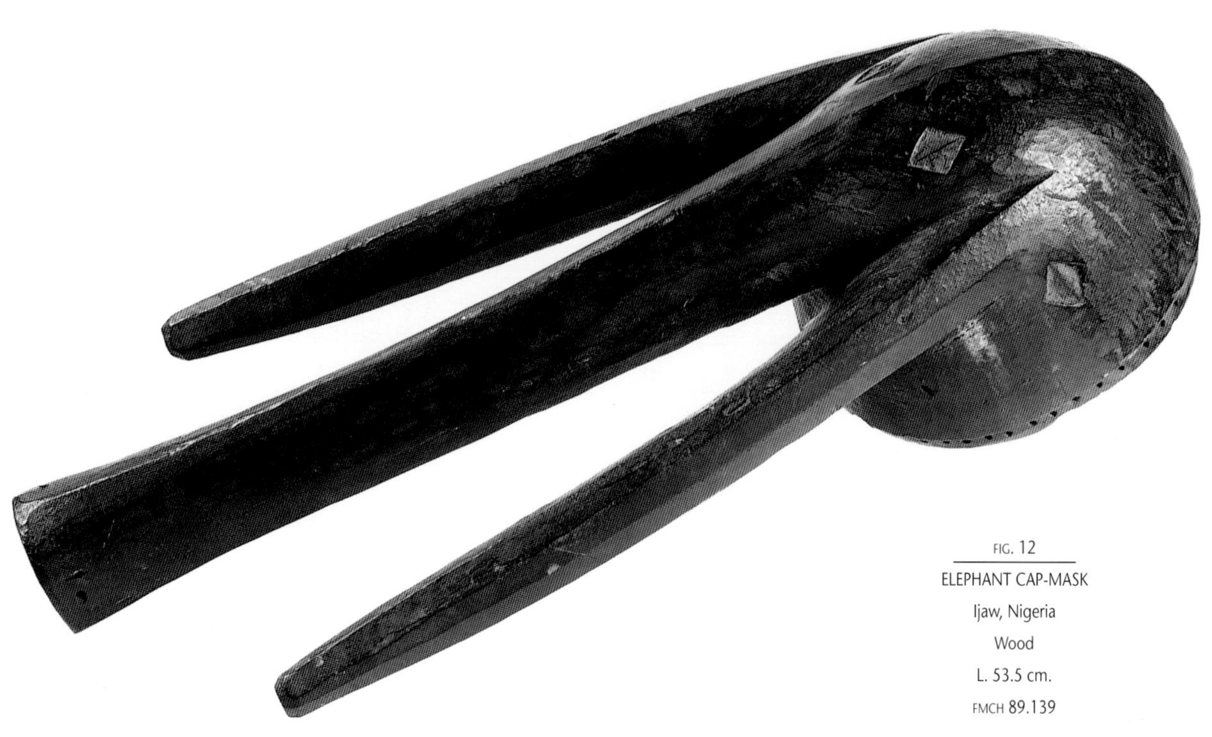

FIG. 12
ELEPHANT CAP-MASK
Ijaw, Nigeria
Wood
L. 53.5 cm.
FMCH 89.139

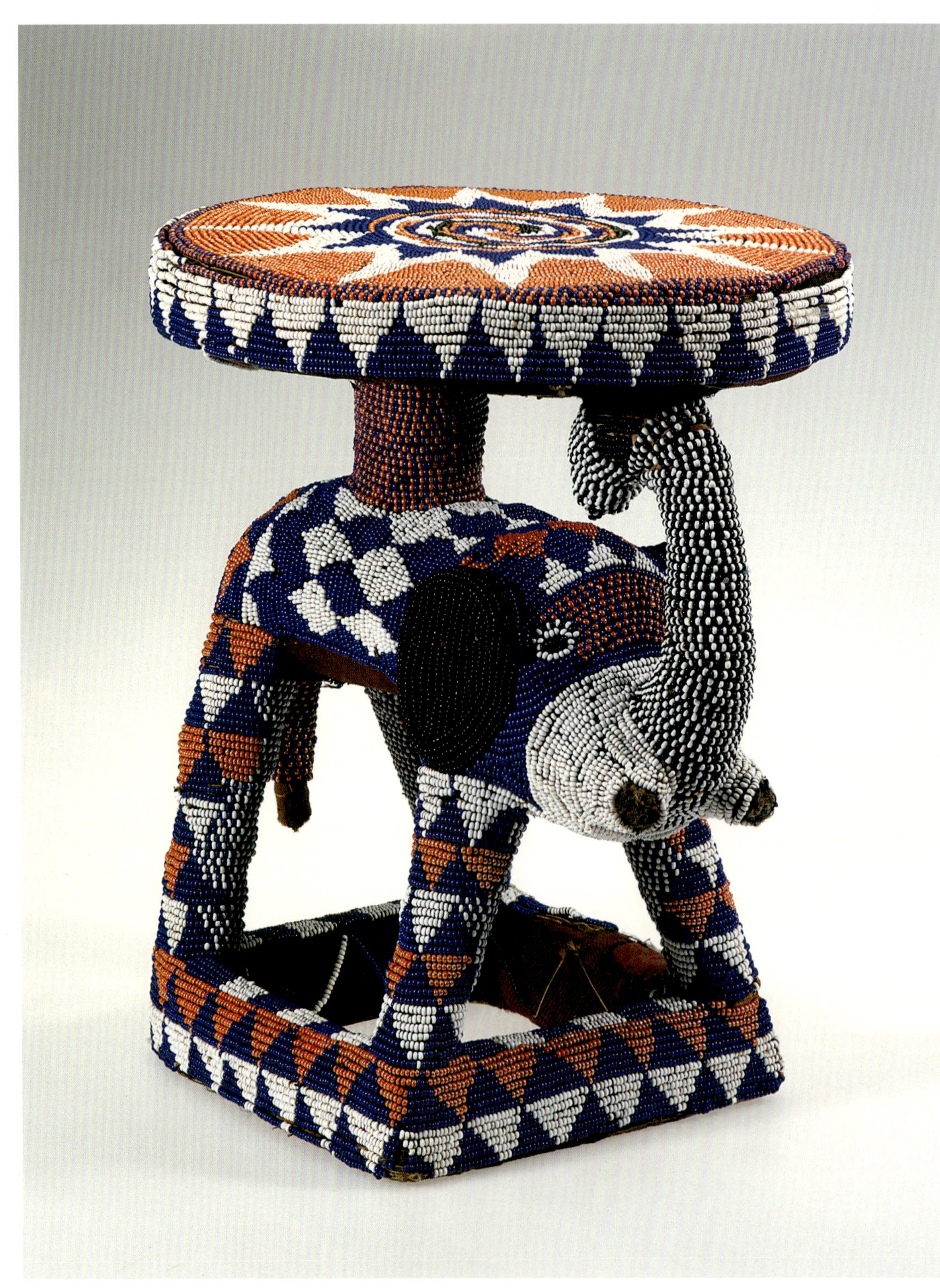

FIG. 13

BEADED STOOL
Bamileke (?),
Cameroon
Beads and wood
H. 30 cm.
FMCH 89.73

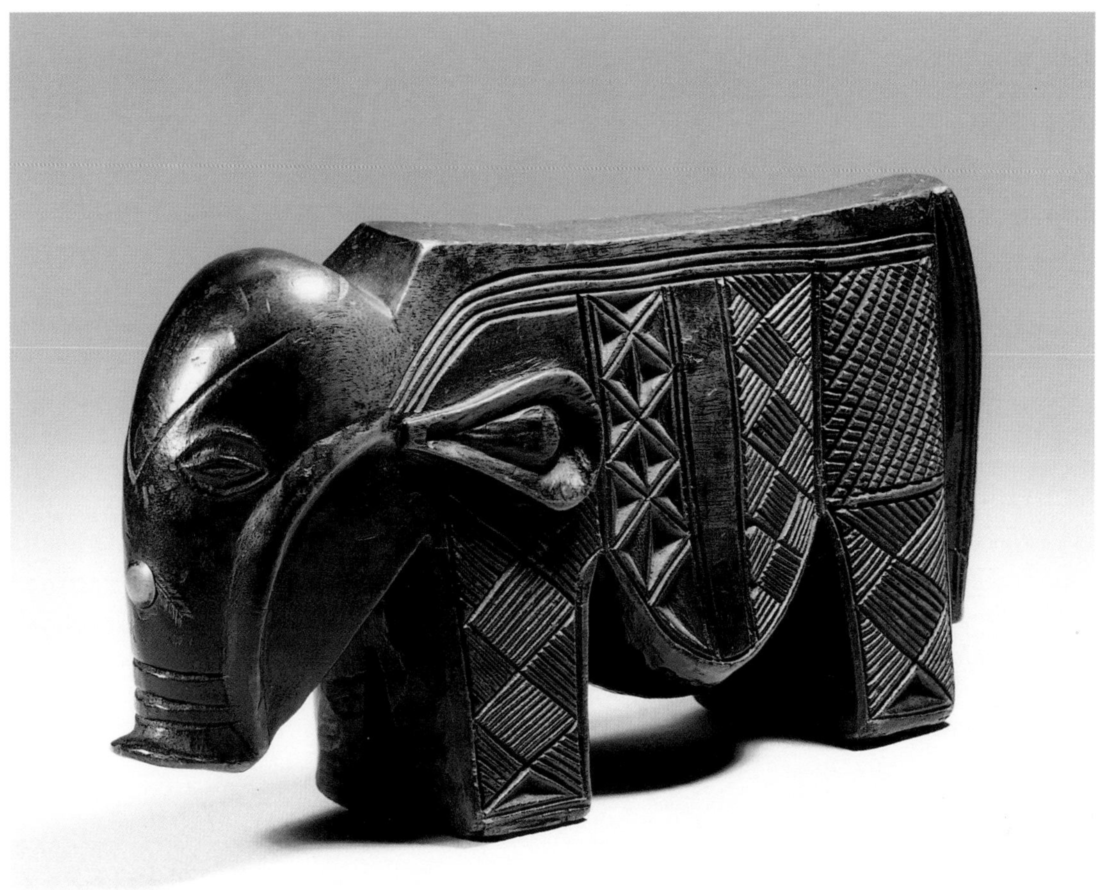

FIG. 14

FRICTION ORACLE

(itombwa)

Kuba, Zaire

Wood

L. 23.5 cm.

FMCH 88.959

SOME RARE OR UNUSUAL PIECES

Aside from the objects discussed in the catalogue of this volume, there are a number of unusual or problematic pieces in the collection. A common and much discussed genre in African art is the mother-and-child image, which typically depicts the mother nursing the child or carrying it on her back. An example is the small but delightful Lobi divination figure in the Joss collection (Fig. 15). The Joss collection also includes an example of a very rare related image of a male with what appears to be a child on his back. The Joss figure is attributed to the Songye-derived Nsapo Nsapo peoples of south central Zaire (Fig. 16). Although the Nsapo Nsapo are well known for seated "maternity" figures (Timmermans 1962 & Christies 1992:82), there are no known examples from this area that are comparable to this male with a much smaller female figure on its back. The dramatically projecting belly of the figure might at first glance suggest pregnancy rather than corpulence, but is nevertheless typical of male figures from that area. The beard, penis, and iron-tipped arrow running the length of the torso through the coiffure and nesting in the hip also clearly identify the figure as male.

The Joss figure joins a thematically related male Teke image from the Wellcome collection in the Fowler Museum (Fig. 17). The Wellcome figure is also quite clearly male and has a similarly posed diminutive figure of indeterminate sex on its back. The interpretation of these images is complicated by the fact that both "children" are unsupported and face in the opposite direction of the nearly pan-African mode of carrying a child pickaback with a cloth wrapper. To my knowledge the configuration represented on these figures has not been documented in the field or recorded in the literature. Without assuming that the explanation for both figures is the same, and ignoring for the moment the lack of support and the back-to-back position, there

are a number of documented contexts for men carrying younger males or females in different parts of sub-Saharan Africa. In the Kasai of Zaire, a father will carry a sick child on his back to the doctor, whether it be a traditional healer or Western doctor (Elisabeth Cameron, pers. comm. 1993). Among several peoples, a senior male will carry a junior one as part of initiation rituals (Kecskesi 1982:52-55). Among the Tabwa a chief was carried on the shoulders (not the back) of a slave or retainer (Neyt 1985:80). The diminutive stature of the secondary figure in both the Joss and Wellcome examples would seem to argue against this explanation.

All three of the above explanations depend on ethnographic analogy and a certain leap of faith to circumvent a literal reading of the "carried" (attached) figures as they are depicted. Individuals who are carried on the back are typically supported by the arms and hands of the carrier, or in the case of the child, by a cloth wrapper. Such is obviously not the case in the two figures under consideration, suggesting that explanations rest more in the realm of the supernatural. The backward facing miniatures may represent some kind of tutelary deity functioning in support of the larger figure, similar to the way little patron spirits of hunters (*mahamba*) precariously perch on the headresses of Chokwe figures of the culture hero Chibinda Ilunga (Bastin 1982:142-43). If these smaller pickaback figures represent a spiritual entity, their nature or character remains unknown.

Another poorly understood sculptural tradition is represented by a figure from the Metoko peoples of Eastern Zaire (Fig. 18). Metoko sculptures apparently functioned within the context of an initiation society called Bukota which is related to the Bwami association of the nearby Lega. Biebuyck classifies Metoko figures according to four functions: initiatory, funerary, peace-making, and circumcision rites (1977:52-53). The sawn-off bottom of this "pole"

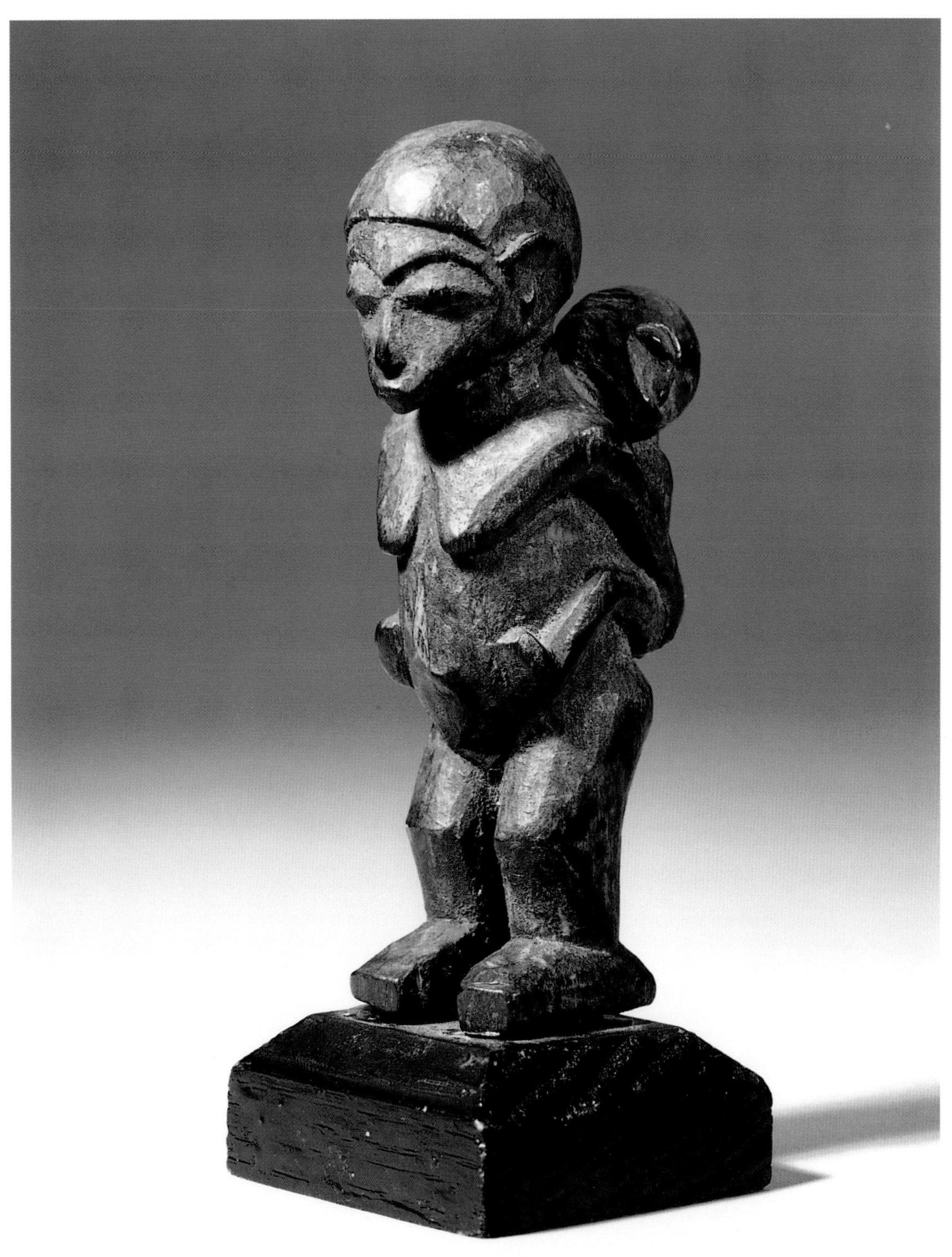

FIG. 15
DIVINATION FIGURE
Lobi, Burkina Faso
Wood
H. 12.2 cm.
FMCH 92.5

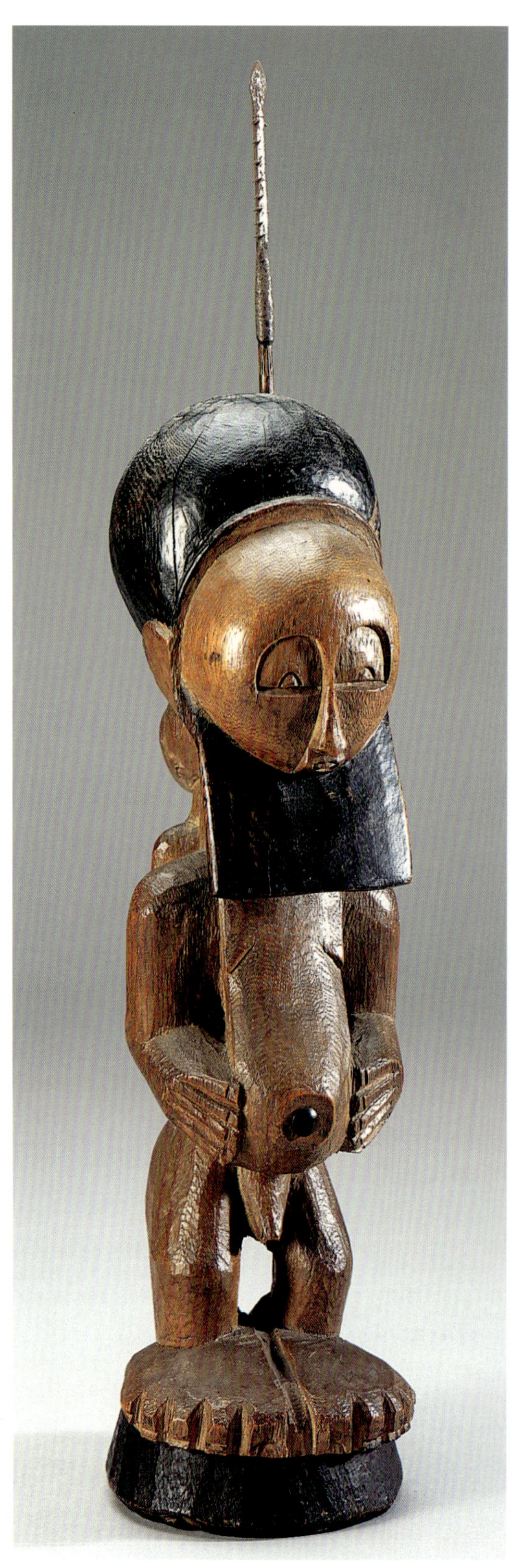
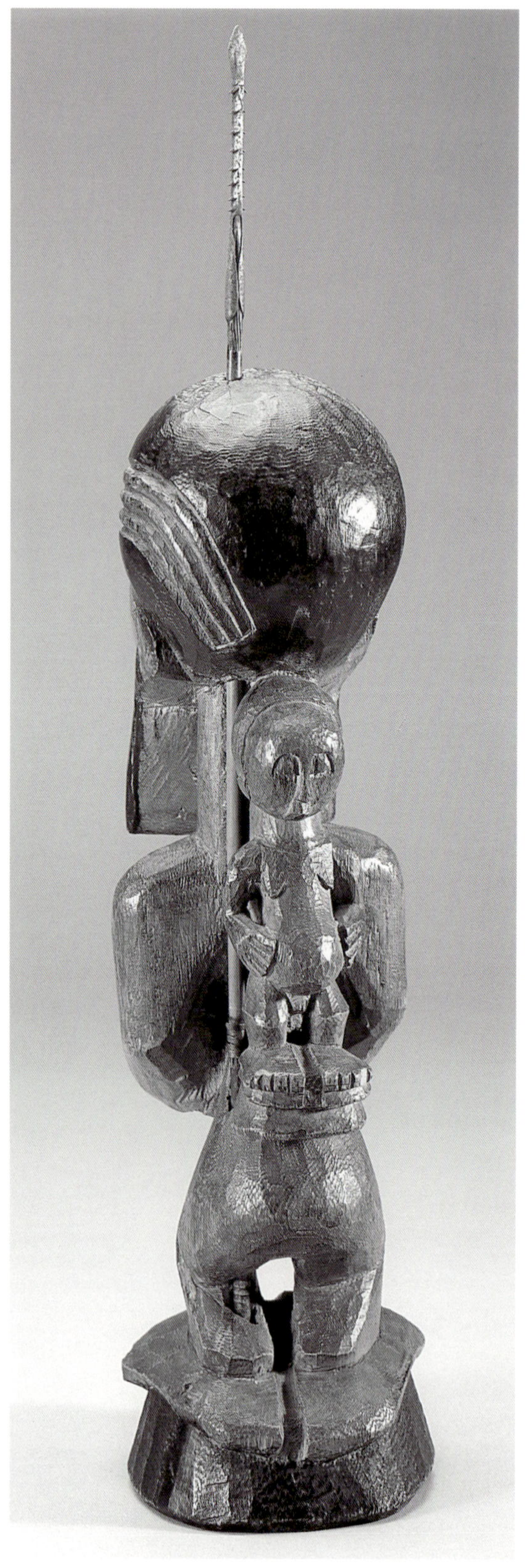

FIG. 16
MALE FIGURE
Nsapo Nsapo, Zaire
Wood and metal
H. 49 cm.
FMCH 86.1726

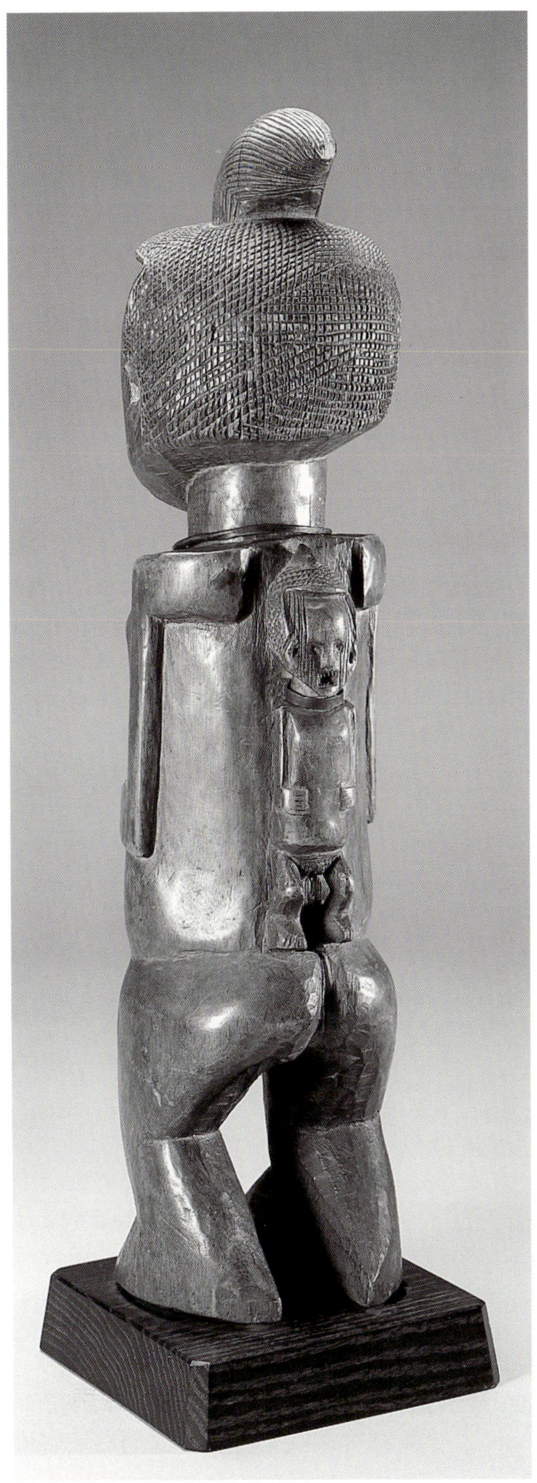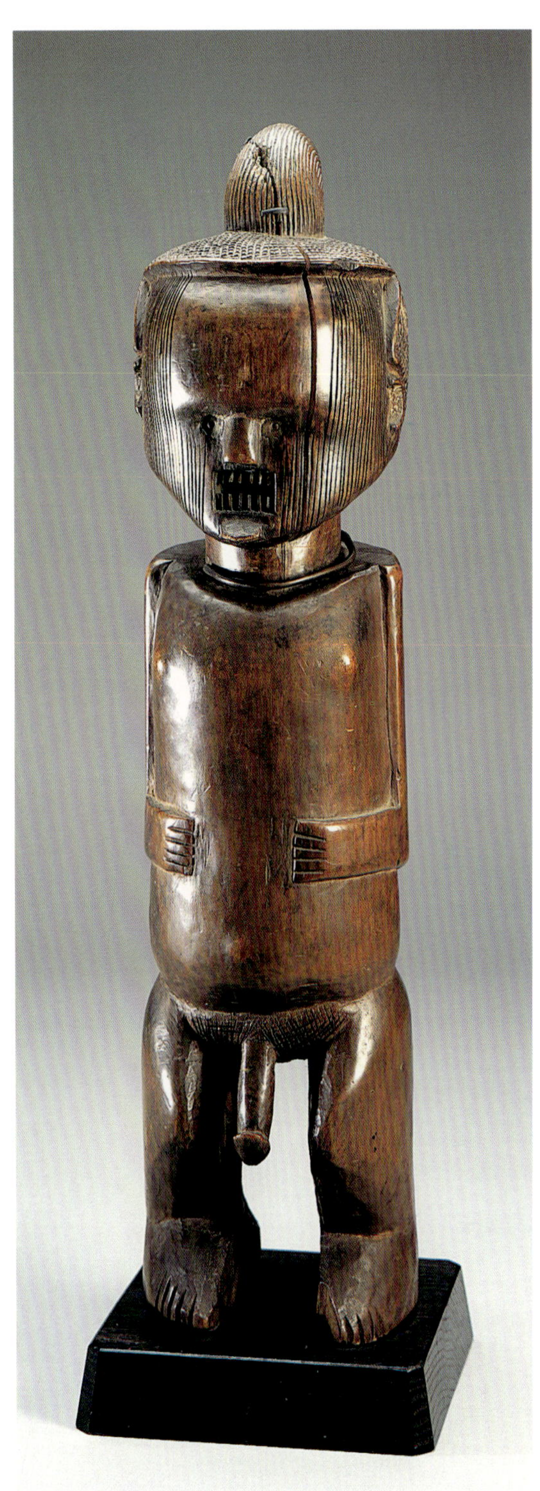

FIG. 17
MALE FIGURE
Teke, Congo
Wood
H. 53.3 cm.
FMCH 65.5463
Gift of
The Wellcome Trust

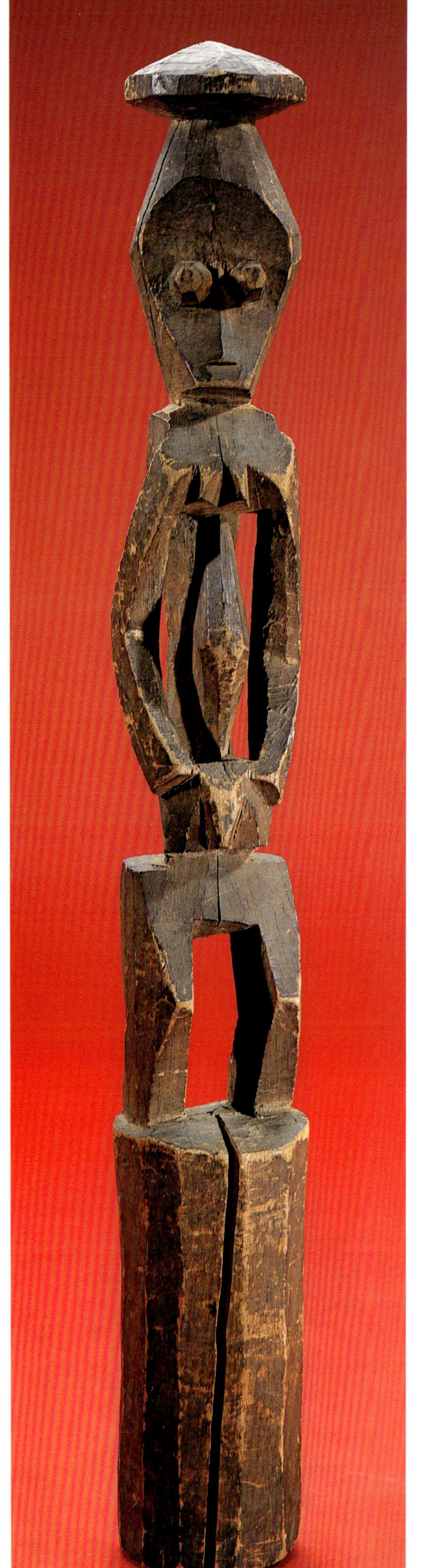

figure suggests that it once was associated with the tomb of a high initiate. A house-like construction was built over the grave in the plaza of the village and the exterior sides of the tomb were lined with figures (*kakungu*; Biebuyck 1977: Figs. 1&5). About one month after internment, the construction is dismantled and the pieces, including the figures, are abandoned in the forest. If this figure was once part of a tomb ensemble it must have been rescued before being discarded since it shows little signs of exposure.

In addition to the masks discussed in more detail in the catalogue, the Joss collection includes three relatively rare Zairian masks, the identification and function of which remain problematic. Although previously associated with the Holo, the mask in Fig. 19 is now more firmly attributed to the Lula peoples of western Zaire (Roy 1985:131; Christie's 1992:92). The influence of mask styles from the neighboring Yaka is evident here. Roy, citing Arthur Bourgeois, suggests that the masks may have served a similar function of protecting initiates by warding off witches from the initiation camp (Roy 1985:131).

The distinctive masks of the Boa (Bua) of north-central Zaire, with their large ring-like ears and alternating light/dark patterning (Fig. 20), are also something of an enigma. Schildkrout and Keim (citing a Tervuren catalogue entry) wrote about a similar mask collected by Armand Hutereau between 1911-1913:

> This mask, said to give power over the enemy, was from a Bua war dance called by Hutereau *pongdudu*. During a Bua rebellion against the Belgians, a colonial officer, Commandant Christians, was wounded by a Bua sorcerer who was wearing this mask. Christians managed to seize the mask, however, and then fled to Magombo Island taking it with him (1990:241).

The accuracy of this "war story" cannot be confirmed. While there are scattered references to masks being worn in battle in the old Belgian Congo,

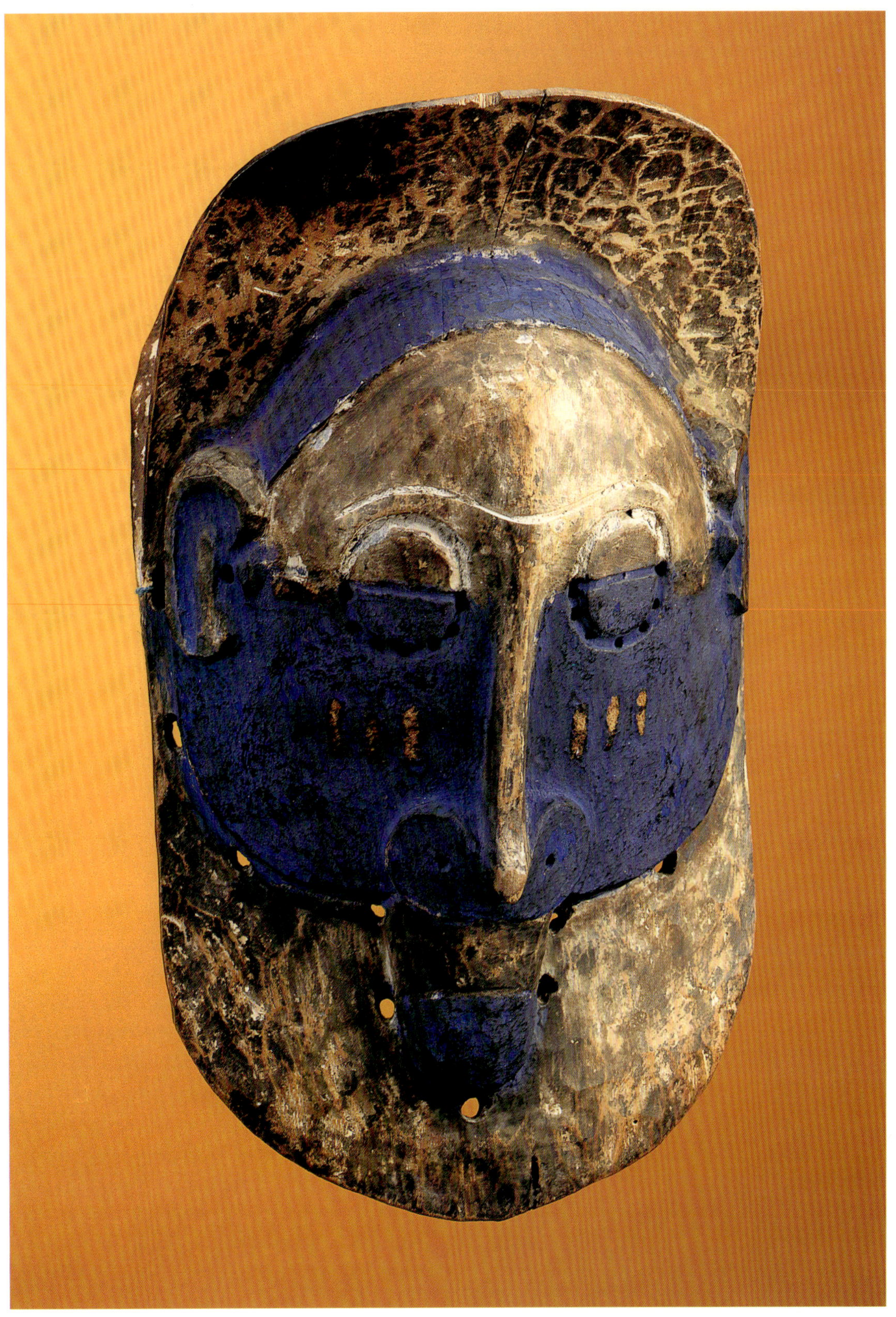

FIG. 19
MASK
Lula, Angola
Wood and pigment
H. 39.5 cm.
FMCH 87.1497

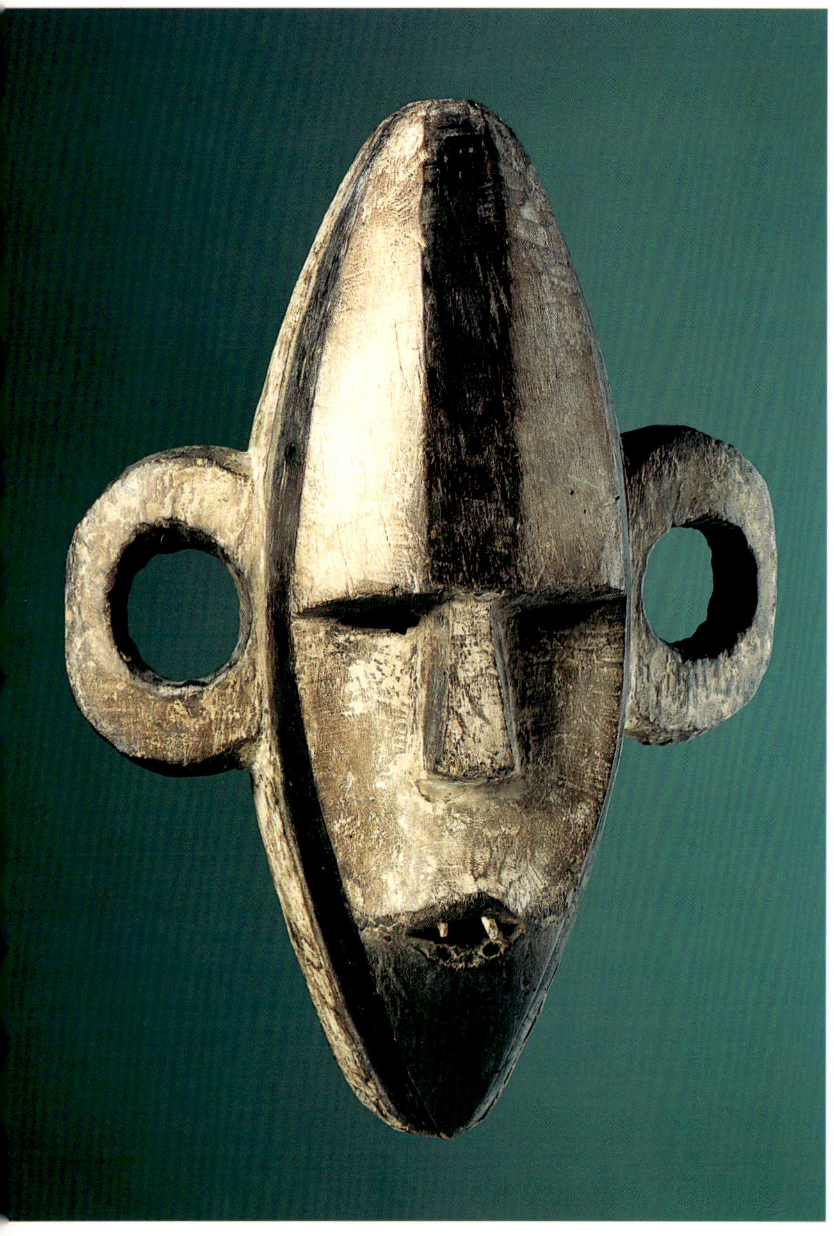

masks would seem to be a major physical handicap in combat.

To my knowledge, the third Zairian mask has no direct counterparts in the literature (Fig. 21). Tentatively identified as Pende, it does share some vague similarities with a mask published by de Sousberghe (1959: Fig. 99). Both have cylindrical eyes and a pinched mouth but the Joss mask is much more crisply executed, has different proportions, and has a well-defined ridge outlining the face, which is painted white. Clearly more research is required.

Yet another unusual genre is represented by the terra-cotta lion from the Mbaka (Ambakista) peoples of Angola (Fig. 22). It is one of three lions found with other ceramic figures in cemeteries south of Vila Salazar in northwestern Angola, a little more than 100 kilometers east of the capital of Luanda. A catalogue entry by Oliveira summarizes what is known about these terra-cottas:

> Vases and above all the small baked clay figures collected from a few cemeteries to the south of Vila Salazar, reveal an unsuspected facet of the Ambakista. At a ceremony held by the family some time after the burial, the dolls, which emphasized a quality or function which the dead one had while alive, were deposited in the grave for commemorative purposes. The variety of styles shows the diversity of periods and authors (the name of the last doll maker is known: Mandamba) who reproduced scenes of maternity, players [of *quadricula* or *alé*], horsemen, soldiery, drum beaters, etc. (1972: Entry 377).

Oliveira considered the lions to be the "outstanding" examples of the collection, which is now largely held by the Overseas Museum of Ethnology, Lisbon. As I have argued elsewhere, the image of the lion is generally rare in the pre-colonial art of sub-Saharan Africa (Ross 1982). When it does appear in the late nineteenth and twentieth centuries it is often influenced by European heraldic models, as appears to be the case in the Mbaka piece.

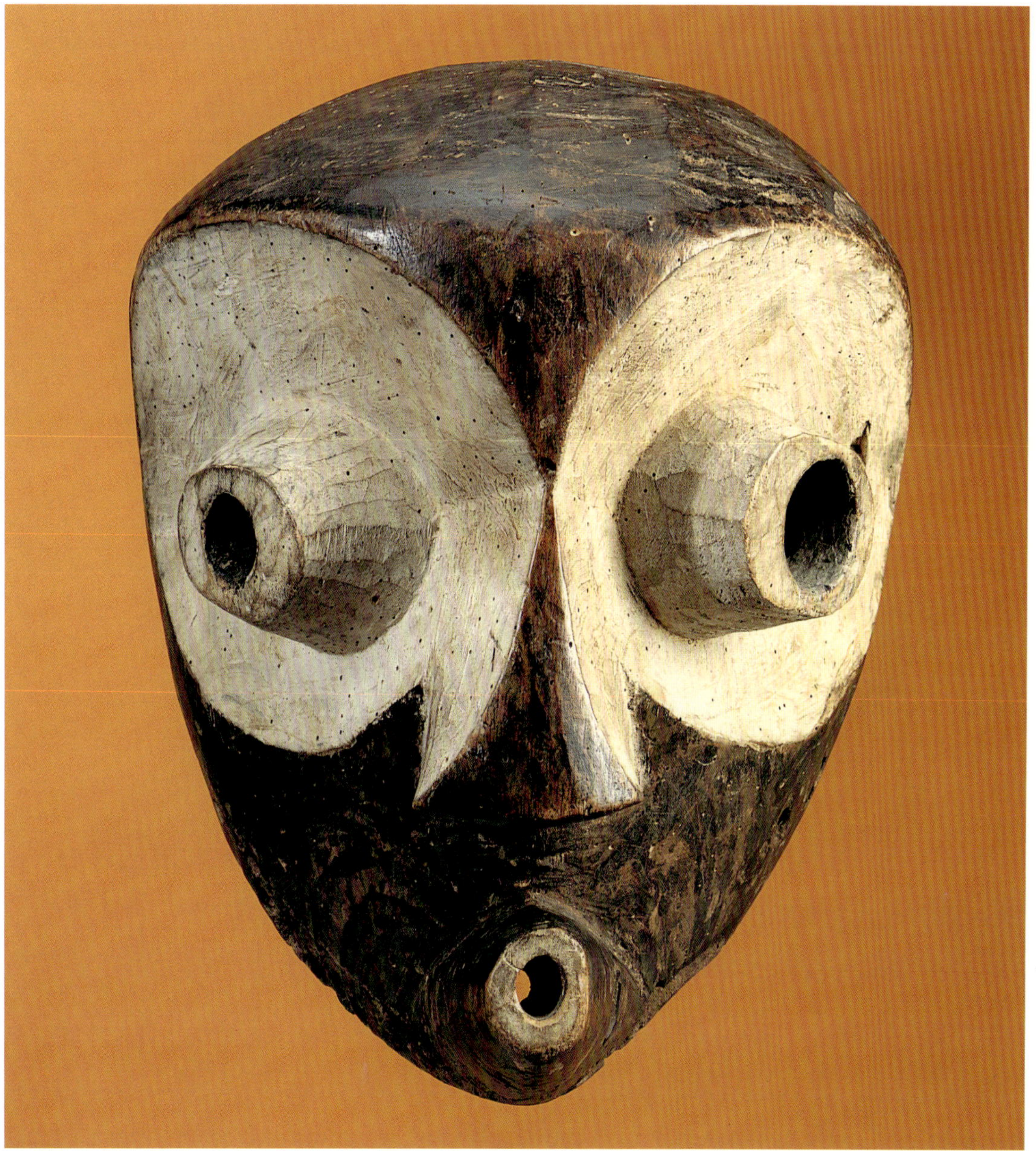

MASK
Pende, Zaire
Wood and kaolin
H. 25.3 cm.
FMCH 89.789

Much of the above discussion about poorly understood objects must remain speculative. These are some of the many challenges that African art presents to those who strive to re-create meaning for material detached from meaningful contexts. Documentation of the above objects and those that follow in the catalogue will undoubtedly evolve as more information is recorded, uncovered, or otherwise added to our understanding of African art.

Aside from the high artistic quality of many pieces, one of the principle values of the Joss collection for a university museum is its potential for research. To this end we invited scholars working in various areas of African art to add their views on selected objects from the collection. The authors were not guided in any specific direction from the Museum, but were encouraged to look at each object from their own perspective. Thus some of the catalogue

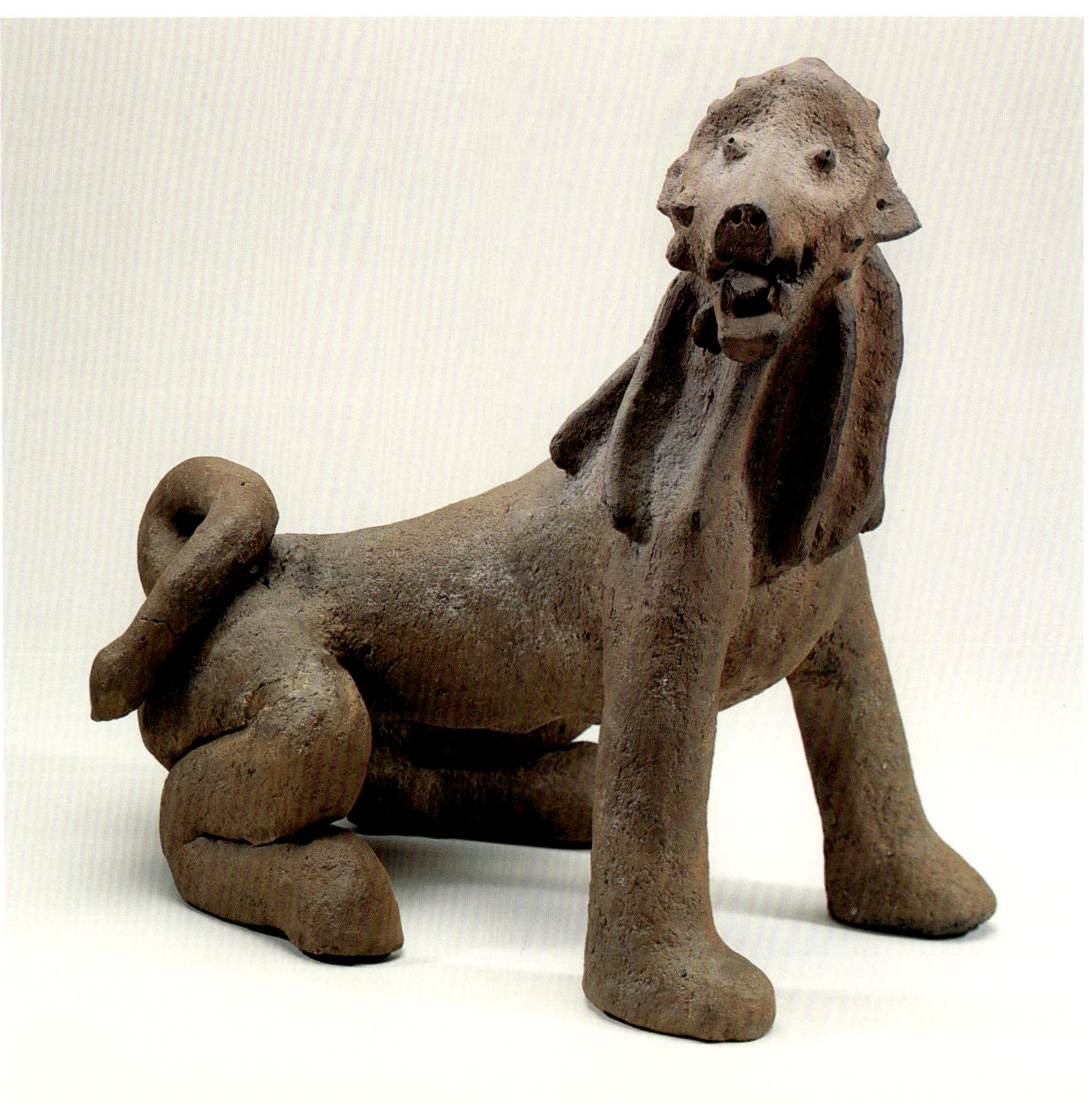

entries consider historical or iconographic issues, others deal with problems of provenance and attribution, and still others emphasize function and context. In keeping with this flexible approach, the entries of Henry Drewal are prefaced by a brief framing essay dealing with "form-words" among the Yoruba.

A Note on Organization

The organization of a volume such as this always presents problems. It has long been recognized that the artificial national boundaries of modern African states are an inadequate means of ordering a discussion of the artistic traditions of Africa. Although it is increasingly clear that division by ethnicity is also problematic, this has been the convention for the vast majority of catalogues of African art and is followed here for ease of access and to keep adjacent peoples as close together in the catalogue as possible. We begin with the Sahel and then move west to east along the nations of coastal West Africa. Central Africa comes next followed by East Africa.

CATALOGUE

1. Kore Mask, Bamana, Mali or Côte d'Ivoire

Although a number of scholars have studied Bamana sculpture, there is still relatively little information published on it. This is partly because of the nature of research to date. Scholars have not always worked (or worked extensively) in areas where some of the better known mask and figure types in western museums originate. And because Bamana sculpture is made by full time professional artists and used in fairly specialized contexts, scholars have frequently found it so cognitively and functionally complex that it was absolutely necessary to concentrate on one or a very limited number of sculpture types, still feeling by the end of their research time that vast amounts of information have not yet been acquired or explored.

But the Bamana themselves do not make analysis of their arts easy. Bamana clans inhabit Mali and northern Côte d'Ivoire, in which they overlap and intermingle with many other ethnic groups. Bamana sculpture tends to be highly adaptable, moving in and out of spiritual and social contexts as well as geographic regions. And Bamana people who view

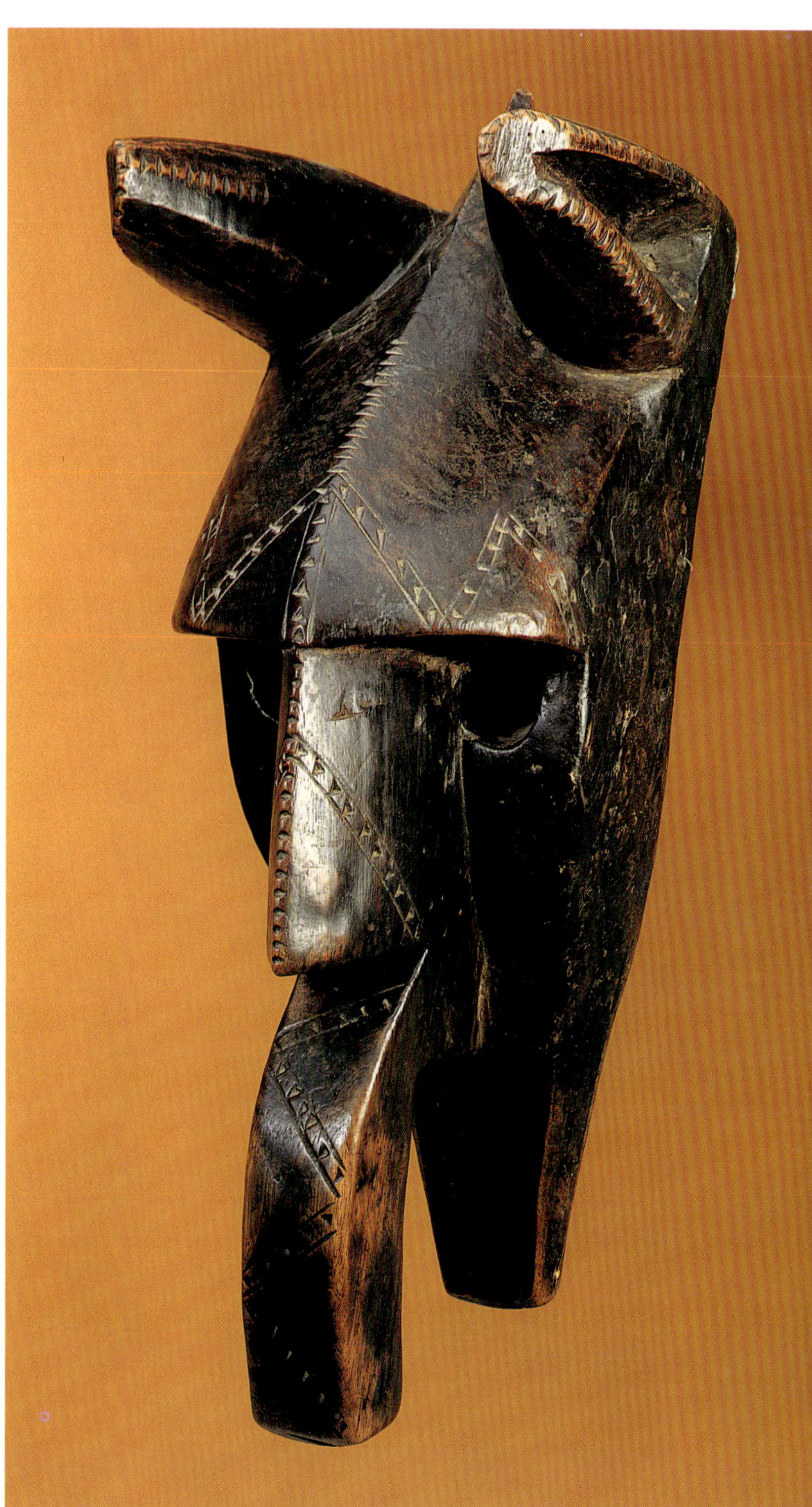

▼▲▼

1

KORE MASK

Bamana, Mali or

Côte d'Ivoire

Wood

L. 40.5 cm.

FMCH **86.1728**

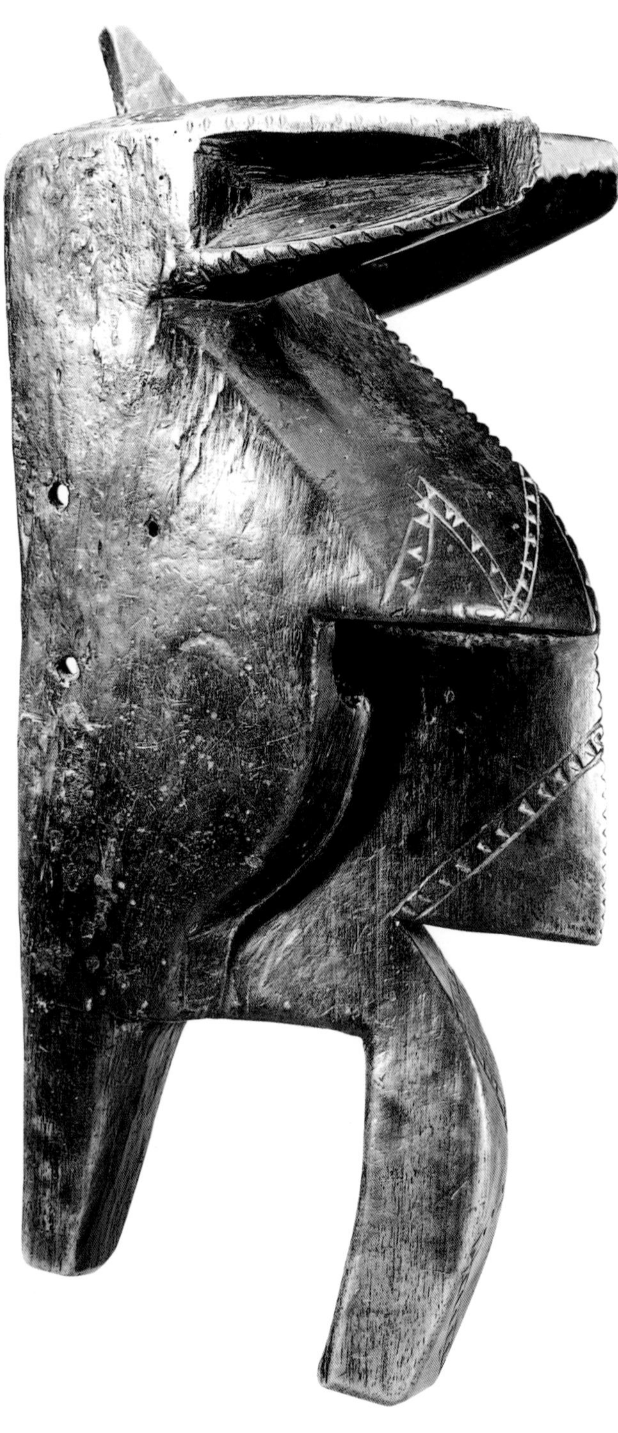

1

KORE MASK
Side view

and use sculpture often tend to be very situational in their approaches to the interpretation of images and symbols, preferring not to speak in general terms about artworks but rather to use specific events (this dance, that ritual sacrifice, etc.) as frames for their views on the meaning and quality of particular pieces. Finally, many Bamana individuals feel quite at liberty to develop very complex, esoteric and even rather personal interpretations of the sculpture they experience, as if they were philosophers asking reflexive, analytical questions of themselves and their society through the vehicle of their art. Thus, published information on Bamana sculpture should always be viewed as partial, subjective and sometimes fragmentary. But that should not be too upsetting, given the nebulous character of art.

Dominique Zahan spent considerable time and energy on the study of Kore association and its sculpture. He considered the association to be at the pinnacle of a hierarchy of six Bamana initiation associations through which the male population passed, gaining in each a progressively complex view of the world and acquiring in several specific bodies of expertise and understanding that relate to such social domains as farming or sorcery. Zahan viewed the Kore association as particularly mystical and esoteric, suggesting that it was the arena where mature men could come to grips with their own mortality and the nature of God, while at the same time acquiring great spiritual and intellectual freedom.

He described the masks of Kore as presenting a visual discourse on the nature of human wisdom and the development of personal reflexivity and self knowledge. This mask appears to combine features of a person's face and a hyena's head. Zahan says that in the context of the Kore association, hyenas symbolize foolishness, incredulity and naiveté. Thus, by likening people to hyenas, he suggests that this mask type refers to incomplete knowledge of human beings, which contrasts with God's infinite wisdom.   PATRICK MCNAUGHTON

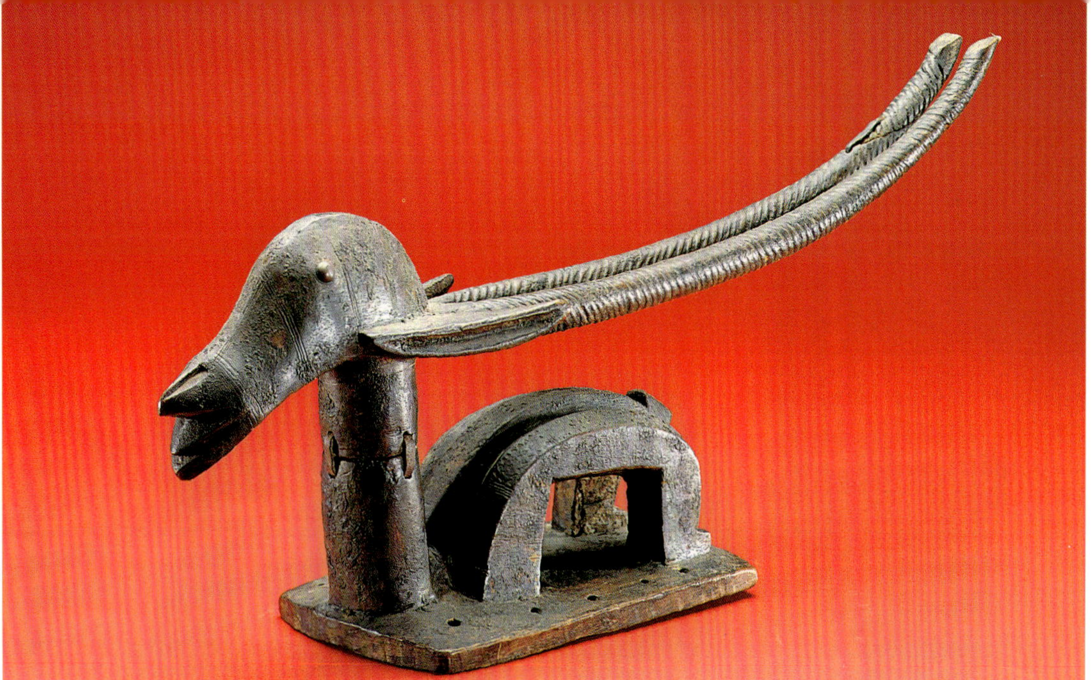

2. ANTELOPE HEADDRESS, BAMANA, MALI OR CÔTE D'IVOIRE

Scholars who are interested in reconstructing (or constructing) the histories of African art types almost always face great adversity at every turn. Evidence is often ahistorical, or historical in a kind of patchwork of fragmented data that are suggestive of complex processes of stylistic and conceptual changes but gallingly incomplete and contestable.

Nowhere is this better illustrated than with the well known "antelope" or "animal" headdresses that hail from Mande language groups such as the Bamana, Maninka and Wasaluka and neighboring groups such as the Voltaic language-speaking Minianka. One need only peruse a handful of publications—by Kjersmeier, Lem, Goldwater, Imperato (whose work is marvelously detailed) and Zahan—to realize how complex the history of related art forms can be, from its diaspora to its constantly changing formal, iconographic, contextual and functional manifestations. Imperato, for example, names three institutions (the spiritual Ci Wara initiation association, the secular Ton youth association, and the Gonzon voluntary work association) in which these sculptures perform, each with its own variations of the ideas, lore and patterns of use that are broadly associated with these headdresses. A correlation with agriculture is a major hallmark of the headdresses, one that reinforces the notion maintained by many scholars that they are historically related.

Farming is the principle occupation for many of the ethnic groups living in this western savannah region. Ci wara, Ton, and Gonzon and the "antelope" and various other "animal" headdresses associated with them are all oriented towards successful cultivation and bountiful harvests. Members carry out communal farming and the associations undertake various activities, including propitiation of spiritual forces linked to agriculture, teaching farming techniques, the celebration and glorification of good farming and even annual cultivation contests. Well to the east, the Voltaic language-speaking Mossi use an antelope headdress called *zazaido* which is also associated with agriculture.

Headdress symbolism seems to refer to agriculture in a round about way. Animals are respected and admired for their strength and toughness. For example, Ci wara is a praise name meaning "farming beast" as well as being the name of an institution and the headdresses associated with it. Some authors (such as Imperato, de Ganay and Zahan) say it is also the name of the spiritual creature that gave human beings the gift of agriculture. Brink notes that animals depicted in the headdresses suggest certain values associated with competent farming. Aardvarks are perceived as determined and conscientious. Roan (depicted in this example) and dwarf antelopes are perceived as very graceful and strong. As Brink also notes, institution events also emphasize sexual union an social cooperation between women and men, and this is one reason the antelope headdresses generally perform in male-female pairs. PM

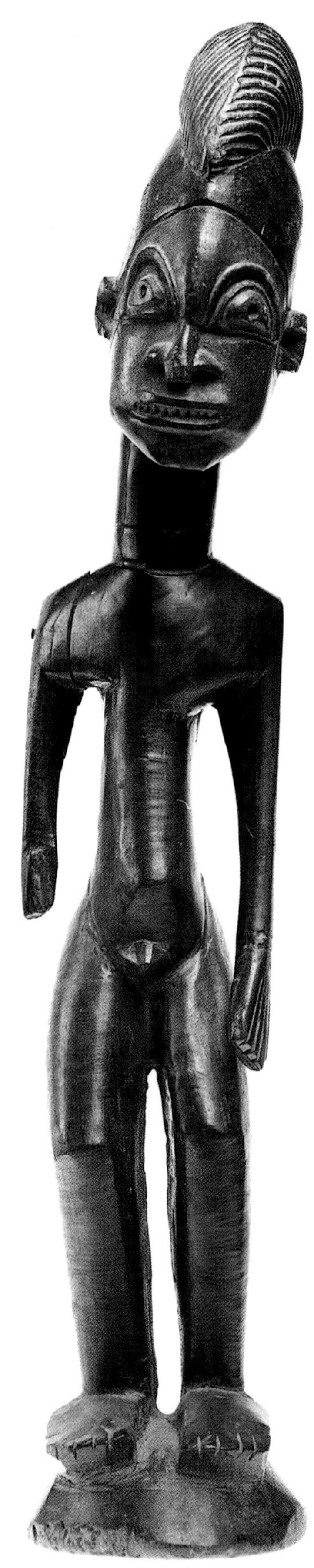

(left)

3

FIGURE

Lobi, Côte d'Ivoire

Wood

H. 59 cm.

FMCH 87.1200

FIG. 23

(right)

Masks, stools,
and axe handle
thought to be
carved by
Sikire Kambire and
collected by
Henri Laborret.
(Laborret 1931:
Plate XVI)

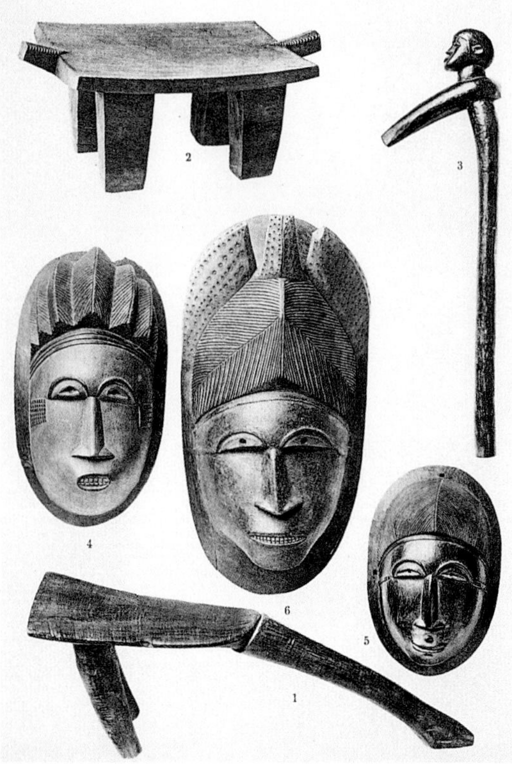

3. FIGURE, LOBI, CÔTE D'IVOIRE
4. STOOL, LOBI, CÔTE D'IVOIRE

These two carvings are attributed to the Lobi sculptor Sikire Kambire (1896–1963). Citing the research of his translator Biwathe Kambon, Piet Meyer has provided the most detailed description of Sikire's life and work (1981:127–133). Sikire was born in 1896 in Gongombili in what is now Burkina Faso. He began carving at the age of sixteen and by the early 1920s he had moved to the district capital of Gaoua where he earned a reputation as the finest carver in the area. Sikire's work captured the attention of several colonial officials who favored him with numerous commissions including doors, tables, chairs, stools, figures, and masks. In 1931 the colonial official Henri Laborret, who was commissioning carv-

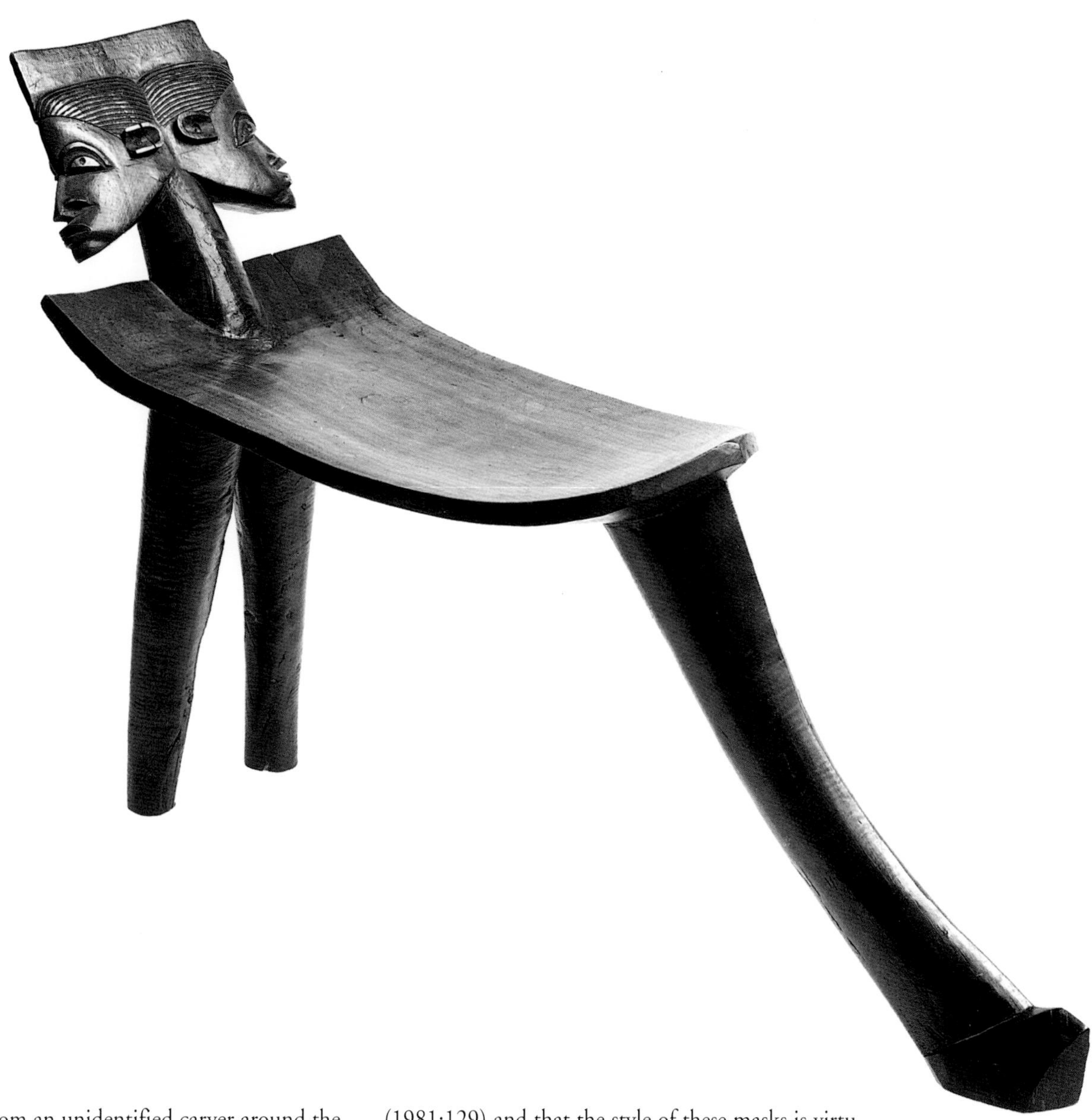

ings (Fig. 23) from an unidentified carver around the same time, wrote about the Lobi:

> The art of sculpture was not practiced by specialists but by many natives who are relatively talented. One of them was asked by me to copy a Baule mask which I brought back from the Ivory Coast. Since then he has made a considerable number of such masks to sell to the Europeans. He has even trained students who work for export. This was a technique formed whose origins will be forgotten in a few years. Its existence will give rise to the supposition that the Lobi were familiar with wood masks earlier. This supposition is however false (1931:188, XVI).

Meyer convincingly argues that the unidentified carver of the masks was indeed Sikire Kambire (1981:129) and that the style of these masks is virtually identical to that of a cluster of figurative carvings, stools with carved human heads and dance staffs. The two carvings illustrated here are certainly part of the same body of work and belong to the artist's earlier work, which Meyer distinguished from his "plumper" more "schematized" later work of the 1950's (1981:133). Meyer identified two of Sikire's numerous students, cautioning that until we have further documentation it is probably more appropriate to use the attribution "school of Sikire Kambire" than to attribute works to the master himself. Although the carver died in 1963, in the late seventies he was still regarded as the finest Lobi sculptor in the Gaoua area.

DORAN H. ROSS

▼▲▼

4

STOOL

Lobi, Côte d'Ivoire

Wood

L. 52 cm.

FMCH 87.1216

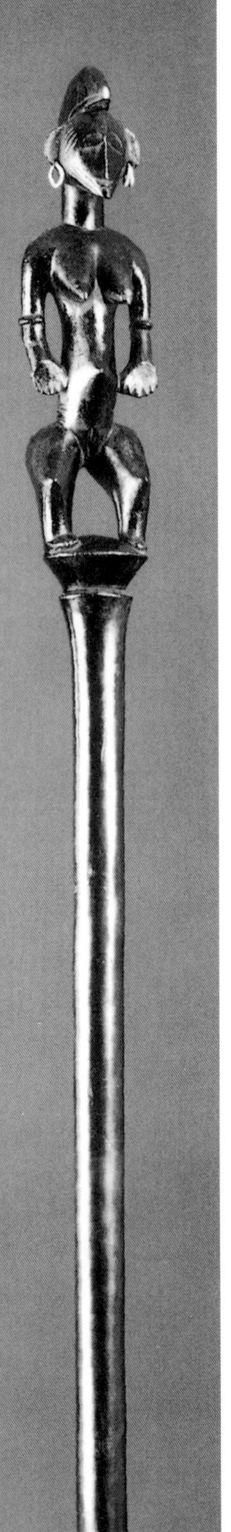

5. Staff with Standing Female Figure, Senufo, Côte d'Ivoire

Designed for portability and mobility, the very nature of the figurative staff implies movement, drama, gesture and dance. Staff types used primarily in ritual tend to be short for ease of carrying, while those intended for periodic display in an exterior or architectural space tend to be long with iron tips for anchoring in the ground.[1] Staff configurations and contexts vary widely but the most common are: 1) champion cultivator staffs used in hoeing contests, for funerary display and dances (long, iron-tipped and with a seated young female); 2) staffs featuring the female icons either sitting or standing that served as guardian spirit figures in shrines and altars or in motion as escorts for masquerades (short, blunt, usually with a standing female power figure); 3) numerous varieties of Poro Society trophy staffs carried by initiates honored by special titles or status, (e.g. lead vocalists and "champion singers" in Poro song ceremonies); and 4) female guardian staffs (with tip and figures in both seated and standing poses) for personal *yasungo* medicine shrines. Sadly, most staffs collected are without the beads, string, feathers, fur, quills, ritual paint or other materials that would have completed the correct iconography and intended aesthetic presentation of the object. This beautiful old staff is difficult to assign to any one category without further data. Longer than normal, the staff has a richly oiled patina and iron tip, which suggest a multiple-setting purpose. The staff appears to have been created for a Poro context rather than as a champion cultivator staff, and to have been handed down from one Poro age grade to the next. This is particularly suggested by the standing pose of the figure and the hole on the crown (rather than on each side of the coiffure) for the addition of materials such as feathers.

The staff was probably carved by a blacksmith sculptor, although much remains unclear about the stylistic relationship of blacksmiths to Kulele work before the 1930s. The figure is notable for the artist's deft articulation of the three strong masses of head, shoulder and thighs along the vertical axis and the ancient device of a knobbed section between figure and staff.

Anita J. Glaze

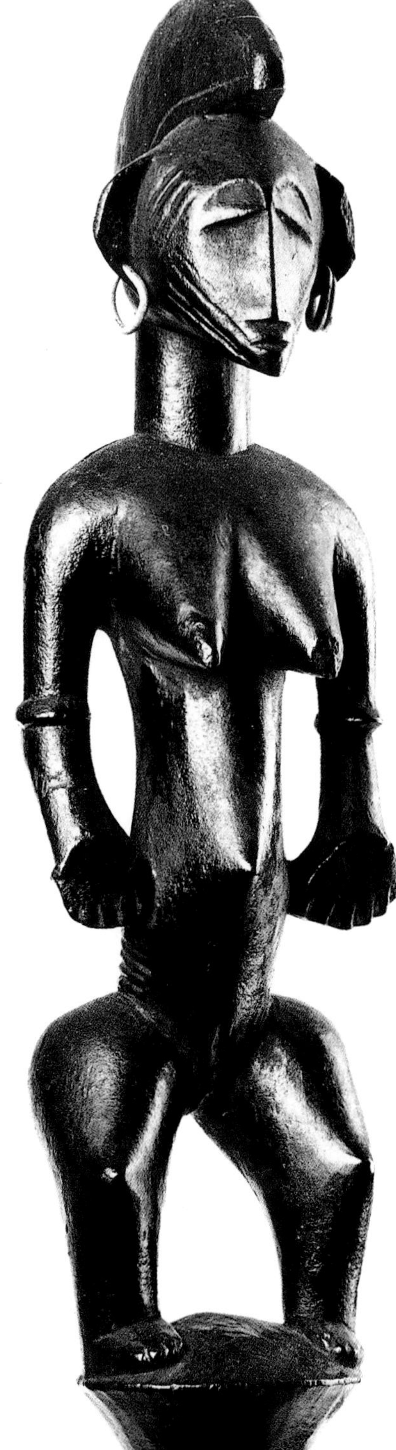

[1] Staff categories have been poorly documented in the literature. One problem is that countless standing and seated figures in collections have been cut off from staffs to facilitate packing and shipping.

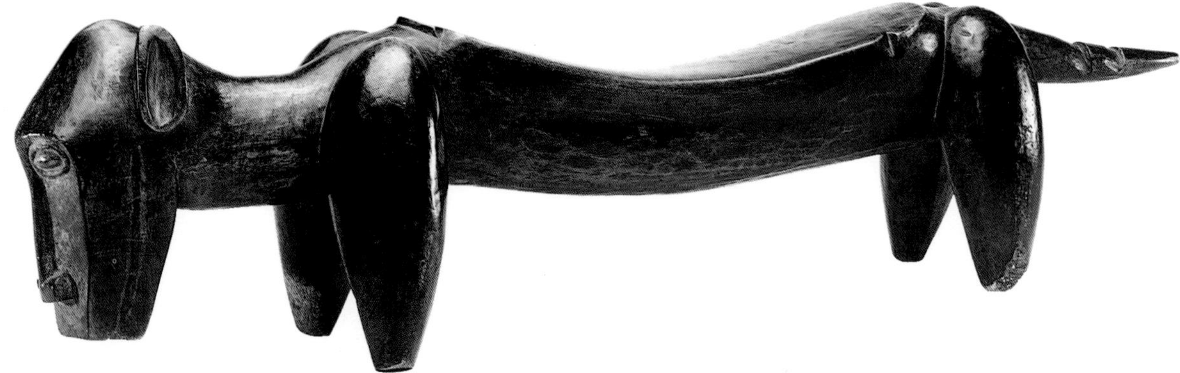

6. DANCE HORSE, PORO, SENUFO, CÔTE D'IVOIRE

Gɔrɔ is a festival of joy and celebration that takes place during the dry season following Kafwɔ, the final graduation ceremonies of the Poro Society. Gɔrɔ is derived from the phrase "I am tranquil, at rest" and refers to the relief and gratitude the recent graduate feels about his release from the exacting demands of the twenty-year initiation cycle. Lively music, dancing, singing, clowning musicians in comical attire, and feasting are all part of the exuberant spirit of freedom that is inherent in Gɔrɔ.[1]

The Gɔrɔ dance horse (*syòóngɔrɔ*) is designed to be straddled by an agile dancer and, as the stool-like legs suggest, can be used as a seat. "Horse" is equated with status and praise rather than an exact image of a horse (rarely seen by Senufo). Chosen as the "champion" dancer of his age-group, the *syòóngɔrɔ* rider jogs and dances round the musicians of a balafon and horn orchestra. A long shoulder strap attached to the horse allows the dancer's hands to be free to carry a horsetail dance whisk and a flintlock rifle. A multi-colored raffia collar adorns the neck, and a smaller one the tail of the horse (notched for the purpose); a large, cast brass bell is tied around the horse's neck to underline the dancer's movement and add *tana* or prestigious display. By sculpture and gesture the danced "horse" honors selected individuals in the audience. A beautiful young woman is greeted as the rider leaps and twists about in the air to land about-face in front of her. Poro leaders and helpful elders are singled out by the rider galloping up and then sitting down before him with songs of praise.

Technically not part of the Poro initiation system, the Gɔrɔ festival is not universally celebrated throughout the Central Senufo region, and the dance horse occurs even less commonly.[2] The origin and center of the dance horse tradition appears to be the Boundiali region, although the festival itself is an old tradition, which extends as far as the Gbato area to the southwest. The Gɔrɔ horse is characteristic of the dance horses carved by the Kulele sculptors in workshops such as Kolia and Sienre of the Bagoe River Valley north of Boundiali.[3]　　　　AG

[1] The highlight of Gɔrɔ is a beautiful dance featuring the young girls selected by the recent graduates (*kafwɔkɔnbele*) as the best dancers. For all the young girls who have been chosen as the graduates' ritual partners during the festival, it is a time of gaiety and "youthful beauty" before the serious duty of arranged marriages to older men.

[2] Data on Gɔrɔ in the Dikodougou district document the pattern of borrowing from one Senufo dialect area to another and the introduction of new cultural traditions and forms within the recent history of a particular area. In 1969 in the Kufuru or Dikodougou district, Gɔrɔ was said to be relatively new, and only one village in the entire area was reported to possess a dance horse. The concept of Gɔrɔ and the style of dance and music had been introduced to the Kufuru from Dagba and other Kafiri villages of the Sirasso district and to neighboring Kufuru villages such as Nɔɔkata'a, Langoka'a and Pindoka'a. The Gɔrɔ of Nɔɔkata'a was still linked by exchanges with Dagba, a Kafiri village famous for the quality of its week-long Gɔrɔ festival. However, according to Nɔɔkata'a elders (March 1970), the best Gɔrɔ music was to be heard at Kanaroba, Gbatoso, Diari and Boundiali, all villages where the Gɔrɔ is "very old."

[3] The articulation of the head varies greatly from one sculptor to another; in this case, the head has been carved wider and larger in proportion to the rest of the body than is usual.

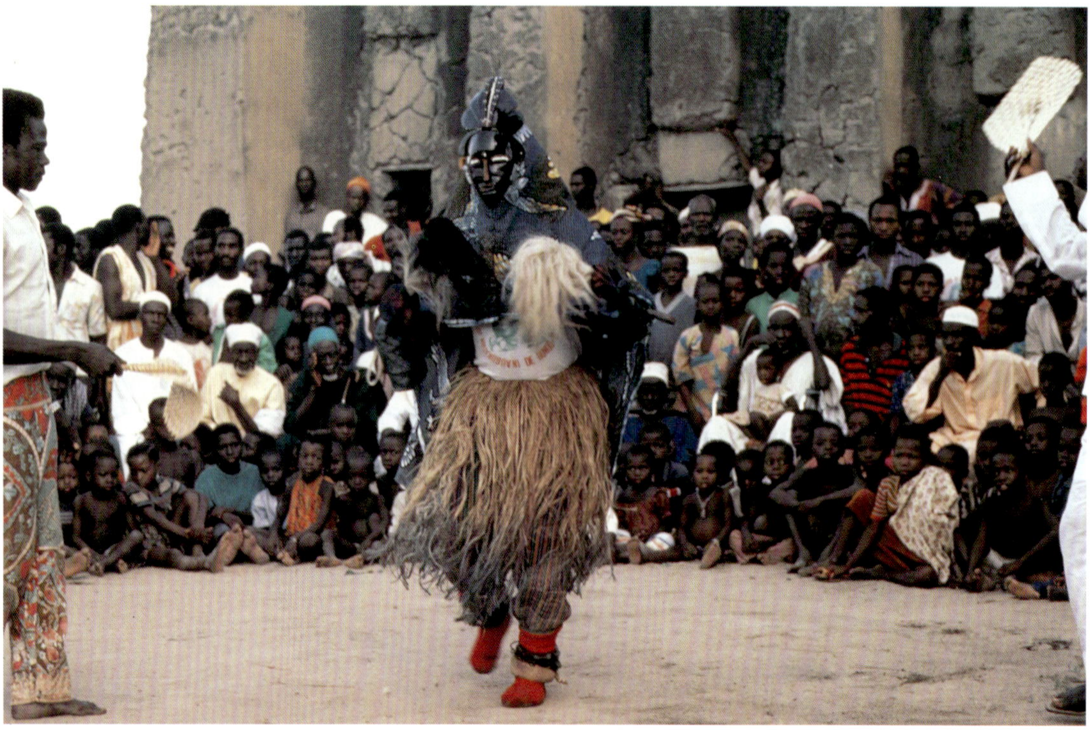

7. *Do* Mask Surmounted by Reverse Head, Djimini or Dyula community (?), east-central Côte d'Ivoire

This mask, which is surmounted by a reversed head, and the one that represents a wart hog (see Cat. 8, FMCH 86.1729) were used in *do* performances in the Mande or Mande-influenced communities of east-central Côte d'Ivoire and adjacent areas of west Ghana. *Do* performances have also been documented further to the east in and around the towns of Kong and Dabakala.[1] Attribution of these masks to specific ethnic groups is often difficult because the mask-type crosses ethnic boundaries. Nevertheless, based on the limited knowledge of the stylistic attributes of *do* masks produced by peoples living south of the Senufo region, this mask may have been used by either a Djimini or Dyula community in the region around the town of Dabakala.

The word *do*, or *dou*, is a Mandekan term that conveys the notion of secrecy or something that is hidden.[2] Many peoples in Côte d'Ivoire, Burkina Faso and Ghana use the term to describe a variety of masked performances. The first Europeans to visit the Bondoukou region of eastern Côte d'Ivoire reported witnessing *do* performances, but it was not until 1974 that the art historian René Bravmann (1974:147–72) produced the first substantive account of the tradition.[3]

Do performances usually feature a number of stock characters, the most common of which is the (beautiful) woman *(domuso)* (Fig. 24). The tradition is flexible, however, allowing local, even idiosyncratic variations. The depiction of a human face surmounted by an inverted smaller face on the *do* mask is iconographically unique. The closest analogy is a mask documented in a Ligbi community near Bondoukou, which presents a human face surmounted by the upper torso and head of a woman. The female figure is said to represent a *nanguini*—the Dyula term for a small, malevolent being that inhabits the forest and is especially dangerous to children who may "pick one up without knowing it."[4]

Before each performance, *do* face masks are generally oiled to attain a shiny surface, and pigments, in this case blue, red and white, are applied to highlight various features of the mask. This treatment is likened to using cosmetics to enhance the beauty of the human face.   RAYMOND A. SILVERMAN

[1] Prouteaux (1925:628–629) and Green (1987) have documented the tradition in Kong. Suthers has collected information about the tradition in the area around Dabakala where it is found in both Dyula and Djimini communities (pers. comm. 1988).
[2] For a fuller discussion of the meaning of this term see Silverman forthcoming.
[3] The early references to the tradition are cited in Silverman forthcoming.
[4] I was told that "in the olden days when children went to the bush to play, the *nanguini* sat on the heads of the children. If the children stayed in the bush without having the *nanguini* removed from their heads they would die. This is why the *nanguini* is depicted on the top of the head of the mask." Interview, Bondo Dyula, June 22, 1988.

8. *Do* Mask Representing a Wart Hog
Bondoukou region (?), Côte d'Ivoire

In the past *do* performances possessed religious significance, but today they are considered primarily entertainment, staged to celebrate special occasions. Since most of the peoples who maintain the tradition (or who have maintained it in the recent past) are Muslim, masquerades are held during festivals like *id al-Fitr*, the holiday marking the end of Ramadan, the month of fasting, and *id al-Qabir*, the celebration of the sacrifice of Abraham. *Do* masquerades also may

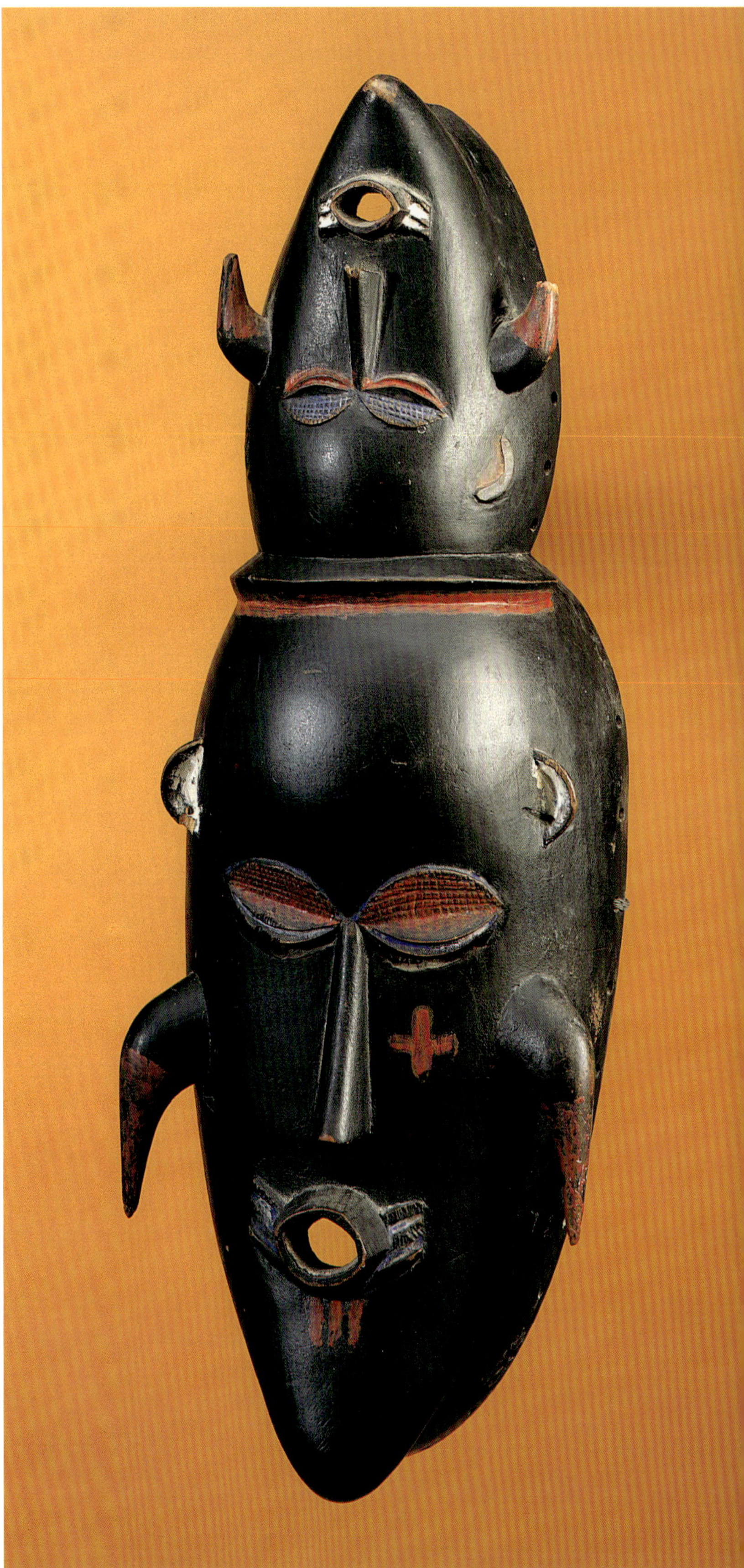

▼▲▼
______
7

DO MASK
SURMOUNTED BY
REVERSE HEAD
Djimini or
Dyula community (?),
east-central Côte d'Ivoire
Wood and laundry bluing
H. 39 cm.
FMCH 87.1494

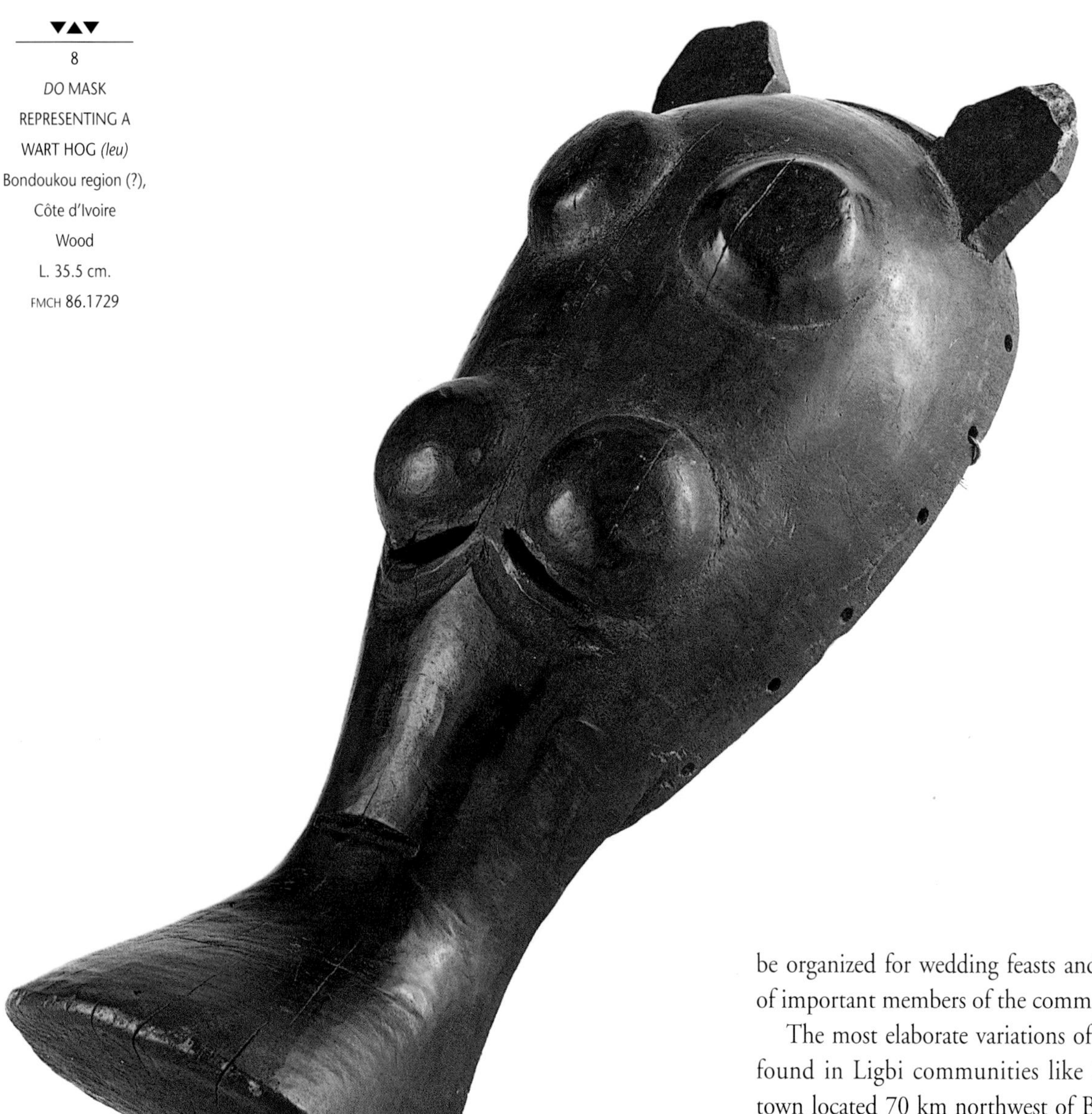

▼▲▼

8

DO MASK
REPRESENTING A
WART HOG *(leu)*
Bondoukou region (?),
Côte d'Ivoire
Wood
L. 35.5 cm.
FMCH 86.1729

be organized for wedding feasts and for the funerals of important members of the community.

The most elaborate variations of the tradition are found in Ligbi communities like Bondo Dyula, a town located 70 km northwest of Bondoukou. Here *do* performances may best be described as theater, similar in structure to a play in which there are several acts with intermissions. The performance generally begins after the mid-afternoon prayer (about four o'clock) when the masked figure called *nafiedou* walks through the town, followed by a crowd of children, announcing that the play will soon begin.[1] The play itself is comprised of several acts during which masked dancers perform either singularly or in pairs. At performances attended in 1988, masks represented a variety of stock characters: beautiful woman

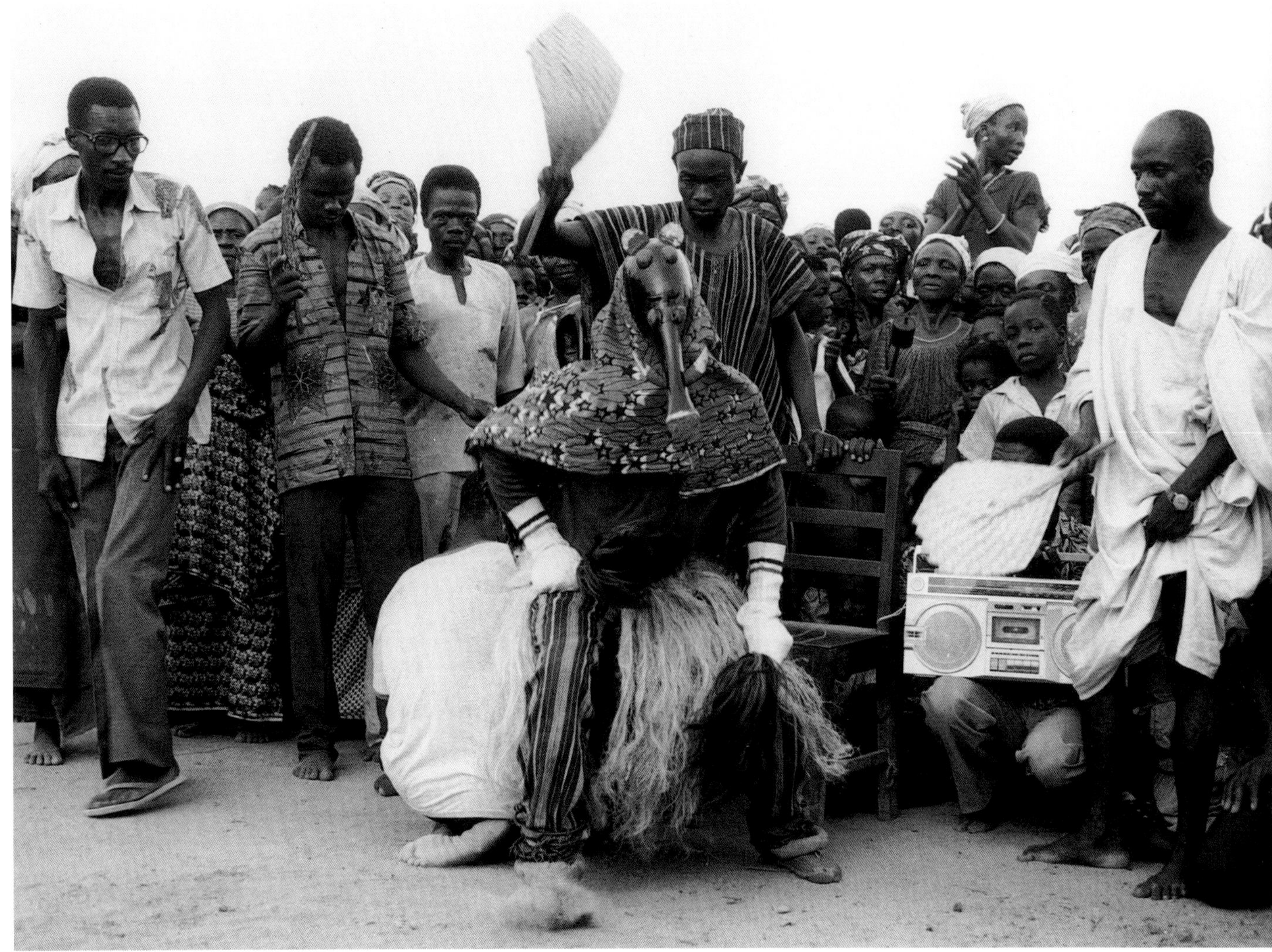

(*domuso*) (Fig. 24), bush cow (*siguin*), hornbill (*yangariya*), pygmy (*nanguini*), and finally wart hog (*leu*) (Fig. 25).

In the performances seen in Bondo Dyula in 1988, this latter character appeared in the final act of a pantomime of a hunter stalking a wart hog. In this reenactment of the hunt, after several minutes of careful maneuvering, the hunter shoots his gun but misses his target, and the wart hog attacks the hunter. The act was extremely popular, and though the audience knew the outcome, it took great delight in seeing *leu* prevail.

The mask is similar to two other published *leu* masks. The first was collected by C.H. Armitage at the turn of the century, the second was documented in 1967–68 in Bondo Dyula by René Bravmann.[2]

Although it was carved without the tusks seen on the other two examples, the general proportions and other stylistic features of the mask suggest that it is a product of the *do* traditions of the Bondoukou region.   RAS

[1] *Nafiedou* also plays the dual role of clown and policeman once the performance begins.

[2] The Armitage mask, which is now in the collection of the Museum of Mankind, London, was first published by Underwood (1948:pl. 25) and is also reproduced in Bravmann (1974:fig. 61). Bravmann (1974:figs. 62 & 75) also published the Bondo Dyula mask, which he had documented during his research in the Ligbi village in 1967–68. This mask was apparently sold or stolen for it appeared (repainted) in a 1979 Paris auction and was illustrated in the catalogue (Loudmer-Poulain 1979:56). I would like to thank Philip Ravenhill for drawing my attention to the Loudmer-Poulain sale of the Bondo Dyula mask.

FIG. 25

Do mask representing wart hog *(leu)*. Photo: R. Silverman, 1988.

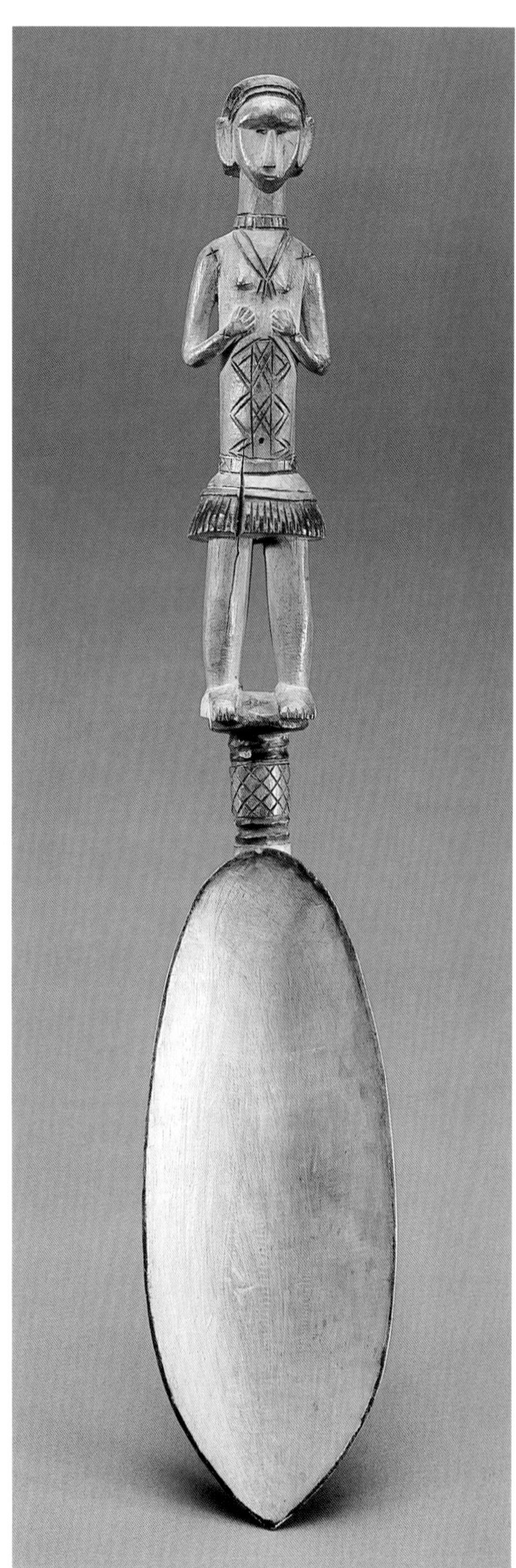

9
LADLE
Bidjogo,
Bissagos Archipelago,
Guinea-Bissau
Wood
L. 41 cm.
FMCH 86.1733

9. LADLE, BIDJOGO, BISSAGOS ARCHIPELAGO, GUINEA-BISSAU

This ladle belongs to a complex of ritual utensils used by the Bidjogo in the preparation and serving of ceremonial meals during initiation (*fanado*). Iconographically, Bidjogo ladles occur in a range of sizes and shapes and exhibit a variety of decoration on the finials and handles. Ladle motifs may incorporate intricate geometric patterns, zoomorphic heads, human heads, partial female torsos, as well as the fully articulated female form. In this example, the age and status of the female figure is signaled by her coiffure, elaborate scarification and fiber skirt (*candi*). Abdominal scarification signals that a female has completed her initiation cycle and is ready to marry. In addition, patterns of scarification specific to an individual village also signal lineage affiliations (Gallois-Duquette 1983:93, 151). Shoulder scarification has erogenous implications, further accentuating the sensuality of an adult woman.

The repeated use of female imagery as a symbol of fertility and prosperity within the Bidjogo ritual art complex highlights the importance and respect given to women in Bidjogo society. Women are viewed as central to the socio-religious equilibrium of the society. Agriculturally, women play an active role in the production of their primary subsistence crop, rice (i.e. planting, harvesting and preparation). On a spiritual level, a female priestess (*oquinca*) serves as the caretaker of the principle village shrine, the custodian of specialized knowledge and obligations used to determine the needs and appease the wrath of the spirits (*unikan*). Within the initiation cycle, female initiates may also serve as intermediary links (*defuntos*) between the world of the living and that of the dead. According to Bidjogo belief, if a boy dies before completing his initiation, his soul is destined to wander and suffer within a dangerous liminal zone (Gallois-Duquette 1979:31). Wandering souls (*oshó*) are considered a serious threat to the

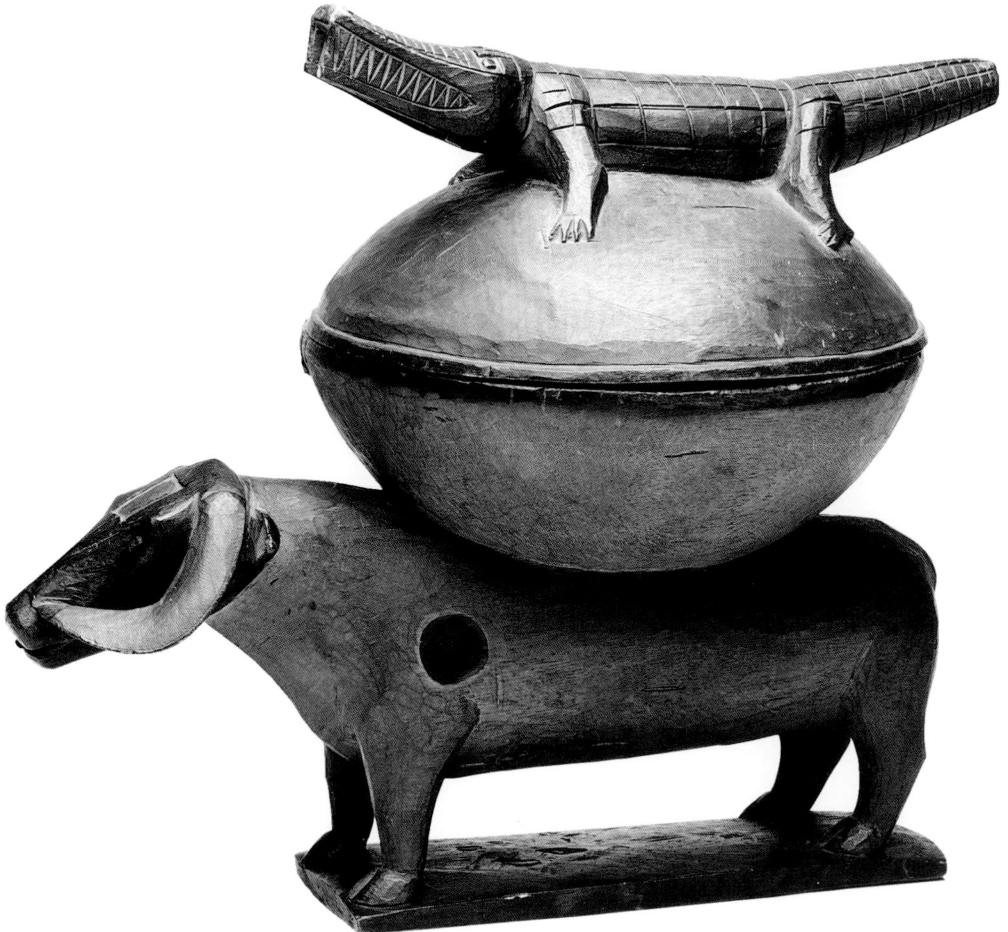

10
CARYATID CONTAINER
WITH LID *(tagara)*
Bidjogo,
Bissagos Archipelago,
Guinea-Bissau
Wood
A (container), L. 44 cm.
B (lid), L. 33 cm.
FMCH 86.1735A,B

community. It is only through the female initiation cycle that the *oshó* are allowed to gain access to adult status, restoring the community to a safe spiritual balance.

JERI BERNADETTE WILLIAMS

10. CARYATID CONTAINER WITH LID, BIDJOGO, BISSAGOS ARCHIPELAGO, GUINEA-BISSAU

Containers such as this one are used primarily during the initiation cycle (*fanado*) to prepare and serve ritual meals. The imagery of the containers metaphorically reflects the opposition of the uninitiated/initiated through contrasts of land/sea or village/bush. The container juxtaposes a crocodile lid, representing the unpredictable and untamed forces of the aquatic realm, with the domesticated village ox (*dugn'be*) base, reinforcing the concept of the pre-initiate as an undisciplined being whose strength has just begun to be tamed. The choice of imagery is characteristic of the Bidjogo preference for aquatic and bovine themes, which are charged with the wild and uncontrolled energies of both the land and the sea. Although not numerous, similar wooden caryatid containers and ritual utensils[1] from the last quarter of the nineteenth century are in German and Portuguese collections (Krieger 1969:figs. 19–24; Bernatzik 1933:figs. 375-376 ; Galhano 1971:figs. 1–18).

JBW

---

[1] Sculptural examples range from stools, staffs, spoons, ladles and containers to the art of masquerade.

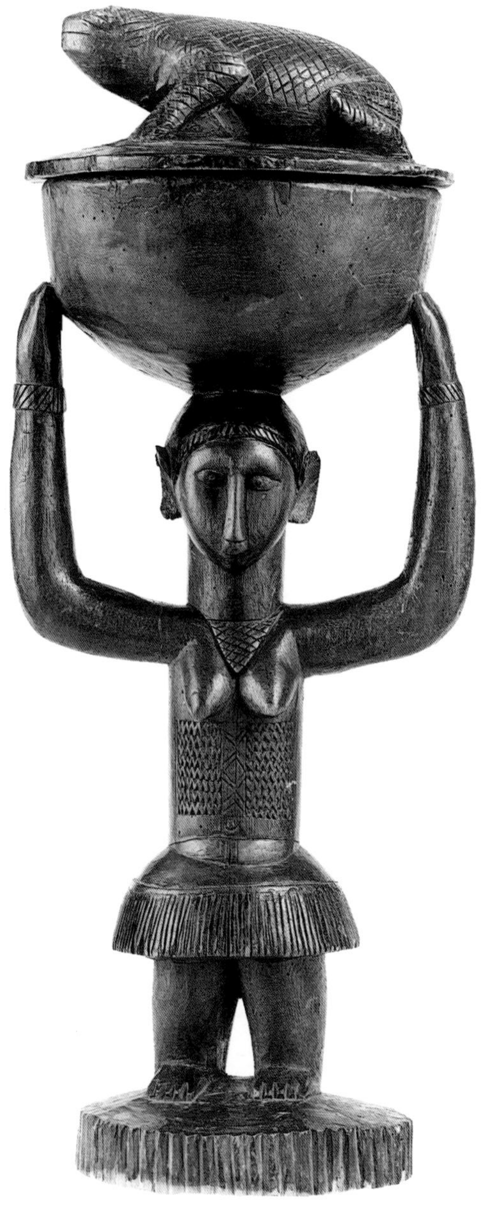

11
CARYATID CONTAINER
WITH LID *(tagara)*
Bidjogo,
Bissagos Archipelago,
Guinea-Bissau
Wood
A (container), H. 47 cm.
B (lid), Dia. 18.2 cm.
FMCH 86.1734A,B

flux and transformation. The female caryatid is the perfect metaphor to complete the nature-village dialectic. Coiffure, extensive abdominal scarification and distinctive fiber skirt (*candi*), suggest that she has already completed the initiation cycle and has successfully passed into adult status.   JBW

12. FIGURE, BIDJOGO, BISSAGOS ARCHIPELAGO, GUINEA-BISSAU

Religion is a vital and dynamic part of Bidjogo life. The spiritual and physical well-being of both the individual and village depends on a positive relationship with the world of the spirits. A clear distinction is made between the two divisions of the cosmos. The first level is characterized by the most powerful sacred energies. Nindo, the supreme creator god, is a distant and ethereal being who is responsible for man's general welfare. The second level includes several types of *unikan*, or spirit manifestations. According to Bidjogo belief, *unikan* possess the power to either harm or protect and are the only agents who can serve as intermediaries between the gods, ancestors and man.

These spiritual essences, *unikan*, which are more commonly referred to by the creole term *iran*, may be interpreted by a range of artistic forms (Williams 1992:21–27). The concept of *iran*, both as spirit and tangible sculpture, permeates all aspects of reality within the Bidjogo community. Serving as key extensions of the social and cosmic order, *iran* are present at rites of birth, death, initiation, periods of crisis and at agricultural festivals. They are omnipresent and omnipotent; adored as well as feared.

The *iran* represents the most powerful spirit, Orebok-Ocoto ("The Great Spirit"). Considered the spiritual guardian of the village, Orebok-Ocoto serves as an indispensable intermediary between the inaccessible Nindo and the world of the living. Stylistically this piece, distinguished by a partially hollowed cylinder surmounted by a anthropomorphic head/neck, is associated with the most versatile and art historically rich categories of *iran* sculpture (Williams 1992:Chart 2, Style X). The headgear,

11. CARYATID CONTAINER WITH LID BIDJOGO, BISSAGOS ARCHIPELAGO, GUINEA-BISSAU

A carved wooden female figure supports a container on her head. A frog squats on the lid of the container. This caryatid container functioned as a ceremonial food bowl during the initiation cycle (*fanado*). The sculptural composition metaphorically reinforces the concept of transition experienced by the initiates by representing the contrasting realms of the land and sea. The selection of an amphibian motif as the handle stresses the marginality of the initiate's new status during his transition into adulthood. Just as the frog is neither solely associated with land or sea, the initiate is neither child nor adult, neither bush nor village, but is in a liminal zone of cloth additions, metal eye inserts, and application of prescribed pigments are status markers, which further enhance the majesty and prestige of the figure.

The specifics of form, obligatory preparations, choice of woods, pigments and specialized accouterments of the *iran* are determined during the initial consultation with a diviner and/or herbalist. It is only after this meeting that an *iran* can be translated into its tangible form. During the first stages of fabrication, an *iran* sculpture is referred to as *boneca* (literally, "doll"), an object without value. It is only after the body of the *boneca* is properly anointed that the sculpture can be transformed into an *iran*, which bears its own unique name (Scantamburlo 1978:83). The role of a particular *iran*, whether to commemorate, control or persuade, can be deduced by its appropriate sacrifice (*ronia*). The *ronia* is the key component which invigorates an otherwise "lifeless" carving, localizing sacred energy into a tangible and accessible form and transforming the profane into the sacred. When an *iran* sculpture has deteriorated beyond repair or has been sold or stolen, the spirit is asked to pass into a new sculpture with the introduction of *ronia*.   JBW

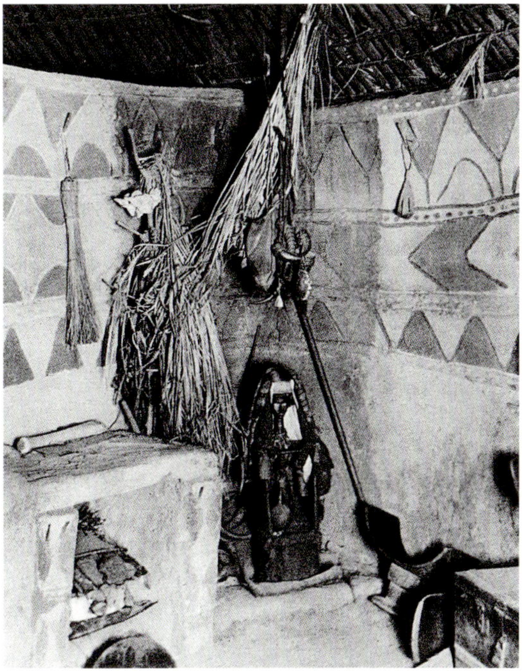

Figure (*iran*) in a shrine in the village of Bijante. (Bernatzik 1933: between 192, 93)

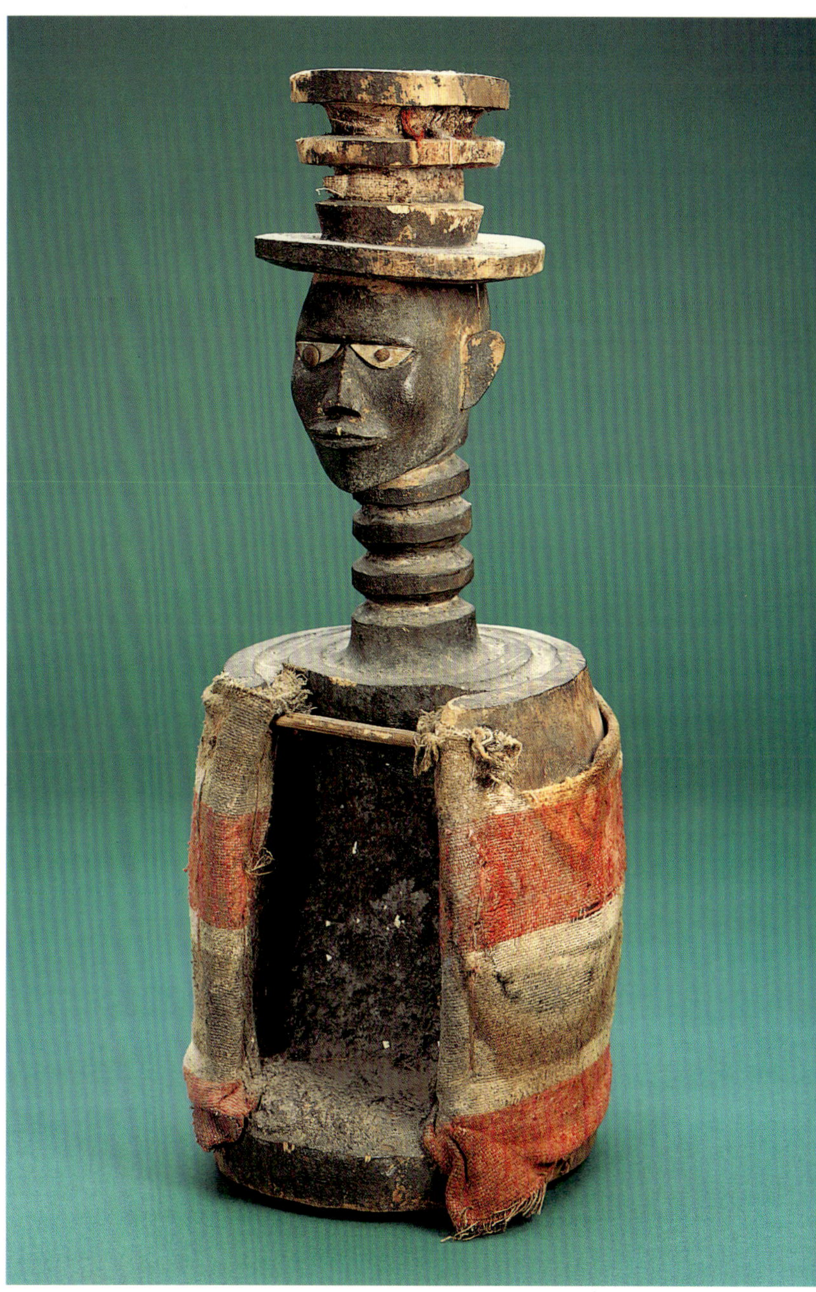

▼▲▼

12

FIGURE (*iran*)
Bidjogo,
Bissagos Archipelago,
Guinea-Bissau
Wood, fabric, metal,
tacks, nails and pigment
H. 43.8 cm.
FMCH 87.607

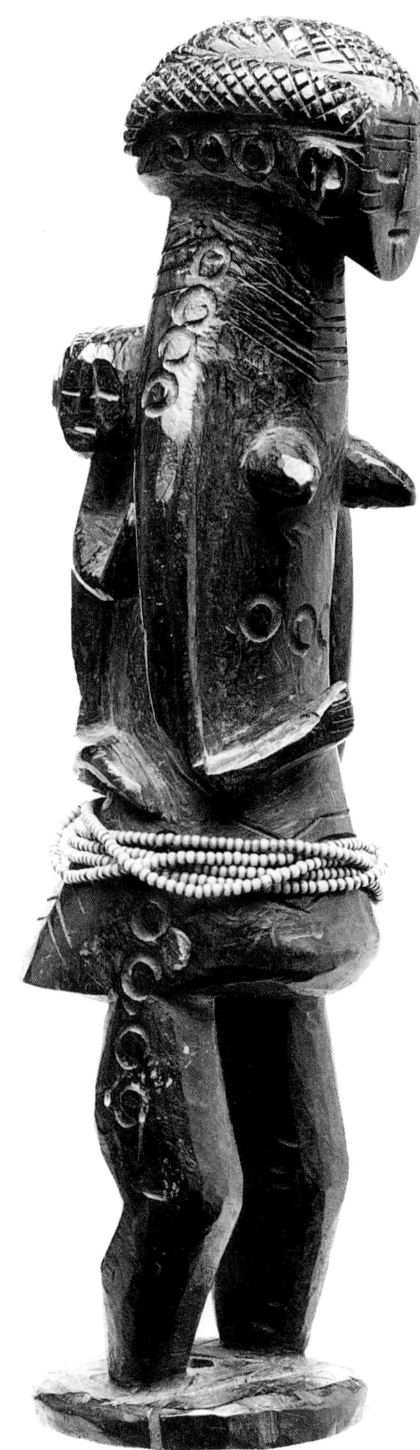

13
MOTHER AND
CHILD FIGURE
Limba,
northern Sierra Leone
Wood, beads and cord
H. 27.5 cm.
FMCH 87.55

13. MOTHER AND CHILD FIGURE, LIMBA, NORTHERN SIERRA LEONE

The figure of a mother and child has many characteristics found in carvings of the Limba of northern Sierra Leone.[1] The thick, solid neck, extended rump cut sharply at the end, the asymmetrical position of the arms against the body and the position of the infant with its head turned to the right are typical of Limba carvings. Also characteristic of Limba figures are the shape of the legs with a slight bending at the knees as well as the sharply projecting breasts, which emphasize her nurturance. Typically, the mother's strong face, the upper part of which is emphasized, has a peg-like nose and a blockish, semi-abstract quality. Raised ridges running from front to back of the head suggest hair. In contrast to these similarities, the striking length of the mother's head, as well as the cross-hatching on the head, are unusual for Limba sculpture.

The somewhat crudely carved scarification marks on the face and body of the figure of the mother are typical of those found on Limba women. The carved circles on the body, legs and neck of the sculpture, however, are decorative and do not represent actual human body scarifications. The line cuts and circles give the surface a somewhat rough quality. This roughness is increased, particularly on the legs, by adze or knife marks, which have been left visible on the surface rather than smoothed out.

The function of this particular piece is not known, although it probably was related to fertility. It may have been associated with Bondo, the Limba female secret society, or with a private women's shrine. More research is needed to determine the exact function of this carving and the precise Limba group from which it came.[2]   SIMON OTTENBERG

[1] These features are also sometimes found in the carvings of other northern Sierra Leone groupings, particularly the Yalunka and the Kuranko, and in those of some northern Temne peoples of the central part of the country. They contrast sharply, however, with the characteristic carvings of the Mende in the south.
[2] This figure joins a collection of 13 Limba figures in the Fowler Museum collections.

14. Dance Headdress (Banda)
Nalu or Baga, Guinea or Guinea Bissau

This massive wooden headdress represents Banda, a high and powerful spiritual being of the Nalu or Baga people of Guinea and Guinea Bissau. A century ago the Banda masquerade appeared only to privileged elders for whom it was danced at male initiations, marriages, harvest celebrations and new planting rituals, and at the appearance of the new moon. A single village might have had two or three Banda headdresses that could appear separately or together. Today, Banda's dance is regarded largely as general entertainment and may be performed on any special occasion.

The Banda headdress is a composite of a number of animal and human forms. The face, scarification patterns and coiffure of braided hair with a high crest are anthropomorphic. Zoomorphs include the jaw of a crocodile, the ears and horns of an antelope, the coiled tail of a chameleon (between the horns), and the body of a serpent (looping through the chameleon tail). The model two-story building on the Joss Banda, and on several masks in other collections, reflects the European style of architecture erected by the numerous traders who settled along the rivers during the mid-nineteenth century, as well as by the Catholic missionaries (Les Pères du Saint-Esprit), who established their first mission in the Baga area in 1875.

Under the formidable weight of the headdress, Banda performs an astonishingly vigorous dance. Over the course of several hours various dancers take turns performing. Movement includes a rapid shuffling in place of the feet; mime roles of a predator bird fishing in the sea, a bird in flight, a serpent undulating, and a fish swimming; and a dizzying and weightless spin, twirling the headdress aloft and then repositioning it on the head without missing a beat. Banda alternates dancing with another masked figure, Pende-Pende. Costumed entirely in brightly colored cloth and raffia, Pende-Pende represents, on the one hand, the buffoon, and on the other, a punisher. He is the opposite of the spiritually noble and benevolent character of Banda.

FREDERICK LAMP

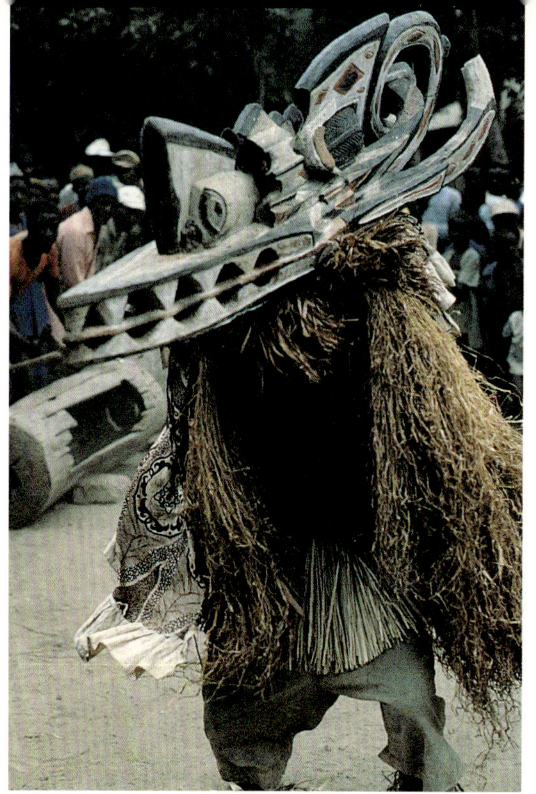

Banda masquerade
performance.
Baga Mandori.
Photo: F. Lamp, 1987.

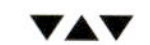

14
DANCE HEADDRESS
(Banda)
Nalu or Baga, Guinea or
Guinea Bissau
Wood and pigment
H. 135.5 cm.
FMCH 87.54

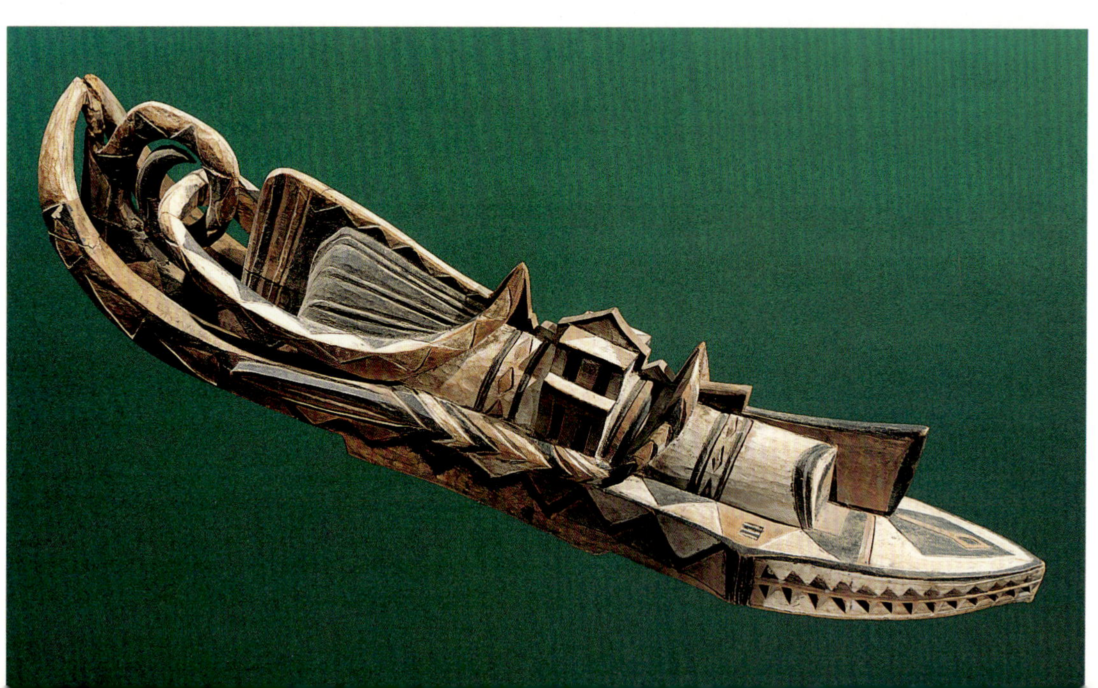

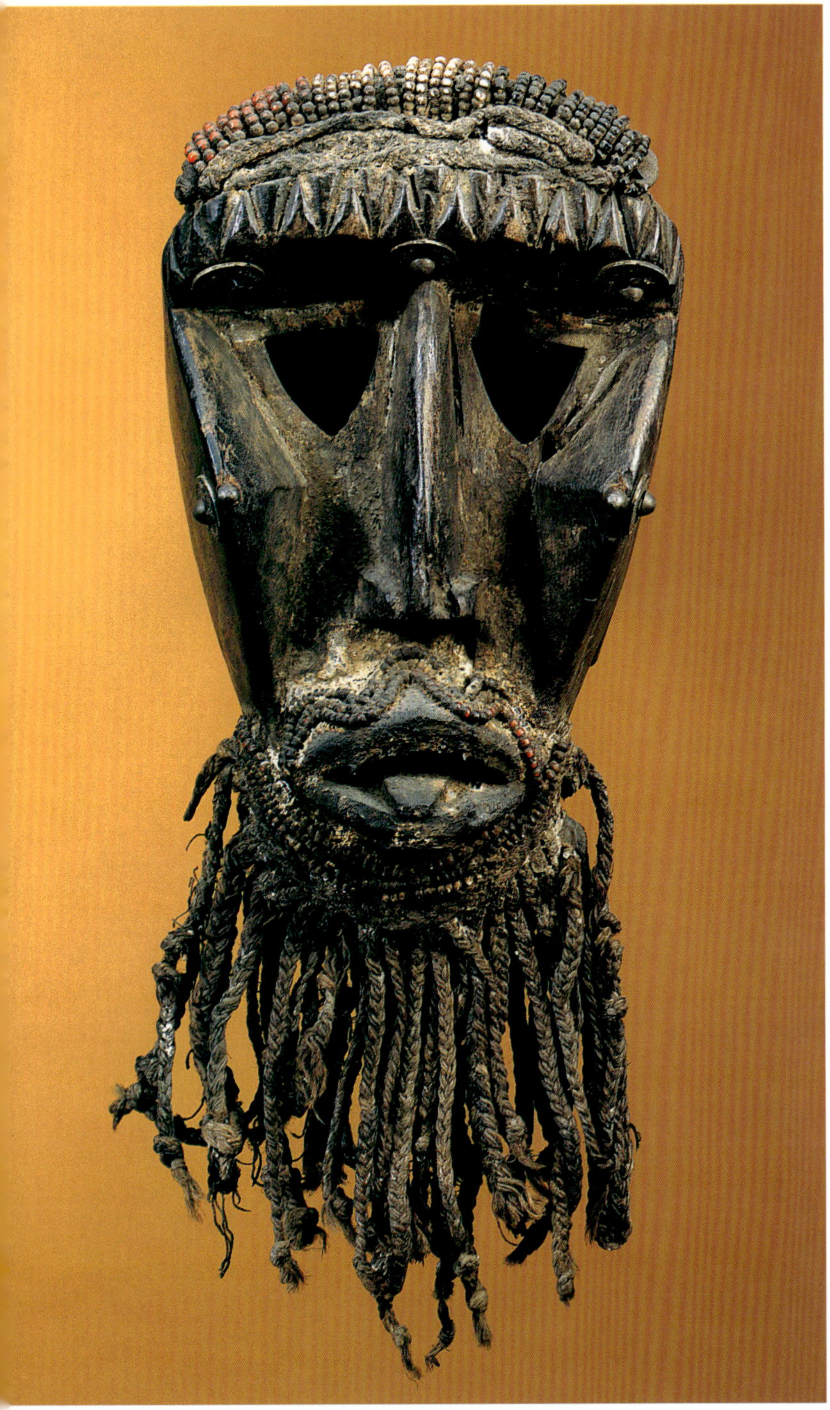

15. *KAOGLE* MASK, DAN, CÔTE D'IVOIRE OR LIBERIA

Among the Dan, the system for naming masks and the relationship between mask names, forms, and functions are extremely complex. It is almost impossible to associate specific functions or names with masks unless they have been documented *in situ*. This mask belongs to a type known as *Kaogle*, which is one of the rare exceptions to the rule. It is characterized by a cubistic treatment of form and a dynamic interaction of planes. The cheeks, which commonly have a pyramidal form, and the nose are highly angular and pronounced. The brow is low but bulges over the cheeks and the recessed eyes. The eyes of *Kaogle* masks typically are shaped like trian-

▼▲▼

15
KAOGLE MASK
Dan, Côte d'Ivoire
or Liberia
Wood, coins, iron, beads,
nails, cloth and plant fiber
H. 43.2 cm.
FMCH 87.1462

FIG. 28
Kaogle mask
performance.
Photo: W. Siegman,
1983.

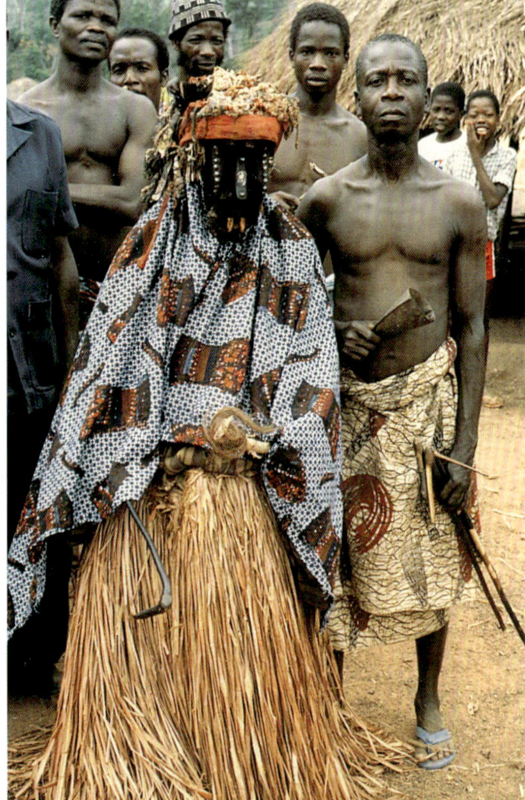

gles, like those seen here, although they may sometimes appear as tubular forms.

A *Kaogle* dancer wears a mask with a headdress known as a *blua*, a piece of cotton cloth to which other narrow strips of cloth are stitched to form a mop-like wig. A small bunch of feathers or leaves is normally attached to either side of the headdress in the temple area. The mask also has beads around the mouth and on a band across the forehead. The remainder of the costume consists of a voluminous raffia skirt and a cotton cloth mantle over a shirt with wide sleeves sewn shut at the ends.

Kaogle masks belong to a larger category of masks known as *Kagle*. The similarity in pronunciation of the terms *Kaogle* and *Kagle* has led to considerable confusion in the published literature. The term *Kagle* means "hooked-stick spirit" and refers to the hooked sticks that people wearing these masks carry and frequently hurl at spectators as they rush through the town frightening people and animals and being generally disruptive. Such behavior, which consciously violates cultural norms, serves a social function by teaching the value of order and discipline through its negative example. WILLIAM SIEGMANN

16. BIRD MASK, DAN, LIBERIA

The frequent appearance of bird forms in the Dan pantheon of masks reflects the prominence of birds in Dan mythology. In general, birds are thought to have supernatural powers, but little is known about specific references to birds in Dan mythology or about the iconography of birds on masks.

The band at the top of this mask simulates a row of small duiker horns, which frequently appear on Southern Dan masks as symbolic references to medicine and supernatural powers. The single slit, which replaces the usual double eye holes, is extremely rare but not unique. It allows the wearer to look directly ahead, while the openings in the beak also function as eye holes. The performer thus has increased peripheral vision and a view of the ground in front of him without having to lower his head. WS

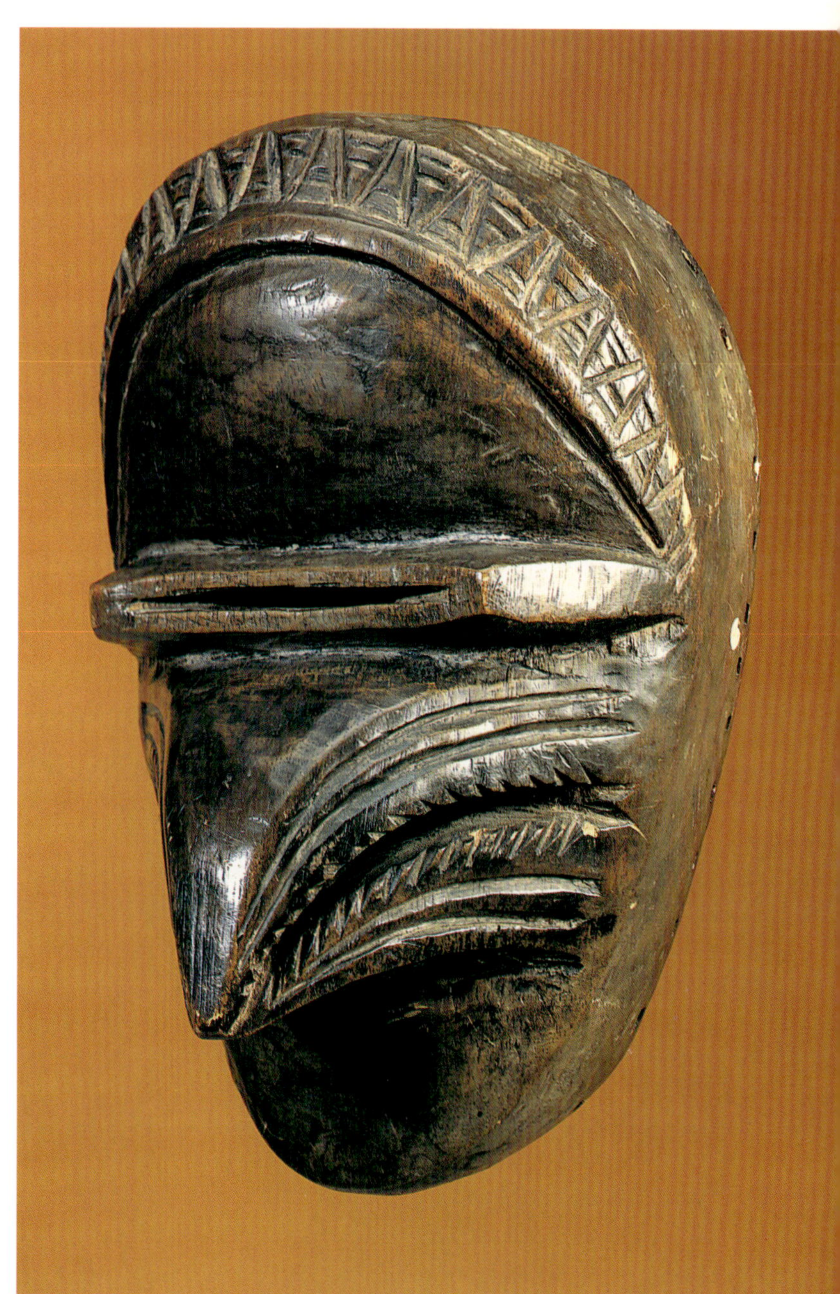

▼▲▼

16

BIRD MASK

Dan, Liberia

Wood

H. 24.5 cm.

FMCH 86.1732

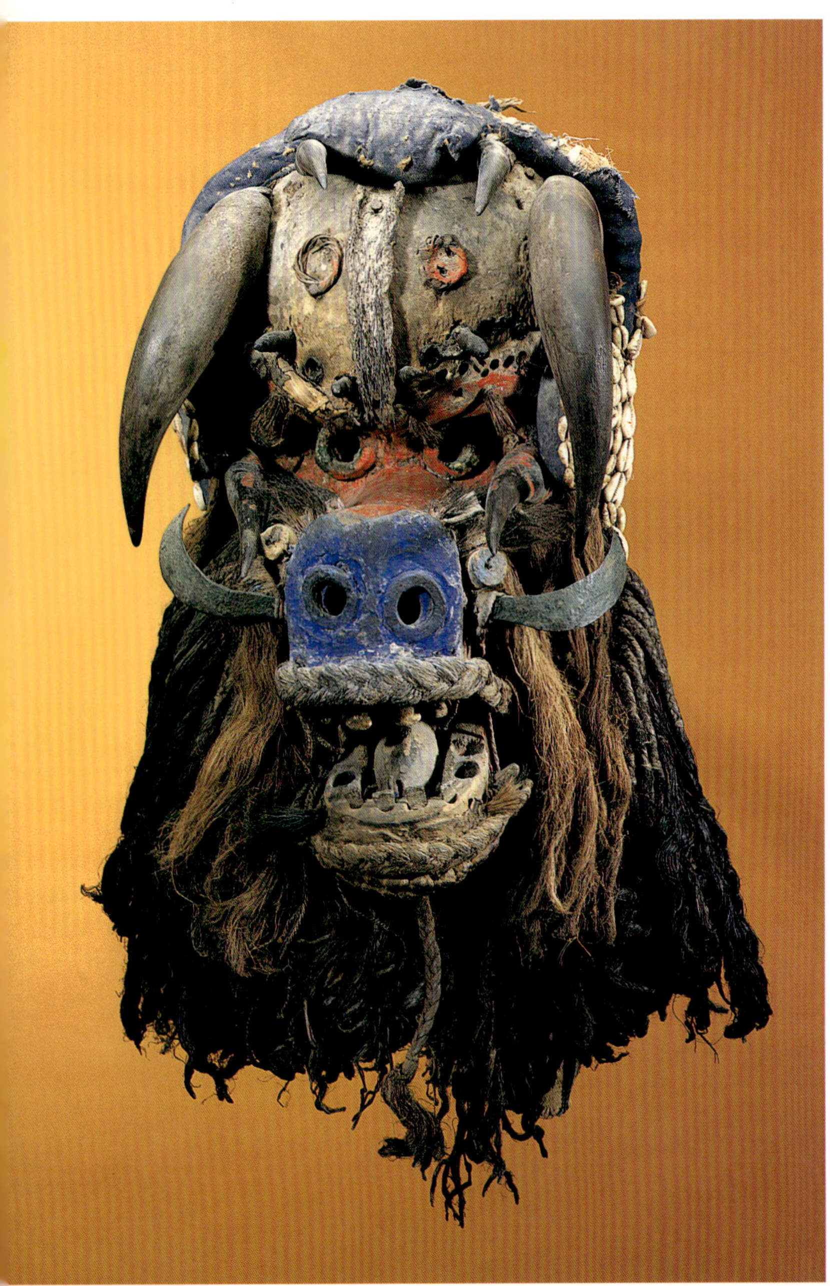

▼▲▼

17

JUDICIAL MASK

Sapo, Liberia

Wood, cloth, pigment,

cowrie shells, animal teeth,

metal, animal horn, rope,

vegetal fiber and hair (?)

H. 71.5 cm.

FMCH 87.1506

17. JUDICIAL MASK, SAPO, LIBERIA

The Sapo see themselves as a distinct ethnic group among the We-speaking peoples of Liberia. They live in a heavily forested and sparsely populated region along the Cestos River. Although they share many features of social organization and artistic style with neighboring We groups, their comparative isolation and distinct dialect have reinforced a strong sense of separate identity.

The Sapo generally refer to all masquerades as *Gela*. While many masks function as entertainers and can be seen by anyone, others, such as this one, perform judicial roles. Little is known, however, about the details of these roles or the circumstances in which they appear. Today the once important judicial role of masks is greatly diminished.

Sapo judicial masks are characteristically large, aggressive and meant to terrorize. Like other We-speaking peoples, the Sapo use masks that incorporate both human and animal features. Most We groups carve features such as horns and teeth as part of the wooden face of the mask and then add details, including bells and wooden simulations of leopards teeth. The Sapo, however, almost always incorporate real animal horns, cow teeth, and animal tails as integral parts of the mask. This mask has an articulated jaw with inset cow teeth, a nose suggestive of a wild boar snout and multiple horns from various antelope, as well as the "bush cow," or wild water buffalo. The beard, mustache, and eyebrows of the mask combine raffia and other vegetal fibers with animal hair, probably from a cow. Like the cowrie shells and cloth-covered packets containing herbal medicines, all of these features are meant to represent, individually as well as collectively, the awesome powers of the mask and the society which controls it.   WS

18. Naw Mask, Bassa, Liberia

Both men's and women's societies of the Bassa use masks. The men's society, Naw, performs a mask known by the same name. The term *naw* is impossible to translate and is usually glossed in Liberian English as "devil," a general term used for men's societies and for all masked performers. The mask is also frequently called a *Gela*, which means "big spirit."

The *naw* or *gela* mask may be present at closed meetings restricted to initiated members of the men's societies as well as at open, festive occasions where anyone may see it. Its performance consists of an exceptionally smooth, gliding dance to the music of slit drums; dancers move rapidly (even over rough terrain), as if floating on a cushion of air. Occasionally the performance has been referred to as "the Bassa Hovercraft."

The facial part of the mask is normally a little smaller than a human face and is attached obliquely to a rattan basketry, cap-like structure. Thus, the wearer does not see out through the eyes, even when they are carved through, but rather sees through a slit in the cloth that is suspended beneath the mask and the headdress.

The features of the mask, like its movements, are refined, graceful, and generally regarded as feminine. Consequently, although the mask is worn by men and is conceived of as the spirit force of a genderless order, it is simultaneously thought of as having feminine attributes. The eyes, which are narrow, half-closed, and close set, as well as the elaborate coiffure, with its central plait or crest and its rows of similar, smaller, odd-numbered, symmetrically arranged forms, match Bassa's canons of feminine beauty. The vertical pattern on the forehead, nose and chin represents a traditional tattoo.   WS

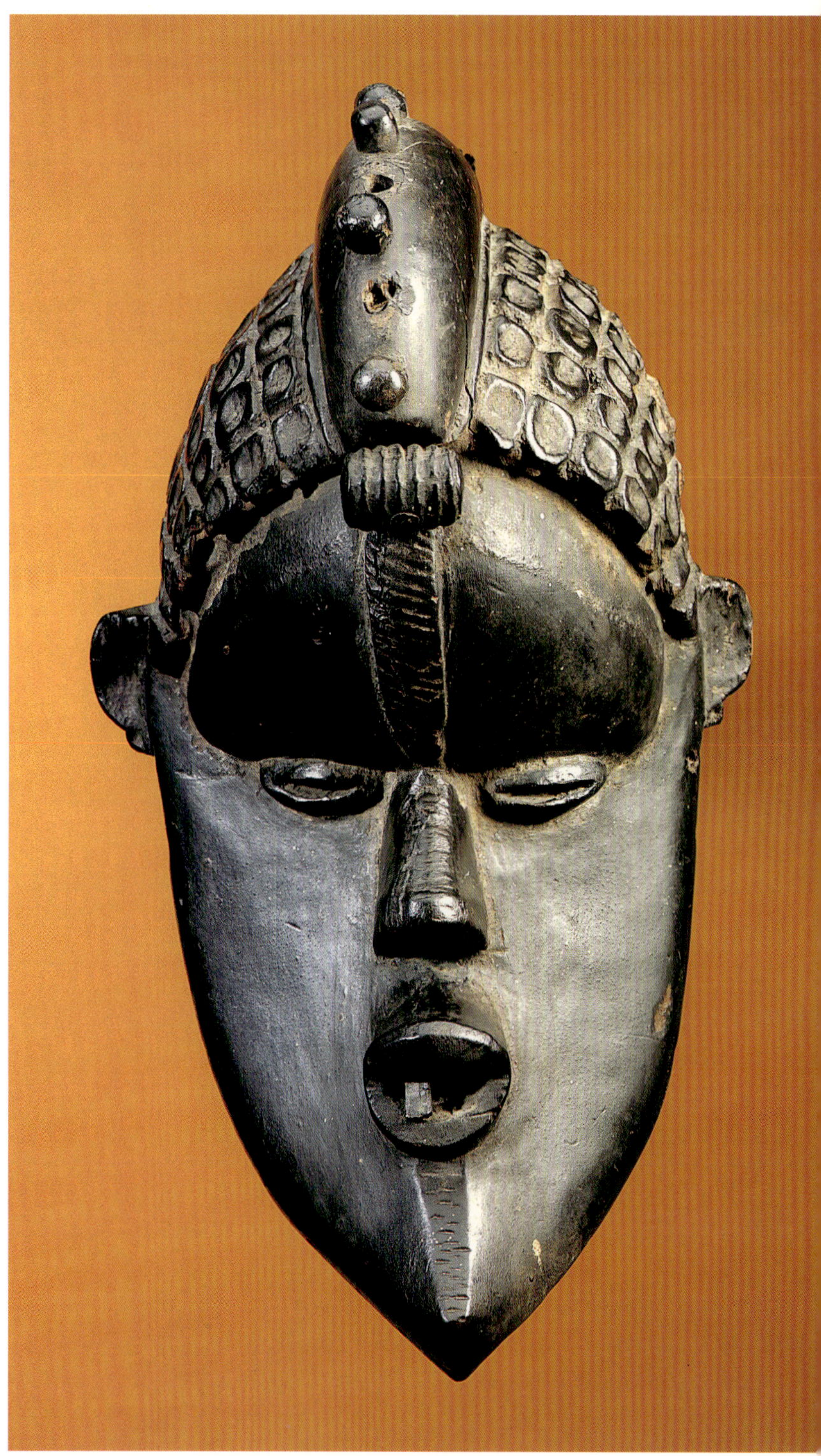

▼▲▼
18
NAW MASK
Bassa, Liberia
Wood and iron
H. 30.5 cm.
FMCH 87.1709

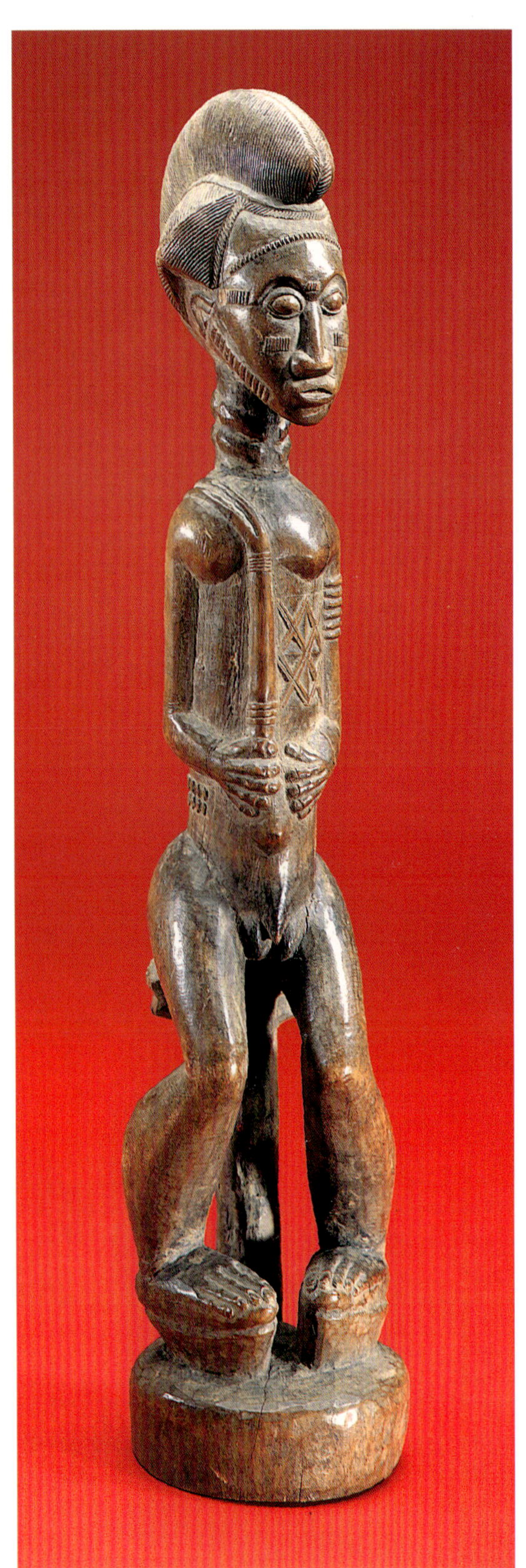

19
SEATED MALE FIGURE
(blolo bian)
Baule, Côte d'Ivoire
Wood
H. 45 cm.
FMCH 87.1454

19. SEATED MALE FIGURE, BAULE, CÔTE D'IVOIRE

This seated male figure was probably carved to represent "the other world man" (*blolo bian*) of a Baule woman. Such figures are carved at the recommendation of a diviner for both women and men to resolve crises associated with marriage, sexuality, or social well being (Vogel 1977). The figure becomes a stand-in for the other-world (*blolo*) mate who has a one-to-one relationship with the person who lives "here on earth" (*asiɛ'n su wa*). Offerings presented to the sculpture formally symbolize recognition and acknowledgment (Vogel 1980; Ravenhill 1980).

The Baule consider the other world to be equivalent to the visible world, and its inhabitants to have the same form as their real world partners. Hence *blolo* figures are carved as idealizations of human beauty (Ravenhill 1980; Vogel 1977, 1980). Great emphasis is placed on the beauty of a well-delineated face, elaborate and carefully rendered coiffure, and beauty scarification (Vogel 1988). Other world figures frequently bear symbols of power, both social and magical: the flywhisk held by the right hand and extending over the shoulder of this figure is an insignia of chieftaincy; and the amulet armbands (*banzrɛ*) on the upper left arm signal power derived from a spiritual agent. The seated position of the figure indicates social seniority and individual prestige. In use, this figure would have been properly dressed: he would have worn a miniature cloth *cache-sexe* suspended from a beaded or corded waist band and passed through the cavity below the genital area. In the privacy of the owner's bedroom, the figure would have been a constant reminder of the ongoing presence of the "other man" in the "other world" whom she could not neglect. PHILIP L. RAVENHILL

20. BUSH SPIRIT FIGURES, BAULE, CÔTE D'IVOIRE

Among the Baule, figures carved as pairs represent bush spirits (*asiɛ usu*), the denizens of the wild world beyond the edge of the village. They may arbitrarily intervene in the lives of individuals, possessing a person, disturbing the previous order and compelling him or her to act in abnormal ways. One result may

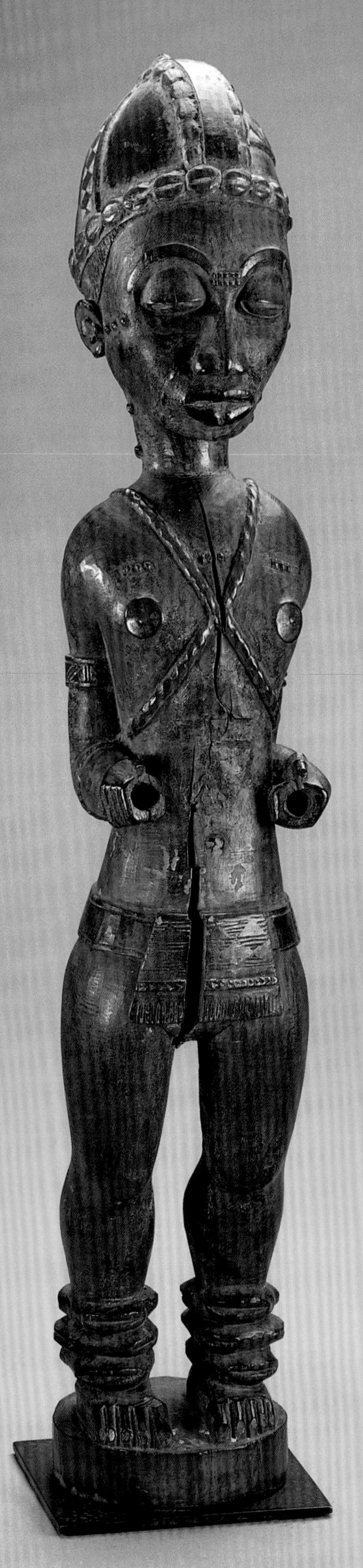
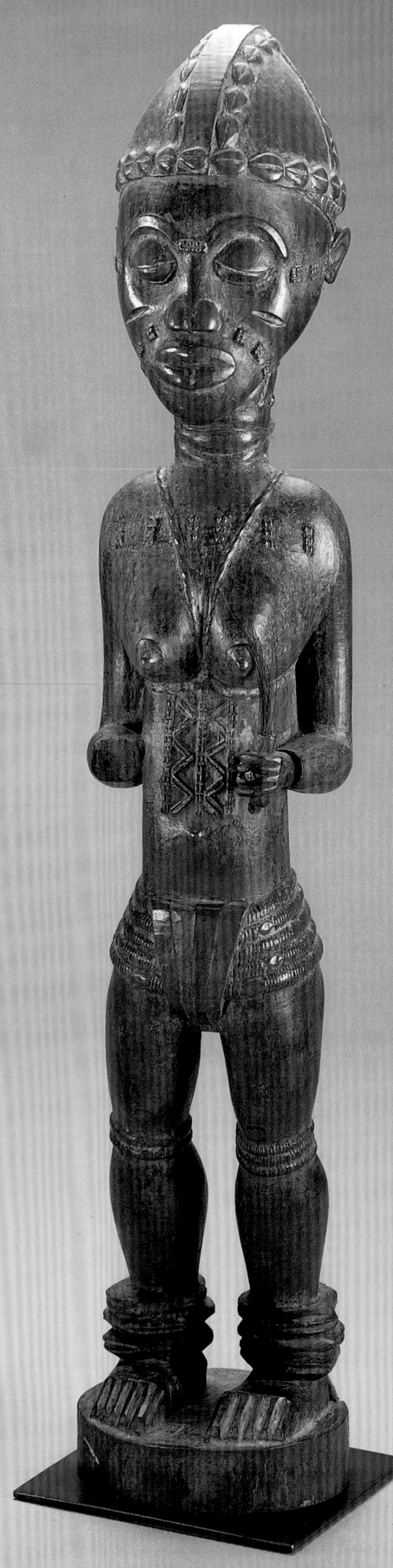

▼▲▼

20

BUSH SPIRIT FIGURES

(asiɛ usu)

Baule, Côte d'Ivoire

(Male)
Wood and kaolin
H. 48.5 cm.
FMCH 86.1739

(Female)
Wood, animal hair
and wool
H. 50 cm.
FMCH 86.1740

be madness; another result may be the gift of clairvoyance, which makes a person into a trance diviner (*komien*). To reestablish order, figures may be carved as intermediaries acknowledging the spirits.

The Baule consider the public performances of the Baule trance diviners not only as divination but also as a form of lively entertainment. Although other types of Baule figures are usually kept in private shrines and are rarely seen by non-family members, the figures representing a diviner's *asiɛ usu* are often publicly and eye catchingly displayed near the diviner—an explicit assertion of the diviner's connection to the invisible world of spirits.

On display next to the diviner, these two figures would have echoed the visual impact of the diviner's costume and accouterments which they accurately depict: a cowry shell decorated leather cap, "medicinal" cords worn in bandolier style, anklet bells, and hand held accessories. The female figure holds a flywhisk in her left hand, and the grasping hands on the male figure indicate that originally he probably held a metal gong (*lawre*) in one hand and in the other a gong beater (*lawre waka*) used for percussion accompaniment to the trance dance. Each figure is also depicted with a *cache-sexe*, which is no longer worn. Today male diviners wear a short cloth wrapped around their hips and females a single wrapper.

Like the figures carved by Baule artists to represent the invisible inhabitants of the other world (*blolo bian*, "other-world man," and *blolo bla*, "other-world woman"), these figures epitomize the Baule aesthetic canon of human beauty (Ravenhill 1980; Vogel 1980). The faces of the figures are finely carved with downcast eyes; scarification, a mark of civilization (Vogel 1988), appears between the eyebrows, on the temples and cheeks and next to the mouth. The neck of the female figure is carved to represent the horizontal striations or "beauty-lines" favored by the Baule. The male figure has strong pectoral muscles, while the female has the high breasts of a young woman. The full calves of both figures are expected of a person of beauty and character. In short, these figures depict beautiful and proper humans. Active wild spirits are controlled through skillful personification; each becomes, as it were, a human (*sran*) thanks to being represented as a statue: *waka sran*—"a person (or human) in wood." PLR

21. PAIR OF BUSH SPIRIT FIGURES, BAULE, CÔTE D'IVOIRE

This pair of figures represent bush spirits (*asiɛ usu*), possibly *bo usu*, forest spirits with whom hunters establish contractual relationships to improve their success in hunting. *Bo usu* figures may be carved as entire families of four, five, or more figures and are usually minimally sculpted. The head may be shaped as a sphere or ovoid separated from the body by a constriction representing the neck. The body may be relatively undifferentiated, with no break between

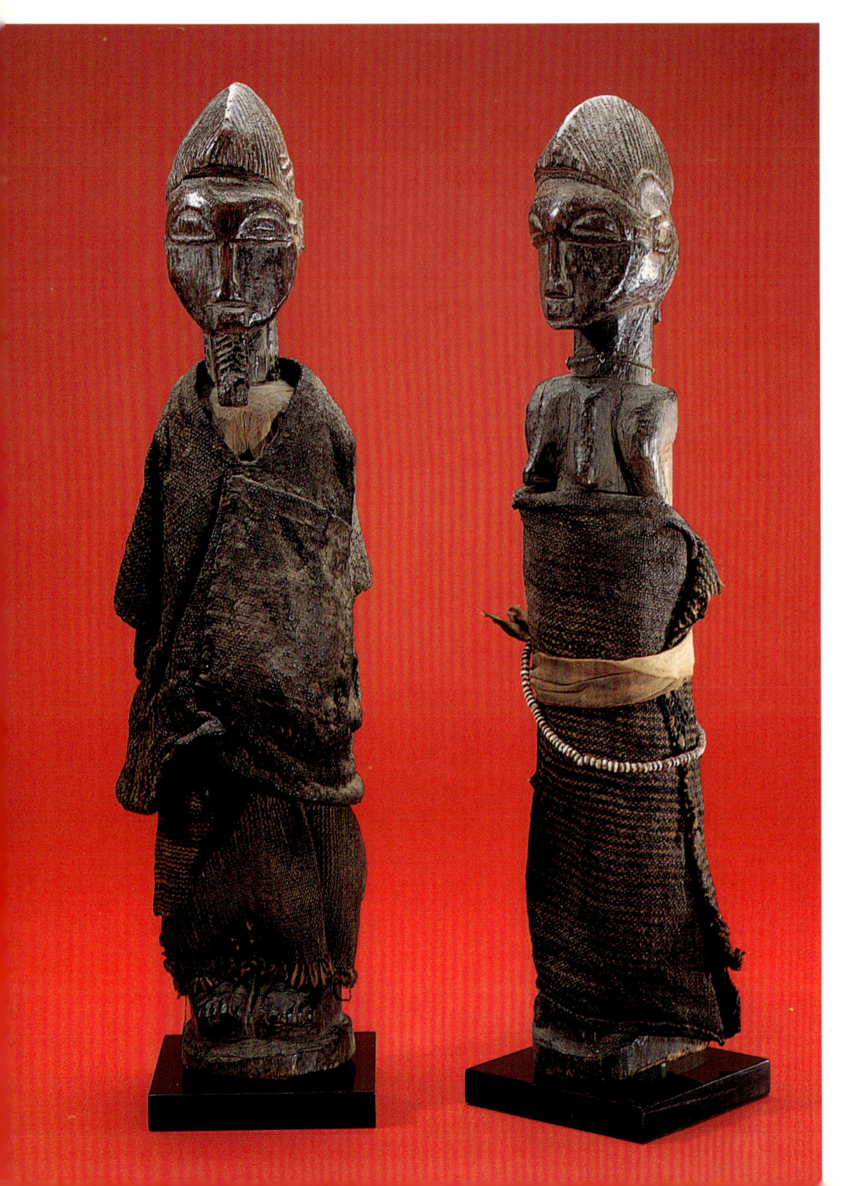

torso, buttocks and legs. The arms are often barely indicated, while the legs form a unitary block. This minimal depiction of an anthropomorphic form may be because the sphere of influence of spirits is still thought to be the bush, the place where game is found. *Bo usu* figures often receive offerings of kaolin or blood, which produce a crusty patina.

The execution of this pair of figures is less elaborate, refined and detailed than many other Baule figures. Their cloth covering and patination indicate, however, care and frequent handling. The addition of a gold bead on a cord necklace also seems to indicate that the figures were particularly revered and may have represented bush spirits more important than *bo usu*.   PLR

22. MASK, BAULE, CÔTE D'IVOIRE

Various sets of anthropomorphic, zoomorphic, and abstract discoid masks function within the pantheon of masks collectively called Goli by different ethnic groups in central Côte d'Ivoire (Ravenhill 1988). The Goli masquerade originated among the Wan, but its forms and function have changed significantly

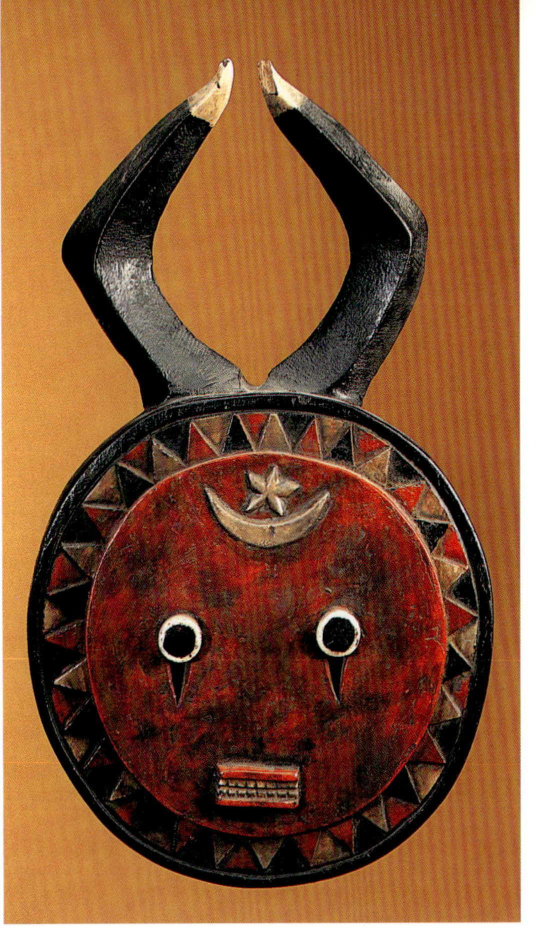

22
MASK
(kplekple)
Baule, Côte d'Ivoire
Wood and pigment
H. 41 cm.
FMCH 86.1741

as it has spread among the Baule; most notably, Baule masks are carved as male and female pairs (Vogel 1978). The Baule have also been particularly interested in disc masks and have added features unknown among the Wan.

For both the Wan and the Baule, the *kplekple* is the least important mask; the Wan consider it the delegated "messenger" sent out to prepare the way for the others. Yet, paradoxically, it is the one most often seen. Widely known in contemporary Côte d'Ivoire, its schematized form appears on posters and in advertising, especially for tourism.

The mask has interesting features related to the original form of the *kplekple* mask among the Wan. The angular treatment of the horns is a reinterpretation of the inverted pear-shaped horns of the Wan *dandi kplekple*. The holes pierced in the mask for the dancer's vision are reminiscent of the concentric, inverted tear-drop lines used by the Wan to define the eyes of this type of mask. The decorative border of low relief triangles, as well as the crescent moon and star motif, may indicate a Baule re-interpretation of the disc as a lunar form, for such treatments and motifs do not occur on disc masks among the Wan.   PLR

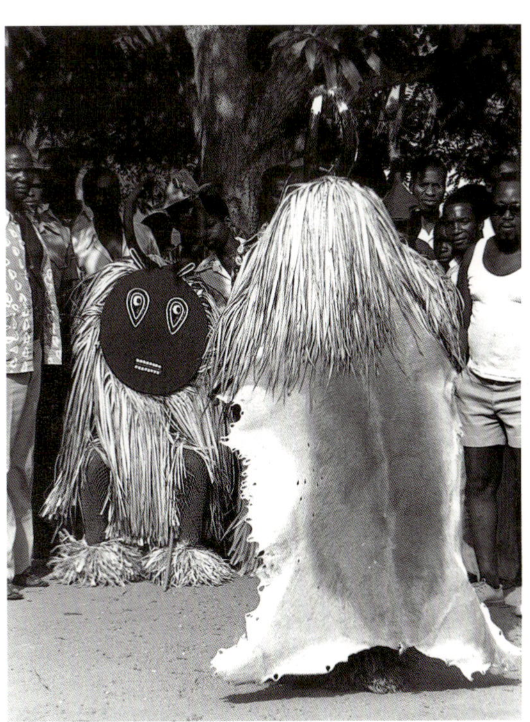

FIG. 29

Goli mask performance.

Photo: P. Ravenhill,

1977.

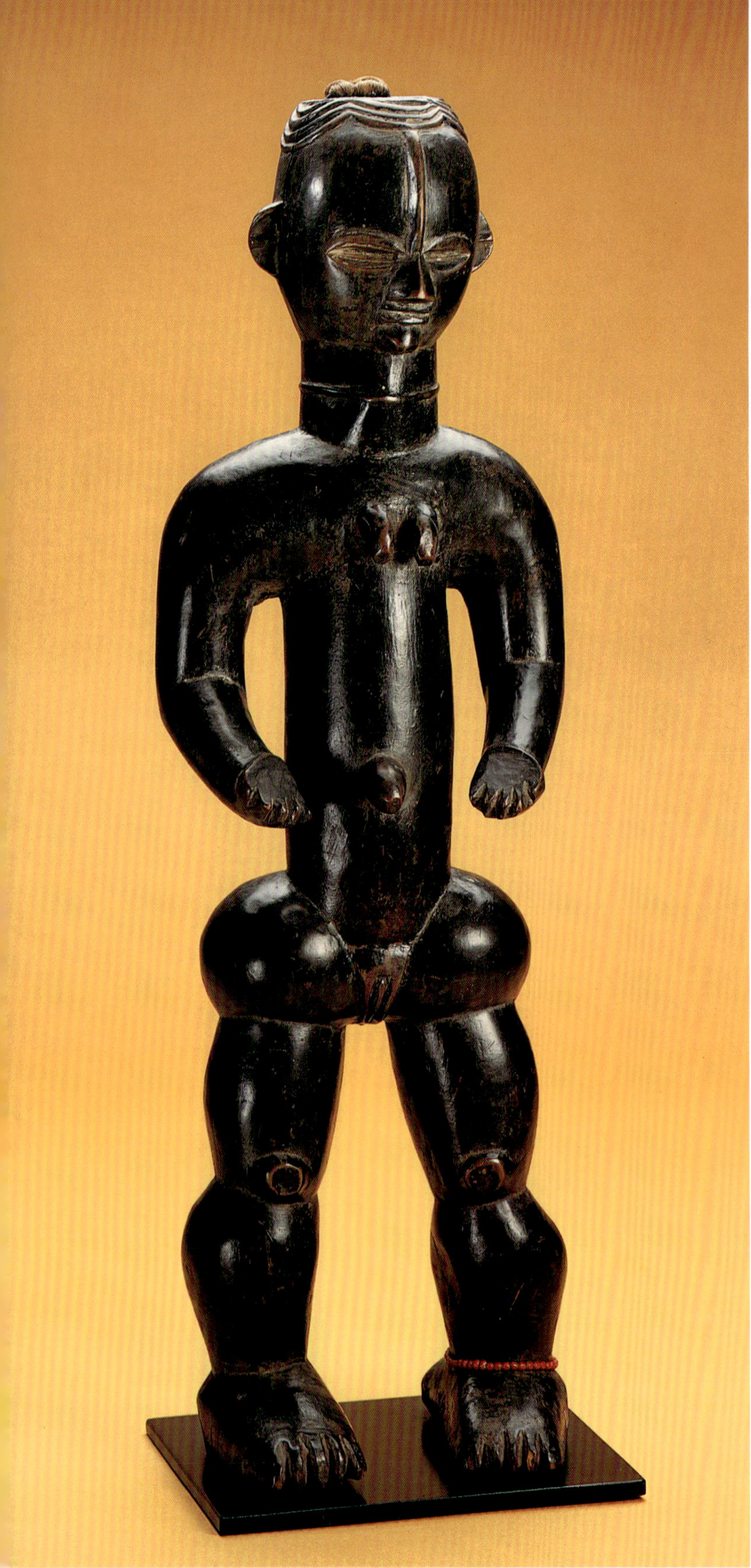

23. FEMALE FIGURE, BETE, CÔTE D'IVOIRE

Erich Herold noted (1985:81) that the first appearance of a Bete sculpture identified as such occurred in 1964 with William Faggs' *Africa: 100 Tribes–100 Masterpieces*, and wryly commented that this was undoubtedly due to Fagg's goal of "presenting 100 various tribes" (Herold 1985:82). Herold in this essay on "Traditional Sculpture of the Bete Tribe, Ivory Coast" sought to summarize and question existing knowledge on Bete sculpture and to present objects known in museum collections.

This female figure is characteristic of Bete sculptures.[1] According to Eric Herold, the majority of known Bete sculptures are female and, he hypothesizes, "are related to the cult of ancestors, perhaps stressing the role of female ancestors…" (Herold 1985:117). Most of these figures are impressive in size, ranging from 50 to 136 centimeters, and show signs of age and wear. They have in common a more lifelike sense of proportion than other African figures—the head is more in proportion to the body; the arms are typically oriented to the front with upraised hands; and the torso shows rather elaborate scarification. Also, these wood sculptures often have the appearance of having been "built-up" and modeled rather than carved.

This sculpture, like the Bete figure on loan from the Brian and Diane Leyden Collection to the National Museum of African Art, Washington, D.C., has braids of fiber representing hair. The flatness of the top of the head of this figure is puzzling; some figures that stylistically relate to the figure originally supported bowls or plateaux (Herold 1985:ill. 24; Rubin 1984:289). It is possible that the top of the head of the figure was modified from an earlier form, although judging by the signs of wear, any such change would have occurred in its original milieu.

PLR

▼▲▼
_____

23

FEMALE FIGURE

Bete, Côte d'Ivoire

Wood, beads,

fiber and iron

H. 51.8 cm.

FMCH 86.1727

[1] The comparative rarity of Bete figurative art may be due in part to the fact that the Liberian prophet William Wadé Harris traveled through this region of lower Côte d'Ivoire at the end of World War I and destroyed by fire those "fetishes" he thought hindered peoples' belief in the true God.

Bete works have been grouped together on the basis of shared stylistic characteristics rather than by any defined ethnic affiliation. Jean-Pierre Dozon has argued, in fact, that the "Bete" did not exist prior to colonization and that the Bete ethnicity was only created in this century (1985). The history of Bete art and the possible connections between the "Bete" style and the styles of neighboring groups, such as the related Kru groups to the west and the Guro to the north, are still little known.

24. MASK, GREBO, CÔTE D'IVOIRE

Although little is known about the actual historical use of masks among the Grebo, it seems that they may have functioned primarily as a significant part of the war costume worn by official Grebo war leaders; some of them may have been worn on basketry frames over the head rather than in front of the face (Siegmann 1977:27). Whatever their original function, they have gained a place in the history of African art because of their form. They have been invoked, for example, as having had a major influence on the art of Picasso and the development of cubism (Varnedoe 1992).

Compositionally, this mask exhibits the Grebo propensity for geometric shapes: rectangles, cylinders, and triangles connect and contrast differing planes. The plane of the face supports the tubular projections of the eyes and the rectangular block of the mouth; the triangular nose bridges the negative space between forehead and cheeks; and the oblong forehead itself provides a planar frame of reference for the projecting elements of the eyes, nose, and mouth. The chin, with its highlighted triangular motifs, accentuates, in turn, the receding plane, which supports the fringed raffia cape. The inset mirrors in the eyes also play with notions of receding and projecting planes.

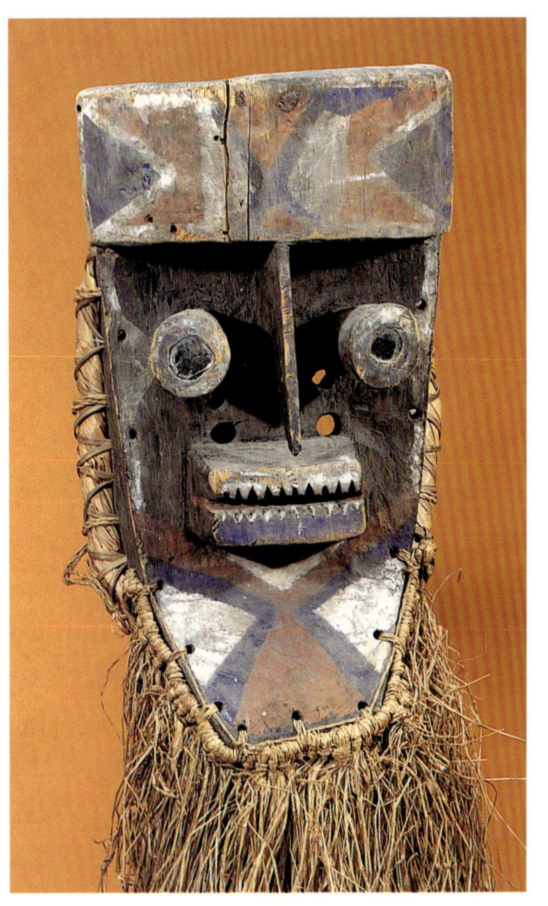

▼▲▼

24

MASK

Grebo, Côte d'Ivoire

Wood, mirror,

paint and raffia

H. 78 cm.

FMCH 88.960

The planar composition of some Grebo masks may be related to the construction techniques of a number of masks found among other Kru groups. These masks (two of which are found in the collections of the Musée National in Abidjan, Côte d'Ivoire) are formed of a tightly woven basketry frame to which are attached separate elements carved in wood—forehead, nose, eyes, and mouth. Assemblage *avant le fait*, these masks have a powerful resonance with certain forms of Western art in the twentieth century, which in turn evoke the abstract composition of wooden Grebo masks.   PLR

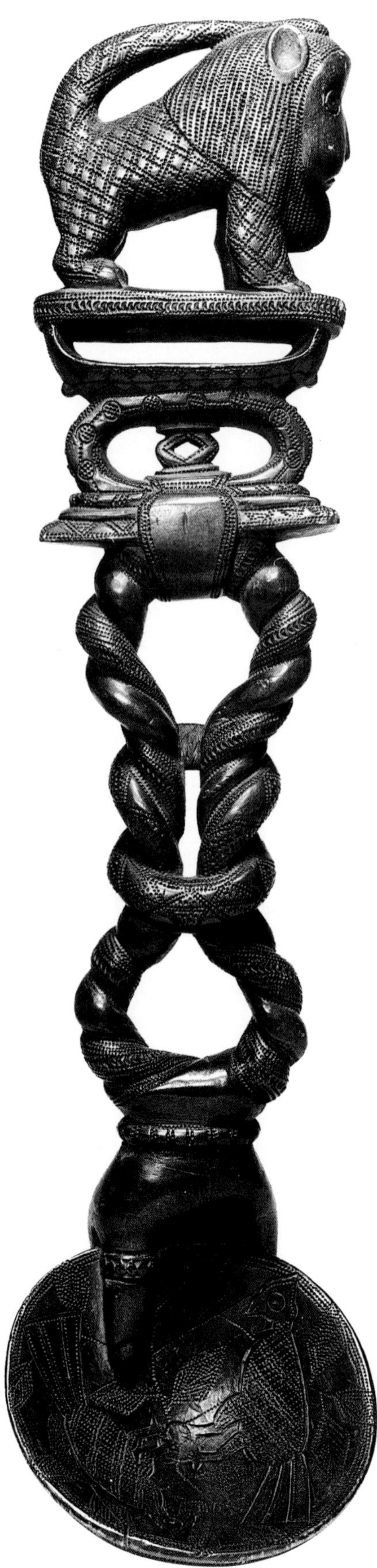

25
SPOON
Effutu (?), Ghana
Wood
L. 57 cm.
FMCH 83.1003

25. SPOON, EFFUTU (?), GHANA
26. MALE FIGURE, EFFUTU (?), GHANA

At least thirteen carvings by the artist of these two works are known: seven male or female figures either standing or seated on stools; four animals standing on stools (a deer, two eagles and a rooster); and two large, elaborate spoons. All of these carvings are characterized by a profusion of punctate surface decoration representing patterns on clothes worn by the people or the fur, feathers, or skin of the animals. Some of this decoration is clearly pyro-engraved. The human figures typically have round heads and widely placed eyes with three evenly spaced vertical scarification marks between them. One horizontal scarification mark appears on each cheek of the figures. This pattern of scarification is not Akan. Since I photographed one of the carvings at the Effutu town of Winneba and the spoon in the Berlin Museum für Völkerkunde (Kreiger 1969:27, fig. 43) was collected as Ga, it seems likely that the carver was from one of the small non-Akan coastal groups.

The artist appears to have been active during at least the first quarter of the 1900s. The spoon in Berlin was collected in 1905, and one of the male figures has the date 1924 incised on it. Despite this apparent age, none of the carvings shows any real signs of use. According to auction records (Christies

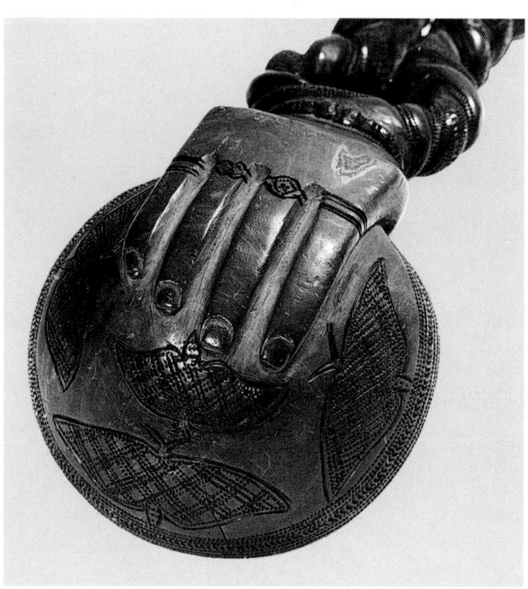

1989:65), this seated male was acquired by John Valentine, R.N. in 1948–1949 as a finial on an intact chair, which was subsequently destroyed in a warehouse fire. Indeed, all the figure and animal carvings have holes in the bottom indicating that they were once mounted on some other structure. In a previous discussion of one of the animal figures, I (1983:97–98) argued that these works were associated with elaborate drum stands and/or were the finials of staffs. Figurative carvings, staffs, chairs, and elaborate drum stands were often part of the displays of voluntary musical associations in southern Ghana (see Cole and Ross 1977:170–179). The spoons may also have played a part in these groups.

One of the human figures in a private collection has the name "Kwaku Dabow" incised on its left arm, and a second figure has "Dr. Kodjoe Kuma." These may be the names of the patrons who commissioned the carvings and who are represented in them. Names on southern Ghanaian carvings typically represent either the artists or their patrons. Although a doctor is not likely to be a carver, it is possible that Kwaku Dabow is the artist's name. Until the corpus of carvings with inscriptions is expanded, this issue cannot be resolved.

The positions of the arms on this figure convey two separate messages. The upraised right arm with an extended index finger invariably represents the expression "Except God," recognizing the ultimate authority of a supreme deity. The gesture of the left hand grasping the head of a snake represents the proverb, "Without the head a snake is nothing but a rope," a metaphorical reference to leadership and problem solving.   DORAN H. ROSS

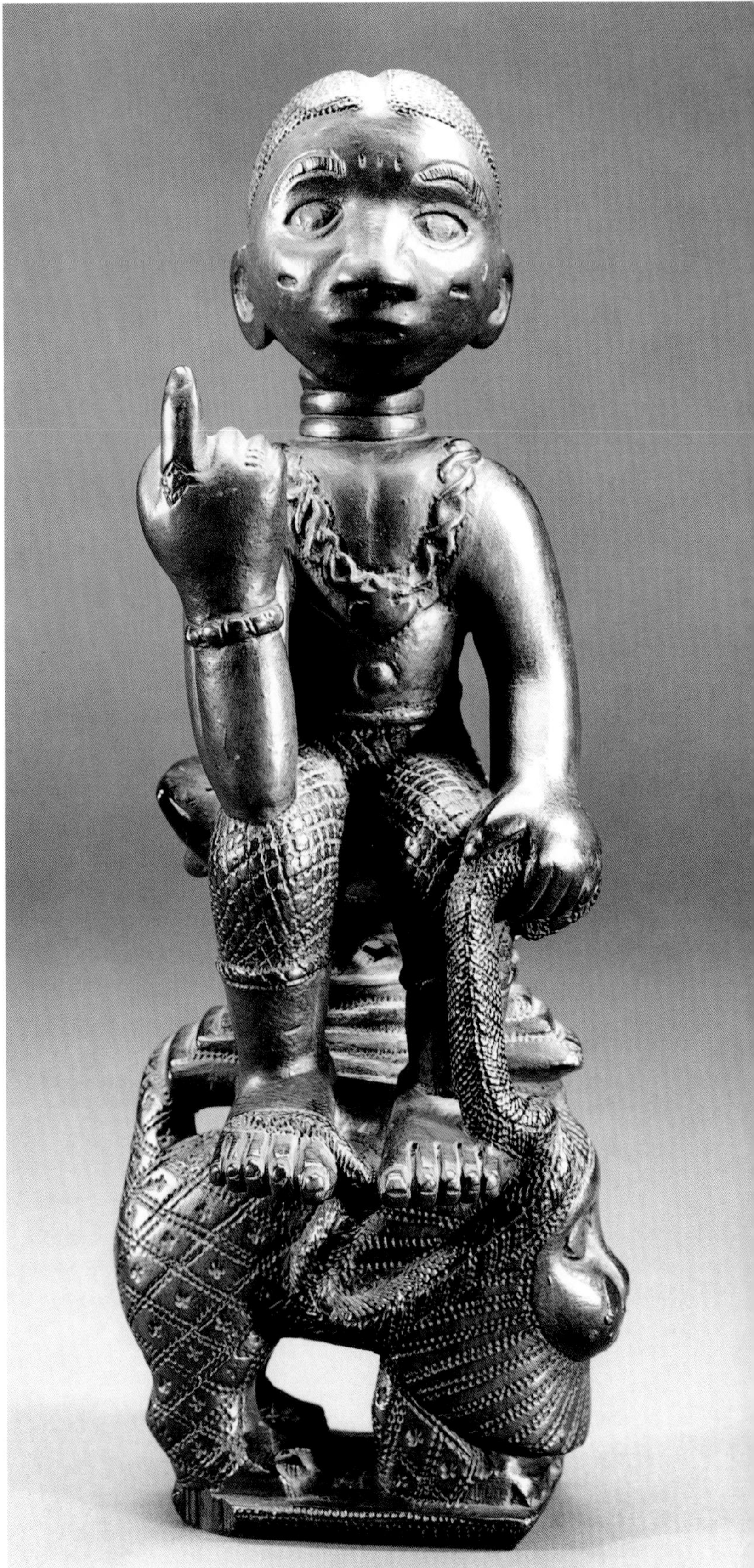

▼▲▼

26
MALE FIGURE
Effutu (?), Ghana
Wood
H. 36.2 cm.
FMCH **89.788**

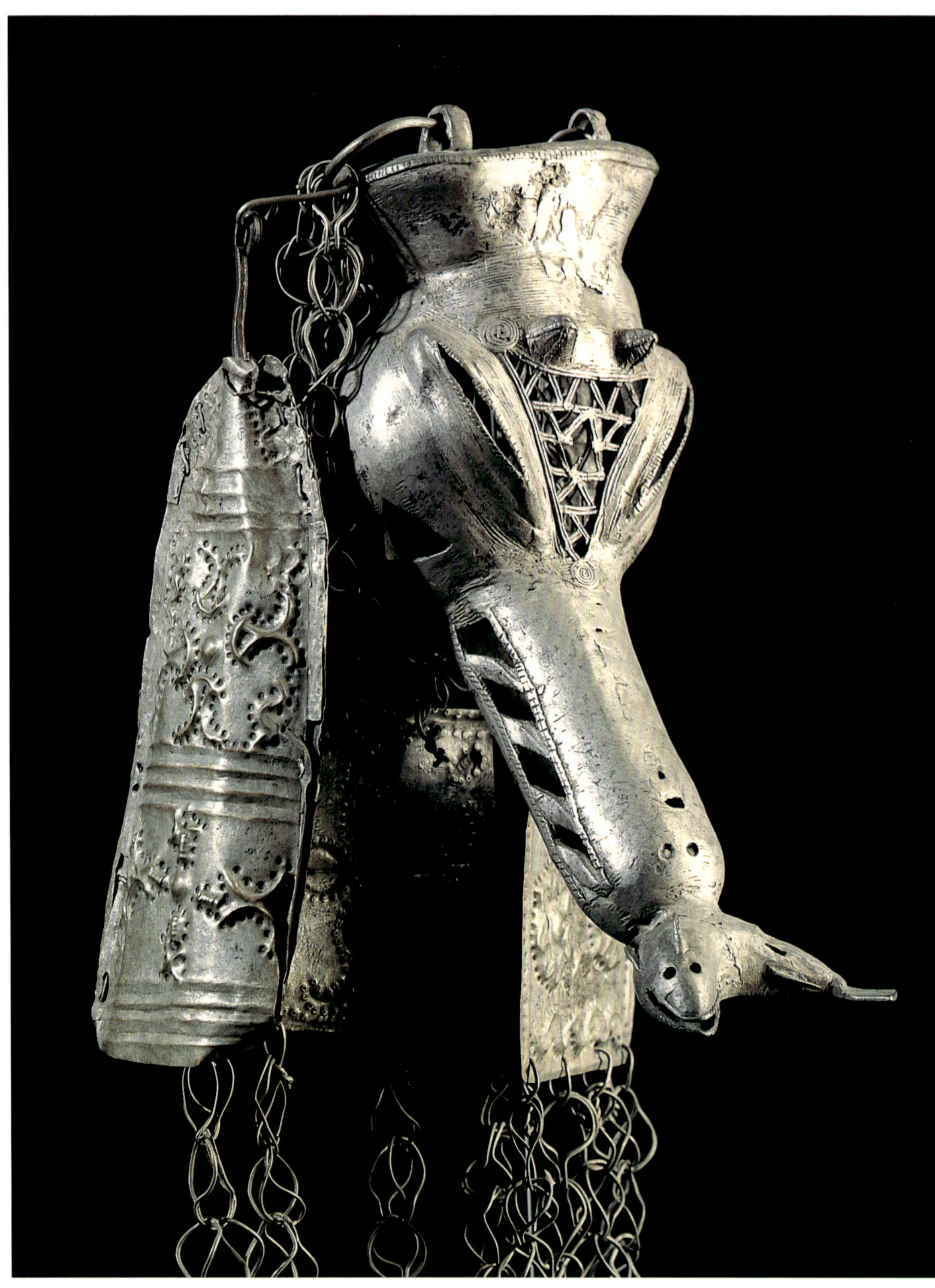

▼▲▼
27
PENDANT
Mamprussi or Asante,
Ghana
Silver
L. 15 cm.
FMCH 87.1710

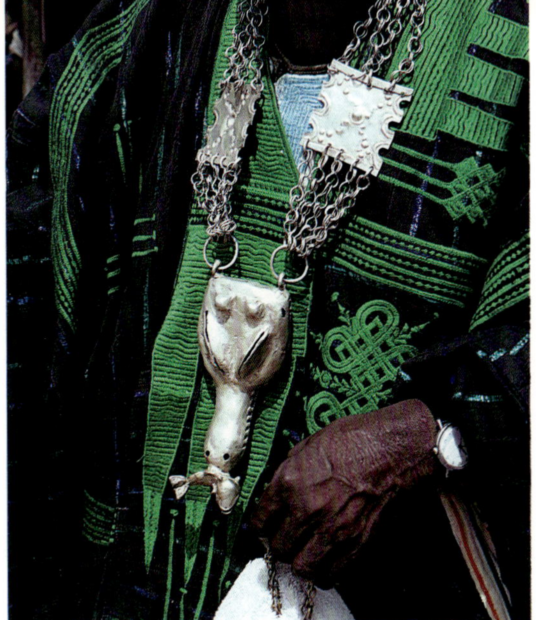

27. PENDANT, MAMPRUSSI OR ASANTE, GHANA

Cast silver pendants depicting a mudfish or a crocodile head, alone or with a mudfish in its mouth, are the prerogative of chieftaincy among several northern Ghanaian peoples. Most of the pendants are modeled in the style of Asante cast gold sword ornaments (see Ross 1977). These pendants originated as gifts from the Asante to selected leaders among their northern neighbors and were subsequently copied by northern casters. In 1976 Adam Badimsogoro of Nalerigu, the Mampruga Na, stated that he had commissioned two of the crocodile head pendants (Garrard 1984:Fig. 6) in his treasury from local casters and that his father had commissioned a third, which is shown being worn in Figure 30. Timothy F. Garrard, who has discussed these ornaments in some detail, has identified four pieces of "undoubted Akan workmanship" (1984:52) presumably on the basis of their quality and their affinity with documented Akan prototypes. This conclusion underestimates the skill of northern casters and their ability to replicate a model which they could study closely. Until the criteria are refined for distinguishing northern work

from that of the Akan, any specific attribution must remain problematic. DHR

28. CEREMONIAL CHEWING STICK, ASANTE, GHANA

Ceremonial chewing sticks (*asakyimannua*) are carried by young female initiates on the sixth and final day (a day of thanksgiving) of the nubility or initiation rites of the Asante (Sarpong 1977:45). Thomas Freeman observed this event at the court of the Asantehene in Kumase in 1841:

> Between the King's sister and his wives, there appeared about twenty-four girls, from eight to twelve years of age...each carried a small stick, covered with gold, about a foot long, one end of which was placed in their mouths (Freeman 1844:125).

In addition to gold-leafed examples, intricately sculpted wood chewing sticks like this in the Joss collection, are also known. Although based on utilitarian chewing sticks used to clean the teeth, the ceremonial examples are not actually chewed. According to Okae (1971:21), the initiate holds the stick in her mouth as a reminder to remain silent. They are presented to the initiate by her parents or by a suitor. The excessive length of several examples, including this piece, suggests that the function of "chewing sticks" was similar to that of staff of achievement, proclaiming the coming of age of its holder (see Cole and Ross 1977:fig. 97a). The female figure seen here is one of the most common motifs on this form and undoubtedly refers to the Asante ideal of feminine beauty and the potential for procreation. DHR

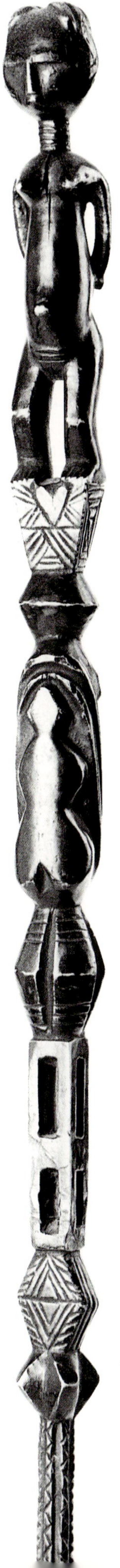

PREFACE TO THE YORUBA ENTRIES

FORM-WORDS AND SENSES IN UNDERSTANDINGS OF ART[1]

Frequently in discussions of objects called "art" we attempt to separate "form" from "content" or "meaning." While "form" generally considers *how* a particular object was created (colors, shapes, volumes, lines, textures and composition, its "style"), and "content" considers *what* an artist represents (or doesn't), a work's evocative qualities constitute both. Form is content, and content, form. An object's colors, shapes, and other stylistic elements have their histories and associated ideas/concepts, which, if explored from multiple perspectives, can help deepen and enrich our understandings of artists, artistic processes and objects, as well as our own responses to them.

If these observations are valid, then explorations of the visual connotations of certain words, what I call **form-words**, would consider the histories or etymologies of such words in order to uncover how *naming* reflects and shapes perceptions and understandings of things (and persons). This is what I propose to do in an exploratory way with several Yorùbá **form-words**. But, as I have argued elsewhere, "while the study of language is a means, it is not an end. Language-based approaches, such as semiotics, are just that, *language*-based, not *vision*-based. Art communicates and evokes by means of its own unique codes, and these need our attention" (Drewal 1990:35).

Recently, Yorùbá artist and art critic Moyo Okediji (1992:119–123) outlined such a vision-based approach, which he imaginatively terms *semi-optics*—an approach that recognizes the limitations of the linguistic basis of semiotics and seeks to uncover the ways in which the sense of *sight* shapes our perceptions and understandings of the world. Distinguishing between the broader term of semiology, the study of signs, and the narrower, linguistically-based field of semiotics, he writes, "Drawing from the treasures of critical resources replete in semiology, semioptics is a dynamic composite approach to critical inquiry, specifically designed to address the challenge of visual arts" (Okediji 1992:120). I have attempted to illustrate how this perspective on visual and verbal signs might be useful in the discussion of certain Yorùbá **form-words** and objects that follow.

I see this exercise, however, as only part of what needs to be a much larger investigation of a *multi-sensorial* basis of understanding. I would contend that while language, for example, is one of the ways we *re-present* the world, before language we began by perceiving, reasoning, theorizing, and understanding through *all* our senses—sight, sound, touch, smell, and taste. Although we may often be unconscious of them, the senses continually participate in the ways we literally *make sense* of the world. Seeing (hearing, tasting, etc.) is thinking, seeing is theorizing. In the beginning, there was *no* word.

In stressing the importance of the senses in the constitution of understanding, I have been influenced by the arguments of Mark Johnson, who wrote in *The Body in the Mind* (1987:xiii, xv, xvi) that "any adequate account of meaning and rationality must give place to embodied and imaginative structures of understanding by which we grasp the world." He goes on to say "contrary to Objectivism, I focus on the indispensability of embodied human *understanding* for meaning and rationality. 'Understanding,'...is here regarded as populated with just those kinds of imaginative structures that emerge from our experience as bodily organisms functioning in interaction with an environment."

Having briefly stated this theoretical position, I turn to an analysis of specific *objects* in the environment of Yorùbá-speaking peoples. A full exposition and illustration of the sensorial/bodily basis of understandings about objects is not possible here. I hope, however, my discussions are provocative. I focus primarily on envisioned attributes of objects and the effects of language/naming, but where possible, I try to suggest the role of hearing, touch, and smell in experiences of form.

For many Yorùba persons, words—*spoken words*—have the "power to bring things to pass," to accomplish things, a power termed *àṣẹ*. The nature and scope of the *àṣẹ* of words depends, of course, on how, where, when and by whom they are voiced (see Drewal and Drewal 1983:chapters 1–3; Drewal and Drewal 1987:225–7).

From the very start of a Yorùba individual's journey through life, he/she is defined by names (Drewal et al. 1989:26). Thus when babies are born, they receive special names expressing their spiritual nature as revealed by the *ways* in which they arrived and their origins. Such names, called *orúkọ àmútọ̀runwá* ("names brought from the otherworld") reveal the special qualities and potential of an individual. For example, children born inside the caul (that is, masked) are called *amúsan* (male) and *ato* (female) are thought to have special affinities with their ancestors, and are expected to become active members in the Egúngún or ancestral masking society.

Other names given after birth, called *orúkọ àbísọ*, provide additional clues to the nature of the person. *Orúkọ àbíkú* are names given to those who are reincarnations of themselves, that is, "children-born-to-die" and to be reborn frequently, and *orúkọ eya* are names that refer to the partial reincarnation of ancestors, generally a grandmother or grandfather. All such names indicate the spiritual qualities and propensities of an individual, stressing her/his uniqueness and connection with the past, the ancestors, and the spiritual forces in the universe.

Such names become a focus in the verbal arts of appellations (*oríkì*) (see Barber 1991) and songs (*orin*). These arts embellish the imagery associated with names, names that serve to integrate persons in a lineage, an unbroken chain of relations from departed ancestors to living relatives, to celebrate the distinctive qualities and uniqueness of the individual, to invoke the spiritual essence of the person, and to elevate the person by encouraging perfection and "faultless performance" (Akinnasọ 1983:15). When such praises are voiced, the head becomes "inspired" or "energized" (*wú*) with the spirit of one's noble ancestry, which is calculated to encourage high achievement. Naming is important because as Yorùba say, "a person's name directs actions and behavior" (*orúkọ ni nro ni*) (Akinnasọ 1981:51). It also encapsulates the history of the individual and his family, for names are used to reconstruct historical circumstances.

If naming is so important among Yorùba, then words that refer to object types or forms, what I am calling **form-words**, should contain associative ideas, evocative resonances related to various senses (touch, smell, etc.), allusions to the past, glimpses of potentiality, that can provide insights into the import, the evocative, affective qualities of a form as it is experienced by its audiences.

In the following discussions of specific Yorùba objects, I have tried to suggest some of the possible resonances evoked by certain **form-words** and how these might lead us toward a richer sense of these objects as art, that is, evocative form, for Yorùbas and for us. In the catalogue entries that follow, I have selected several form-words—*ògo, ọ̀pá, òpó, ọpọ́n, ìrùkẹ̀rẹ̀, idẹ*—and developed brief expositions of their etymologies and fields of associative ideas to suggest the possibilities of such an approach. The paucity of systematic studies in Yorùba etymology is lamentable, especially since there is a tradition within the language itself—the oral artistry of Ifá diviners whose recitations of *odù* verses filled with idiophones provide a wealth of etymologies (Yai, pers. comm. 1992). Work on the sensorial basis of experience among Yorùbas remains unexplored. These entries are but beginnings.

HENRY JOHN DREWAL

[1] I acknowledge with gratitude funds from the Graduate School of the University of Wisconsin-Madison, a 1990 NEH Summer Stipend, and a Newberry Library/NEH Fellowship, which gave me time to work through some of the ideas in this essay and catalogue. I am particularly indebted to Professor Ọlabiyi Babalọla Yai for information, comments, and suggestions on various points, and to Margaret Thompson Drewal for her advice and counsel throughout. All shortcomings are of course my own, *o kàwé ni, ó ò kà ọgbọ́n.*

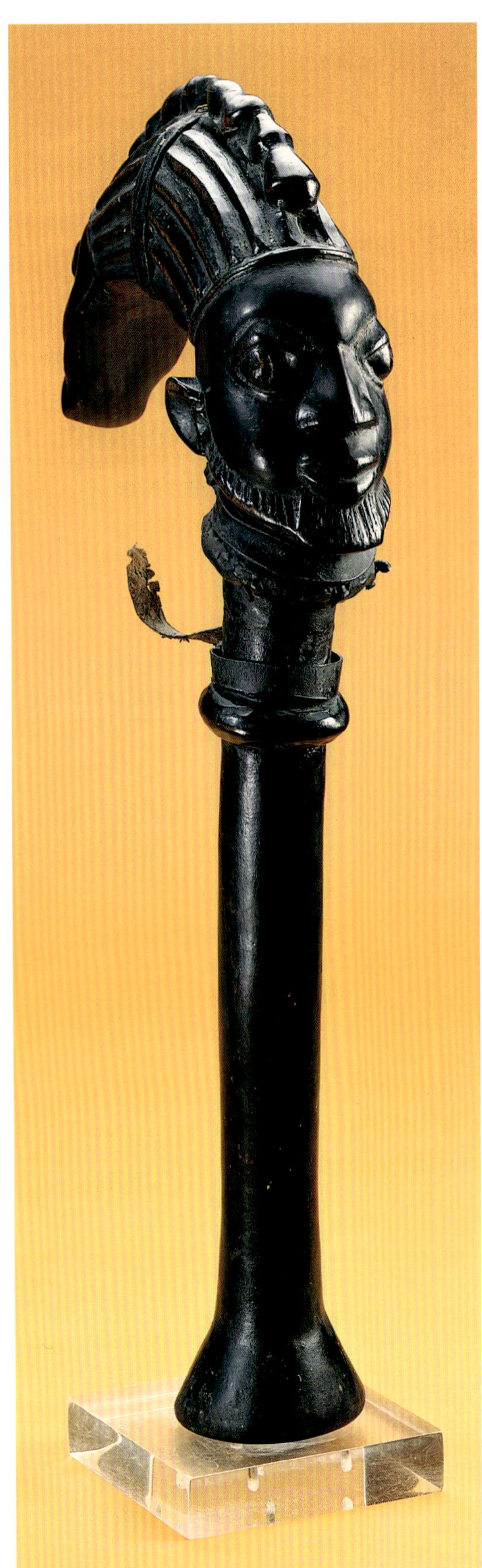

29. Dance Staff for Èṣù/Ẹlẹ́gbá, Yorùba, Nigeria

Èṣù Láàlù, okiri oko!

> Honor to the one who throws a stone today
> and kills a bird tomorrow,
>
> Who struggles to climb a blade of grass, yet
> whose shadow darkens a mountain.

During a performance, the dance staff is worn over the left shoulder (side of sacred, awesome matters) of a priest; at other times it is displayed on an altar. The staff is carved to honor Èṣù/Ẹlẹ́gbá, divine mediator, trickster, and question mark, who stands at the crossroads of human lives. The double identity of the "confusionist" Èṣù/Ẹlẹ́gbá, emphasized by his double name and multiple identities, reminds people that things and events in this world (and the next) demand careful observation, perception, interpretation and action and must be done with patience (*sùúrù*) and composure (*ìfarabalẹ̀*). Note how certainties are shaken in his transgression of time and scale in the verses above and in the iconography of his ritual form where two heads face in opposite directions, with Èṣù/Ẹlẹ́gbá you never know whether you're coming or going! Èṣù/Ẹlẹ́gbá is undomesticatable energy, ready to wreak havoc. Thus, Yorùba say (Abraham 1958:166): "*Èṣù kò ní ìwà, a kọ́ ilé rẹ̀ s'ìta*,"—"Èṣù lacks [positive] character, we build his/her shrine outside" (my translation).

Ọ̀gọ, the **form-word** for this object type, incorporates a network of resonating ideas and themes. In the earliest dictionary written by a Yorùba, Samuel A. Crowther (1852:231) defines *ọ̀gọ* as "a short knotted stick or club for self-defense ; believed to be used by the devil [Èṣù/Ẹlẹ́gbá] who is therefore called *Agongo ọggọ*, 'The man of the knotted club.'" According to Abraham (1958:508), *ọ̀gọ* is translated as "cudgel" and related to another club/weapon type called *kùmọ*. He goes on to give a sentence using *ọ̀gọ—ó ju ọ̀gọ nùn*, which he translates, "He gave up the struggle as fruitless ... he died." My literal translation is, "He threw away/abandoned his cudgel." As I interpret this, throwing away one's club/weapon is a sign of capitulation, whereas the brandishing/display of one's weapon signals life, action, and continued struggle. Elsewhere Abraham (1958:166-7) states Èṣù goes "about with a knobbed club (*ògo Ẹlẹ́gbẹ́ra*)...with which he attacks his enemies." He also notes, "Some images are male, others female. The image of a man with a horn on his head curving backwards and carved in wood and ornamented with cowries is often used by devotees who beg for alms on public roads." Thus the sight and significance, the form/content of the form-word *ògo* conjure up confusion with simultaneous suggestions of supplication *and/or* coersion/punishment, attack *and/or* self-defense, begging *and/or* beating—mixed messages and ambiguities that are at the very core of Èṣù/Ẹlẹ́gbá conveyed powerfully yet perhaps subliminally by the form-word *ògo*.

The Joss *ògo* is carved from a carefully chosen knotted, branching piece of wood (the same as is used for the handles of hoes, adzes, and clubs). Traditionally the sculptor transforms the staff handle into a primary figure, and the subsidiary portion of the staff into a partial figure or, as here, tailed coiffure. Gourd containers (*àdó*), which line the crest of the curving coiffure, signal magical substances that cause things to happen. Leather strands of cowrie shells probably originally encircled the shaft, but have either been removed or lost.

The physical characteristics of the branching, intersecting form of the staff connote multiple directions, paths—the crossroads that are Èṣù/Ẹlẹ́gbá's domain. Support for this supposition is found in the unfigurated forked staffs for the divine mediator Leggua (Èṣù/Ẹlẹ́gbá) among the Lukumi, Cubans of Yorùba descent. As in Africa, these staffs are carried over the shoulder, ready to "hook" or capture the unsuspecting, the unaware.   HJD

30. Dance Sculpture for Èṣù/Elẹ́gbá, Yorùba

Doubling or multiplicity associated with Èṣù/Ẹlẹ́gbá is often imaged in paired figures, one male, one female. Despite graphic phallic themes in much of the oration and sculpture honoring Èṣù/Ẹlẹ́gbá, the deity's gender, like much else, remains uncertain. Here the images are of male and female devotees.

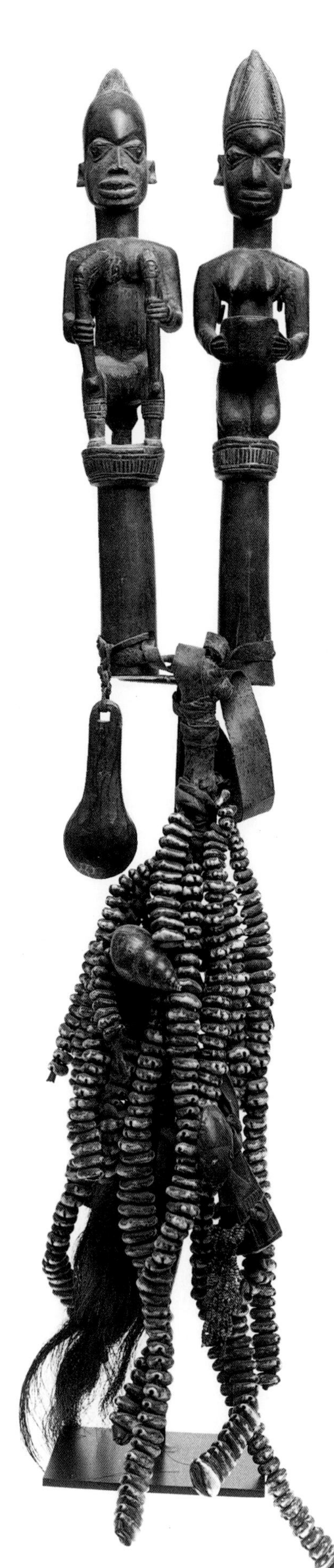

▼▲▼

30

DANCE SCULPTURE
for Èṣù/Ẹlẹ́gbá
(*ògo* Elẹ́gbéra/Ẹlẹ́gbá)
Yorùba, Nigeria
Wood, animal tail,
cowrie shells, leather,
glass beads, string,
metal, shell and bluing
H. 96 cm.
FMCH 87.1223

The man holds paired *òg̣o* in his hands and sits on a flute, a highly surprising act in itself. The flute symbolizes Èṣù's aspects as messenger/provocateur. The female kneels and presents an offering bowl. Both wear elaborate, conical coiffures, perhaps a reference to the tufted, tailed hairstyles that signal the presence of activating materials containing *àṣẹ*. Attached among the strands of cowrie shell-money are a miniature spoon with which to offer the deity its due, a small wooden wristlet in the form of a half figure with tailed hairstyle, and a snail shell, like those used as tops by children, the spinning of which is likened to the whirling of a dancer (*jíjó bi òkòtó*).

The style of the figure recalls northern Ọ̀yọ́ style generally, perhaps in the area of Ìlọrin.   HJD

31. STAFF-SPEAR, YORÙBA, NIGERIA

A staff—*òpá*—is a widespread symbol of authority, which in a Yorùba context is usually associated with age. According to Abraham (1958:522), *òpá* refers to a "walking stick." Walking sticks are associated with elders, those who lean on a cane when walking. Age connotes wisdom (*ogbọ́n*), and wisdom connotes intensified *àṣẹ* or the power to accomplish things. Two examples may illustrate this point. First, among the *òrìṣà*, the aged one, Ọbàtálá, is the only one to dance with a staff (*òpá oṣóòro*) (Yai, pers. comm.1992). And second, among Ìjèbu-Yorùba there is a powerful society known as Ọpa, literally "Staff-Society," or Awoọpa, "Secret/Esoteric-Knowl-edge-Society." Members are termed *abọpa*, "worship-pers-of-staff" who *bú ọpa*, "swear-*ọpa*-oath." The primary symbols of Awoọpa are wooden staffs, the features of which are masked by a thick, blackened coating of sacrificial residue, which exudes a powerful odor. Smell as well as sight contribute to one's experience of their aura. Their texture, opacity, and scent together evoke the idea of an awesome, hidden knowledge and power whose presence is made all the more palpable by the open display of secrecy. In sum, the form-word *òpá* evokes age, wisdom, status, initia-tion, ritual preparation, and both signals and sub-stantiates power and authority, *àṣẹ*.

Figurated staffs with one or more spear blades (*òkò*) at the summit are carved in honor of various *òrìṣà* in western Yorùbaland among the Kétu-, Ọhọrí-, Anago- and Ègbádò-Yorùba, as well as among the Egun people of Ajaṣé (Porto-Novo). Kevin Carroll recorded a figurated staff for Òṣùmàrè, deity of the rainbow, at Ilara-Kétu (Carroll 1966:Plates 30,36). According to Carroll (1966:159), "[The staffs] are carried in procession or stuck in the ground during ceremonies for the cults of Oṣumare (the god of the rainbow), Babaligbo (or Ṣoponna, the god of smallpox), and Momogre (*oriṣa Egun*). The worshippers of these gods take part in each others' ceremonies and lend their implements to each other." I have also documented among the Ègbádò-Yorùba a spear-staff in honor of the water goddess Yewa.

The carving of the staff represents a seated mother, who holds her breasts in a gesture of greeting and offering. Her child looks out to her left, a triangular protective amulet around its neck. Below the figurative group is a hollowed rectangular box, which originally had a removable cover, and below that a female kneels within an enclosure. She faces to the mother's right, in the direction opposite to that of the child. The interlocking forms below her suggest two entwined fingers, an ancient and widespread Yorùba gesture of intimate friendship, togetherness, a sacred bond. Together these images, each facing in different directions, suggest vigilance and preparedness, ritual or otherwise. The box probably originally concealed an empowering substance containing *àṣẹ*. The theme of potential aggressive/protective power culminates in the iron blade of the spear. Like the *òg̣o* of Èṣù/Ẹlégbá or the *òpá ọsun* of Ifá diviners (see Drewal and Drewal 1983:65-66), this *òpá-òkò* is a sanctified weapon of action—protecting and naming those who stand with it.   HJD

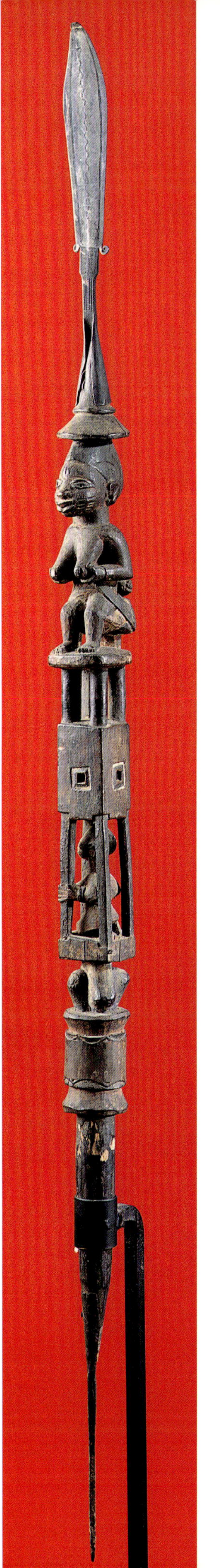

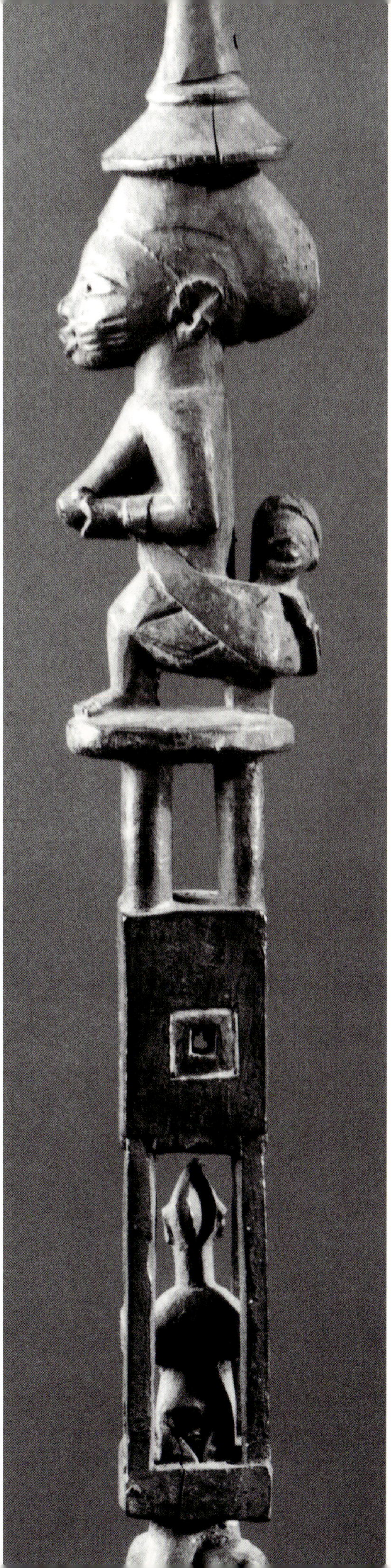

▼▲▼

31

STAFF-SPEAR

(ọ̀pá-ọ̀kọ̀)

Yorùba, Nigeria

Wood and metal

H. 121.92 cm.

FMCH 92.6

32. Houseposts by Obembe Alaye (ca. 1869-1939), Yorùba, Nigeria

Òpó or "post" connotes something that supports, literally as well as figuratively. *Òpó* is part of several prominent lineage totems (*orúkọ ìdílè*), like Àjàdíòpó and Òpómulero. "Òpómulero" consists of the sentence *òpó mu ilé rò* meaning "post sustains the whole edifice" (Yai, pers. comm. 1992). This conveys the notion of unfailing support and sturdiness as in the saying, *ìwọ lo jé òpó ìfaratì fún mi,* "you are a tower of strength to me" (Abraham 1958:478). It is thus most appropriate that *òpó* be transformed by images of those who support, sustain, and shape culture and history—women, mothers, elders, chiefs, rulers, foreigners, warriors, priests and others.

The workshop of the master carver Obembe Alaye (ca. 1869-1939), the Ologunde of Èfòn-Àlàyè, was a prolific producer of veranda posts with a varied repertoire of images. These images record primarily ordinary people among the Èkìtì-Yorùba during the early colonial period. The arrangement of these superposed images implies no narrative, rather the images form a serrate or segmented composition of autonomous themes meant to give each subject its space and to attract the attention of viewers (Drewal and Drewal 1987). The subjects of one of the houseposts (FMCH 91.29), include a standing female, who wears a triangular amulet (possibly a reference to ones made by itinerant Muslim clerics) and holds her breasts in a gesture of welcome, respect and nurturance; a mother who tightens her baby sash (*òjá*) as her baby looks outward from behind; and a male, possibly an elder or chief (suggested by the bracelets he wears), seated in a folding camp chair introduced into Yorùbaland by the British in the late nineteenth century.

The second housepost (FMCH 91.30) depicts a kneeling female wearing multiple strands of waistbeads; a bearded male who smokes a pipe and carries a cane, probably a European; and a standing male. Despite the segmented, non-narrative composition, Obembe Alaye playfully suggests the continuity of the vertical form by subtly overlapping the segments. For example, in FMCH 91.29 the red-colored diminishing diamond motifs at the side of the top section descend to the neck of the seated male, and in FMCH 91.30 the kneeling female at the bottom steadies the base of the image above her.   HJD

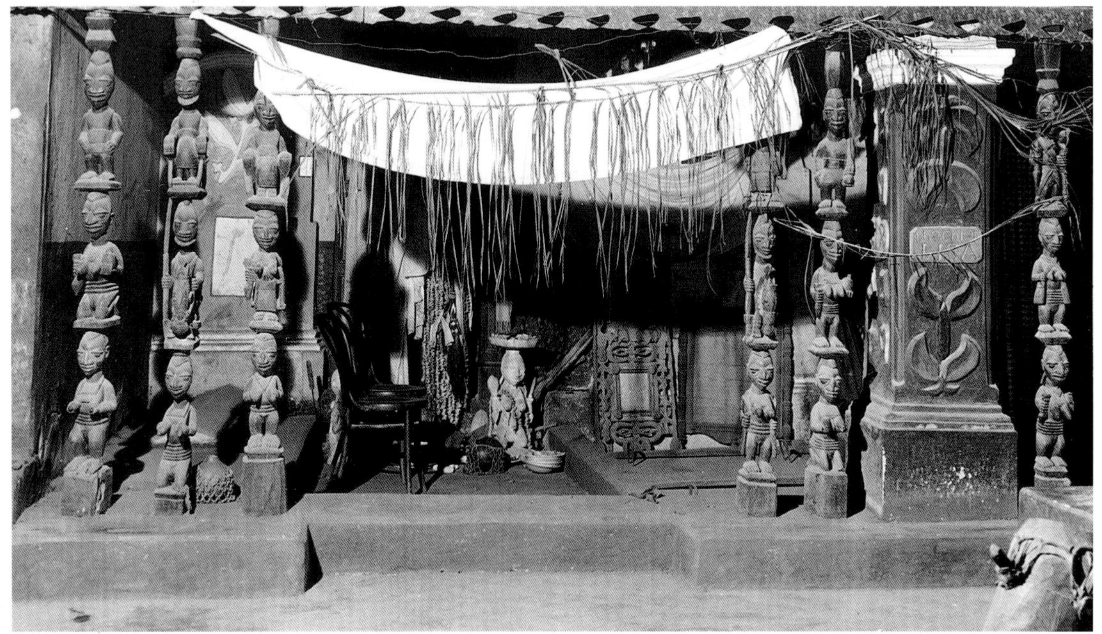

FIG. 31

Tomb of former Chief Lisa. Ondo, Nigeria. Photo by W. Fagg, 1959. William B. Fagg Archive, FMCH.

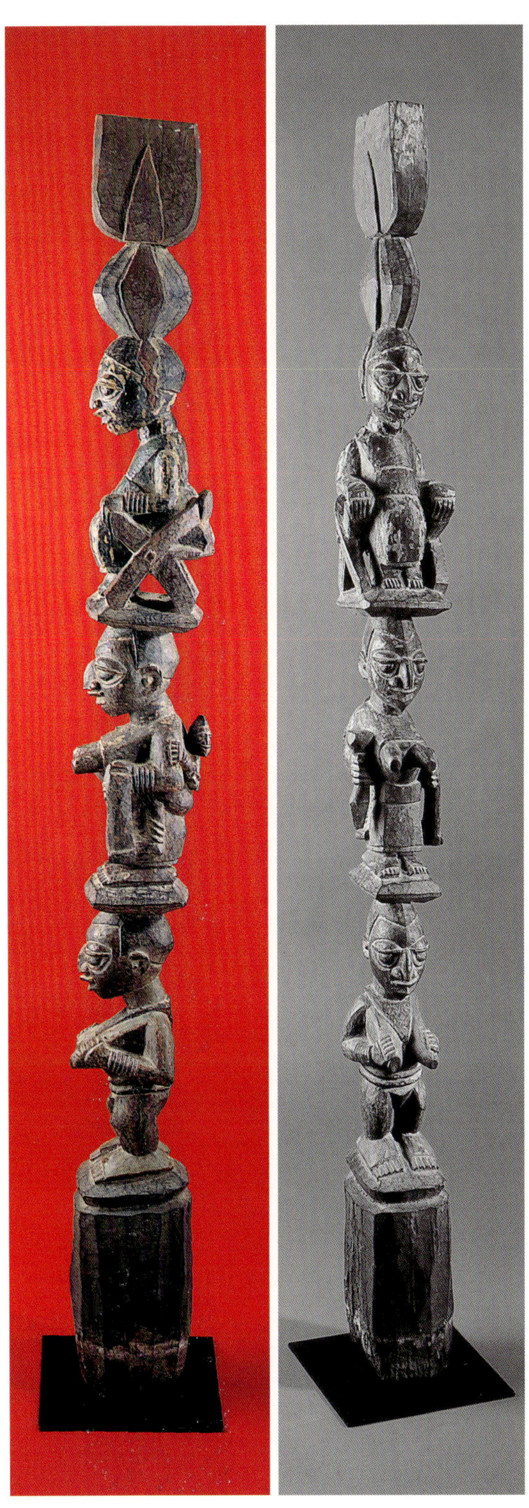
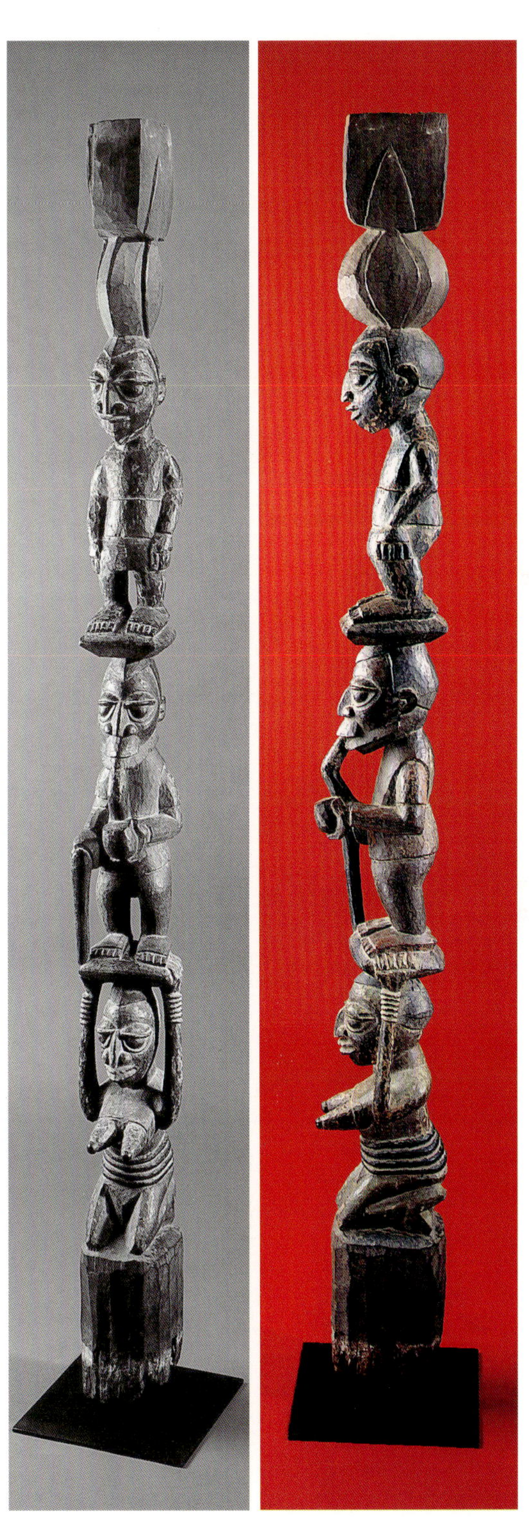

32

HOUSEPOSTS
(òpó) by Obembe Alaye
(ca. 1869-1939)
Yorùba, Nigeria
Wood and paint
H. 213 cm.
FMCH 91.29 and 91.30

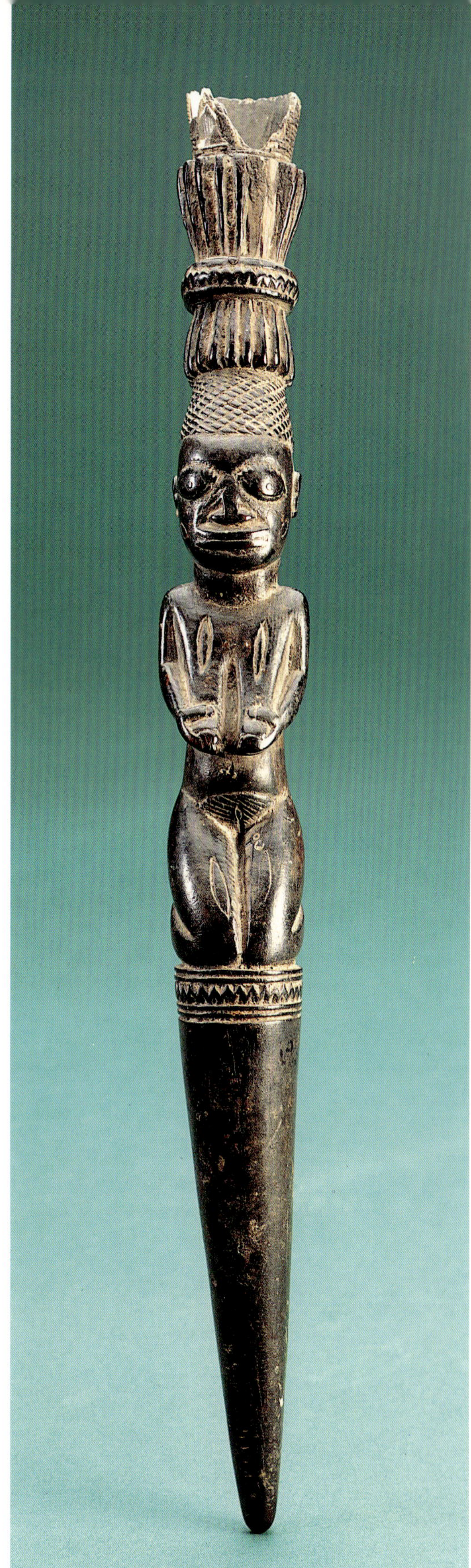

▼▲▼
33
IVORY IFÁ TTAPPER
(*iroke* Ifá)
Yorùba, Nigeria
Ivory
L. 32 cm.
FMCH 87.434

▼▲▼
34
DIVINING CHAIN
(*ọ̀pẹ̀lẹ̀* Ifá)
Yorùba, Nigeria
Ivory and brass
L. 106.5 cm.
FMCH 90.693

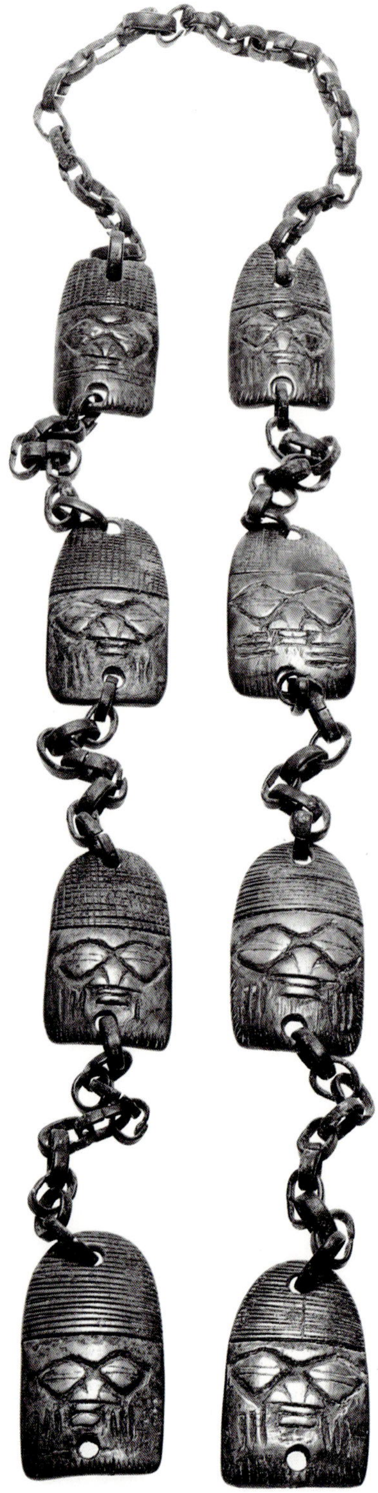

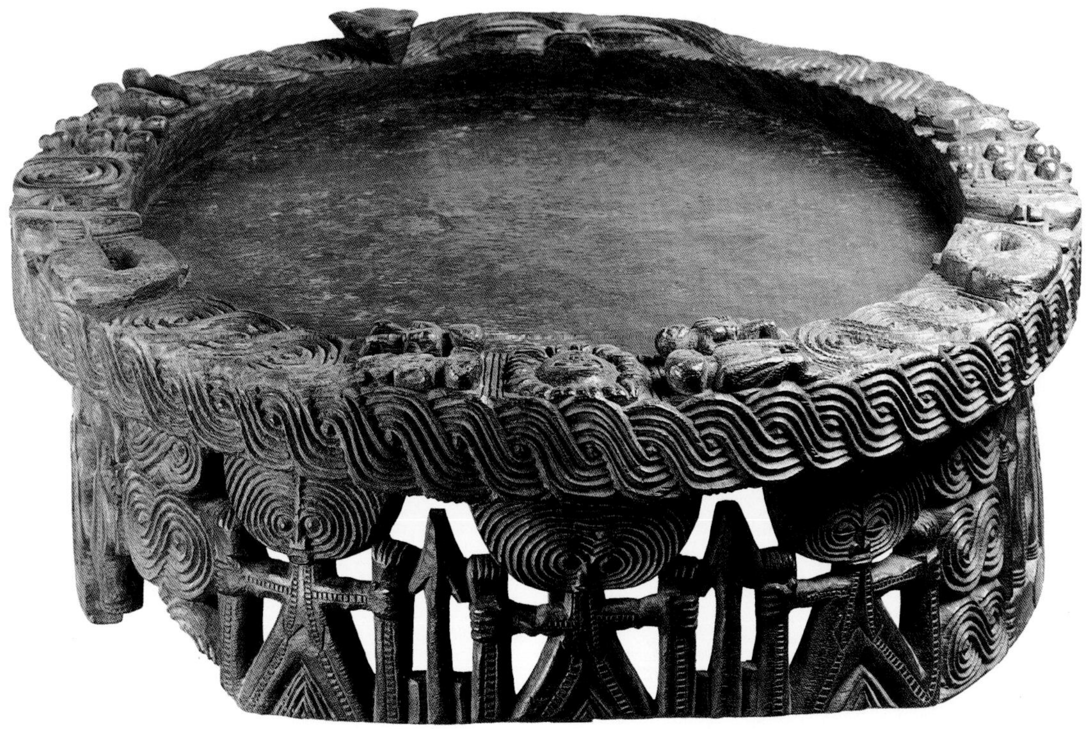

33. Ivory Ifá Tapper, Yorùba, Nigeria

The worn surface of this Ifá tapper (*iroke* Ifá) is evidence of long use by a diviner, a "father of ancient wisdom" (*babaláwo*). Diviners use the tapper to strike the center of the divination tray at the outset of divination to invoke cosmic forces and to emphasize points during their commentary and interpretation of Ifá orature. The broken and incomplete open end of the tapper may have had a clapper, thus transforming the tapper into a bell and providing another sound for invocations and songs during ceremonies. The motif of a kneeling female holding her breasts is a gesture of supplication, greeting, respect and devotion, all attitudes appropriate for one who comes to Ifá to address important matters. The marks on her cheeks, above her breasts, and on her thighs may indicate regional, community, or lineal affiliations, royal/non-royal status, or permanent beautification (Drewal 1988). HJD

34. Divining Chain, Yorùba, Nigeria

Ifá diviners use the divining chain (*òpèlè* Ifá) to obtain the number combination/signatures of the *odù* Ifá verses more quickly. Holding the chain at the center between the two rows of *òpèlè* seeds (here represented by convex, carved ivory faces), the diviner gently tosses the ends toward himself, allowing the eight elements to land either face up or face down. He then counts these to determine which *odù* has come to speak. HJD

35. Ifá Divination Tray, Yorùba, Nigeria

A famous carver of Ifá, Chief Alaaye of Ikerin, told Rowland Abiodun (1975:435-6) that "*opón* is designed to flatter and honor Ifá." The word *opón* means "tray," something made to display or present something openly, plainly, and clearly. *Opón* Ifá, by its flattering "designs," extends presentation to revelation.

One of the ways forces operating in the Yorùba cosmos reveal themselves is on the face of divination trays (*opón* Ifá). A "father of ancient wisdom" (*babaláwo*) manipulates sixteen sacred palm nuts (*ikin*) or an *òpèlè* divining chain (see FMCH 90.693, cat. 34) and then marks certain number combinations in a thin layer of *iyèrè òsùn* wood dust spread

35
IFÁ DIVINATION TRAY
(*opón* Ifá)
Yorùba, Nigeria
Wood
D. 71.5 cm.
FMCH 90.168

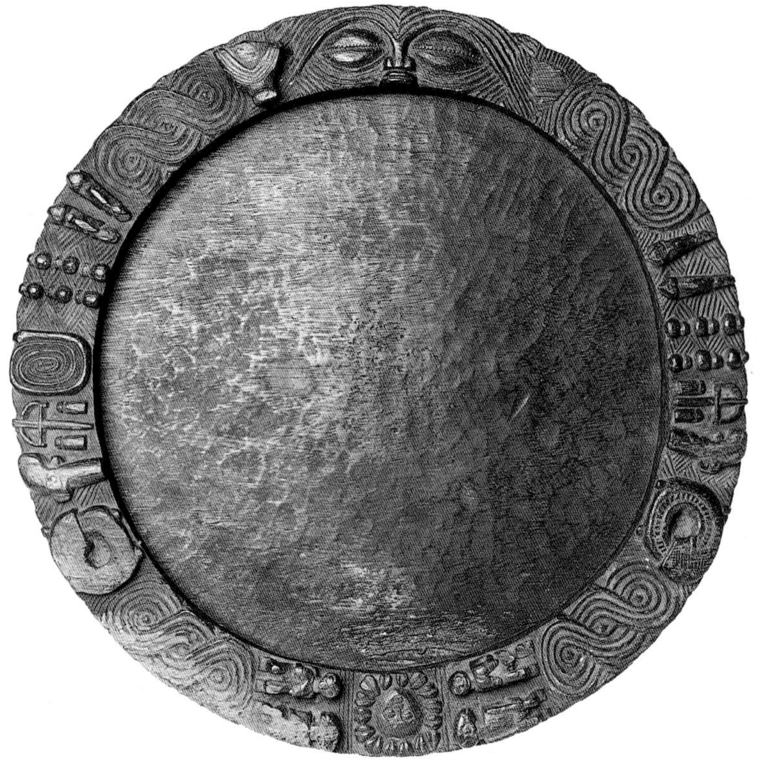

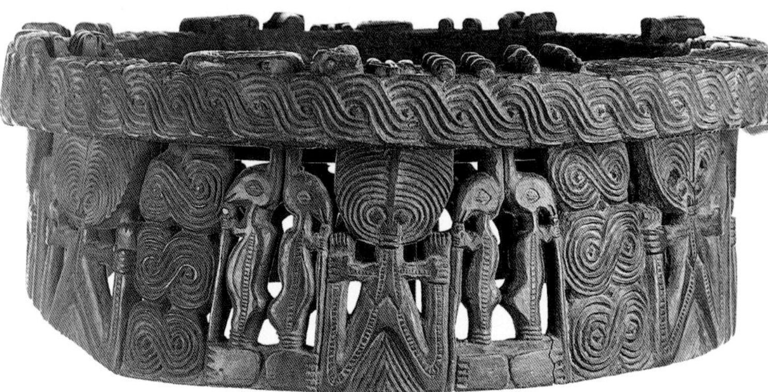

▼▲▼
35
IFÁ DIVINATION TRAY
Alternative views

over the tray's surface to obtain the "signature" of a divination verse or *odù*. Forces, such as gods and ancestors, speak through the *odù*. The diviner's clients must listen to the stories, reflect upon and interpret their implications, and then take appropriate action to bring good fortune to their lives.

This large, elaborately carved divination tray is elevated on a circular stand with openwork imagery. The tray plus stand may also have served as the lid for a large container in which the diviner kept his paraphernalia. The carved decoration of the stand and that around the raised edge of the tray itself, is serrate in composition but reflects a four-part division. No narrative links one image to the next, rather, each motif, or group of motifs, is separate and autonomous, a visual means of invoking, evoking, and marshaling the diverse, often competing forces in the Yorùba world (Drewal 1977; Drewal 1987; Drewal and Drewal 1987; Drewal et al. 1989:16-26).

The carving on the tray's edge is dominated by one face, which one diviner (Kolawole Oṣitọla, pers. comm. 1982) has identified as "the face of the tray" (*ojú ọpọ́n*). Others interpret this face as a reference to Èṣù/Ẹlẹ́gbá, the divine mediator; still others, especially when there are fish-legged figures represented (as in the openwork stand of this tray), consider this to be a reference to Olókun, goddess of the sea. The face is flanked by birds (one broken off). To the right and left of the face and birds are three-part interlaces and a series of ritual objects: two clubs[?]; two rows of three medicine gourds (*àdô*); bows and arrows flanked by containers; pistols; dried fish on skewers; three-part interlaces; and paired female/male figures. Opposite the "face of the tray," on what Oṣitọla called the "foot of the tray" (*ẹsẹ̀ ọpọ́n*), is a face encircled by cowrie shells. This is a representation of the seventeenth palm nut (*olorí ikin*) surrounded by "the money of Ifá," *ajé* Ifá (Bascom 1969:Pl. 15). Each of the images on the tray evokes a range of associations—references to partners, sacrifices, deities, mothers, means of destruction, creation, and transformation, etc.—all of which diviners and clients must acknowledge and respect.

The images around the stand evoke many of the same presences, but others as well. The interlace that encircles the edge of the tray is without beginning or end and may thus evoke a Yorùba world view. In the words of Wole Ṣoyinka (1975), "the universe of the Yorùba mind [is] the world of the living, the dead and the unborn, and the numinous passage which links all: transition." Below the "face of the tray," a female and a male figure with their arms upraised face in opposite directions. Below them are three female fish-legged figures separated by arrows. This ancient motif, which is widespread among the Yorùba and their Edo neighbors to the southeast, is generally associated with Olókun, goddess of the sea. Her presence in this Ifá context is very appropriate because the diviner's spirit dwells in Olókun's realm after departing the world (Kolawole Oṣitọla, pers. comm. 1982). On the sides of the stand, the fish-legged image is flanked by paired profile figures who stand back to back and hold staff-like objects. Three fish-legged figures separated by arrows appear again on the stand at the "foot" of the tray. Such diverse and enigmatic imagery provokes thoughtful contemplation, one of the important lessons of divination, and of life.   HJD

36. Beaded container lid, Yorùba, Nigeria

Rulers in Yorubaland possess a profusion of beaded objects. One object type is the beaded container designed to hold personal belongings and a variety of items such as kolanuts, for distribution to favored guests. The form of this lid plays upon the conical shape of beaded crowns (*ade*), the container for a person's symbol of individuality, identity, and destiny (*ile ori*), as well as the sacred clay sculptures for the riverain deity Erinle. The missing beaded finial figure may have been a bird (see small ones within the open pyramid), often a reference to the mystical powers of women.   HJD

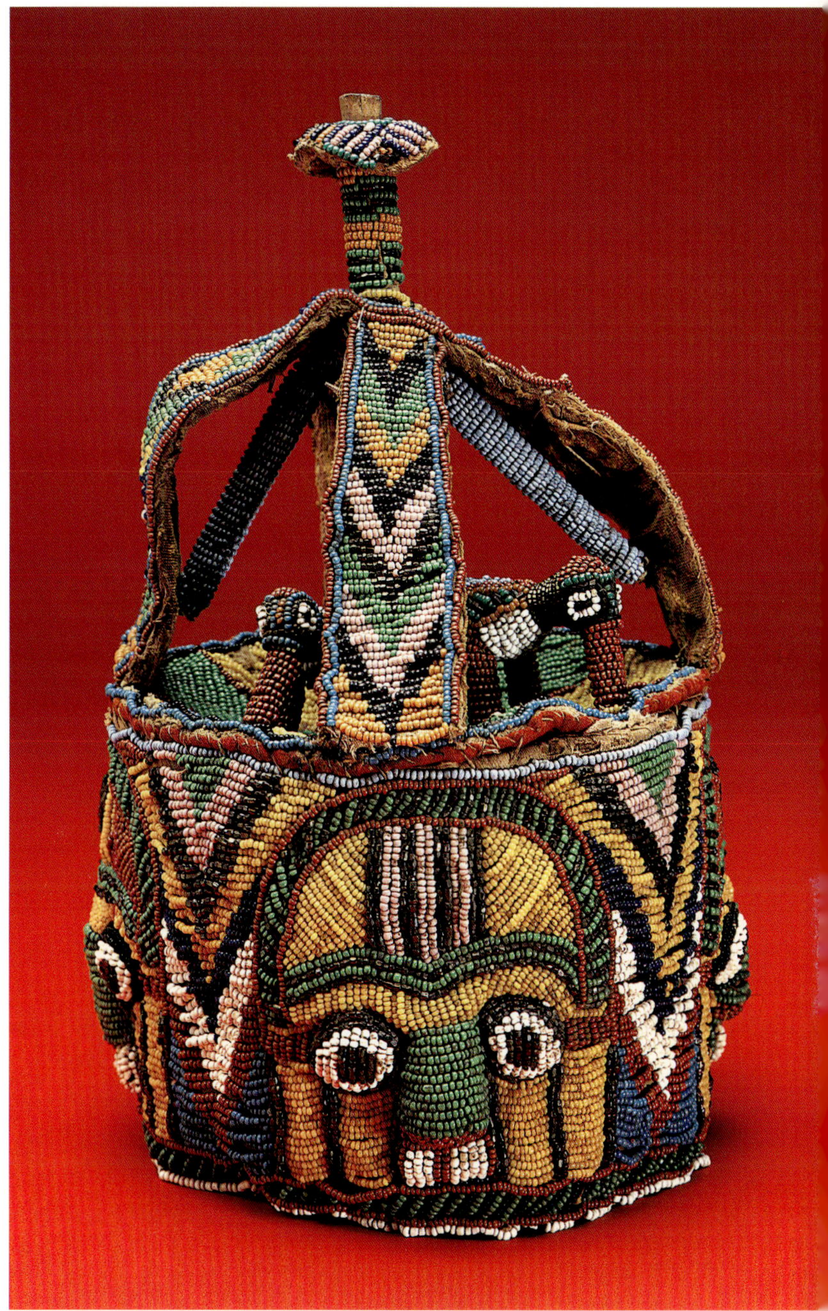

▼▲▼

36
BEADED
CONTAINER LID
Yorùba, Nigeria
Cardboard, wood,
paper, cotton,
burlap, felt,
and glass beads
H. 30 cm.
FMCH 90.700

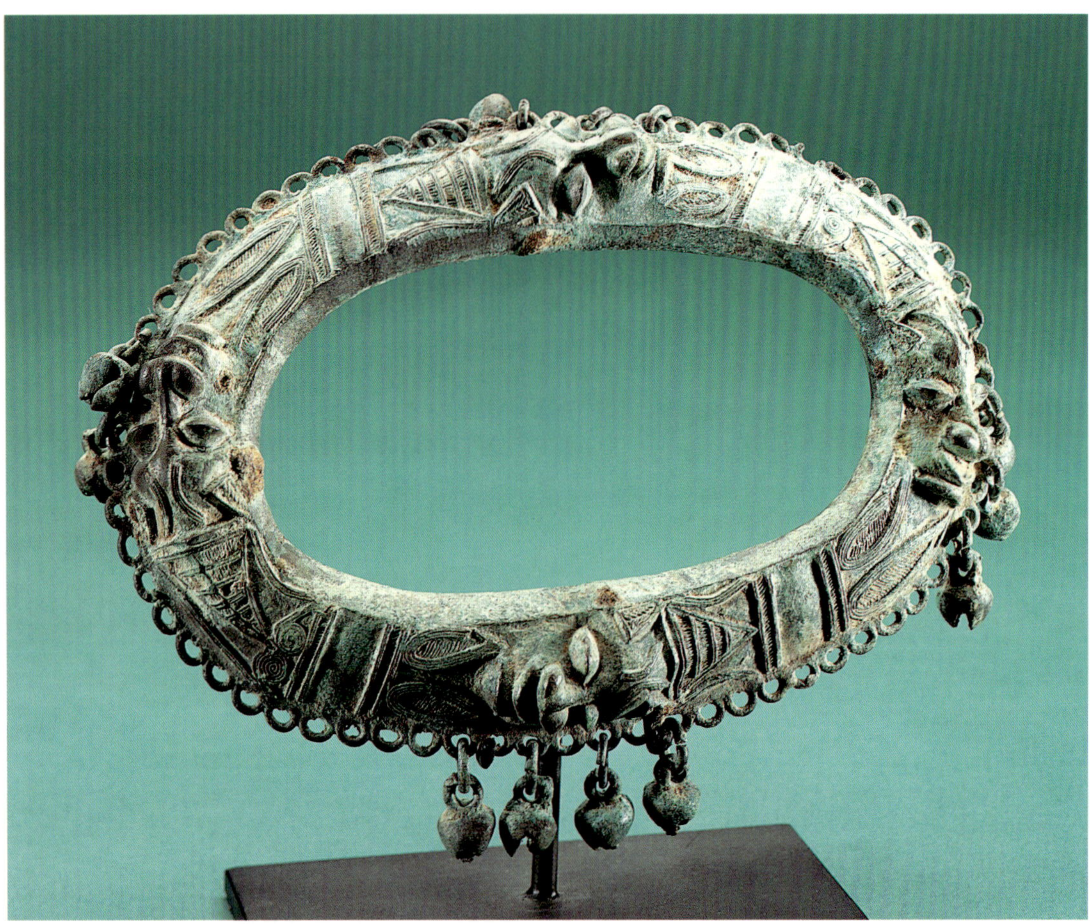

37
Anklet
(*idẹ ẹsẹ̀*)
Ìjẹ̀bu-Yorùba, Nigeria,
early nineteenth century
Bronze
H. 20 cm.
FMCH 87.605

37. ANKLET, ÌJÈBU-YORÙBA, NIGERIA

This bronze anklet (*idẹ ẹsẹ̀*) was probably cast by an Ìjẹ̀bu-Yorùba artist in the early nineteenth century; a very similar work was excavated at Imodi-Ìjẹ̀bu, the burial site of First Otunba Suna (Calvocoressi 1978). Such anklets were worn by important chiefs and elders among the Ìjẹ̀bu. The four faces that adorn this anklet have opposed crescent marks on their foreheads, often a sign associated with Oṣugbo, the Ìjẹ̀bu society of female and male elders who served as the ruler-makers (and breakers) as well as the highest judiciary in the land (Drewal 1989:136-144). Crotals were probably originally attached all around the perimeter of the oval anklet, providing a distinctive sound that announced the approach of an impressive personage. HJD

38. FLY WHISK, YORÙBA, NIGERIA

The form-word *ìrùkẹ̀rẹ̀* refers specifically to a tail (*ìru*), the part that trails behind, that remains like a potent memory. The tails of certain animals, like those of the chameleon (*agẹmọ*) or spiny anteater/pangolin (*arika*), are thought to contain that creature's *àṣẹ* or potency and are greatly sought after for medicinal/protective purposes. The term *kẹ̀rẹ̀* connotes something huge or substantial (Yai, pers. comm. 1992). Thus tails (or their leather substitutes, as here) in whisks may evoke great power and potential.

But *ìrùkẹ̀rẹ̀* conjures up other thoughts as well. Crowther (1852:157) gives the proverbial saying "The horse's tail soon becomes a man's tail: (for) when the horse dies he leaves his tail behind him, *iru ẹsin ki ipẹ idi ìru enia, bi ẹsin ku afi ìru si aiye.*" The key themes revolve around passages—between other-world (*ọ̀run*) and world (*ayé*) and *heredity*. As I learned from another context, the use of horsetail whisks by Gẹ̀lẹ̀dẹ́ Society members at Lagos (Beyioku 1946:4), is "emblematic of hereditary [sic]." The tail left by the departed horse, is what descendants claim from their ancestors. The whisk then signals its owner's connectedness to those departed. It is inheritance visualized.

The motif of a seated monkey consuming an ear of corn is widespread in Yorùba sculpture, occurring in a housepost by Obembe Alaye (Drewal 1977:18), as well as elsewhere. The connotations of this image are, however, poorly understood. It has been suggested that this motif might be a reference to Ṣàngó, since, according to Lawal (1970:99), the grove where Ṣàngó allegedly hanged himself was filled with monkeys. The image may also be connected with a story from the Ifá corpus about monkeys, which is related by 'Wande Abimbọla (1976:200-204). Significantly the story mentions the popular idea that monkeys steal corn from farms. In this story, the *ẹdun* monkey turns a disaster into a success using his quick wit. Because he was too slow to run away from the farmer, he pleaded innocence, saying he couldn't be accused of being a thief because he ate the corn in the owner's presence! The same reference is found in a Yorùba poem, which Beier (1970:83-4) collected and edited. The poem praises the monkey's gaul and wit:

> Child of maize!
> Owner of the farm!
> . . . .
> You continue to steal
> though you are old enough not to steal.
> O no!
> Since he was born
> the red monkey never stole anything:
> he merely picks what he wants
> in the presence of the farmer!
> He does not fight the farmer:
> he only stares at him.

As in other cultures, animals in Yorùba art often serve as metaphors for the attributes and actions of humans, and as allusions to proverbial and divinatory wisdom. The motif of the monkey on this fly whisk, an accouterment of elders, may thus have been intended both to delight and enlighten those who saw it.   HJD

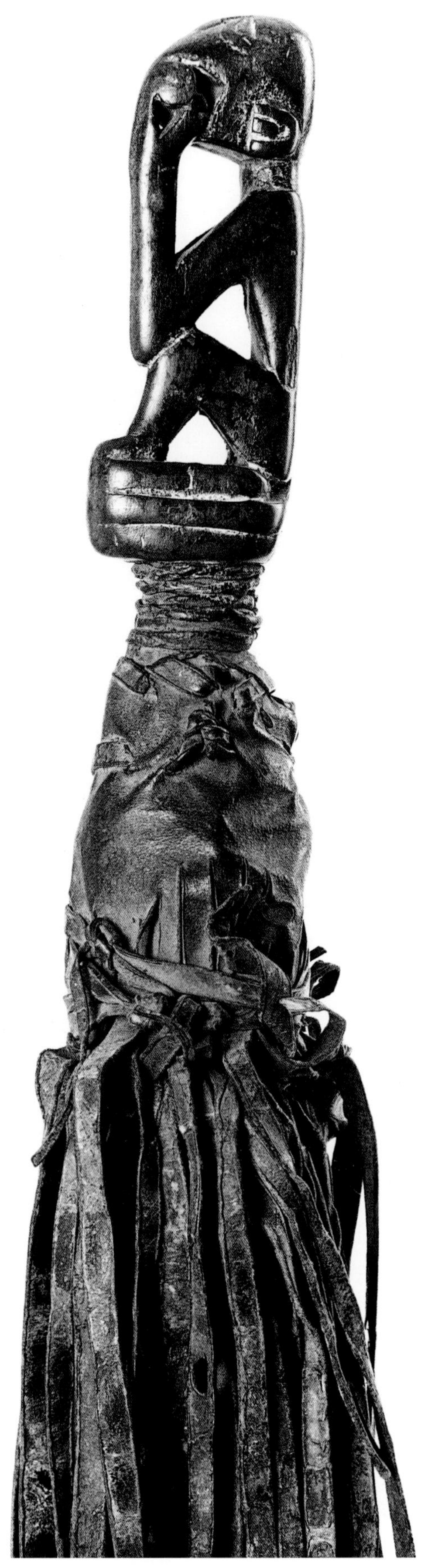

▼▲▼

38

FLY WHISK

(ìrùkèrè)

Yorùba, Nigeria

Wood and leather

L. 71 cm.

FMCH 87.1486

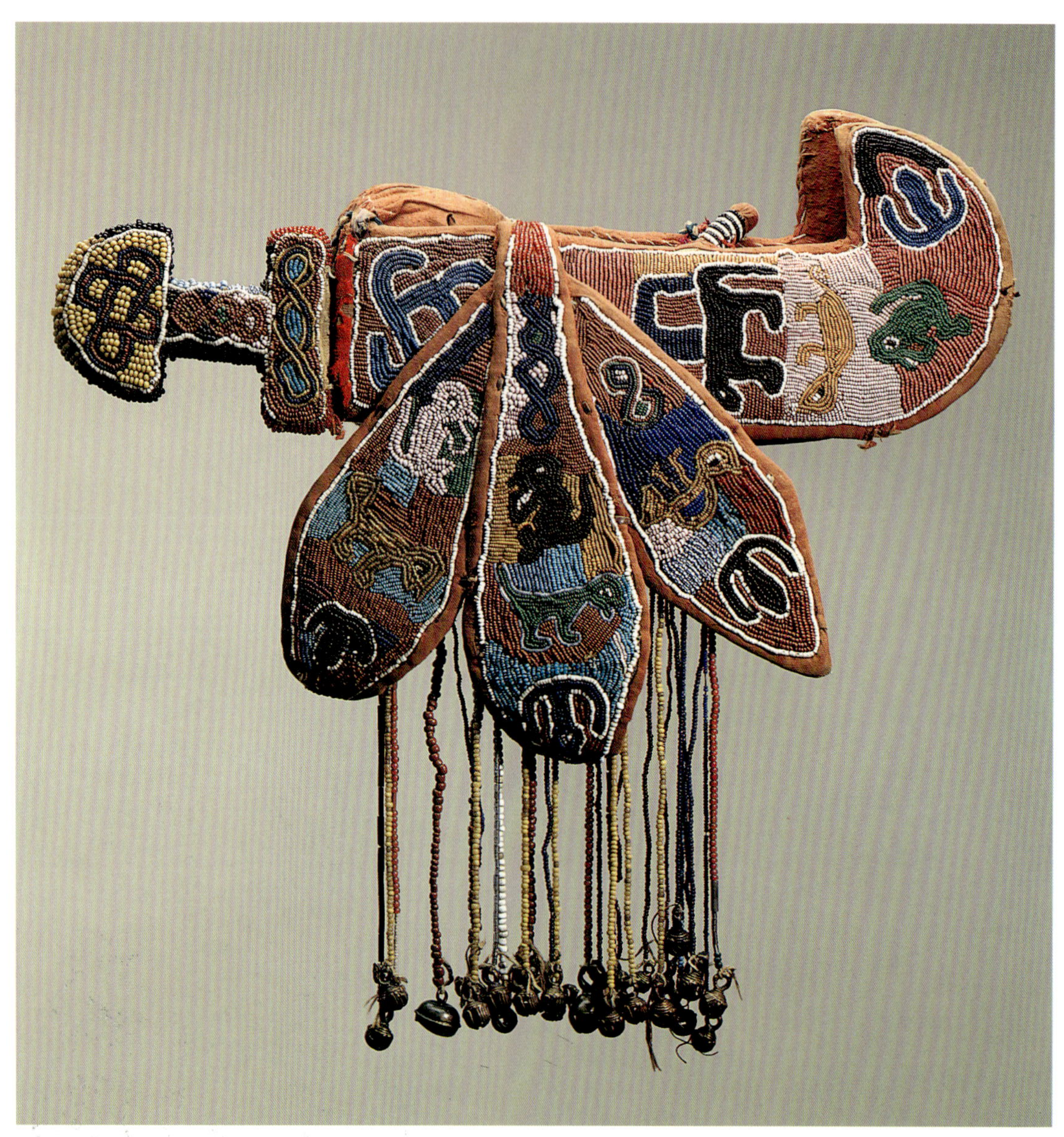

▼▲▼

39

CEREMONIAL SWORD
(udámalore) AND SHEATH
Òwò-Yorùba, Nigeria
Iron, wood, textile, glass
beads, flannel, bamboo,
copper alloy and leather
A (knife), L. 40.5 cm.
B (sheath), L. 40 cm.
FMCH 90.421A,B

39. Ceremonial Sword and Sheath, Ọ̀wọ̀-Yorùba, Nigeria

The *udámalore* ceremonial sword is reserved for use by the Olòwò, the ruler of the Ọ̀wọ̀-Yorùba, and his highest ranking chiefs (Abiọdun 1989:109). These titles seem to be related to military (and magical) prowess, not only because the emblem is a sword, but also because the imagery covering the beaded sheath refers to equestrian warriors and clever, powerful animals such as the monkey, leopard, chameleon, and ram. The rendering on the sheath of a black rider by his mount suggests that the bead artist has not seen many equestrians. Below the rider is a chameleon, identified by its distinctive spiral tail. Chameleons are renowned for their powers of transformation, changing their appearance for protection and survival. Below the chameleon is a seated monkey eating corn (see Fly whisk, Cat. 38, for a discussion of this motif), and below that is a ram's head. For the Ọ̀wọ̀-Yorùba, the ram is the supreme symbol of ancestors because of its associations with "alertness and strength, and its ability to defend itself" (Abiọdun 1989:113). Several of these motifs reappear on the blade-shaped panels attached to the sheath. HJD

40. Staff, Yorùba, Nigeria

Examples of this distinctive type of staff of authority were first photographed at Ilé-Ifẹ̀ in 1931 by District Officer H. L. Ward Price. He was shown a remarkable group of ancient terra cotta sculptures at the Iwinrin Grove by "Chief Obalara and other priests of the cult of Owinni, an early hero whose shrine is a sanctuary for smallpox sufferers..." (Fagg and Plass 1966:60). Price's photograph shows the chief and priests holding staffs and wearing pendant necklaces and conical headdresses. While the staff is different in terms of the figuration at the top and the open loops of braid along the shaft, the upward curving "handle" terminating in a head is identical to those in the photo. Very little has been published on the status and authority of Chief Ọbalara, or on chiefly regalia at Ilé-Ifẹ̀. This iconographically rich tradition of leadership arts dates to at least the eleventh century. HJD

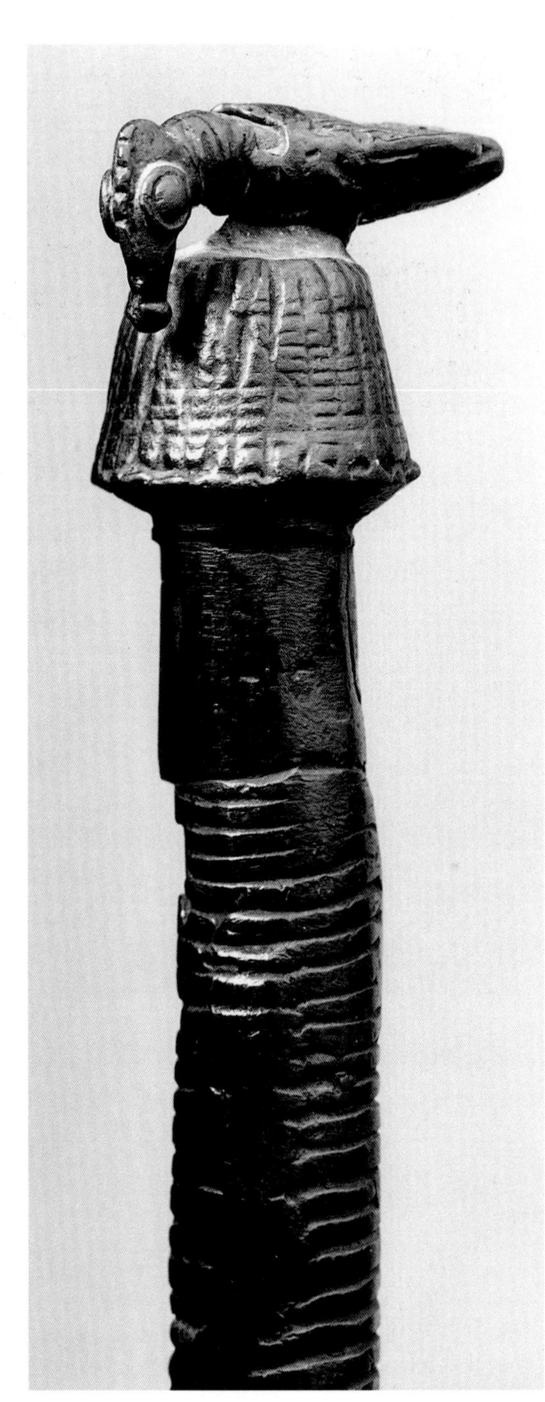

40
STAFF
Ilé-Ifẹ̀,
Yorùba, Nigeria
Brass and iron
L. 132 cm.
FMCH 87.1513

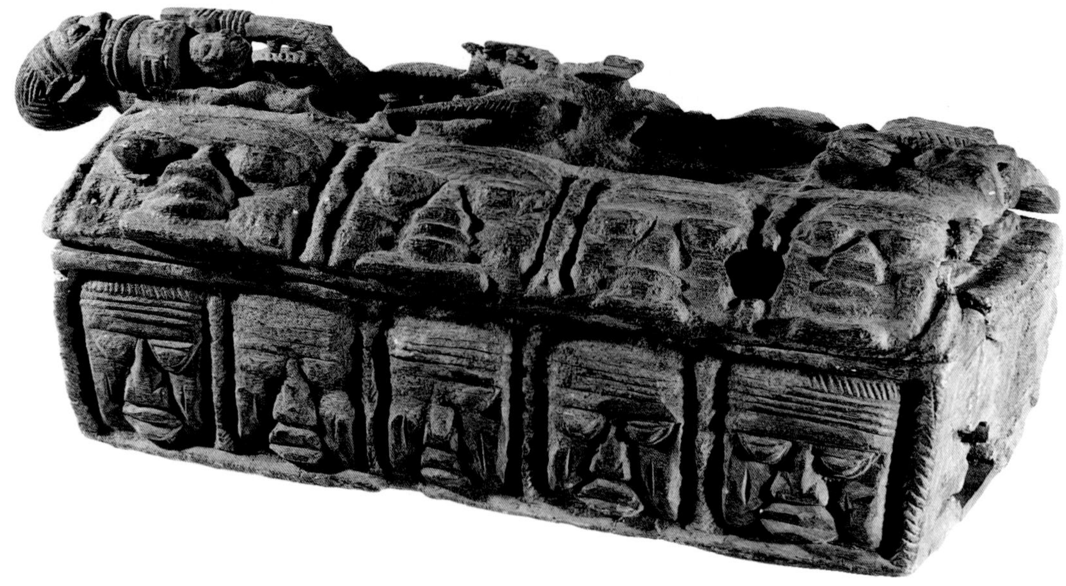

41. DOLL BY OLOWE OF ISE-EKITI (CA. 1873-1938), YORÙBA, NIGERIA

Yoruba girls, like girls around the world, play with dolls in imitation of their mothers caring for their children. Before the introduction of European dolls, girls played with small carved wooden figures called *omolangidi* ("child[ren] of wood"). These are minimal objects depicting a human head on a flat, rectangular body with few, if any, anatomical details. The average height of an *omolangidi* is 28 cm. Their small size and flat bodies allow the dolls to be carried on a child's back, tucked into the wrapper and secured with a "baby tie" cloth like real children. In addition to being toys, *omolangidi* may also be used as substitutes for memorial figures representing deceased twins (*ere ibeji*).

Omolangidi were often practice pieces for apprentice carvers, allowing them to perfect the coiffure, head and facial features before attempting full figures. However, some dolls, like this one, display a professional artist's design sense and carving skill. Such dolls are characterized by naturalistic, three-dimensional heads with carved details of facial scarification and coiffure. Their bodies are decorated with elaborate incised or relief designs. The high, laterally crested coiffure, facial scarification, and elongated neck of this *omolangidi* are also characteristics of the large kneeling female Figure with Bowl (Bequest of William A. McCarty-Cooper to the National Museum of African Art, Smithsonian Institution, Washington, D.C.), of which this seems to be a miniaturization.

The Joss *omolangidi* was carved by Olowe of Ise-Ekiti (ca. 1873-1938), the most important Yoruba sculptor of the twentieth century. He is known for his unique style, which is characterized by large-scale, elongated, dynamic, angular forms and exceedingly high-relief carving. Olowe of Ise served the Arinjale of Ise as a court artist and honored *emese* (messenger), but he also executed commissions from other Yoruba kings and men of wealth in northeastern Yorubaland. Olowe's repertory included dolls, game boards and mirror frames, as well as architectural sculpture, masquerade headdresses and figures with bowls and other types of containers (Fig. 32). His art was first exhibited outside Nigeria in 1924 when a set of doors and a lintel he carved for the Ogoga's palace at Ikere were displayed in the Nigerian Pavilion at the British Empire Exhibition at Wembley. The British Museum authorities considered Olowe's doors to be the finest example of West African art to reach England and subsequently acquired them.

ROSLYN A. WALKER

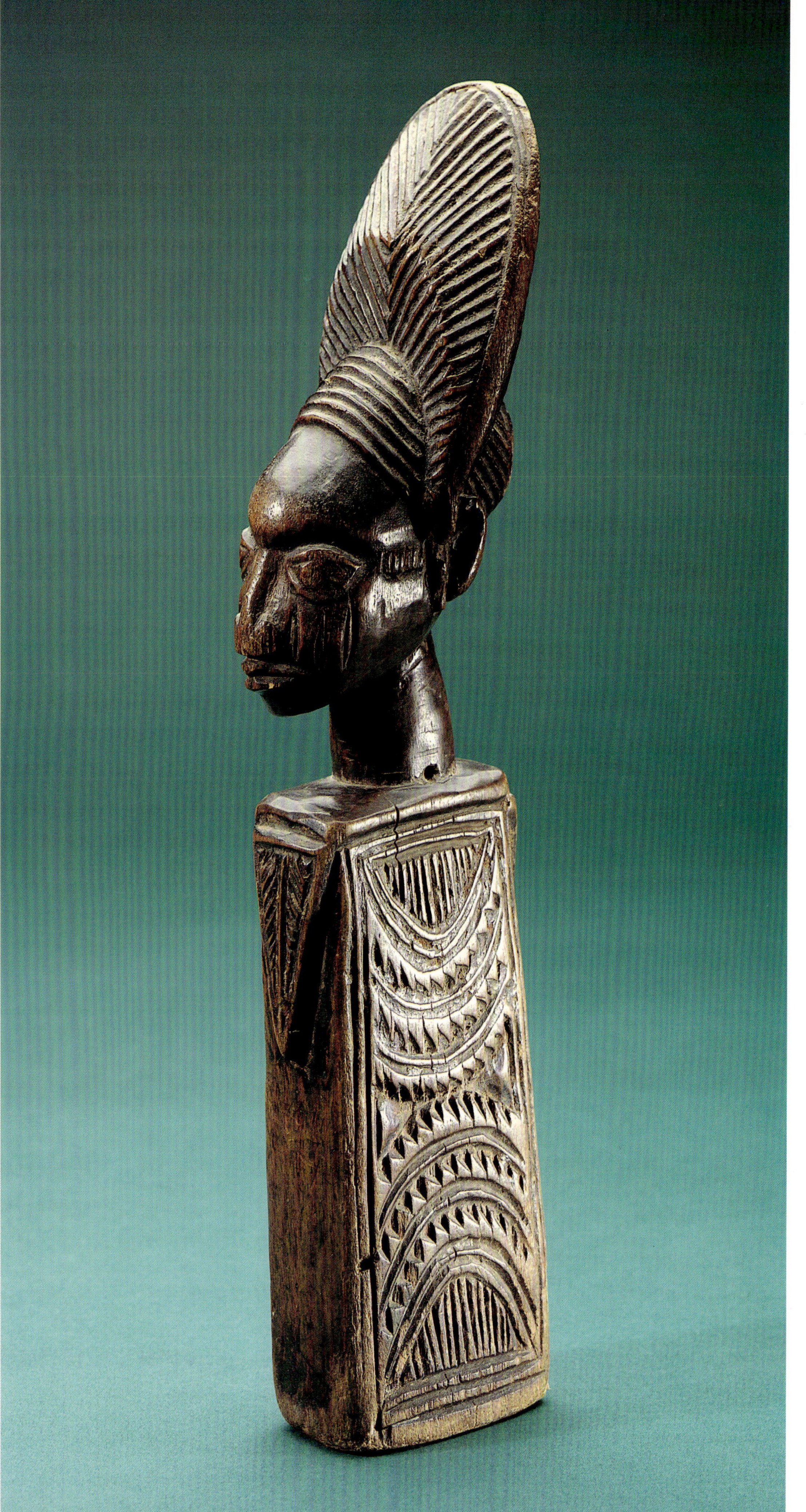

41
DOLL
(omolangidi)
carved by
Olowe of Ise-Ekiti
(ca. 1873-1938)
Yorùba, Nigeria
Wood
H. 31 cm.
FMCH **88.1024**

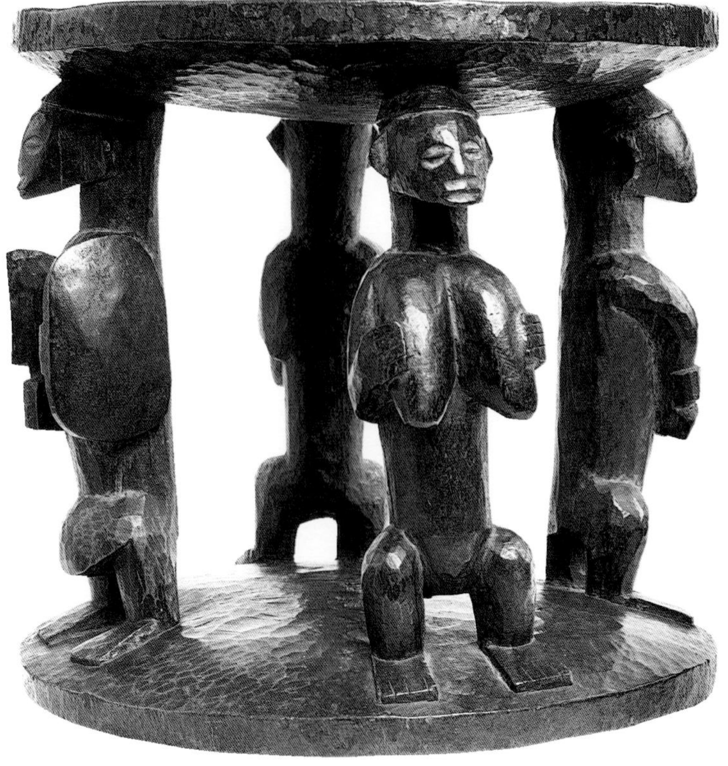

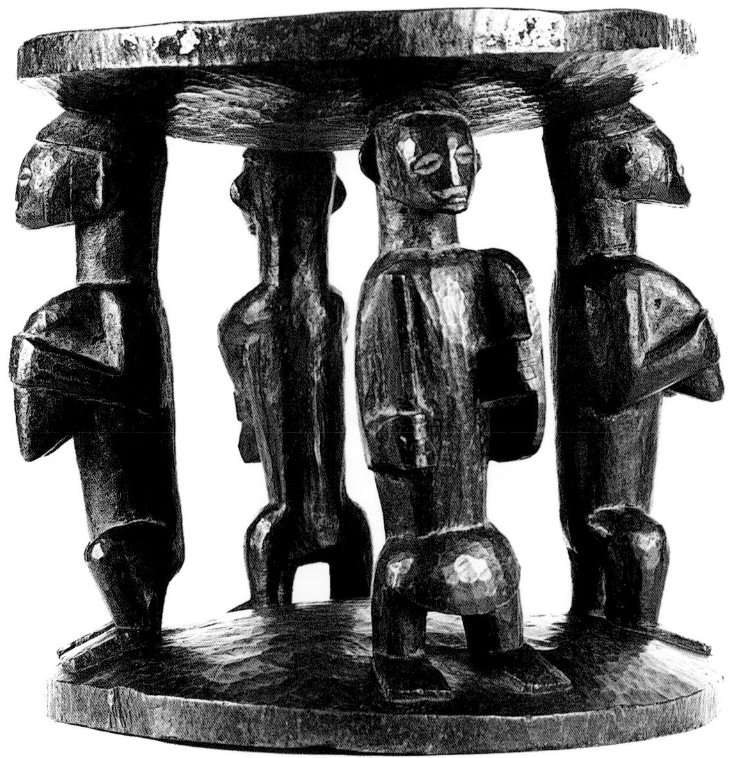

▼▲▼
42
STOOL
Abinu or Ijumu,
Yorùba far north-east
Wood
H. 36.5 cm.
FMCH 86.552

42. Stool, Abinu or Ijumu, Yorùba far north-east

Wooden stools are ubiquitous items of furniture in the households of the Yoruba far north-east as well as in those of Ebira and northern Edo. This stool, which is embellished with both figurative and non-figurative sculpture and is larger than that of the purely functional common stools, is typical of the more elaborate stool produced for a lineage elder or titled man. These were commissioned both for the elder's own personal use and as his memorial after his death. Stools are one of the characteristic productions of this region in which large-scale sculpture is only occasionally found. In addition to stools, local artisans carve staffs for elders and titled men and face masks for certain forms of masquerade, displaying a wide range of schematizations of the human figure.[1] Although the area is characterized by social and cultural diversity, an overall artistic unity is mediated by the Ineme (or Uneme), the smiths. Of Edo-speaking ancestry, the Ineme are now found throughout the region. Not all sculptors are smiths, but most smiths engage in some aspect of wood sculpture.

The supports for the Joss stool are composed of two double sets of paired figures. The pair of male figures on the stool, a prisoner and a man holding a cutlass and shield, reflects the prevalence of feuding in the area of the Yoruba northeast. The motif of the two female figures is, however, unusual for this region where women are usually shown with their arms raised above the head, a gesture originating in the Akoko-Edo ceremonial of the marriageable young woman. This iconographic difference suggests an origin beyond the culture of northwest Edo communities. In 1964 I photographed stools by the same or a closely related hand (not identified by name) in villages of the Abinu and Ijumu groups to the east and south-west (respectively) of the local government administrative center of Kabba; and in 1966 I photographed another in an Ebira village. This indicated to me that there was a local distribution (through trade, chiefly patronage, or looting as a result of conflict) of decorative works of this kind (Picton 1991:41).[2]

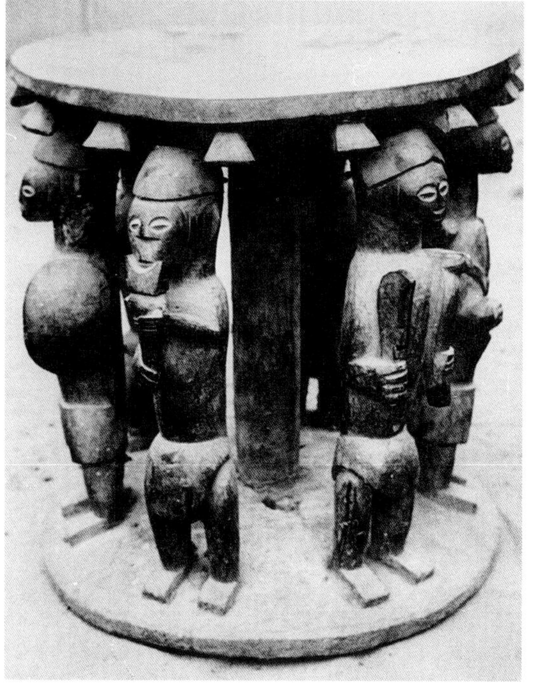

Stool *(opo)* for a titled man. In 1964 this was said by the Olokoro of Okoro ward to have been made for his grandfather. 48 cm. Ogibi village, Ijumu. Photo: J. Picton, 1964.

This stool was already in the collection of W.O. Oldman, London, by 1908, only shortly after the region of Yoruba north-east was brought under colonial administration. Its patination suggests that it had not been recently commissioned but had been produced some years prior to its arrival in London, probably during the latter half of the nineteenth century. It is one of the earliest surviving works of the region (the Ebira mask in the Royal Scottish Museum, Edinburgh, which was formerly labeled Asante, was acquired in 1903) and has added significantly to the known canon of Yoruba sculptures pre-1900. The strong ancestral association with these stools, which often become shrines through the application to them of sacrifices to the deceased man who had owned it, has meant that they have rarely been put up for sale. Rather, they have remained part of a living social and cultural matrix from which they were not to be extracted (even for the National Museum, Lagos). Extensive documentary work (recorded in the Lagos Museum archives) has been conducted by Kenneth Murray, Philip Allison and myself.

JOHN PICTON

[1] The schmatization of the stool, which seemed to defy ethnic classification, puzzled the late William Fagg, who suggested the origin was Senufo, Yoruba, or maybe Zaire (FMCH documentation).
[2] See Obayemi 1976 for a map of the Yoruba far north-east.

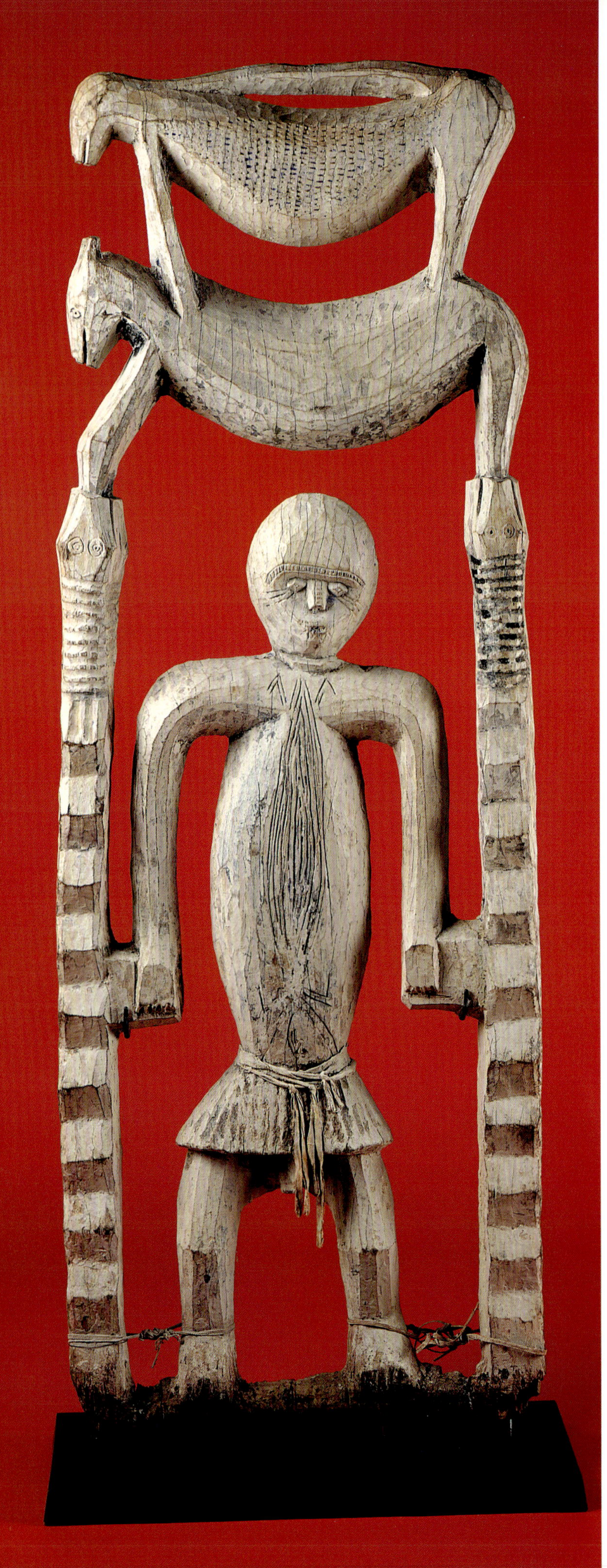

43. Figure Group, Esan (?), Nigeria

This sculpture of a standing male figure, framed laterally by two snakes (pythons?) and above by an antelope (?) with a leopard on its back, was apparently cut out of a single board. The rigid, frontal orientation and two dimensional quality of the composition are reminiscent of door panels carved in relief, especially those in the Edo-speaking region to the north and north-east of the Benin kingdom.

The condition of the base of the sculpture indicates that it either stood on, or was embedded in earth. The overall structure of the sculpture, however, makes it unlikely that it was intended to serve as a support for the roof of a house. More likely, it was originally intended, perhaps together with carved posts, for the decoration of the house of a titled or otherwise well-to-do man. Ulli Beier has published a series of stylistically related sculptures in the palace of the Obi of Agbor, the Ika-Igbo community immediately east of the Edo kingdom (Beier 1963). Agbor was within the hegemony of the Edo state for much of its history, although in 1896 it rose up against Benin. The figure group shares with the Agbor posts a schematic character, the fact that they are essentially flat carvings from thick planks of wood, and the carving in relief of the scarification on the forehead and nose of the male figure. Both groups also share the manner of suggesting the spots of the leopard by small rectangles carved in relief.

In spite of these similarities, the Joss sculpture is distinguished from the Agbor carvings by its roundness, which it shares with other sculptures recorded

43

FIGURE GROUP

(*izemize*,

"the human figure

that cannot speak")

Esan (?), Nigeria

Wood

(probably iroko)

H. 201 cm.

FMCH 92.78

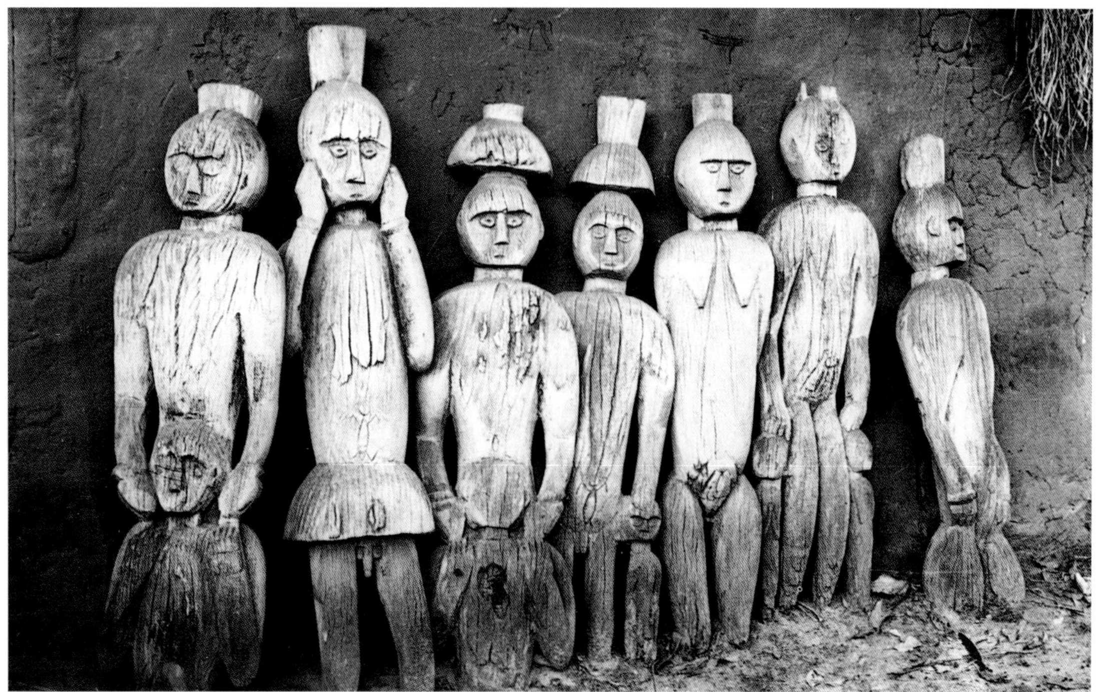

FIG. 34
Izemize
veranda posts at
Iubiadan-Emu, "Ishan".
Photo: Philip Allison, 1960.

in the Lagos Museum archives by Philip Allison. Allison identified the provenance of these sculptures as the Esan communities to the northeast of the Benin kingdom and north of Agbor, where it was apparently also fashionable to use sculpted posts to ornament the house of the incumbent of a senior inherited title. These ornaments also had vague ancestral associations. According to Allison, they were sometimes known as *izemize*, a human figure who cannot talk; but it is unclear whether this name is generally used throughout the area. Allison's photographs also show posts as external ornaments to an ancestral shrine, and the occasional figure, itself, as the focus of ritual attention.

It is now conventional within the literature of African art to label all such works as those discussed here as Ishan, though it would perhaps be more accurate to associate them regionally (rather than by an ethnic label) with the area east and north-east of Benin, dominated by Esan yet also including Igala and Igbo communities.[1] Comparison of Beier's and Allison's photographs reveals a tendency towards the cutting out and flattening of forms in the south within this area. In his diary for 16 April 1960 Allison describes "flattened" figures at Uhro including one in which the central figure is "arched over by two beasts."

It is debatable whether the figure group should be regarded as provincial derivatives of Benin City, or as part of a wider range of schematic northern Edo forms, survivals within a stylistic configuration that in some sense preceded the evolution of Benin City High Style. The image of the leopard is common in the arts of southern Nigeria, but here it appears to be pouncing on the back of another animal. The image is reminiscent of eastern Yoruba sculptures of Oloko, the lord of the farm, such as the *epa* and *aguru* masks of Ekiti and Ọpin. Leopards and pythons are well known as emblems of authority in the art of Benin (Ben-Amos 1976). Nevertheless, one is reminded, without assuming formal continuity, of the traditions of large-scale work that characterize eastern Yoruba and northern Edo.   JP

[1] R.E. Bradbury lists thirty-four distinct political units within Ishan (1957:65) and notes that "the word Ishan is a corruption of *esan*, which is said to be derived from *esanfua*, meaning 'those who fled'. Many of the Ishan communities and immigrant elements within them claim to have been founded by people who left the Benin kingdom to evade justice or escape oppression" (Bradbury 1957:61). The Esan dialects are closely related to Edo, and this area has, like Agbor, largely subsisted within the Edo hegemony for much of its history. Some Esan districts, however, are of mixed origin.

44. Male Half-Figure, Kingdom of Benin, Nigeria

The Joss miniature half-figure may be unique among the 4,000 or more Benin works of art known in public and private collections. Intentionally partial figures of miniature size are not typical of Benin brasswork. As William Fagg noted (1979:34,#192), however, the smooth base of this small brass piece seems to be original, suggesting that it was intentionally cast to represent only the upper part of a human form. In his discussion of the piece, Fagg suggested that it might have been part of a game, such as the "War Game," which was popular in past Benin court circles.

Two representational game pieces of a size similar to this half figure are known (Fagg and Plass 1964:110). Each portrays the head and torso of a helmeted official in elaborate regalia. The nearly identical pieces are cast in the style typical of rectangular Benin brass reliefs produced in the seventeenth century. Both game pieces were apparently made for a specific brass game board about thirty inches long,[1] with hemispherical indentations into which the rounded bases of the pieces fit.

Significant differences between the miniature and the two game pieces challenge Fagg's opinion that they shared the same function. Stylistically, this miniature appears to be much later than the seventeenth-century pieces. Moreover, the level, flat base of the casting indicates that it was not intended to fit into the same type of board. Although it could have been used as a game piece on a table top, more plausible functions can be suggested. For example, figures of this size are often part of multifigured altarpieces (*aseberia*). This well-finished example could have been salvaged from an unsatisfactory *aseberia* and skillfully repaired.

The iconography of the sculpture, however, argues against this interpretation. The clothing portrayed is not typical of *aseberia* figures, which tend to be relatively standardized. The figure, which is apparently male,[2] wears a straight, sewn skirt, trimmed at the waist with a series of rounded forms resembling cowrie shells. While a wide variety of gar-

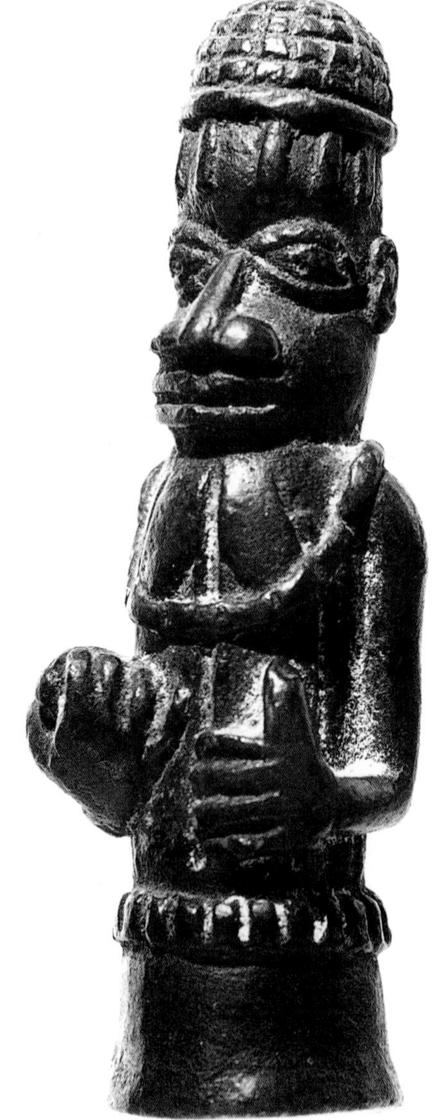

ments appear in Benin art, this straight style contrasts with the usual male wrapper, which is asymmetrical and fastened at the left hip. A straight skirt suggests the garb of a priest (*ohen*) in one of Benin's many indigenous orders. In spite of its small scale, it may have enhanced one of Benin's myriad public or private altars as a representation of a particular type of religious specialist.

The identification of the figure as a priest is supported by the inclusion of a tiny spherical object, which the figure holds in his right hand. Incised lines divide the surface of this object into sections. The object may be interpreted in a number of ways. It could represent a netted calabash rattle, a ball of white kaolin clay, a rounded stone, or a kola nut, which has been peeled to reveal its segments. Any one of these various interpretations would be significant spiritually and ceremonially in Benin. A small netted rattle appears frequently in ritual contexts on Benin brasswork from the sixteenth and seventeenth centuries, but its precise significance is uncertain beyond its obvious musical function. White kaolin clay (*orhue*), is widely used in present-day Benin, where it is customarily molded into small spheres. Incised with lines, the spheres are placed on altars as symbols of spiritual harmony. If the object in the figure's hand is an incised stone, it would refer to a method of divination used by the followers of Olokun (Azaigueni Aghahowa, pers. comm. 1982). A rounded stone is held in both hands at waist level and then dropped carefully so that the manner and direction that it rolls on the floor can be noted for spiritual guidance. The most common type of divination, however, employs a kola nut. During a customary rite of hospitality, the nut is opened and the number of its segments is counted as a general indicator of good or bad fortune.

A priestly figure of this tiny size, portrayed with an object designed to communicate with deities and spirits, would be appropriate in an assemblage of miscellaneous divination aids. Contrary to Fagg's suggestion, this miniature brass sculpture is unlikely to have been a game piece. It is more plausible that it was part of a divination kit used by a religious specialist in Benin.   Barbara W. Blackmun

---

[1] The game board and two miniature partial figures that fit into it are discussed in Fagg and Plass 1964:110. Dark (1982:2.4.4) listed these two miniatures under "figure, game piece" (X6/25 and X8/31); he tentatively included this miniature (N3/7) in the same category. Number X6/25 is in the Fuller Collection at the British Museum (1962.Af.10). Its duplicate, number X8/31, was formerly in the John Russell collection and was sold at auction by Sotheby's on July 11, 1972 (Sothebys 1972:pl. LXIV) (Dark, pers. comm. 1991).

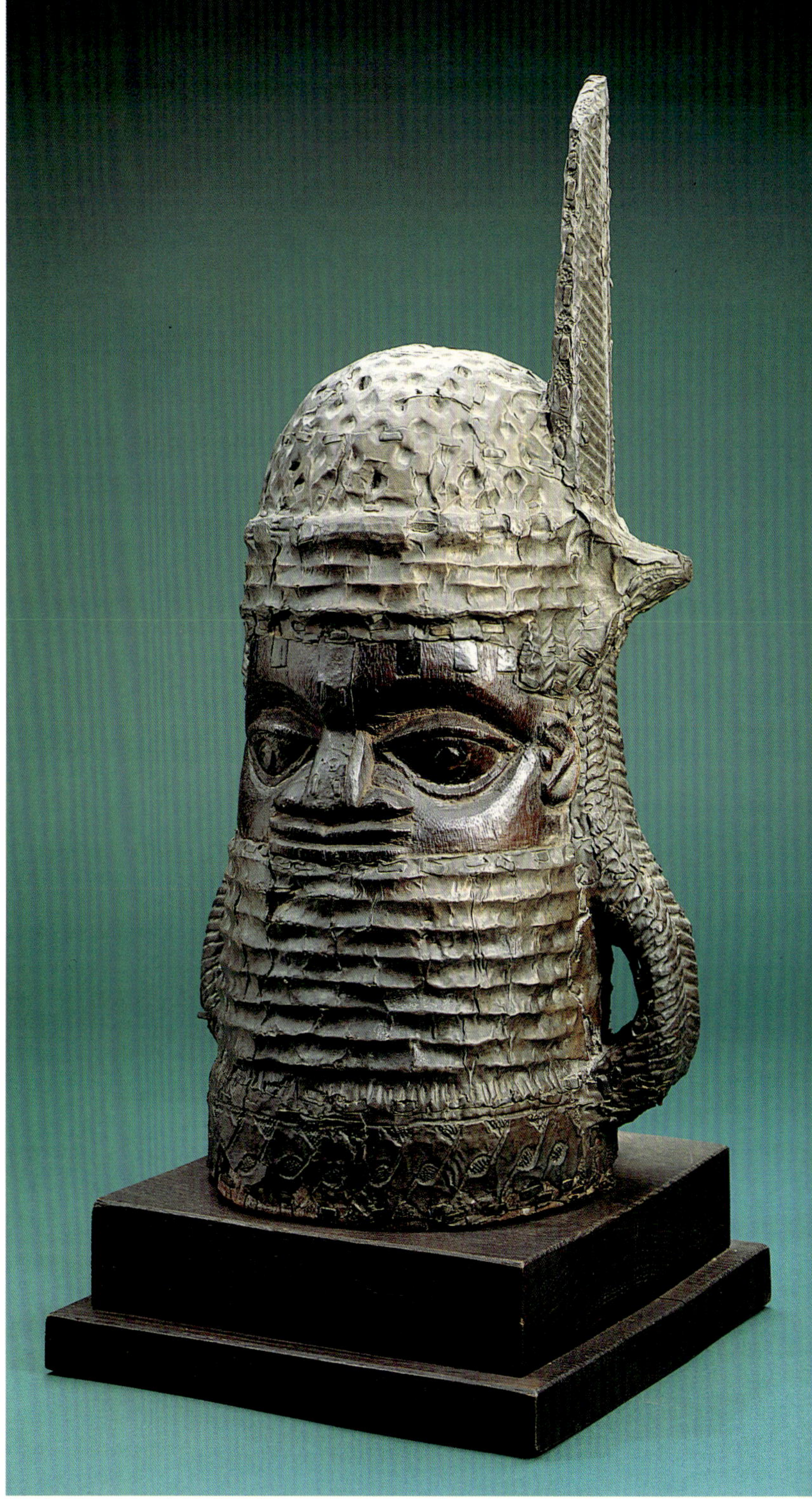

▼▲▼
45
MEMORIAL HEAD
Kingdom of Benin,
Nigeria
Wood, coconut shell
and brass
H. 48.9 cm.
FMCH 87.1456

[2] Although the pectorals resemble flattened pendant breasts, the close-fitting beaded cap on the head is usually associated with males.

45. Memorial Head, Kingdom of Benin, Nigeria

This carved wood head with the elaborate regalia of a chief once stood on an altar maintained by a prominent official in the Edo Kingdom of Benin. The textured cylindrical form covering the chin and throat represents an *odigba*, a thick, high collar made of multiple strands of red coral beads sewn together on a base of stiff cloth. An *udaeha*, a coral beaded band around the forehead, supports a white eagle's feather on the left. On each side of the *udaeha*, a long, spirally-wrapped form descends from an ornamental cluster of coral to the base of the sculpture. A twisted strapwork pattern typical of the hereditary carvers' guild, Igbesanmwan, enhances the base itself. Inlaid pieces of dark coconut shell on the forehead of the sculpture simulate the vertical marks that formerly distinguished Benin citizens from other ethic groups.

In traditional Edo belief, a person's head has a special significance as the locus of wisdom in following one's destiny (Schaefer 1983:71-78). Sculptured heads are traditionally placed on altars, where they serve as focal points for prayers and sacrifices. Most of Benin's hereditary nobles and other prosperous officials who follow the old traditions still maintain shrines dedicated to the head. A wooden head very similar to this example was still in use in the 1970s on a personal altar of the head in Benin City, the capital of the kingdom (Ben-Amos 1980:Fig. 62). Although the condition of the Benin City sculpture has deteriorated through its constant employment in rituals, the proportions and details of the carving and metalwork suggest that it was probably produced during the late nineteenth century by the same group of craftsmen in Benin's hereditary carvers' guild. A third, related altar head is in the Fuller Collection at the Field Museum of Natural History, Chicago (Dark 1982: Plate XXXIX). The Joss head

is also related to the custom among the Edo of the male leader of an extended family furnishing an ancestral altar to commemorate the deceased members of his patrilineage. The earliest written description of domestic altars in Benin was recorded by a Spanish missionary in 1651 (Ryder 1969:314). In later years many European visitors remarked about the richness of the ancestral altars in the palace of the Oba (Benin's hereditary king), which were enhanced with sets of very large carved elephants' tusks. Each ivory tusk rested upon a heavy, brass pedestal cast in the form of a crowned head, which commemorated in a general way a former ruler of Benin.

The Oba has always reserved the exclusive right to use memorial heads cast in brass, but many wealthy chiefs have commissioned wooden heads similar to that in the Joss Collection to support carved elephants' tusks for their own elaborate altars. Sheets and strips of brass added to the wooden heads approximate the effect of the Oba's brightly burnished, cast metal sculptures. BWB

46. STAFF, IGBO, NIGERIA

The *ofo*, a small wood and iron ritual implement, is one of the most important ancestral and spiritual symbols in any Igbo extended family or community shrine. *Ofo* are mandatory and essential to all cults, families, and other social entities, and may also be owned by individual men and some women. Normally *ofo* staffs (as they are often called) are non-figural, comprised of single or bundled sticks of spiritually significant wood heavily encrusted with sacrificial materials (especially blood and chewed kola nut, but also other symbolic substances). Figurated *ofo*, very similar to this example, were first documented in the 1930s by M.D.W. Jeffreys in Anam villages in the northwestern Anambra River Valley (Jeffreys 1956a & b). Figurated *ofo* may refer to the ancestral authority invoked in important ceremonies of Igbo communities people who call themselves Anam.

Rituals and sacrifices made with and to an *ofo* ensure the spiritual, ancestral validity of ceremonies and the integrity of the participants. All agreements, treaties, prayers and other transactions are legitimized in the eyes of the ancestors and the gods by the presence of the *ofo* of the individuals or institutions involved.[1] Participants swear upon an *ofo* to proclaim their innocence or honesty, and believe that the *ofo* is capable of killing persons who bear false witness.

This rare example of a figurated *ofo* is partly anthropomorphized, with facial features comprised of delicate spirals and strips of wrought iron attached to the wood armature. The "body" is wrapped with a continuous spiral strip of iron, with a loop at the lower end. An oval, blade-like piece of iron attached to the upper end serves as a corona for the head. This oval recalls, in miniaturized form, blades of hoes which are crucial implements in the economy of Igbo yam farmers.

Herbert M. Cole

[1] See Bentor 1988 for an extended discussion of *ofo* forms and functions.

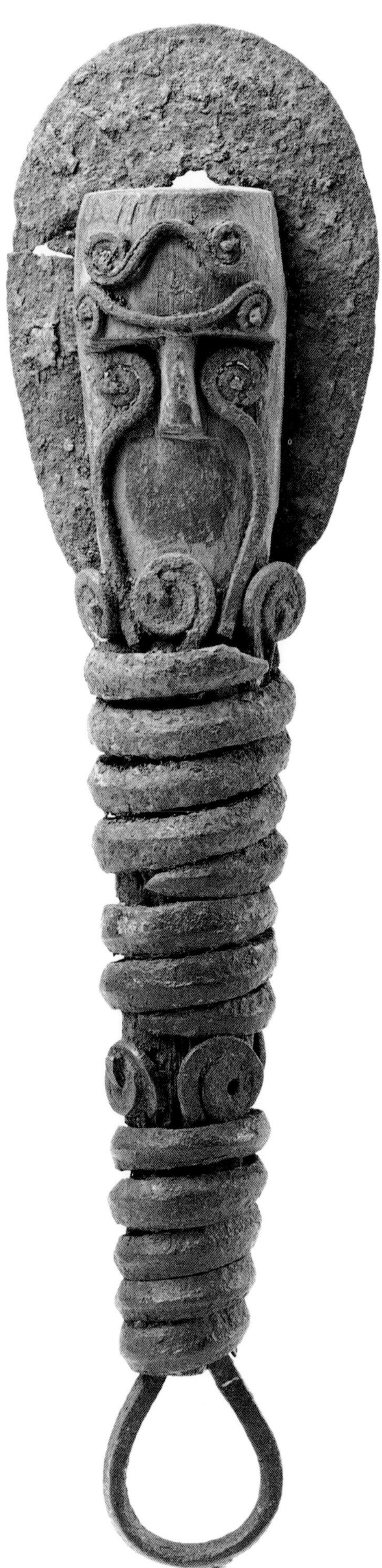

▼▲▼

46

STAFF *(ofo)*

Igbo, Nigeria

Iron and wood

L. 27.3 cm.

FMCH 84.221

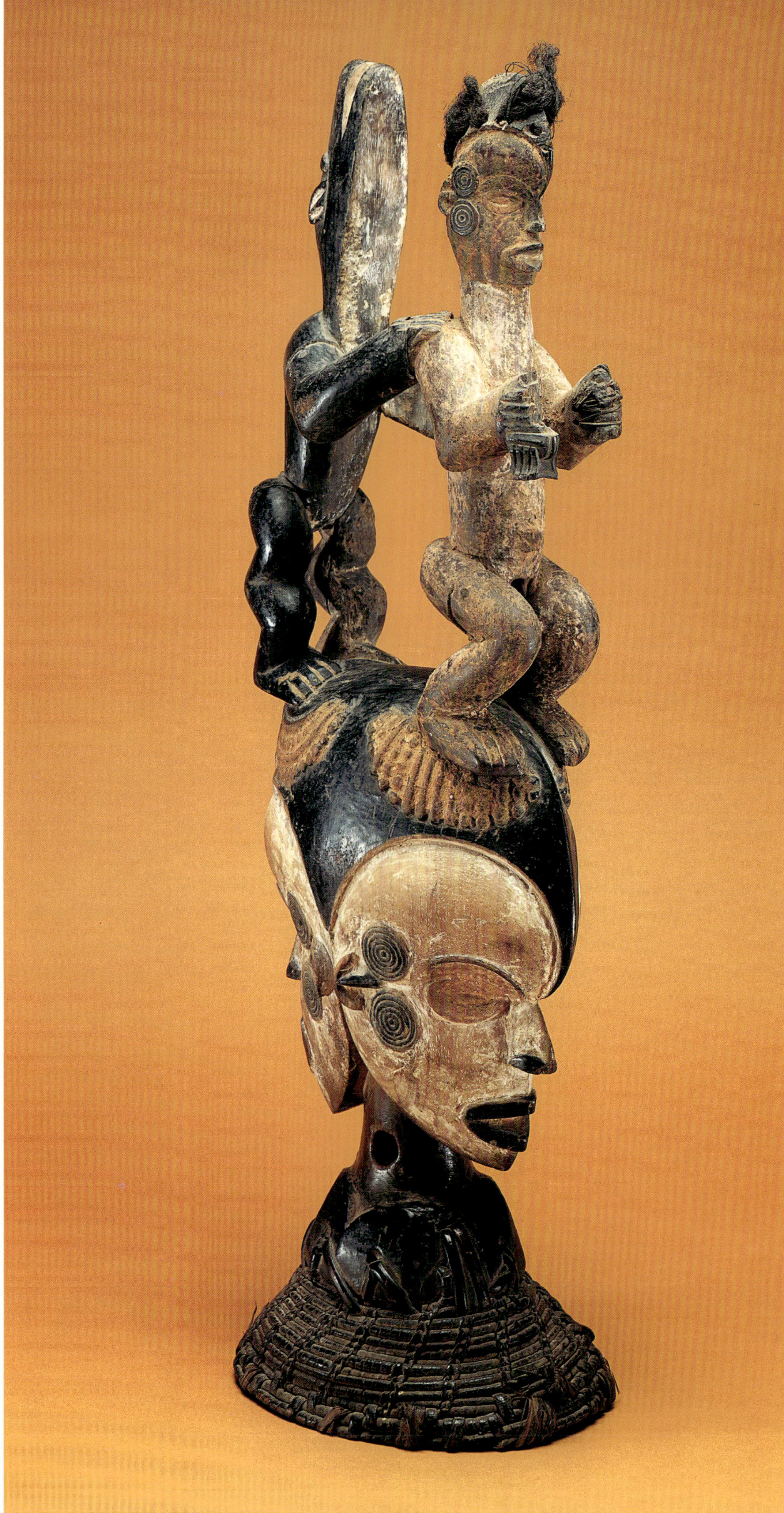

▼▲▼

47

EKELEKE HEADDRESS

Igbo, Nigeria

Wood, raffia,
kaolin, hair,
pigment and
basketry

H. 66.5 cm.

FMCH 89.796

47. EKELEKE HEADDRESS, IGBO, NIGERIA

This finely carved wooden headdress, lashed to a basketry cap, was most probably used in Ekeleke dances among southern Igbo peoples. Its precise provenance is uncertain. However, it may have come from a Kwale or Aboh Igbo community on the western side of the Niger, peoples adjacent to Isoko and Urhobo peoples, who may have originated Ekeleke. Ekeleke, often performed on stilts, is a festival honoring water spirits, Owu; southwestern Igbo claim to have obtained Owu masquerades from non-Igbo riverain communities. As documented in the Agwa village group west of Owerri, Ekeleke is a finely choreographed performance by several men wearing similar headdresses, imported, lace-like cloth head coverings and skirts or wrappers of Indian madras cloth, locally called "George." Virtuosic individual dances alternate with sets danced in unison, activated by a small gong and a drum orchestra playing on the sidelines. Despite initial sacrifices to Owu spirits, performances—at least in recent decades—are essentially secular entertainments repeated on several days and sometimes enriched by a simple play involving other masked characters (Cole and Aniakor 1984:204-210).

The dominant feature of this headdress is a pair of nearly autonomous, but attached, janus heads, painted white and facing outward. A common color for the Igbo masks, white generally refers to the spirit and/or ancestral worlds honored by many masquerades. The heads on the headdress are surmounted by two integrally carved standing figures, a bent-legged human with hair on his head and double temple markings in the form of concentric circles, plus a snouted animal that holds the human's shoulders with its forelegs. While this iconography is cryptic to us, it probably signals the specific name of the spirit character embodied by the masquerader in context. Patterns of wear and a rich patina suggest that this headdress was danced repeatedly over a period of many years.   HMC

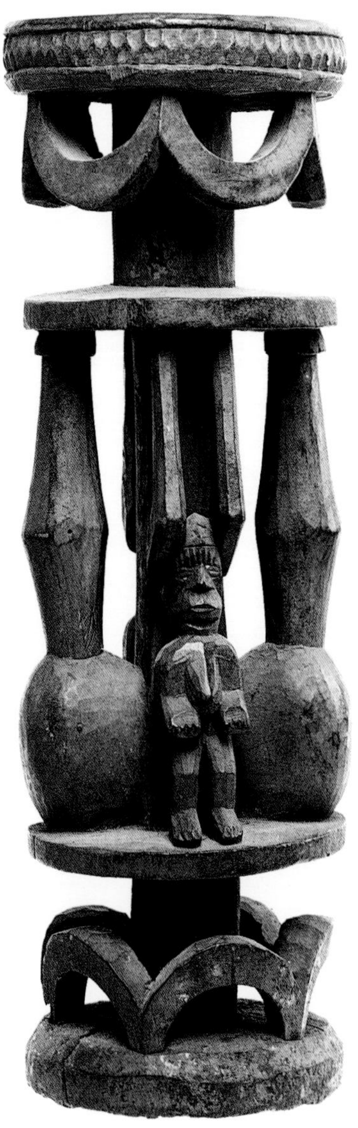

48. ALTAR STAND, IGBO, NIGERIA

The name and precise function of this object are not certain. The two standing figures with horns are characteristic of the imagery of northern Igbo *ikenga* (male personal shrines). However, the carving is more likely an altar stand commissioned for an elaborate community shrine, probably one element of a fairly large ensemble of carvings, medicine bundles, staffs, and varied shrine offerings (Cole and Aniakor 1984:pl. 18). The two long-necked vessels that also decorate the object are carved, miniaturized versions of ceramic or calabash jars for palm wine, which might have been placed on the uppermost flat surface of this object when it was used.

The carving probably was among items of "furniture" provided voluntarily by priests or supplicants of a relatively wealthy, well-appointed shrine of a type that often serves several tutelary nature and/or market deities. A finely-carved, decorative, tiered stand for wine—shared at periodic rituals held to honor the deity—would have enhanced the status and reputation of a shrine and its priest/priestess. Prominent males associated with these shrines may have had their own *ikenga* nearby. Carvings such as this example, or the analogous, if smaller, monoxyl stools of titled men from the north and central parts of Igbo country, may have indirectly referenced the ethos of masculine, physical prowess and success associated with both male deities and *ikenga*. Notably, the parallel grooved forehead scarifications, *ichi*, on the *ikenga* figures are the marks of titled men.

The style of carving suggests that the Joss object originated in the northern region of Igboland, probably between Awka and Nsukka. The openwork, semi-circular decorative patterns at top and bottom, as well as the fine zigzag patterns around the edge of the top platform, recall similar forms on stools carved by Awka and other north central Igbo artists.   HMC

49. OGBODO ENYI HEADDRESS, IGBO, NIGERIA

This Ogbodo Enyi[1] headdress is one of several dozen from northeastern Igbo country that came out of Nigeria around the time of the Nigeria-Biafra civil war, 1967-1970. The large numbers of similar sculptures, differentiated by size and decorative features, such as the compact full figure on the back of the head on the Joss headdress, attest to the former

importance of the Ogbodo Enyi masking cult among several Igbo and neighboring peoples (Ekajuk and other Middle Cross River Peoples). Because collection data is seldom available, it is difficult to attribute definitively any given headdress to Igbo origin.

Among Izzi and Ezza Igbo, Ogbodo Enyi masquerades were danced at dry season festivals by select members of four age grades, starting with young boys and ending with elders, performing individually and at different times. These festivals stress community purification and renewal, as well as communion with revered ancestors and tutelary deities. Accordingly, Ogbodo Enyi maskers visit community shrines to honor the spirits, and they lead age grade members in assigned jobs of community cleanup and other service (Weston 1984:153-159).

Weston (1984:157) noted that "*Ogbodo Enyi* is repeatedly described [by Northeastern Igbo people] as a harsh, violent spirit mask of unusual power." During the early decades of the twentieth century the masker, apparently reflecting dimensions of his former responsibility for social control, actually beat women and members of subordinate age grades but recently his violent demeanor remains only in his frenzied, shaking dances, aggressive strides and bursts of running. Prior to performing, the most important Ogbodo Enyi headdresses, which belong to the senior age grade, are activated and placated with offerings of kola nut and palm wine. The masker's hands and feet are marked with purifying chalk, and young palm fronds (*omu*) are tied to the back of the knotted raffia costume and held in his hands, as ritual signals of the dangerous nature of the spirit. At the end of the dry season, offerings are made to calm and placate the tempestuous spirit until it is reactivated the next year (Weston 1984:157).

Like many Igbo zoomorphic masks, these headdresses are fanciful, rather free interpretations of elephant heads combined with human features. The elephant's trunk is creatively placed as an extension

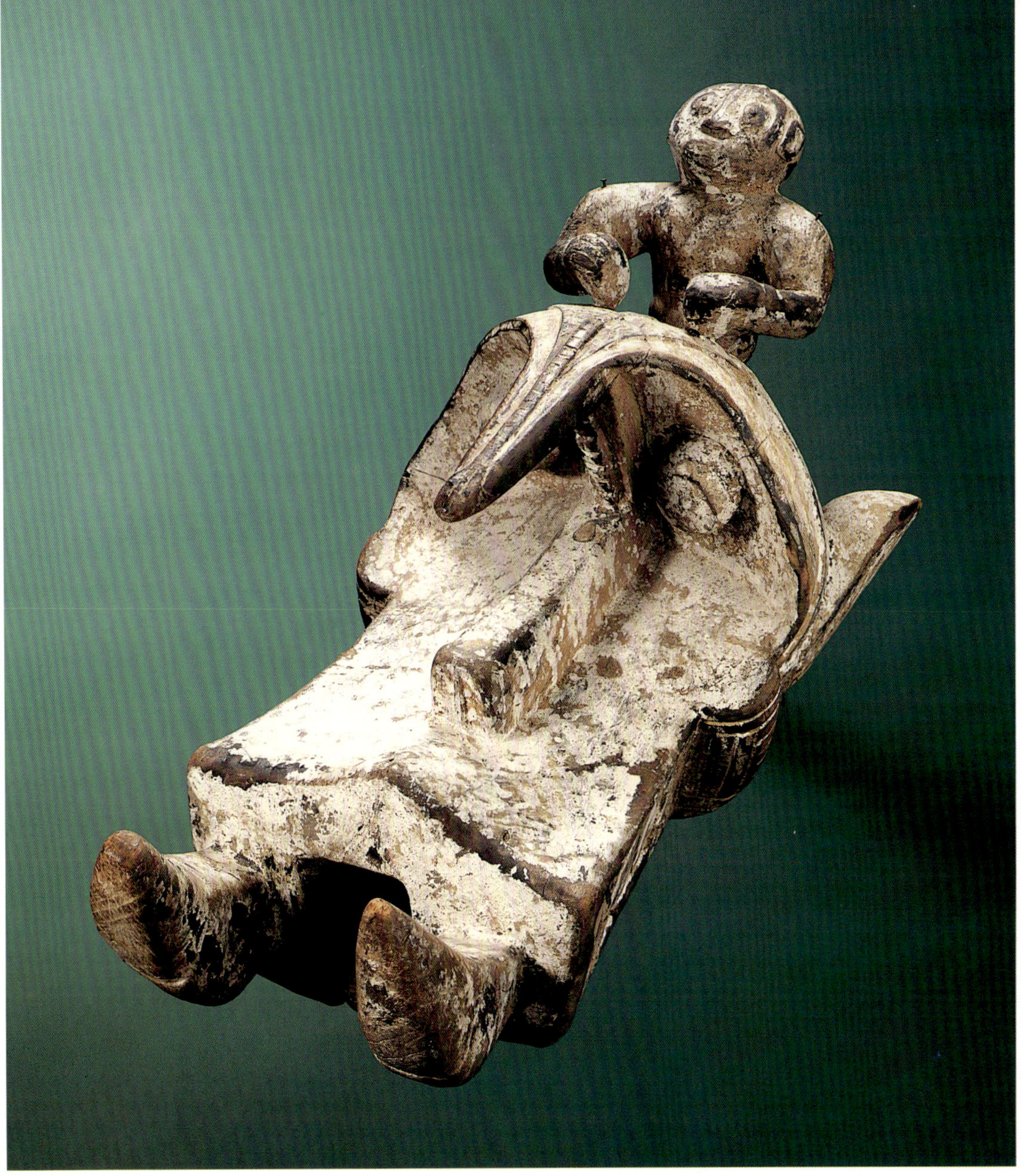

of the forehead and frequently, as in this example, ends in a snake's head. Large ears extend backward from the head, balancing correctly positioned tusks. The human figure seated on the back of the head identifies this Ogbodo Enyi as having belonged to one of the adult age grades, since such features are normally absent on the smaller headdresses of children. Additional figures (or more commonly, heads) on the masks are variously interpreted as simply "decoration" or as generic "portraits" of respected community members. Some informants claim that only the senior, most powerful mask can be so embellished, clearly an indication of the hierarchical nature of the masking cult.

Since 1975, women have danced Ogbodo Enyi in the Nkaliki villages among Izzi Igbo. Representing women collectively, this practice was instituted to honor the deity and oracle Uke, who is credited with averting the deaths of large numbers of children in the early 1970s. This may be a unique instance of women dancing masks east of the well-known complex of Sowei masks and women's societies among several related peoples of Liberia and Sierra Leone. HMC

[1] Literally: "village," "friend" or "elephant", depending on tonal stress.

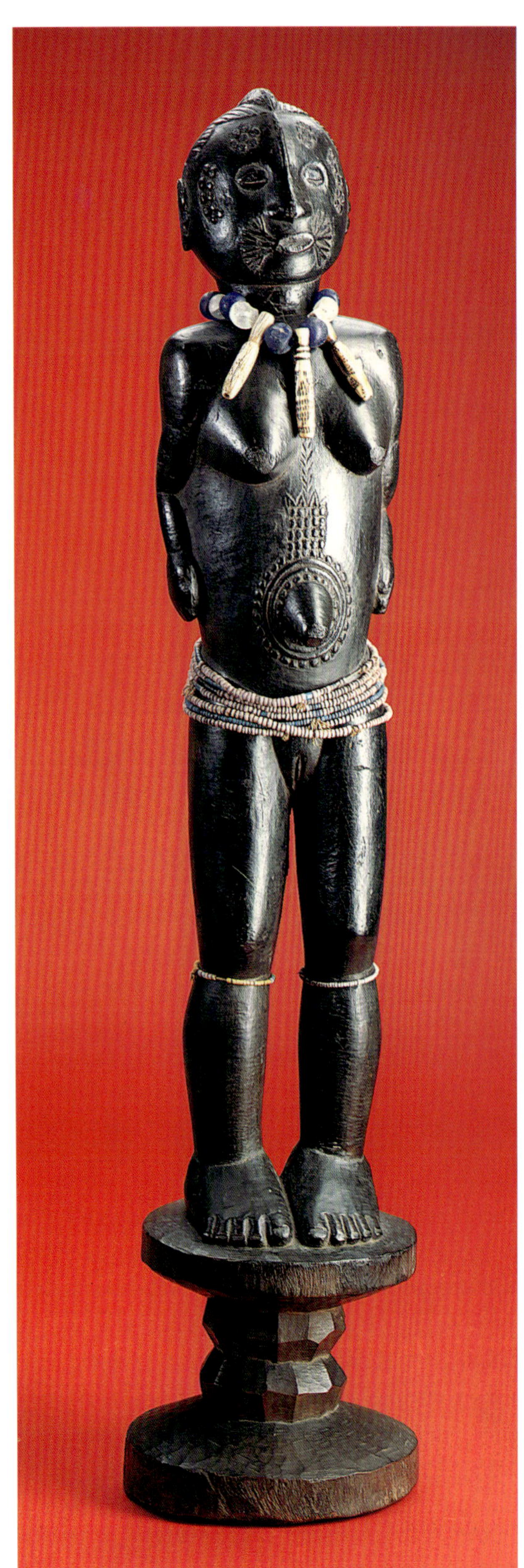

50
FEMALE FIGURE
(*mtam*)
Tiv, central Nigeria
Wood, beads,
ivory and glass
L. 89.5 cm.
FMCH 86.1725

50. FEMALE FIGURE, TIV, NIGERIA

This carving of a figure standing on a pedestal is properly called a *mtam*, part of a group called *ihambe*. Possibly of recent origin, it was made for use in one of the villages of the Tiv people of central Nigeria. *Ihambe* belong to a category of forces and emblems known as *akombo*. These forces are healing if one seeks their protection, or they are harmful if one violates them by acting on them inappropriately. *Ihambe* are amongst the oldest and most important of all *akombo*. They are associated with a good marriage, success in farming and success in hunting, all the things that make up a comfortable life in a rural society. *Ihambe* emblems such as this carving are placed either at the farm, if their power is to be directed towards the protection of the crops, or at the entrance to the home, if their power is to be directed to domestic concerns.

To be ritually effective, the form of *ihambe* only needs to be a stake or post pierced with holes for eyes and a mouth. A stake sharpened to a point represents the male principle (*ihambe*), while a stake rounded at the top represents the female principle (*mtam*). The figure, with its rounded top, appears to be an *ihambe* carved to represent the deceased mother of the senior man in the household. The female figures were often placed without a male counterpart. They can be called either *mtam* or *ihambe*, but the figure represents the female principle of *ihambe*. The elaborate carving of this figure suggests that these objects are viewed as works of art as well as effective vehicles of ritual.

FRANCES HARDING

51. CARVED SPOON, TIV, NIGERIA

Little is known about the large, carved and decorated spoons such as this from the Tiv people of central Nigeria. The spoon is one of a number of domestic utensils carved for its beauty as well as its usefulness. Decorated calabashes were made for women and the spoons may have been made for men. The carving

on the handle may be either a male or a female.
Carved spoons are said to indicate the high status
and social prestige of the owner and the household in
which they are used in welcoming important guests.
Temple (1922:297) referred to a headman offering
an honored visitor a "carved double-spoon containing gari with red pepper in the larger bowl, and salt
in the smaller." In Tiv society, a meal usually consists
of individual portions of pounded yam served to
each person accompanied by a separate dish of meat
and sauce. This type of spoon may have been used to
dispense the portions. The spoon has no known ritual function. The face of the figure of ambivalent sex
on the handle of this spoon is carved in the concave
form commonly, though not exclusively, used in the
atsuku carvings associated with funeral rites; the convex form of the *ihambe, mtam* or *twel* figures was
associated with success in marriage, birth, hunting
and farming. The concave form of the spoon may
thus indicate that the spoon had a ritual use or association in a funeral meal.   FH

52. FEMALE FIGURE, DAKAKARI, NIGERIA

The Dakakari of northwestern Nigeria are known for
their elaborately modeled ceramic grave sculptures.
These figurative works fit within the broad belt of
ceramic sculpture documented across the savannah
and sahel of West Africa. Although such fired clay
sculpture has been documented from the first half of
this century (Harris 1938), it is likely, given other
ceramic evidence from across Nigeria and eastward
to the Chad Basin, that the ancestors of the present-
day Dakakari also made similar works.

In Dakakari society, everyone other than "unim-
portant men and women" had accumulations of
ornamented pottery on their graves (Fitzgerald
1944:44). According to Allen Bassing (1973), the
graves of the most important men in Dakakari society were distinguished by ceramic sculpture made in
the form of humans and animals. The figurative

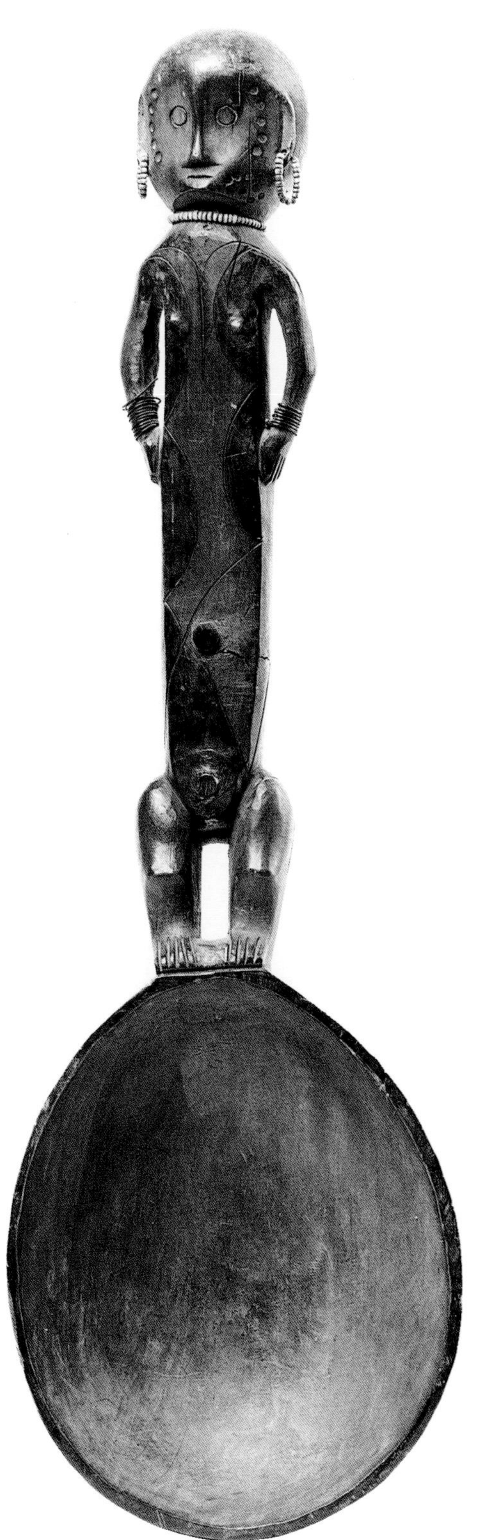

51
CARVED SPOON
Tiv, central Nigeria
Wood, beads,
wire and nails
L. 46.5 cm.
FMCH 83.1002

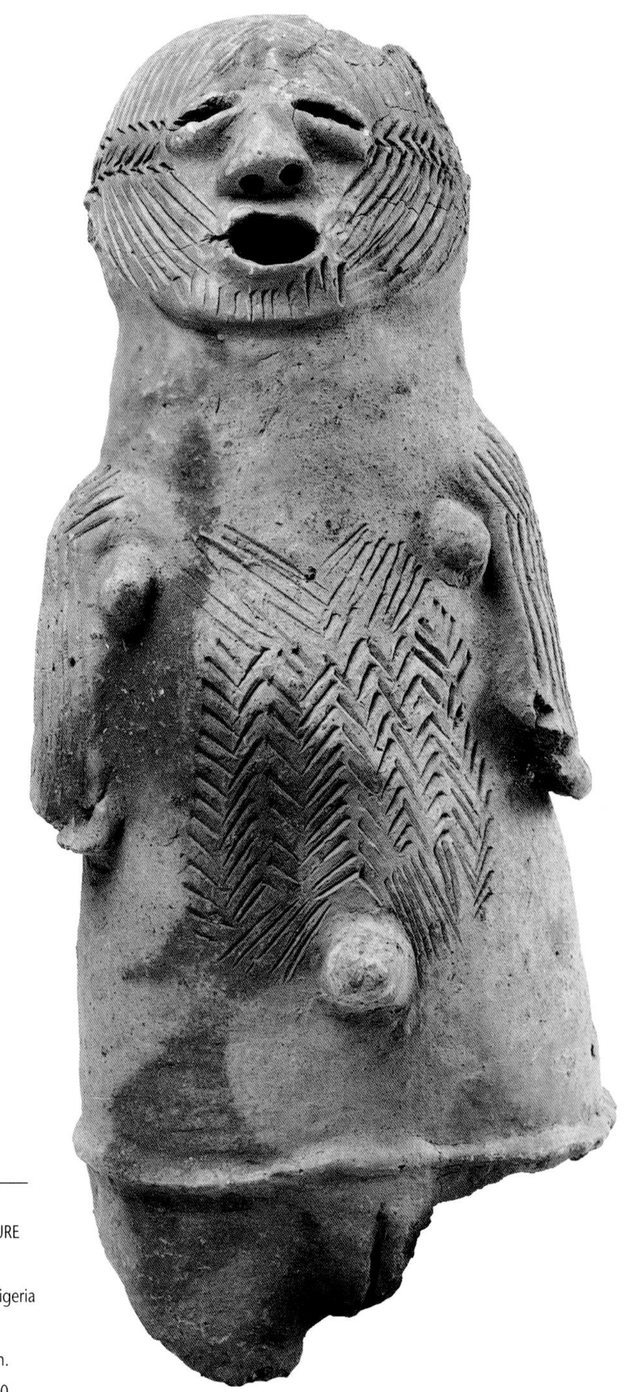

52
FEMALE FIGURE
Dakakari,
northeastern Nigeria
Ceramic
L. 40.64 cm.
FMCH 88.300

ceramics were placed on top of an earthen burial mound, along with household pots and non-functional decorated pots ("pots of the grave"); and the mound was encircled by a wall (up to two feet in height) of roughly dressed flat stones. The strategies underlying the configurations of sculpture placed on top of the mounds (within which a man's wives and unmarried daughters were also interred) have not yet been clarified, however the most elaborate graves belonged to the highest ranking men—village chiefs, great hunters, chief blacksmiths, rainmakers.

This figure of a standing woman is very similar to *in situ* examples published by Bassing (1973:37). Like these male and female figures, which either stand or ride an animal, this figure is very simply conceived with an upturned, spherical head, open mouth, slit eyes, and pierced nostrils. The arms are small and flipper-like. The rudimentary columnar legs were conceived to be embedded in the earthen mound. Typically, the figure's sex is clearly depicted below a band of raised decoration around the waist. The female figure, like others of its type, is also distinguished by striations on her face. These closely reproduce the facial scarifications, which were common ethnic markers among Dakakari women (Fitzgerald 1942:25; fig. 3). The chevron patterns on the abdomen describe the cicatrizations young girls underwent in stages (Harris 1938:132-34).

The manufacture of grave sculptures was the sole responsibility of the Dakakari women. This suggests that women could have produced other figurative ceramic sculptures found archaeologically (see Berns 1993), even though the examples from the inland Niger Delta or from northern Ghana are often different in style, conception or execution.[1] MARLA C. BERNS

[1] The parallels between the Dakakari and Koma sculptures, disposed in "stone circle burial mounds," seem the most intriguing.

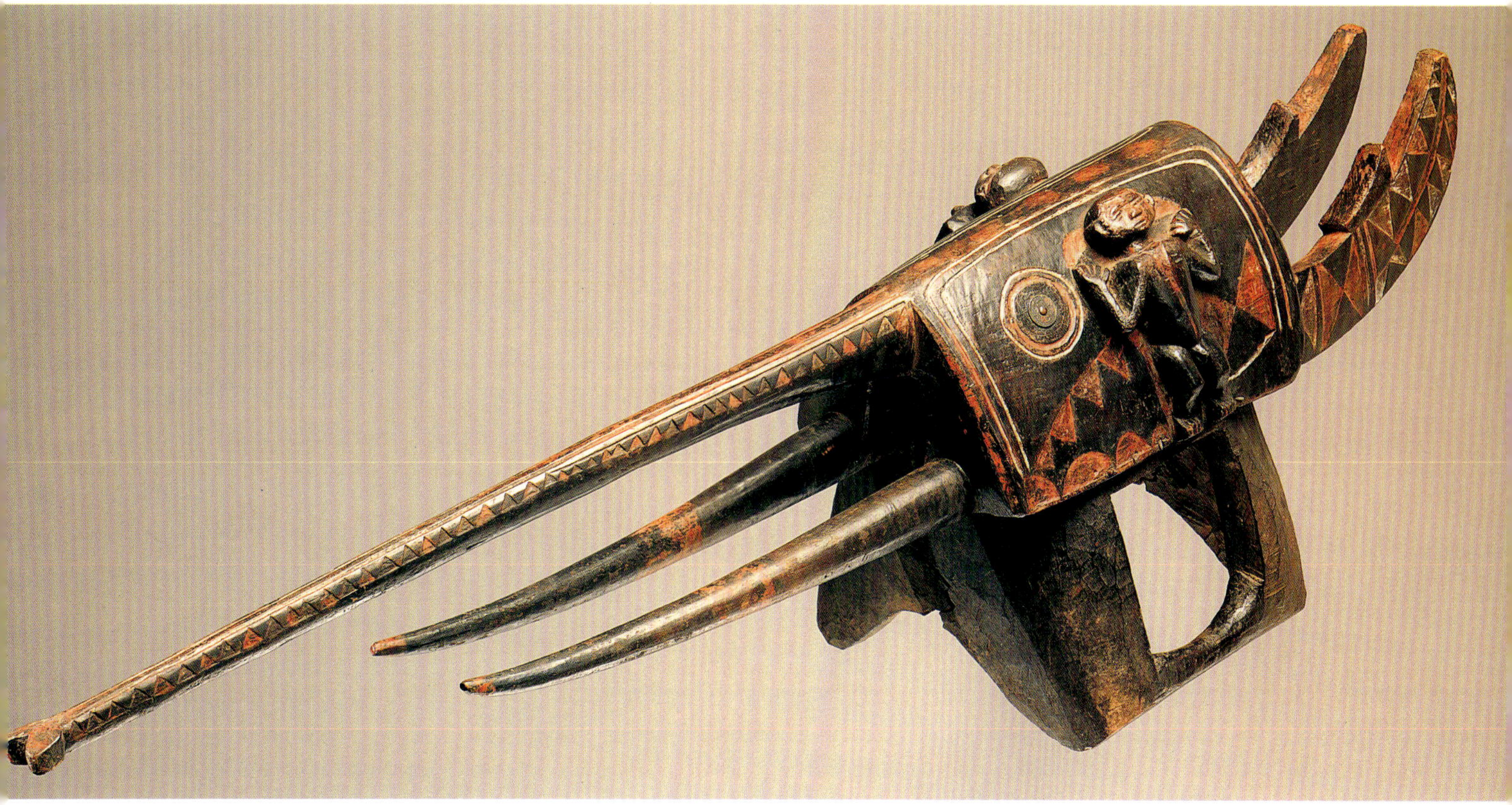

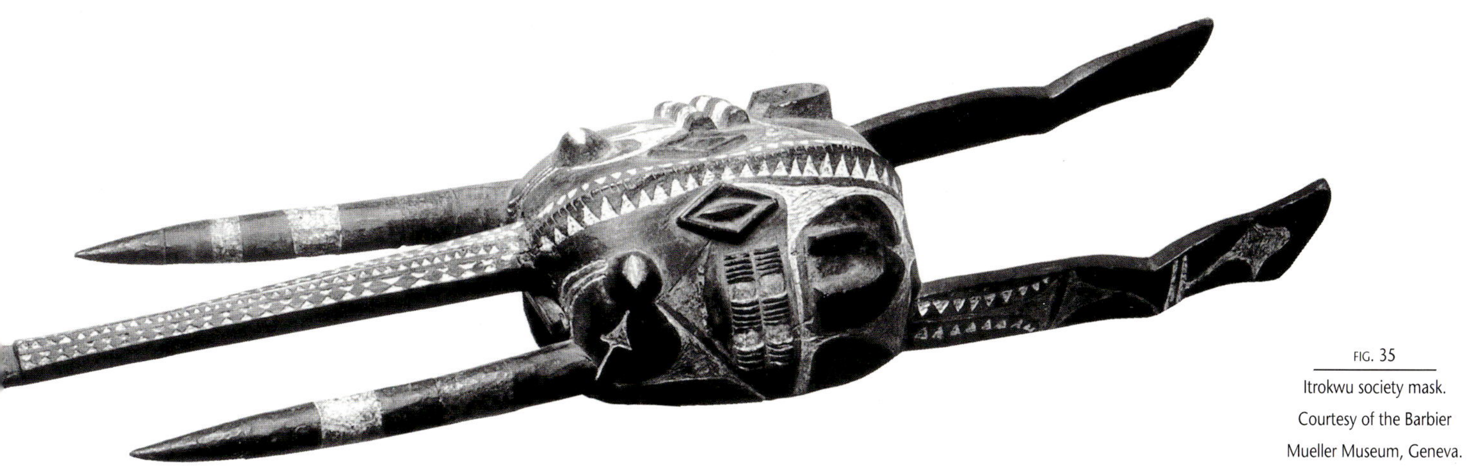

53. ELEPHANT MASK, EKPARI CLAN, NIGERIA

The attribution of this mask, like many objects from Africa, has been complicated by war, migration and resettlement, which have separated indigenous populations who possess similar (or in this case, the same) mask traditions. This mask has been attributed to the Idoma because of its resemblance to two elephant masks first documented by Sieber in 1958 (Sieber 1961:ill. 20, 20a). However, it differs from these two masks in important ways: the supporting structure is different, and the Joss mask has a small human figure carved in high relief on either side of the head. A third distinctive feature of this mask is the use of British West African pennies, one of which is dated 1913, to define the eyes.

These variations may be attributable to time,

▼▲▼

53
ELEPHANT MASK
(*Itrokwu* or *Igllo*)
Ekpari Clan, Nigeria
Wood, pigment,
iron nails and coins
H. 46.5 cm.
FMCH 90.366

FIG. 35
Itrokwu society mask.
Courtesy of the Barbier
Mueller Museum, Geneva.

space, or the hand of the artist or to a different tradition. Sieber attributed the two Idoma masks to Ochai and Oba, two widely known carvers resident in Otobi village during the late colonial period.[1] Otobi is the major lineage village of the Akpa District of the former Idoma Division and the home of the Ekpari, Mbo and Ifu-Akpa clans, which form an Akweya-speaking enclave within Idomaland proper. In addition to Idoma masks, they possess their own clan-based mask traditions, such as this elephant mask in the Joss collection. Despite the overall resemblance of this mask to the type of mask made by Oba, which was then still in the village where Sieber saw it (now in the Barbier-Mueller Collection, Zurich), no one claimed to recognize the mask when a photograph of it was circulated in Otobi in 1989. Two possible explanations exist: first, that while the mask does indeed originate with an Akweye-speaking group in southeastern Nigeria, it is not from the Idomaized enclave in the Akpa District but instead from their fellow lineage members living in Ogoja, south of Idomaland and north of the Middle Cross River. The second is that the mask did originate in Akpa District but a generation or two earlier than the other two masks.

Although they have been separated since the 19th century, the Akweya-speaking Yachi (Yache, Yatye) in Ogoja include the same major lineages as do the Otobi and have many of the same masquerades and cults. The ruling Ekpari clan in Otobi owns the *Itrokwu* mask described initially by Sieber as *Akatakpurapura* (an Idoma designation), while the Ekpari clan in both Akpa and Yachi owns *Igllo*, the most powerful of Akweya clan masks, which closely resembles *Itrokwu* but appears only at the death or installation of a king.

Geographic separation and the absence of Idoma influence are sufficient reasons for the variations in the mask, yet one could also explain these as the work of an earlier sculptor predating Ochai and Oba by one or two generations. In Otobi there is a small figure in the form of a mask headdress, which closely resembles the figures on the Joss mask. The figure, which is said to be by Ochai, thus provides a link in the genealogy of the masks and their carvers in Otobi itself.

In both *Itrokwu* and *Igllo*, the destructive power of the elephant is linked with the spiritual power of the king. This metaphor is played out in the performance of both masquerades as well as in the morphological features of the mask. A high degree of tension is generated by the appearance of either mask in public. *Itrokwu*, which is more frequently seen than *Igllo*, wreaks havoc upon its audience by knocking over cassava platforms, cooking pots and anything else in its path. At the same time its royal associations are indicated by its indigo burial cloth (Akweya: *ochicidi*) and its accompanying stool.

We may conclude that the present mask may be linked with either *Itrokwu* or *Igllo* and can be traced to a probable origin in the Ekpari clan of Akweya speakers. But whether this was in Idomaland or the Middle Cross River can only be a matter for speculation.

SIDNEY KASFIR

[1] I now believe that both were probably made by Oba.

54. Object in the Style of a Reliquary Guardian, Wumbu and Ndasa peoples, People's Republic of the Congo or the Republic of Gabon

This object is related to the reliquary guardian figures made by the Wumbu and Ndasa peoples, who make up the southern-most extension of Kota-speakers. A number of details indicate that its conception and technique closely agree with that of figures from the region north of the town of Mossendjo in the southwest of the People's Republic of the Congo. These large, ornate figures have convex and relatively naturalistic faces. The great predominance of the Wumbu in that region suggests that they may be considered the originators of the convex-face style.[1] Bifrontal figures, representing a merger of the convex-face style with an apparently earlier concave-face style, are also characteristic of the Mossendjo region.[2] The convex face of the figure ties it closely to the convex-face style of Mossendjo figures, but the unusually small scale and incomplete appearance of the sculpture distinguish it from these, marking it as a comparatively rough work. It is also set apart by the absence of the high brow and strong ridges, which define the spacious supraorbital planes of Mossendjo figures.

The function of this object is not known. If it was, like the larger Mossendjo figures, used as a reliquary guardian, its very small size must be explained. It may be a fragment of a complete figure, the form of which is defined by the loss of its neck and "arms," as well as two-thirds of its surmounting crescent. If we extrapolate from the proportions of an arbitrarily chosen figure, number 104 in Chaffins' Group 16 (Chaffin and Chaffin 1979), its original height as a complete figure would have been about 18.6 cm., which would still be remarkably small and unknown among the southern Kota peoples. We have no record of the Wumbu having used small auxiliary figures in conjunction with large reliquary guardians as is documented among the Mahongwe and others.

It is unlikely that this object, replicating in great part a reliquary guardian figure, would have appeared in public as an ornament (such as a pendant) or an emblem of status because the quasi-secret nature of the family reliquary cult restricted the sight of its cult-object to initiates. The same secrecy would probably have precluded its appearance at the top of a dignitary's staff.

Leon Siroto

[1] An Ndasa style has not yet come to our attention, although the possibility of a co-tradition is strong.
[2] Thirteen examples of the convex-faced styles are listed in Chaffins' Group 16 (Chaffin and Chaffin 1979:199-213). Of these only three backs are shown, all of which present concave faces. At least some of the corpus have only a convex, metal-covered face on one side and a simple symbolic motive on the uncovered reverse side.

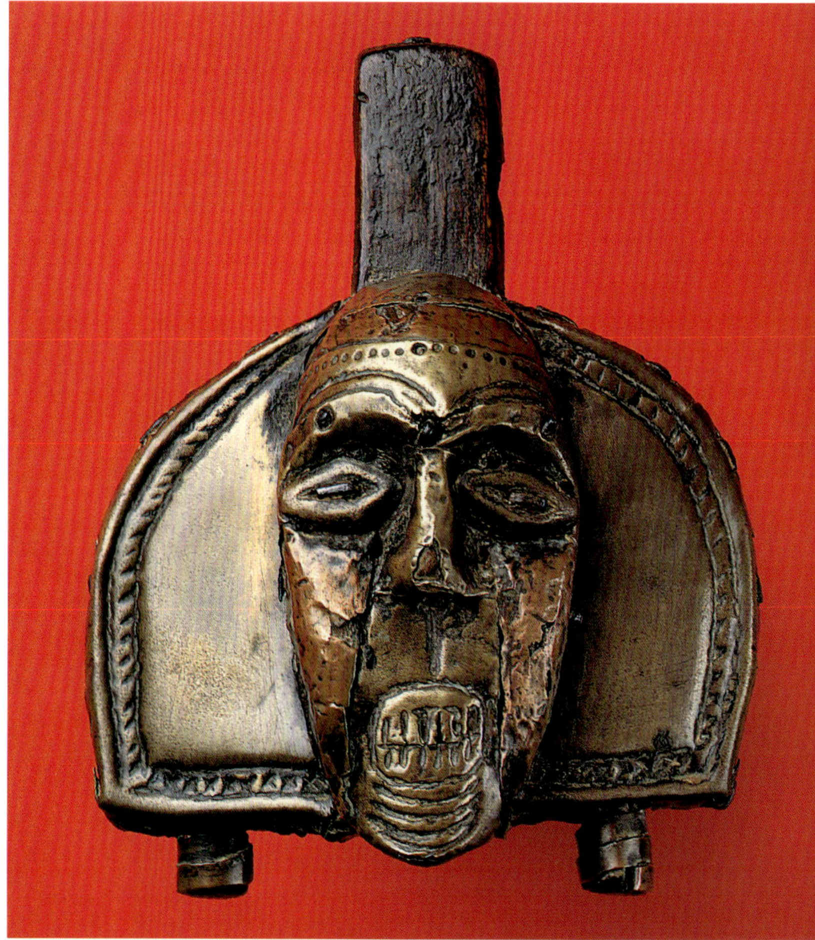

54
OBJECT IN THE STYLE OF A RELIQUARY GUARDIAN
Wumbu and Ndasa peoples,
People's Republic of the Congo or the Republic of Gabon
Wood, brass and copper
H. 11 cm.
FMCH 86.1736

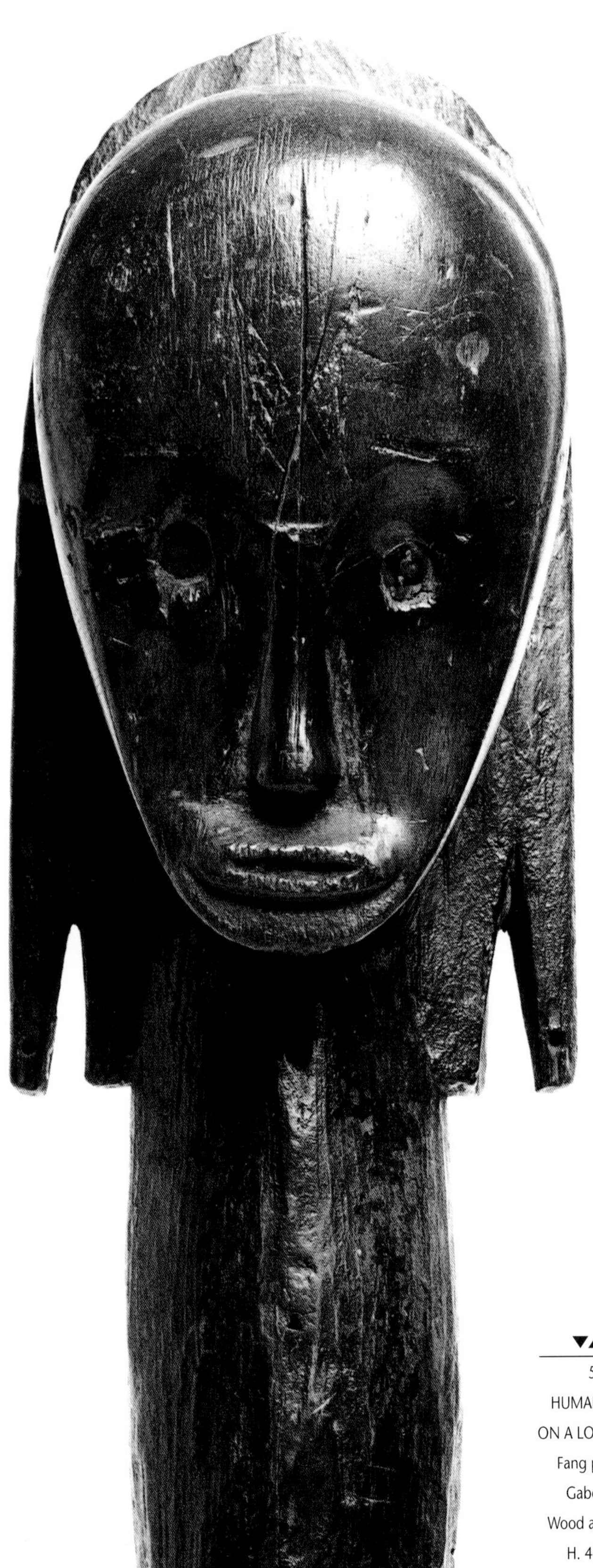

55

HUMAN HEAD
ON A LONG NECK
Fang people,
Gabon (?)
Wood and brass
H. 44 cm.
FMCH 87.1493

55. HUMAN HEAD ON A LONG NECK, FANG PEOPLE, GABON (?)

The Fang cult of family relics employed three kinds of human images to stand guard over its reliquary barrels: an independent head, usually on a long neck; a half-figure ending at the waist; and a full-figure.[1] Most of these images had extensions which, when thrust through the lid of the barrel, served to fix them in place over the relics, which were primarily the upper part of the skull of family leaders. Of these three types of guardian figures, the independent head is the least understood in terms of its origin, distribution and iconography. Its relative obscurity is probably a function of its seemingly greater age, narrower range of occurrence and sparser representation. At the beginning of the twentieth century the traditional Fang seem to have lost (or dissembled) recall of its inception and history.

Recent ethnological and art historical interest in this form centers on its place in the differentiation of Fang reliquary guardian imagery. Perrois's field inquiries among the Fang led him to conclude, however, that the head was little more than a southern variation on a primal Fang theme, contemporaneous and coordinate with the other types (1985:143-46). Other scholars follow instead Tessmann's seminal but laconic scenario for the endemic evolution of the guardian head into the complex full-figure (Tessmann 1913 II:117). J. and R. Fernandez saw the head as a more convenient form for the Fang to have carried about through the many marches and stations on their migration southward (1975:739-41). J. McKesson provides yet another explanation, suggesting that the full-figure guardian to be the inevitable transformation of the long neck of the head into the columnar trunk and thin limbs of the archetypal guardian statue (McKesson 1987:10, 16-19).

However logical and parsimonious these exegeses may be, they rest upon an undemonstrated premise that the Fang family relic cult and its use of guardian images were well-established traditions in pre-migration times. However, there are no significant versions of the family relic cult known among the people who replaced the Fang in their homeland. The Beti, northern relatives of the Fang in southern Cameroon, claim to have received their *melan* cult from the Ngumba, a neighboring but ethnically-unrelated group (Laburthe-Tolra 1985:337). Thus, although nearly all studies of Fang material culture accept the dogma of the migrating Fang as lenders rather than borrowers, it appears that the guardian head was not an invention of the Fang culture.

It appears more likely that as the Fang vanguard came into what is now Gabon and Equatorial Guinea, they borrowed the cult of family skulls, reliquaries and guardian images from the peoples already established there in the mid-nineteenth century. Reconstruction of the origin of the guardian head may be traced by changes in the styles of hair-dress enroute. Paul Du Chaillu, the first explorer to provide an eye-witness account of Fang culture, tells us that in 1856 men of the Fang vanguard wore their hair in either stiff plaits or long, thin queues decorated with beads and metal rings (Du Chaillu 1861:92-93, 104). A suggestion of this latter mode appears very rarely on Fang guardian heads, but it is occasionally found among guardian-figures from the Okak Fang of Equatorial Guinea (Laburthe-Tolra and Falgayrettes-Leveau 1991:118, 124, 126, 145-46).

Writing in 1876 of his visits to the southern Fang around the Gabon Estuary, R.F. Burton mentioned diverse coiffures (Burton 1876:204-205) but failed to touch upon the prevailing hair style found among the corpus of Fang guardian heads. This style of often high sagittal crests flanked by relatively long and broad sidelocks (Fig. 37) appears to go back to at least the seventeenth century on the coast of Gabon (Perrois 1985:32, fig. 26). Its enduring place in the aesthetic of the western edge of the country shows clearly in the iconography of the diverse ethnic groups settled there in the nineteenth century (Krieger III 1969:46, pl. 134; Perrois 1979:224, pl. 234, not necessarily Tsogho). Its absence among the westbound Fang toward the middle of the nine-

teenth century suggests that it may have been borrowed from the skull-cult of the Myéné and Kélé (Ngom) peoples they encountered when they began to settle near the coast (Deschamps 1962:118, 130; Perrois 1985:144, fig. 65).

This extra-Fang perspective is supported by the inconsistency of attributing the origin of the "Fang" heads, which appear to represent female personages (probably protective spirits), to the starkly patrilineal society of the Fang. Attribution to the Myéné, who at least partially follow a matrilineal rule of family membership, seems more appropriate. In addition, in contrast to the Fang, the cultural inclination of the family relic cults of the peoples whom they encountered in the south seems to have been toward using partial images—heads, half-figures, masks and mask-like forms—as guardians for magical materials.

The headdress and decoration of this head seem to recapitulate the early days of Fang acculturation during the 1870s. The explicitly rendered details of its coiffure recall a variety of techniques and materials: hair-braiding in the median band running down the back and cowries stung end-to-end flanking the median band and edging the sidelocks. The circular pits around the edge of the back are less explicit; their shape and size suggest that, if they were whitened, they could be European objects: bone buttons or brass tacks.

The style of the head assigns it to a formal group with deep faces and strikingly shallow occiputs. The flat coiffure seems to be applied to the main mass, rather than forming part of an organic whole. Similar examples are common (see Perrois 1985:168-69, 219, pl. 32).[2]   LS

---

[1] As far as we know, these types did not serve together on any one reliquary.

[2] This head has been published in an auction catalogue (Christie's 1978:50-51, no. 136). Its photographs revealed extreme rodent damage to the mouth and moderate damage to the nose. Afterward, an overly ambitious attempt at restoration failed to recapture the quality of the original features which, even in their ravaged state, suggested a certain delicacy in their carving.

56. HEAD OF MAN WITH LONG NECK ON PEDESTAL, TSOGHO PEOPLES, REGION OF MIMONGO, GABON

This head probably served as guardian for a packet of magical objects and substances, which would have been enclosed by a square of cloth—Tsogho raffia or European cotton—or, more traditionally, the spathe of a palm-inflorescence. The sides of the envelope were brought up around the contents and fastened to the neck of the guardian; the head's pedestal stabilized it at the center of a packet. The objects would have included relics of remarkable persons (both family members and others), as well as symbolic items such as mollusk shells, stones, leaves, and bangles. Barwood powder and kaolin, the most common substances kept in the packet, were thought to absorb the magical power of the objects.

The identities and contexts of these packet-assemblages remains controversial. The most authoritative source says that some are used in the rites of traditional Tsogho *bwété*, the paramount men's cult of a village. In this connection, when the guardian is female, it represents "the mother, the origin of all things." When it is male, it merely repre-sents an "ancestor." The same assemblage could be used in the rites of the cult of ancestors (presumably regarded as separate from *bwété*). Other assemblages were placed in a secret chamber in the *bwété* cult-house. The senior initiates presented them with offerings and prayers so that their candidates for initiation would be granted visions of the unseen world (Gollnhofer et al 1975:78, no. 151; 80, no. 156:82, no. 164).

The Joss guardian head is the most graphic rendering of the hairstyle of the male Tsogho that is known. Paul Du Chaillu, who was among the Tsogho ("Ishogo") June 20-22, 1865, noted the distinctive hairstyle: "The men...have fancy ways of trimming their hair. The most fashionable style is to shave the whole of the head except a circular patch on the crown, and to form this into three finely-plaited divisions, each terminating in a point and hanging down. At the end of each of these they fix a large bead or piece of iron or brass wire, so that the effect is very singular" (Du Chaillu 1867:288). In the same book he included an engraving depicting the hairstyle (Du Chaillu 1867:opp. 289): the "divisions" are flat and in the form of a long triangle (Fig. 37).

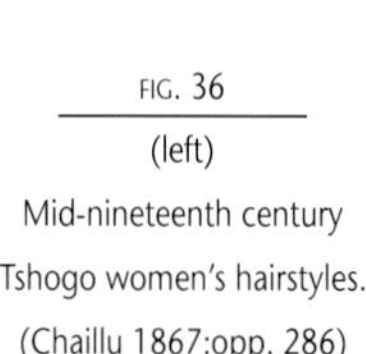

FIG. 36

(left)

Mid-nineteenth century Tshogo women's hairstyles. (Chaillu 1867:opp. 286)

FIG. 37

(right)

Mid-nineteenth century Tshogo men's hairstyles. (Chaillu 1867:opp. 289)

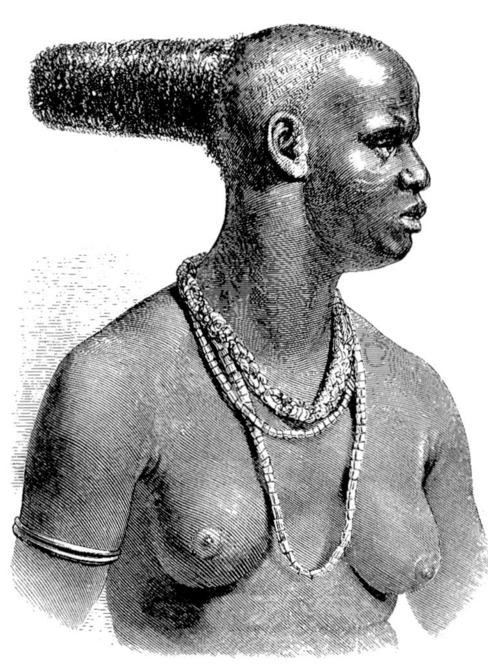

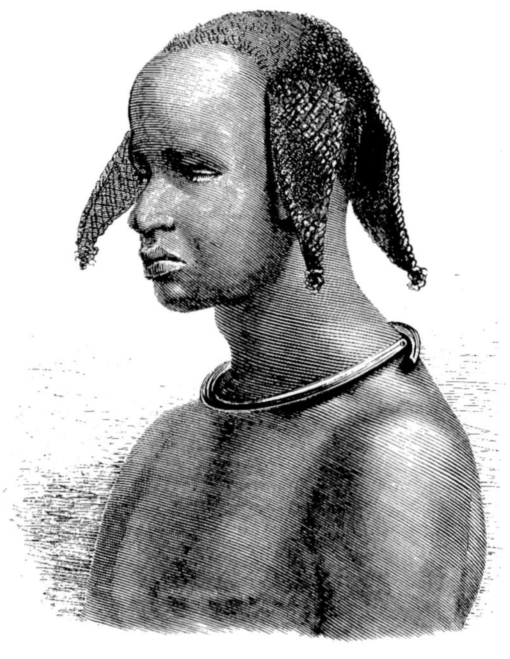

The coiffures of the Tsogho women that he describes were quite different (Fig. 36). While the association of the Joss head with the coiffure does not assure us of its origin as early as the 1860s, the rarity of the depiction of this hairstyle in the Tsogho corpus strongly suggests that it went out of fashion some time after Du Chaillu's visit and that most of the representations of it in sculpture disappeared before the transportation of Tsogho sculpture to Europe began. Other guardian heads may refer to this kind of coiffure (Perrois 1979:222, No. 231), but their carvers apparently preferred to bring the lateral "divisions" toward the rear, thereby sparing themselves the effort of cutting away a larger amount of wood and forestalling the later risk of breakage.

In the same account of Tsogho personal adornment, Du Chaillu reported that women wore no ornaments in their ears (Du Chaillu 1867:287). This observation was probably also valid for men, but it is at variance with the decoration of this head. Perhaps, however, the depiction of protective spirits allowed a margin for flattery by enhancement that transcended prevailing standards of fashion. It is also possible that the earrings were added later.   LS

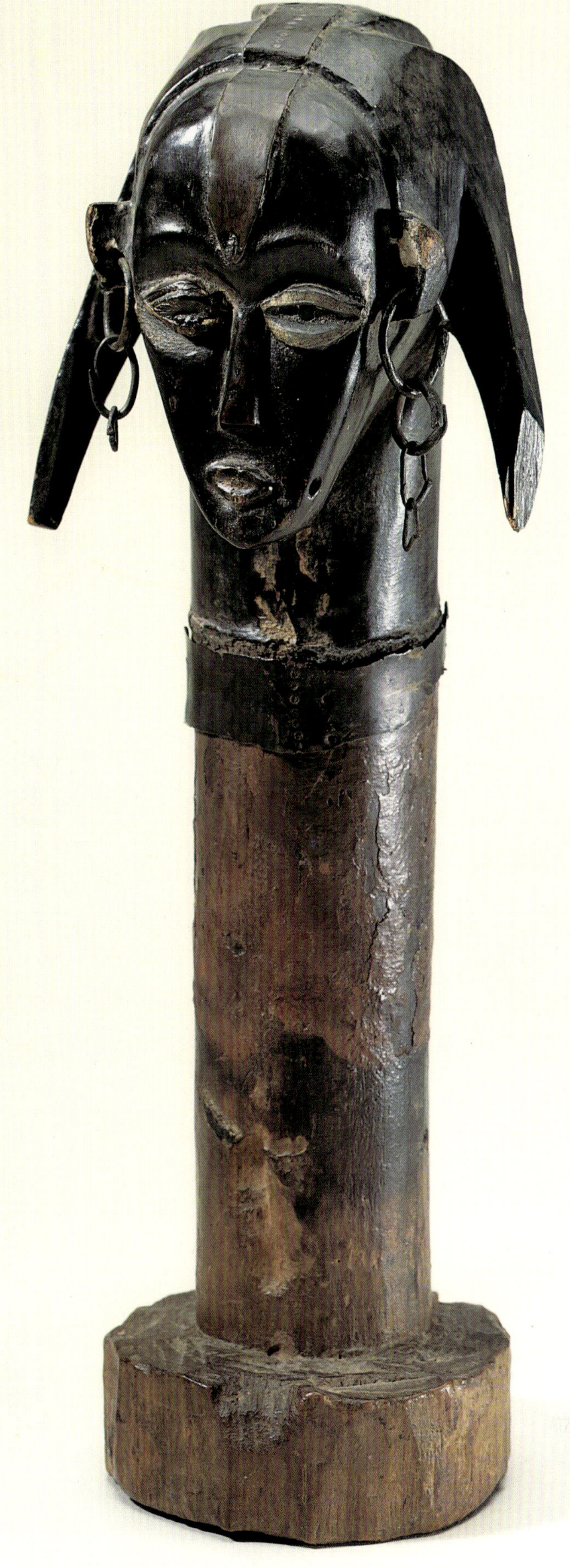

56
HEAD OF MAN
WITH LONG NECK
ON PEDESTAL
Tsogho peoples,
region of Mimongo,
Gabon
Wood, copper
and brass
H. 35 cm.
FMCH 87.1489

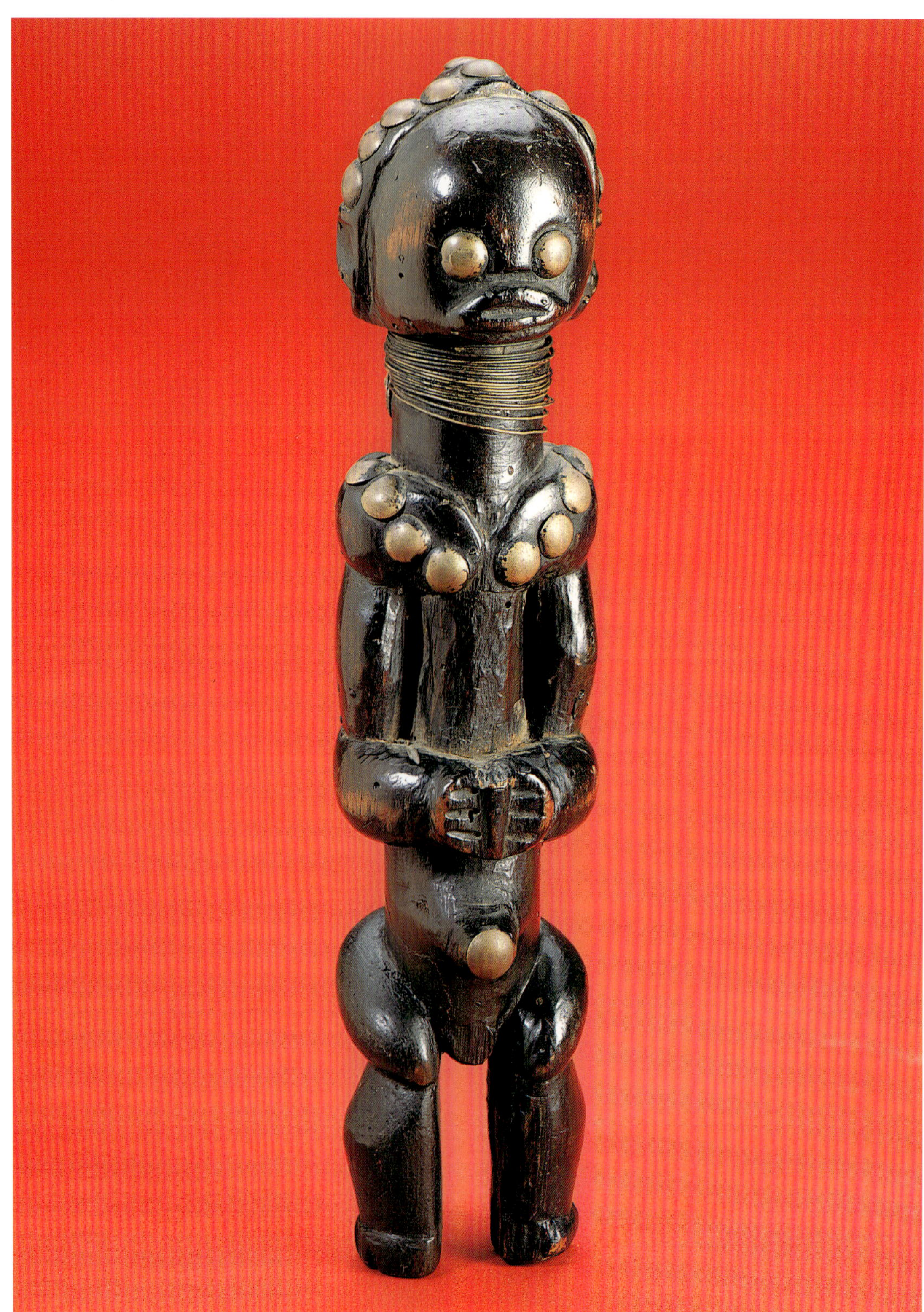

57
STANDING MALE
(DESEXED) FIGURE
Probably Fang people;
Okak or Ntumu
subgroup with strong
Mabea influence;
Equatorial Guinea
Wood, brass tacks
and brass wire
H. 20 cm.
FMCH 87.1472

**57. Standing male (desexed) figure,
Probably Fang people; Okak or Ntumu subgroup
with strong Mabea influence; Equatorial Guinea**

This figure was acquired from an exhibition of the arts and techniques of Spanish Guinea shown at Seville in 1929. The right leg of the figure had been restored sometime previously (Adams 1982:111). Based on this circumstantial evidence, which suggests that the figure comes from the Rio Muni region of Equatorial Guinea, it appears that the figure was produced by a Fang sculptor who was strongly influenced by Mabea style.

The Mabea, who call themselves "Bisio," (administrative term "Bujeba") belong to the Ngumba branch of the Makaa-Njem Bantu languages. Today, the Mabea live in Equatorial Guinea and southern Cameroon, but at the beginning of the twentieth century they lived farther inland. Although ethnically and linguistically distinct from the Fang, the Mabea interacted closely with them, especially the Ntumu and Okak, sometimes retaining their own identity within Fang villages and sometimes assimilating completely into Fang society, where they were known as *akuk* (i.e. Mabea) *fang*. The influence of the Mabea on traditional Fang culture appears to have been greater than the reverse and may have been crucial to the development of the religion and figure sculpture of the Fang. The Mabea were skilled and prolific carvers who worked both for their *melan* cult of skulls and for European colonial collectors and travelers. Mabea and Ngumba figures are usually notable for their verticality, conventionalization of the male breast and shoulder into a unified sculptural unit, elongated arms, and the gradual outward swell of the lower trunk. These features are evident in this figure.

The Joss figure also includes elements of Fang sculpture that rarely come into the Mabea corpus and thus suggest that it was a work of a Fang artist under the influence of Mabea style. Specifically, the highly conventionalized facial features and the strong separation of thigh and shank are characteristic Fang

elements. If not due to damage, the carving of the trunk is also rougher than one would expect from a Mabea carver. In addition, small, independent figures seem to have been rare among the Mabea and Ngumba.[1] They are, however, common among the Fang.

Westerners have tended to identify small wooden figures from the Fang as the finials of prestige-staffs, separated from their shafts for convenience in transportation and display in the West. Tessmann, however, cites two religious contexts for smaller statues. One is associated with the secret skull-cult. For various *ad hoc* reasons, the traditional Fang would occasionally initiate small boys into the ranks of the secret cult. Presumably too young actually to take part in the more serious affairs of the cult, they were allowed to play during its ritual, using small figures of plantain-pith or wood to guard small bark barrels containing the skulls of monkeys and mongooses (Tessmann 1912:261-62). Secondly, Tessmann noted that certain magical agencies are thought to be embodied in small wooden figures. These syntheses probably operate as tutelaries in the world of personal medicine for gaining wealth, love, game, etc.

The style and care shown in carving and decorating this figure suggest that it served as an agent of magic, similar to the presumably small figure of high sculptural quality identified by Tessmann as "medicine against enemy gunfire" (Tessmann 1913:165, Abb. 62, fig. d).[2] The generous use of brass in the decoration of this figure might express a desire for success in trade. Perrois published a comparable figure 27 cm. high that is studded with tacks, festooned with animal teeth and claws and chained to a small mammal or bird skull (Perrois 1979:84, no. 73).   LS

[1] Although Western collections give the impression that these peoples carved only guardian figures, the ethnographic literature tells of other figures—not small—used in the theater of illusion associated with initiation into the *melan* cult (Conradt 1902: 353; Laburthe-Tolra 1985:338, 341-43).

[2] Unfortunately he provided neither the dimensions nor the details of its activation and use.

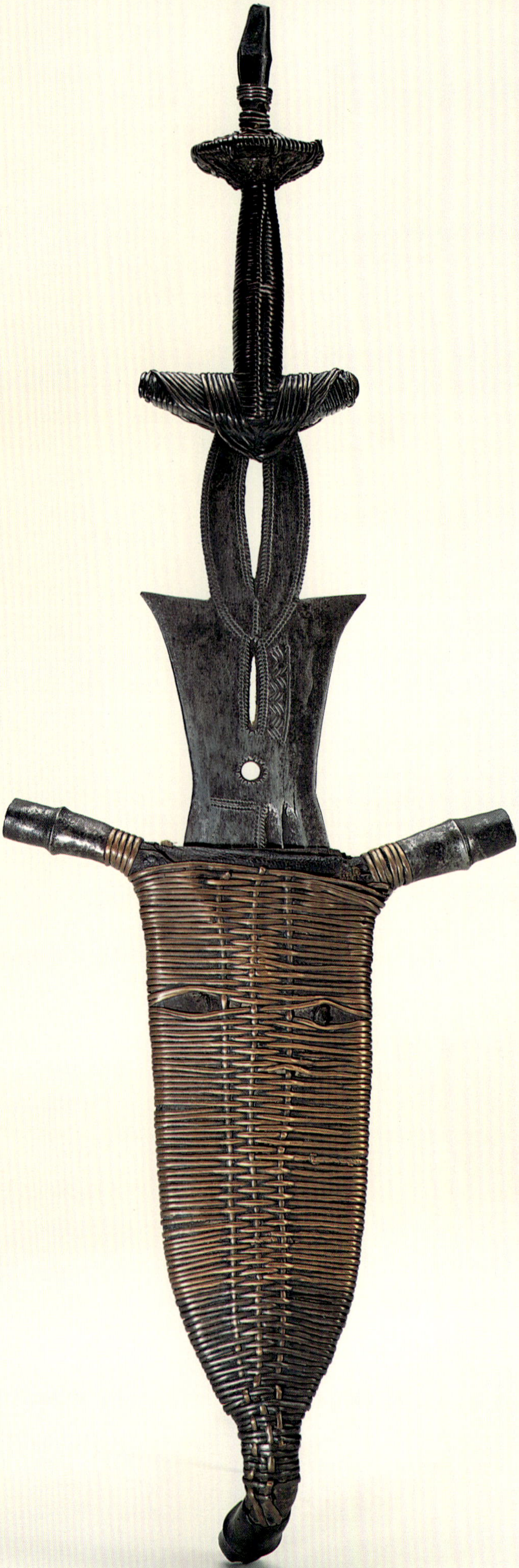

58
DISPLAY KNIFE
AND SCABBARD
Ngbandi or
related peoples,
e.g., Sango and Yakoma;
Upper Ubangi Basin,
Zaire or
Central African Republic
Wood, hide,
copper and brass
H. (knife) 49 cm.
FMCH 87.1458A,B

58. Display Knife and Scabbard
Ngbandi or related peoples, e.g., Sango and Yakoma; Upper Ubangi Basin, Zaire or Central African Republic

This knife and scabbard were made by the Ngbandi, six large ethnic groups who live about 700 miles from the Ogowe-Ivindo confluence, across several great rivers. The Ngbandi, who speak a Nigritic language in contrast to the Bantu ones of the Ogowe-Ivindo, were among the most tasteful and skilled sword smiths of Central Africa. Their inventory included wide sabers with offset, expanded ends and spears with very long blades.

This knife is a prime example of the tour-de-force of the series, a straight knife with a blade divided into three parts. The lower half of the blade is shaped like a long oval, designed without a point and enhanced by stepped, longitudinal contours and some engraving. The form of the leather scabbard is consistent with the shape of the blade and adds greatly to the distinctiveness of the knife. Sometimes left uncovered, the scabbard was often, as in this example, completely covered by wire worked in a pattern that was only a little less masterful than that covering the hilt. Knife and scabbard were carried on a bandoleer slung over the shoulder; with the handle kept upper-most.

The ethnographic record sustains the use of the form as a weapon, if only in display. Although not documented, these knives were apparently at least partly intended for display. As in many other such associations, the Ngbandi ancestor cult honors the weapons of deceased leaders. The Ngbandi, however, did not use weapons as reliquary guardians, a typical practice among the Ogowe-Ivindo. Although previously these knives and scabbards were mounted upside-down by art collectors, there is no support to the suggestion that they were traditionally hung in this manner to represent something other than a weapon.[1]

This knife and the others like it appear to have been produced by either one or only a few ateliers. Although their exact origin has not been localized, some authorities attribute them to the Yakoma (Westerdijk 1984:31, nos. 125, 127). The use of wire covering two different kinds of armature, which is common to this group, probably derived from basketry or matting. In this it differs from the very peculiar Ogowe-Ivindo technique, which seems to have been based on the example of metal stapling. The biomorphic quality of the Ngbandi scabbard, which is pronounced in this example and can be discerned either right-side-up or upside-down, is not consistent within the corpus.   LS

[1] This practice may have resulted from the manipulation of a 1968 article I published on a type of metal-covered reliquary guardian figure made by certain peoples in the Ogowe-Ivindo confluence of Gabon but wrongly attributed to the "Osyeba" people since the beginning of the century. I mentioned the possibility that the image's form could partly refer to the prestige-knives and spears used in that region (Siroto 1968:86, 89). At that time, these reliquary guardian figures were much rarer and more desperately sought than they are today. It is conceivable that between 1968 and 1970 an enterprising dealer inverted the knife to emphasize the resemblance, thereby reversing my premise by giving a literal-minded reading to the "Osyeba" figure as the representation of a weapon rather than a guardian spirit. In 1971 this inversion was honored when Fagg claimed that the Ngbandi knife and scabbard bear, upon my authority, a probable relationship to the Gabonese reliquary guardian: first, the wire wrapping of the former reproduces the technique of covering the latter and, second, the Ngbandi are near neighbors of the peoples of the Ogowe-Ivindo confluence (Fagg 1971:21, no. III-1).

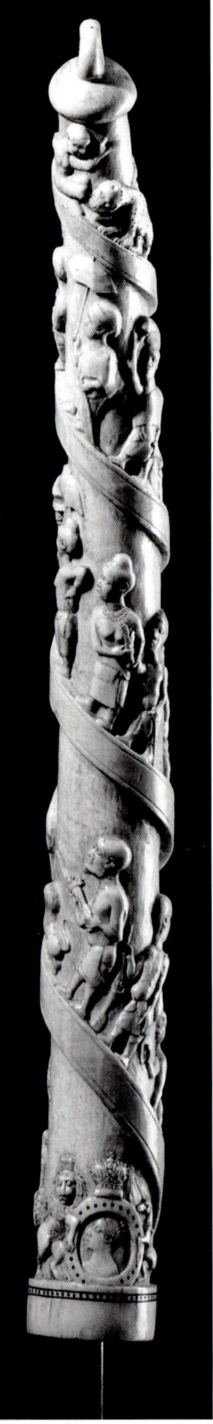

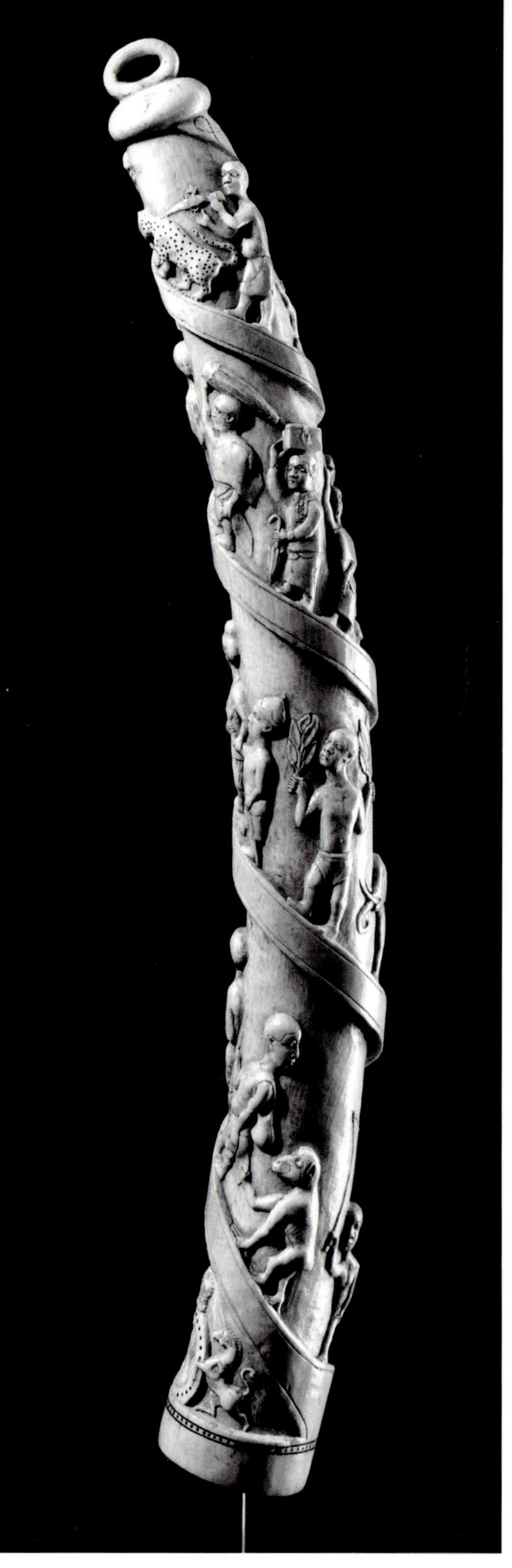

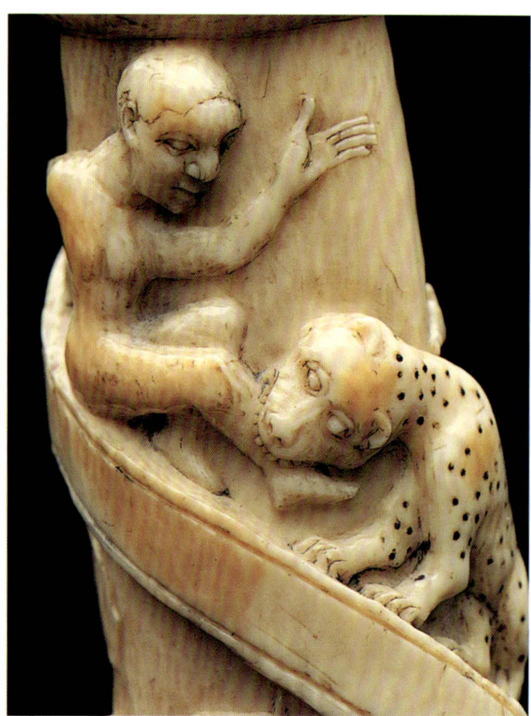

59. Ivory Tusk Carving, Loango Coast of Zaire

This intricately rendered ivory tusk is the early work (circa 1850) of a prestigious carving "guild" on the Loango coast of Zaire. Perhaps as many as 600 of these carvings were produced during the second half of the 19th century, mostly as souvenirs commissioned by employees of various European trading companies. A few were presented as gifts from African to European royalty. Large tusks (84 cm. long with 95 figures) required sixteen months of constant labor by an individual artist (Steckelmann 1889:5), using simple tools such as nails (Bastian 1874:156) or scraps of soft iron (Cincinnati Art Museum 1889) and some type of dividers to ensure consistent proportions of figures on the helical organizing ridge.

The realism and the mixing on the tusk of imagery from two different continents are typical of traditional Loango themes found on combs, baskets, cloth, rock engravings, body scarifications and hammock pins. The tusk also includes a fascinating vari-

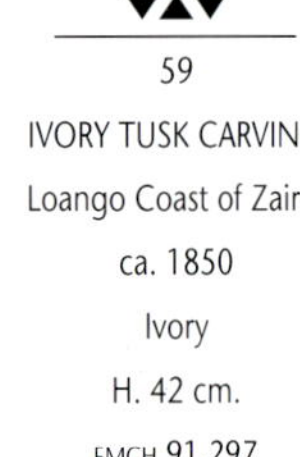

59

IVORY TUSK CARVING

Loango Coast of Zaire,

ca. 1850

Ivory

H. 42 cm.

FMCH 91.297

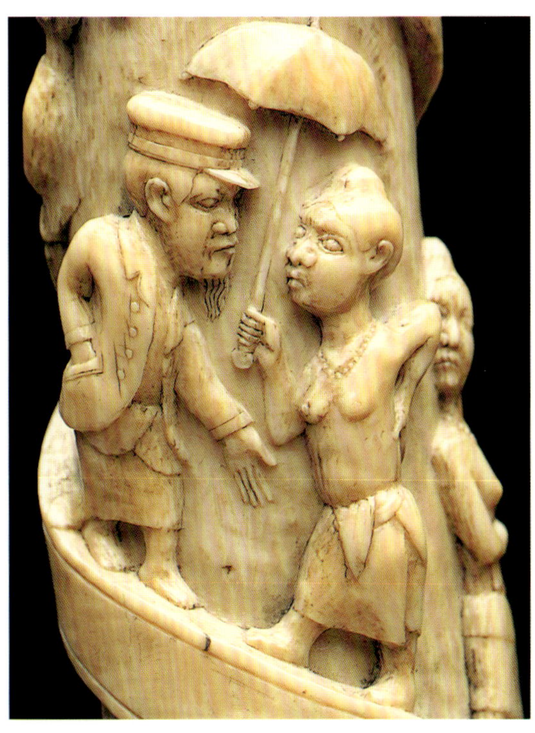

ety of contemporary European images viewed from the perspective of the Congo. The characteristic helical organization of the tusk is narrative in function. The details of each figure reveal much about contemporary African life and the way that the carvers viewed interactions between African and European cultures. Although this piece is unusual in substituting an open loop for a figural carving at the top, it possesses the usual synthesis of African and European subjects; for example, elephants, leopards and chimpanzees share the stage with unicorns and heraldic lions. Traditional knee-length and ankle-length skirts appear with shorts, stocking caps, English jackets, flintlock guns and umbrellas. Traditional drums are carried with padlocked boxes, and a man in European shorts raises a branch in each hand as the traditional symbol of trust and assurance (Tuckey 1818:124). At the base of the tusk, a young Queen Victoria sits in profile within her coat of arms.

DELLA JENKINS

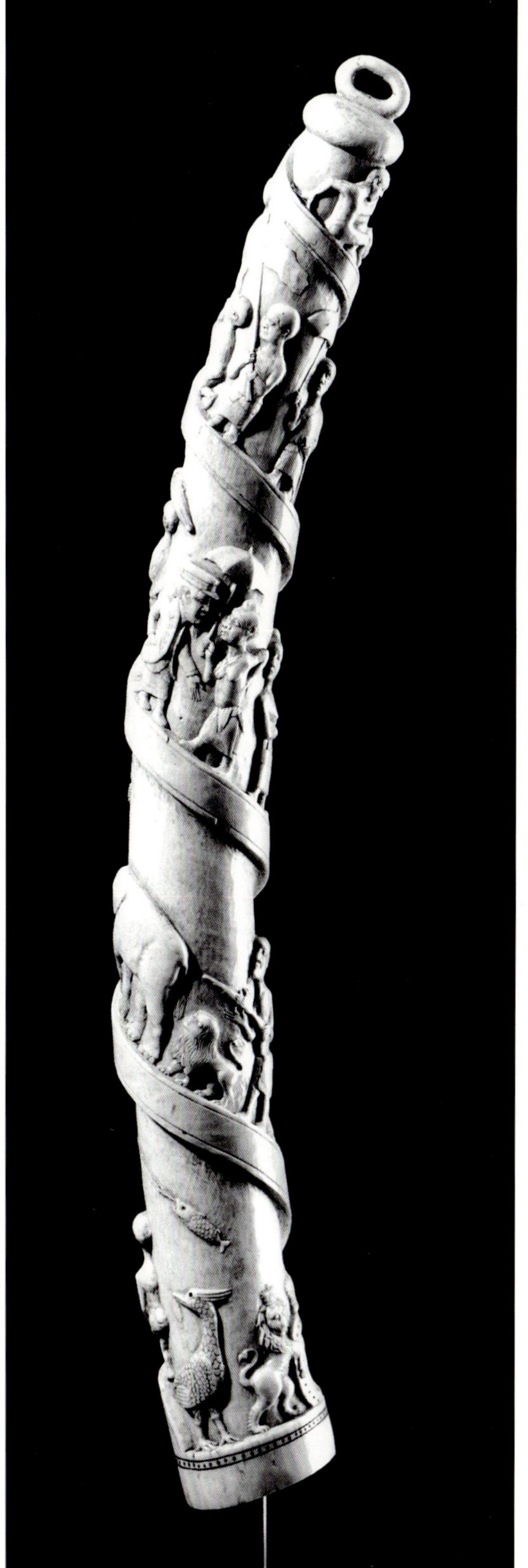

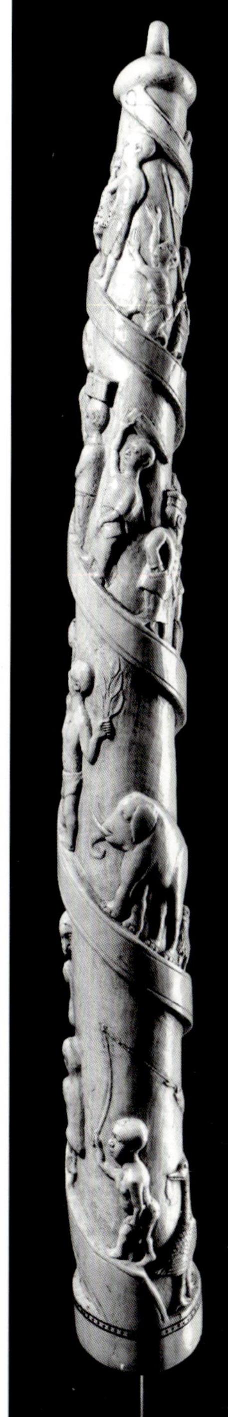

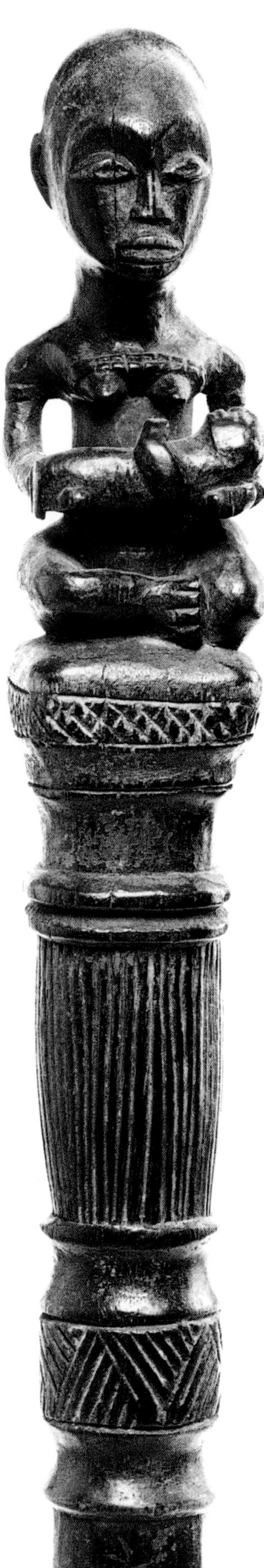

60
CHIEFTAIN'S STAFF
(mvuala amfumu
or *nti mfumu)*
Yombe, Kongo, Zaire
Wood
H. 70.5 cm.
FMCH 87.1500

60. Chieftain's Staff, Yombe, Kongo, Zaire

Throughout the five centuries of Kongo history known to the West, staffs have been associated with governmental and both traditional and Christian religious practices. According to oral tradition, Ntinu Wene, the founder of the Kongo Kingdom, brought nine clans and nine staffs with him when he conquered the autochthonous people and took over the lands that were to comprise his sovereign territory. Whether this account memorializes an actual historical event or legitimizes the power of the throne by creating a myth of foundation, the staff is recognized both as agent and as a symbol of the chief's right to rule. At the time of the kingdom, the staff established a link to the capital, Mbanza Kongo, or San Salvador as it was called by the Portuguese and is known today. It also linked the chief and the clan to the ancestors in a symbiotic relationship of ritual reciprocity. This relationship between the living and the dead still forms the basis of Kongo society.

The staff in the Joss collection is an example of a *mvuala amfumu* or an *nti mfumu*, staff of the chief. Stylistically distinct staffs are associated with different sub-groups and clusters of geographically related groups within the Kongo proper. This chieftain's staff is stylistically related to the Yombe,[1] but it does not obey the strict cannons of that style. The worn and flaking patina of this staff also lacks the thick, layered encrustations of the surface of old staffs, which were often stored where smoke from fires gave them a rich black patina as protection against insects. This staff was, therefore, probably manufactured in the twentieth century rather than in the nineteenth century, possibly as a replacement for an older staff bearing the same motifs or for the market.

The carved top of the staff represents a woman holding an infant. She sits in the *funda nkata* pose, the cross-legged posture assumed by the nobility. This motif is related to *mintadi* grave effigies. Neither on staffs nor on tombs is the image meant to be a portrait. On staffs it legitimizes authority among the predominantly matrilineal Kongo through the memory of a founding ancestress, represented by a woman holding the clan as a child. On tombs it petitions a particular ancestral spirit of a woman of great courage, physical strength, and fertility to intercede for the clan as she journeys among the dead before reappearing in this world as a new life.

The figure sits on a pedestal bordered by lozenge motifs. Field research (1984-86) has demonstrated that similar lozenges were used in a variety of permutations on mat designs among the Yombe for centuries. Abbe Mvumbi Nkonde (Nkonde) found that in that context, lozenge designs, which he called *mabuuinu* (sing. *buuinu*), relate to aphorisms and proverbs commenting on correct social action and responsibility and the values of clan unity. Lozenges also traditionally appear on staffs and on the chief's *mpu*, or bonnet, as well as on the shawl that he wears around his shoulders, a kind of shirt historically worn by the nobility. Field research among the Woyo in 1985 found that in certain contexts the lozenge design may relate to political territory, which is seen as comprising not only the living and their dwellings but also the dead.[2] Thompson's study of the lozenge or diamond form on *maboondo*, funeral stelae found primarily among the Mboma, considerably augments our understanding of the plasticity in rendering and meaning of this design (Thompson & Cornet 1981:876-894). He discusses in detail its formal aspects and permutations, indicating its role as the foundation of a language of signs.

Double bands in relief, descending incised lines, and a single band in relief create the next section of design. Congruences between Yombe and Woyo staffs suggest that their designs carry similar meanings. While in Bas Zaire in 1986, Woyo informant Balu Balila glossed double bands as cords that bind the covenant between the living and the dead (Balila, pers. comm. 1986). Twisting lines on Woyo staffs

(replaced here by straight lines) indicate direct attention downwards to the land of the dead. A single band completes the design, making it a single phrase of a codified idea.

The final band of design is formed by triangular motifs created by diagonal lines in relief. The triangle is a variation on the lozenge or diamond motif of which it is one half. The exact meaning is not known, but it probably comments further upon realms of experience of the living or the dead.

Taken together, the figure and geometric motifs appear to sanction the legitimate right of the chief to rule by indicating that he has the beneficence of the ancestors, represented by the founding ancestress, and that he is the agent who addresses the needs of their living descendants. The geometric designs further suggest the invocation of a covenant with the dead for the sustenance, increase and protection of the living. All the clan's members must live in the community according to ancient precepts for correct social interaction in balance with the capricious forces of existence.

RAMONA M. AUSTIN

[1] The characteristic Yombe style is marked by a large head, slightly inclined backwards, and very pronounced eyebrows that are often serrated, although not serrated here. Eyes are half circles, or coffee-bean in shape, giving the appearance of being half-closed. The head is coifed in specific motifs or wears a *mpu*, the bonnet worn by chiefs or regents, and is sometimes adorned with leopard claws. The mouth is often open, revealing filed teeth. The facial expression suggests a trance. Nlunga, bracelets denoting chiefly and noble status, may encircle the arms. The shortened, and sometimes thick torso, may bear simple raised cicatrices or variations of lozenge motifs. Snakes may appear on the shoulders and at the top of the head, and the breasts may be encircled by double cords which bind them for work and are raised to give suck to infants. Staff motifs usually show the infant being held and not being suckled even though the breast bindings are raised.

[2] Informants from the coastal Woyo explained the lozenge and this triangular motifs on knotted chieftain's shawls (*zamba kya mfumu*; Thompson & Cornet 1981:104-105, 139, 246) as the journey and record of the ancestors from the kingdom of Ngoyo who penetrated what is now Woyo territory, Collectivite de la Mer, Bas Zaire.

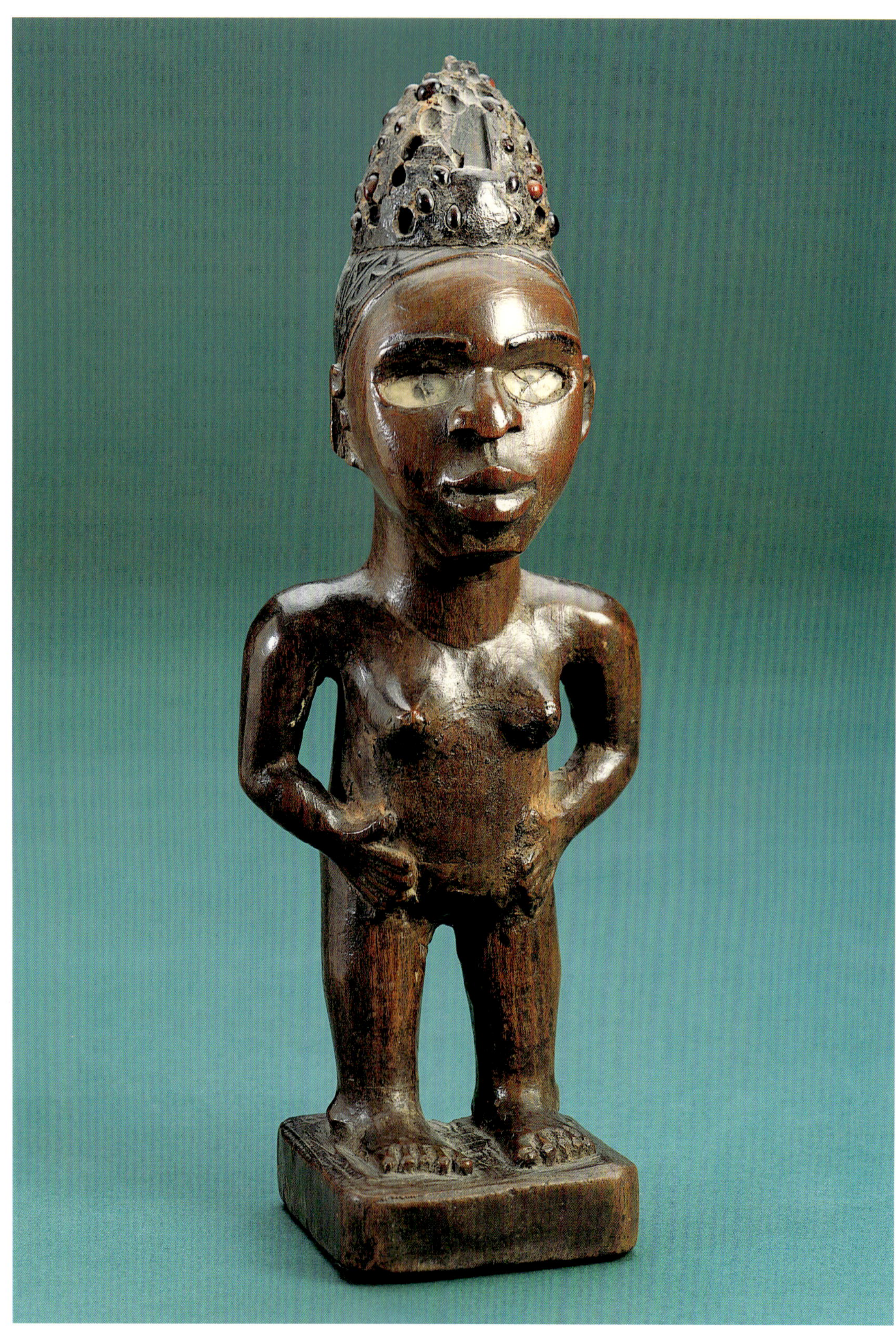

▼▲▼
61
STANDING
FEMALE FIGURE
(nkisi)
Yombe, Kongo, Zaire
Wood, abrus seeds
and glass
H. 23 cm.
FMCH 87.1477

61. STANDING FEMALE FIGURE, YOMBE, KONGO, ZAIRE

Like many *minkisi* (singular, *nkisi*), this figure has hands that are positioned on either side of the belly. Surface evidence indicates that a charge packed in resin was fixed to the abdomen in the same way that embedded materials are fixed in a resin crown on top of the figure's head. The position of the hands is important because the hands emphasize that part of the body as the site of the *nkundu* gland, the gland involved in sorcery. This is the gland that swells when activated, and by swelling, the belly signals that forces from the other world affect the physical and metaphysical well being of the afflicted. By extension, it signals the activation of supernatural force and power, an appropriate valence for an *nkisi*.

The positioning of the resin cone at the crown of the skull also suggests an otherworldly agency. The crown of the head is where the parietal and temporal bones of the cranium fuse. At birth these bones are incompletely ossified. The result is the fontanel, soft membranous intervals, which pulse at the top of the skull. For the Kongo this is one of the special points of the human body where charges are affixed. On this figure the head is covered by lozenge and triangular shapes like the designs found on the chief's *mpu*, or bonnet. The inlaid glass and porcelain eyes continue to reinforce the supernatural agency of the *nkisi*, because the transparency of the glass and the white color of the porcelain (manufactured with kaolin, a fine white clay) visually pun on water and thus on the watery Kalunga, a line that separates the land of the living from the land of the dead in Kongo cosmology (See the discussion of the Kongo staff Cat. 60, and Kongo *nkisi* Cat. 62). If the body itself is a code for the cosmos, the clavicle is the Kalunga line, and the crown of the head and the belly, or *nkundu* gland, represent the reflected mountains above and below the Kalunga line. The two charges, therefore, sit at these important points indicating that the *nkisi* has agency in both worlds. This is reinforced by the fabrication of the *mpu*, or chieftain's cap, the threads of which are bound up at the crown as a knot or tuft, another rendering of the Kongo universe in microcosm. The glass and porce-

lain eyes, by referencing the Kalunga line, also indicate the figure's mystical ability to see into the other world.

The stylization of the head, and its proportion to the rather stout, cylindrical body are classic Yombe. The rigid frontality and strong shoulders, which arch away from the body, are also characteristic of this style.   RA

62. STANDING FIGURE OF A WOMAN HOLDING HER BREASTS, YOMBE, KONGO, ZAIRE

Minkisi (singular, *nkisi*) are generally bundles of wrapped cloth or figurines which hold medicated charges. However in its most reductive meaning, a *nkisi* is a vessel or container for a charge. It can thus be a wide variety of objects, including even persons, as in the body of the consecrated chief. The purpose of a *nkisi* is to heal and to ward off malevolent forces. It can also be an instrument for oath taking to assure the fidelity and concurrence of the parties who make an agreement. Such agreements usually pertain to social contracts, nails driven into the figures and cloth wrapped around nails or small bundles signify that a contract and promise have been bound. Such figures are called *nkisi nkonde*.

The figure of a standing female figure belongs to another of the numerous classes of *nkisi*, that of a standing female figure holding her breasts. Rendered in classic Mayombe style from the area near the Cabinda border, its coiffure of triangle and lozenge designs ends in a top knot not unlike the design of a chief's *mpu*, his royal bonnet of office. As such, its designs extrapolate on the relationship of the living with the dead and the Kongo cosmology (MacGaffey 1986:43). The nail between the serrated eyebrows pierces the center of thought, and a collar of iron encircles the columnar neck. The human body, like the chief's bonnet, can represent the cosmos in miniature. The clavicle marks the Kalunga line, which separates the land of the living (head and neck) from the land of the dead (the body). The head rests at those lines of vertical and horizontal intersection which can be rendered in the abstract as a lozenge shape, a cross, or a spiral. The point of

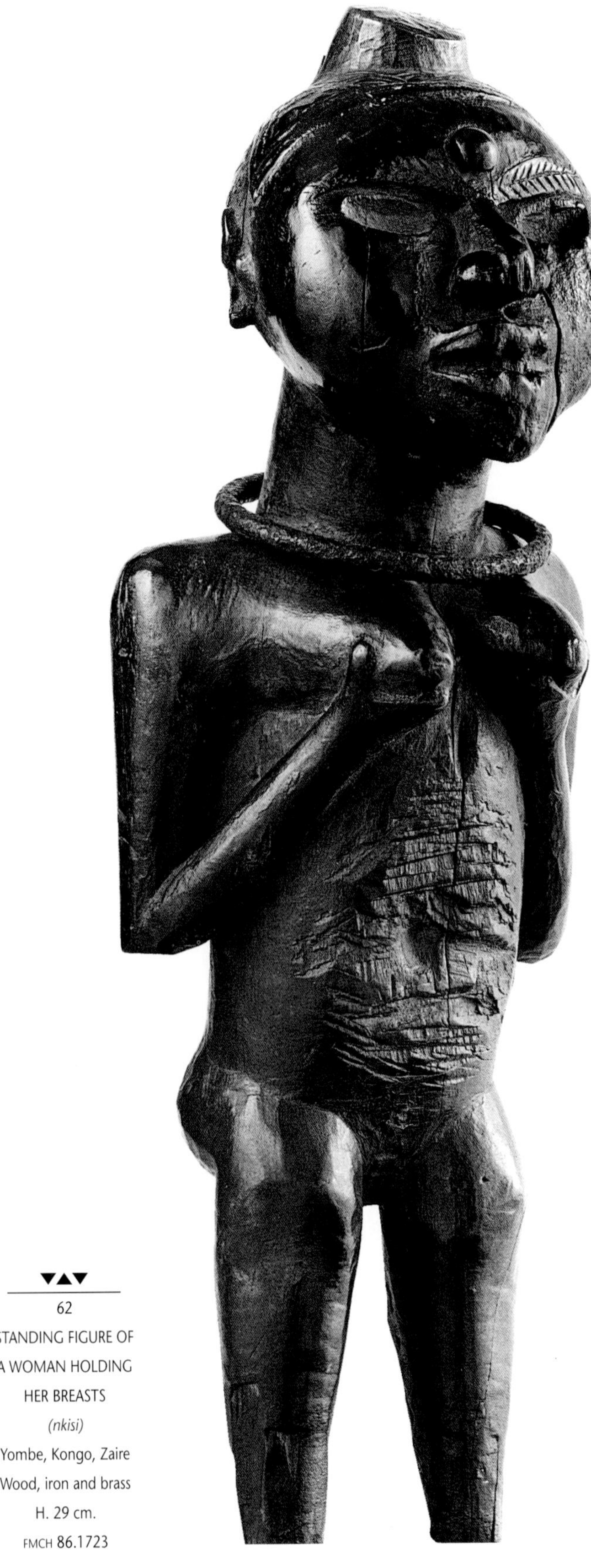

62

STANDING FIGURE OF
A WOMAN HOLDING
HER BREASTS
(nkisi)
Yombe, Kongo, Zaire
Wood, iron and brass
H. 29 cm.
FMCH 86.1723

intersection requires much mystical prowess because it is the point where all the confluent forces of the world come together. Graves are sometimes bound by iron rings to keep the dead bound in the earth unable to roam and adversely affect the lives of the living. The iron collar on the figure suggests a similar purpose to bind the force of the *nkisi* for a special and healing purpose.

The proffered breasts, which represent benediction and nurturance throughout a broad area of sub-Saharan Africa, reinforce the notion of force controlled for the good. Among the Kongo, the white milk of the mother's breasts alludes to *mpemba*, white kaolin. White is the color of the Kalunga line, the watery boundary between the living and the dead (Robert F. Thompson, pers. comm. 1992). Smeared around the eyes it opens mystic sight to other worlds. *Mpemba* is also the white clay that anoints the chief, is the ingredient par excellence of *nkisi*, and is an essential ingredient in the arsenal of sacred medicines at ritual events. The rough-hewn quality of the front surface of the figure's torso is evidence that a ball of resin holding the medicines of a charge was once attached to this figure but has been secularized.   RA

63. MATERNITY FIGURE, PROBABLY MANYANGA, KONGO, ZAIRE

This standing figure of a mother and child has been classed Vili, one of the related chieftaincies of the Kongo.[1] The attenuated physique, long columnar neck, and tubular torso of the figure are, however, stylistically more closely related to the tradition of another Kongo chieftaincy, the Manyanga. The figure is also related to the *mintadi* of the Yombe, who customarily portray maternities seated in a cross-legged position and suckling or holding a child, or more rarely, kneeling with a child at the side. Such figures were placed in or on tombs and referenced the dead woman as exemplary in her physical strength and in her courage to live correctly. The figure was also an intermediary between the land of the dead and the living members of her clan, graphically portrayed by the suckling child who nurses at its mother's breast. The mother is not only rich in life giving force but also generous in her nurturance. The related image of a woman offering her breasts is a traditional sign of benediction throughout much of sub-Saharan Africa.

The ungainly pose of the maternity is not found among Yombe, Mboma or Vili figures. The mother precariously holds the baby with one hand and with her other squeezes milk from her right breast into the baby's mouth. The mother's head tilted to one side suggests contemplation or reflection. The heads of steatite effigies of chiefs found on tombs among the Mboma also incline to the right and rest on one hand in contemplation. Thompson identified this as a pose of sadness (Thompson 1981). During field research in Bas Zaire in 1985, a Yombe fly whisk of old and exquisite manufacture was observed with a handle carved as a seated chief with his head resting on his arms and his legs forming an entwined and closed posture. Thompson (1981) described this pose as the *luumbu* pose of silence and negation.

The figure succinctly captures the primary importance in Kongo culture of the woman as the vehicle through which each generation inherits the wealth of the last, and as the primary source of increase, power, and immortality. It is she who produces the children who are the real wealth of the clan and who will carry in their memories to the next generation those who have gone before.   RA

[1] The others are the Yombe, Bembe, Bwende, Manyanga, Mpangu, Ndibu and Ntandu.

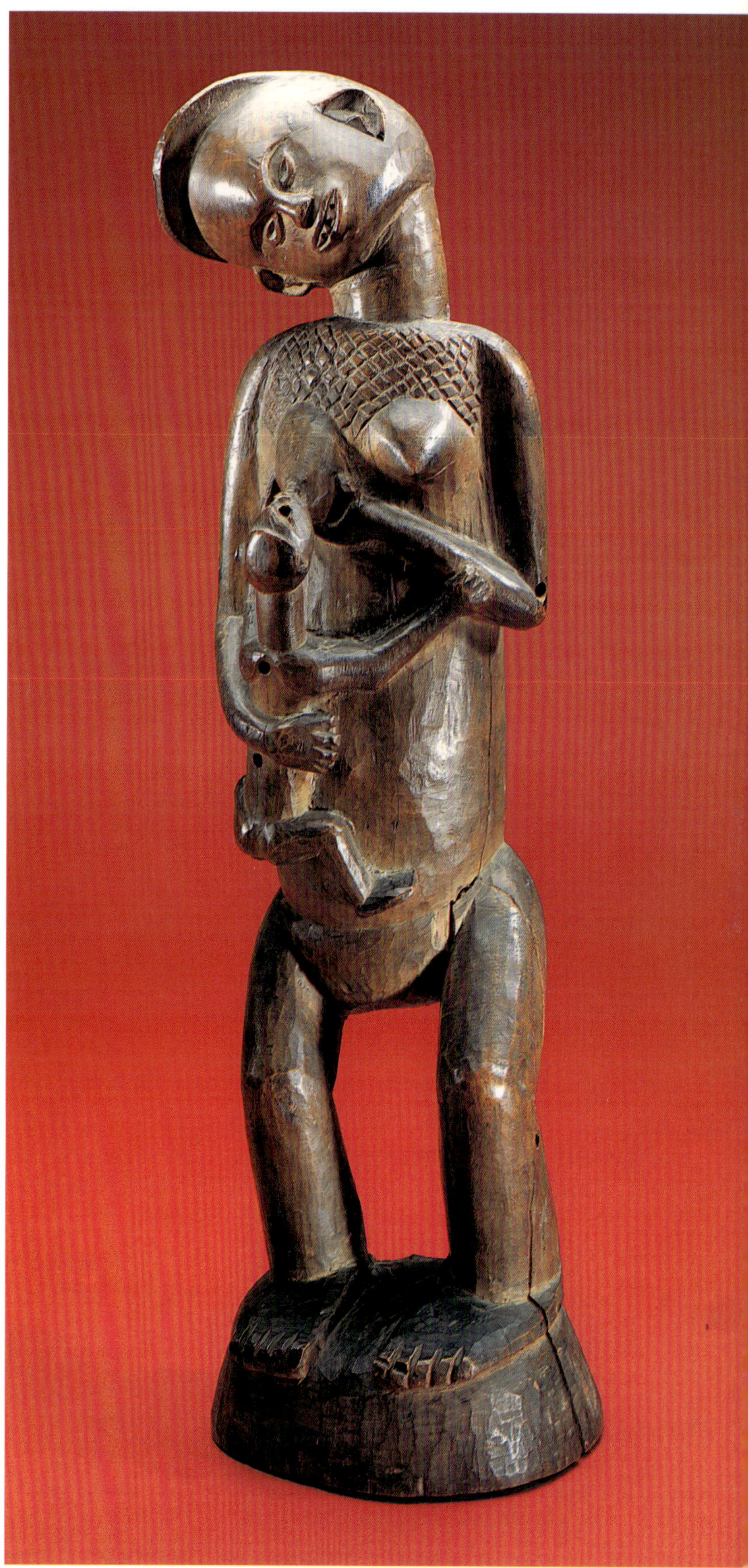

▼▲▼
____
63
MATERNITY FIGURE
(mintadi)
Probably Manyanga,
Kongo, Zaire
Wood, resin and kaolin
H. 56.5 cm.
FMCH **86.1730**

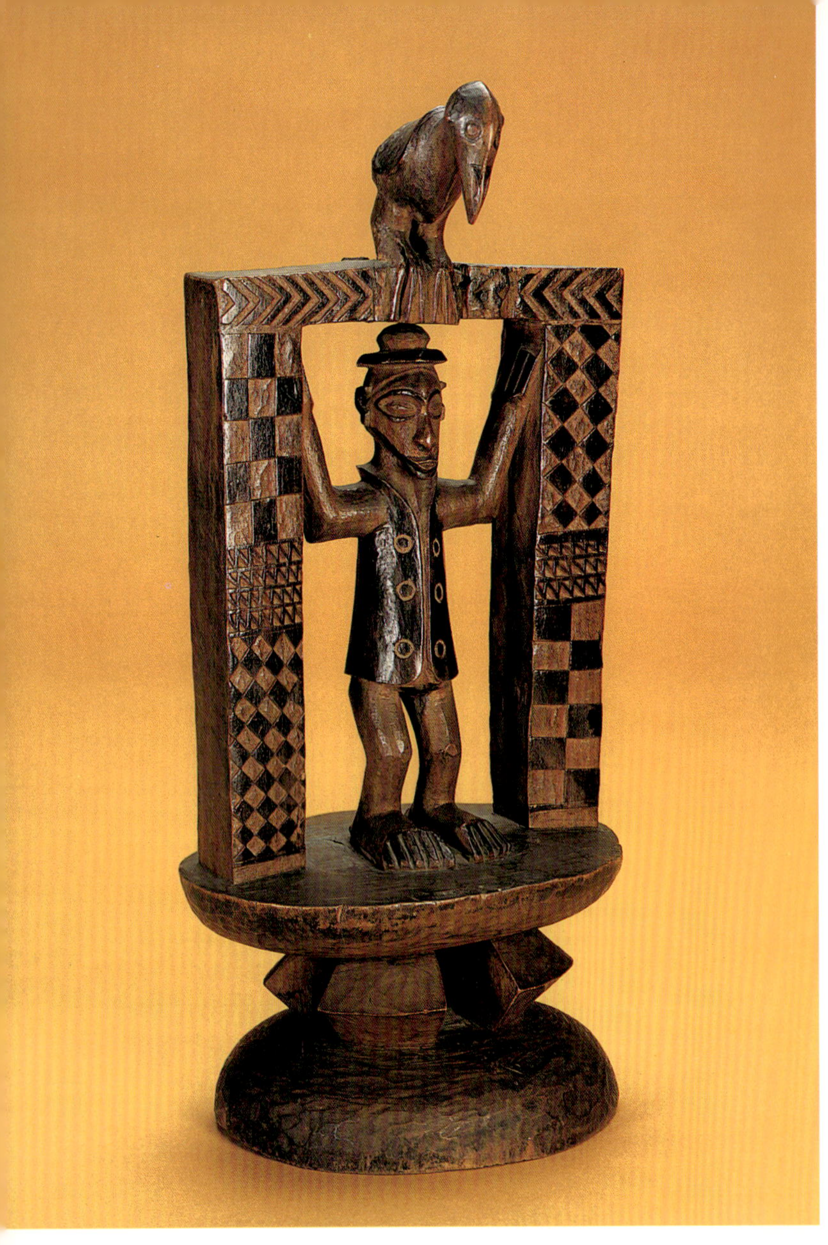

64

FRAMED FIGURE

(nzambi)

Holo, Zaire

Wood and paint

H. 31.5 cm.

FMCH 87.1479

64. FRAMED FIGURE, HOLO, ZAIRE

This framed statuette, with arms extended, stands on a stool; a bird looks down from above him. The Holo, Shingi, Songo and Chokwe call this type of figure *nzambi* after the Nzambi cult of which it is an emblem. The statuette is said to have come from the Luremo, Camaxillo and Lubala region, where Bastin reported the considerable development of the Nzambi cult (Bastin 1979:36), the true nature of which is not fully known.

Scholars are uncertain how early to date the earliest *nzambi* figures. The first explorers who arrived in the region in the nineteenth century reported seeing *nzambi* figures. Capello and Ivens, Portuguese explorers who left Banguelle in 1877 to discover the northern part of Angola and the region of the Kwango, saw a figure of the *nzambi* type in Chiboco,

the Chokwe region corresponding to the area where this figure was found (Capello and Ivens 1969:I,113). The figurine was in a small house or chapel where a local cult dedicated to it presented it with offerings. The local population called this figure *ngana nzambi*, which the two explorers translated as "My God." In inquiring about the origin of this cult object, the explorers were told that *nzambi* had been brought to the region by an Mbaka (Ambakista).[1]

Nzambi figures probably originated in the seventeenth century. According to Maesen, the *nzambi* evoke the Christian crucifix introduced at that time by the Capuchin missionaries who settled at the Saint Marie mission of Matamba (Maesen 1956:44). Influenced by Christian practices, the Holo built small cult houses for the *nzambi* figures and presented them offerings, in a manner similar to the reverence shown toward framed Christian crucifixes and figures of saints, which they call Santu.

The occidental influence on the art of the Holo can also be seen in the frock coat and hat of the Joss figure. The plastic conception of the figure is, however, characteristic of the Holos of Angola: an elongated face inscribed in a triangle; almond eyes; a triangular, elongated, thin nasal plane with well tailored alae; a prognathic mouth; short, bent legs; and carved, geometric motifs decorating the frame. A number of *nzambi* figures represented as standing on a stool have been found in this region of northern Angola. The example at the University of Pennsylvania (Wardwell 1986:135, fig. 67) is similar in many ways to this example. The motifs of the man standing on a stool and the bird on the sculpture glorify two ancestors. The stool is an emblem of authority, the man appears to be an ancestor of high rank whose spirit, transporting vital and vitalizing forces, receives the name of Nzambi. The ancestors are the protectors of the clan; they possess and distribute the lands, forests and all the riches in which they abound. They generate well-being, inflict and cure sickness, and ward off evil curses and spells.

Nzambi surmounted by bird sculptures have also been found in the region of northern Angola. The

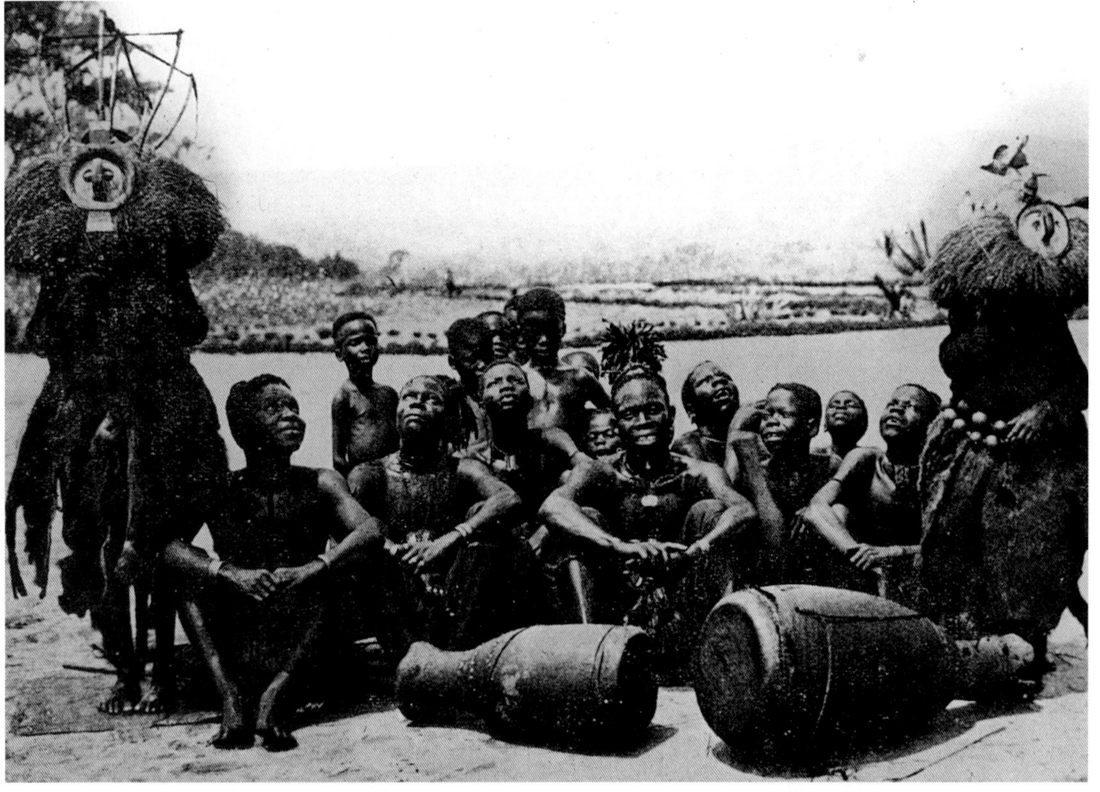

66. MASK, YAKA, ZAIRE

This mask is one of several varieties made by professional sculptors and danced in festivities marking the emergence from the circumcision camp. Essentially charms of good reception, they are worn on the head or held before the face only momentarily, almost as dance wands. The mask is of the *kholuka* variety, which commonly feature puppetry-like imagery on the coiffure. The *kholuka* mask is the most popular Yaka mask, usually worn by a particularly extroverted performer. Imagery surmounting the mask commonly features sexuality and procreation scenes expressed in both human and animal models; mammals, birds, fish and reptiles peering downward; and genre scenes of domestic dwellings, cups and containers or of Europeans or Africans in various roles and uniforms. This imagery partakes of motifs sung by the *kholuka* performer and song leaders in the coming-out festivities. In this mask, the child attempts to wrest a pipe from its mother, apparently an allusion to over-eagerness to assume adult privileges. Tear lines refer to the sufferings of initiation. Although the custom of making these masks was handed down by the elders-ancestors (*bambuta*), the face of the mask does not depict or represent anyone specific.

Painted designs in checker, triangle, camber-shaped, herringbone or cross-hatch, are commonly arranged in encircling panels. Large triangles are painted on the surface of the elevated disks, resulting in star-like configurations. The different designs do not have individual names but are collectively referred to as *bibemba bia nkanda*. Such arrangements conform to the broader classification of African cellular design. As defined by Denyer (1978:122), this is made up of two alternating, serially repeated units, one of which is the "positive" and the other its "negative" replication, one dark, the other light. APB

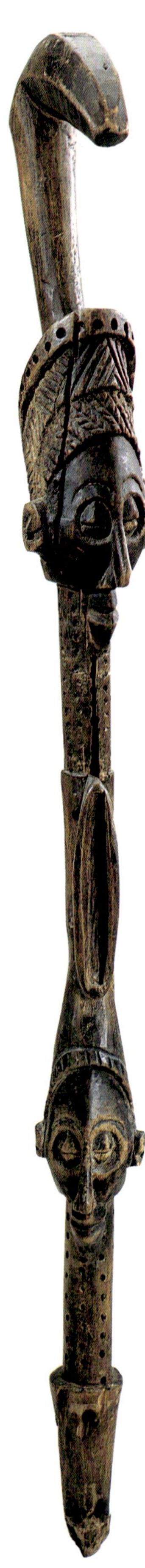

67. DIGNITARY'S STAFF, NKANU OR SOSSO, ZAIRE

The large, circular eyes and long, tapering nose of this staff relate it to several masks which have emerged from Angola over the past ten years and apparently derive from either the Nkanu or Sosso. The double heads, each with a high coiffure, a protuberance with three holes and a hooked top are, however, unique to this object.

In contemporary African political life, canes have replaced staffs as emblems of authority. This example, with its handle, appears to syncretize a standard European walking cane with the more elaborated staffs of traditional chiefs. The vertical rows of small holes likely featured brass tacks, while the extended element at the center of the staff was undoubtedly used to suspend attachments.   APB

68. CHARM CONTAINER, YAKA, ZAIRE

The Joss charm container is similar in form to the much larger *n'koko ngoombu* percussion instrument, which is part of the paraphernalia of a diviner. The head surmounting the handle appears to objectify the role of elders in mediating misfortune, sickness, and death. There is an implied reference to the powers of extravision attributed to those in authority, which enables them to see past the appearances of ordinary life into the nefarious world of envy, witch-

▼▲▼

67
DIGNITARY'S STAFF
Nkanu or Sosso, Zaire
Wood
H. 74 cm.
FMCH 86.1724

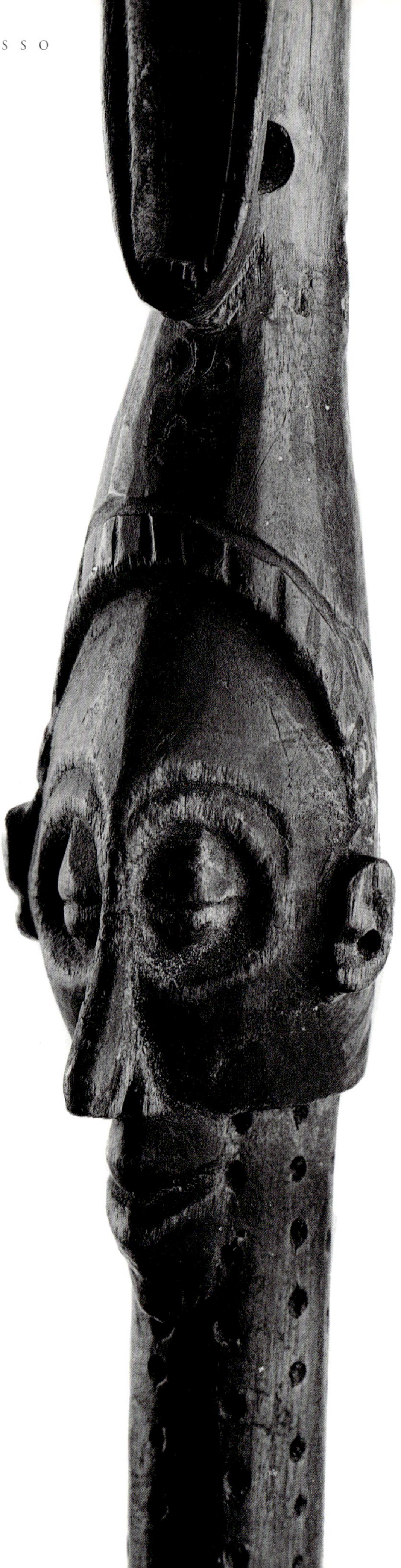

craft and sorcery. The diviner's vision is an internal vision, which is most clearly revealed only when he or she "dreams" on a given matter. The charm ingredients originally inserted in this object were determined by the needs of the maker and user. Some elements appealed to the goodwill of elders and ancestors, others asserted how and in what direction the power charge was to act, and still others had cosmological referents uniting dyadic opposites, mediatory categories, and two of the triadic colors. This bundle of charm ingredients was then triggered by appropriate verbal formulae.   APB

FIG. 40
Northern Yaka diviner
(nganga ngoombu)
Mahunda Malaku sounding
a *n-kooku* slitdrum and
wearing neck pendant
containing charm
ingredients pertaining to
diviners of the *wefwa
muyaka* and *wefwa musuku*
traditions.
Masala-Yalama village,
Bandundu, Zaire.
Photo: A. Bourgeois, 1976.

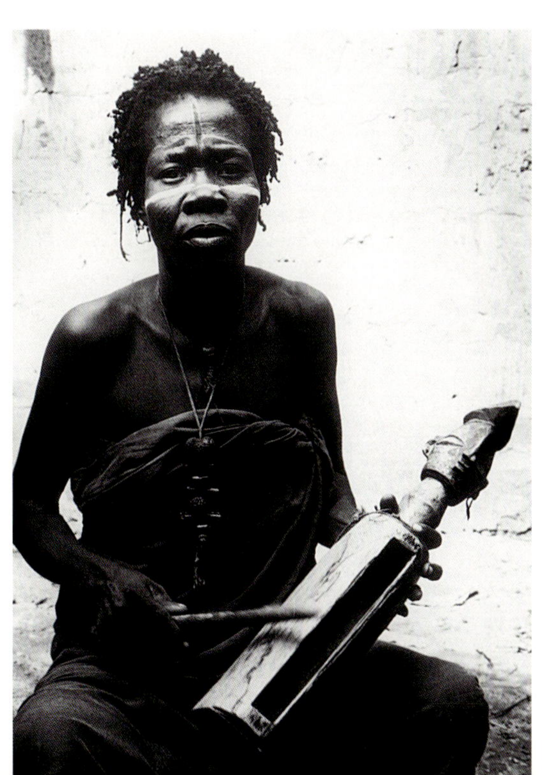

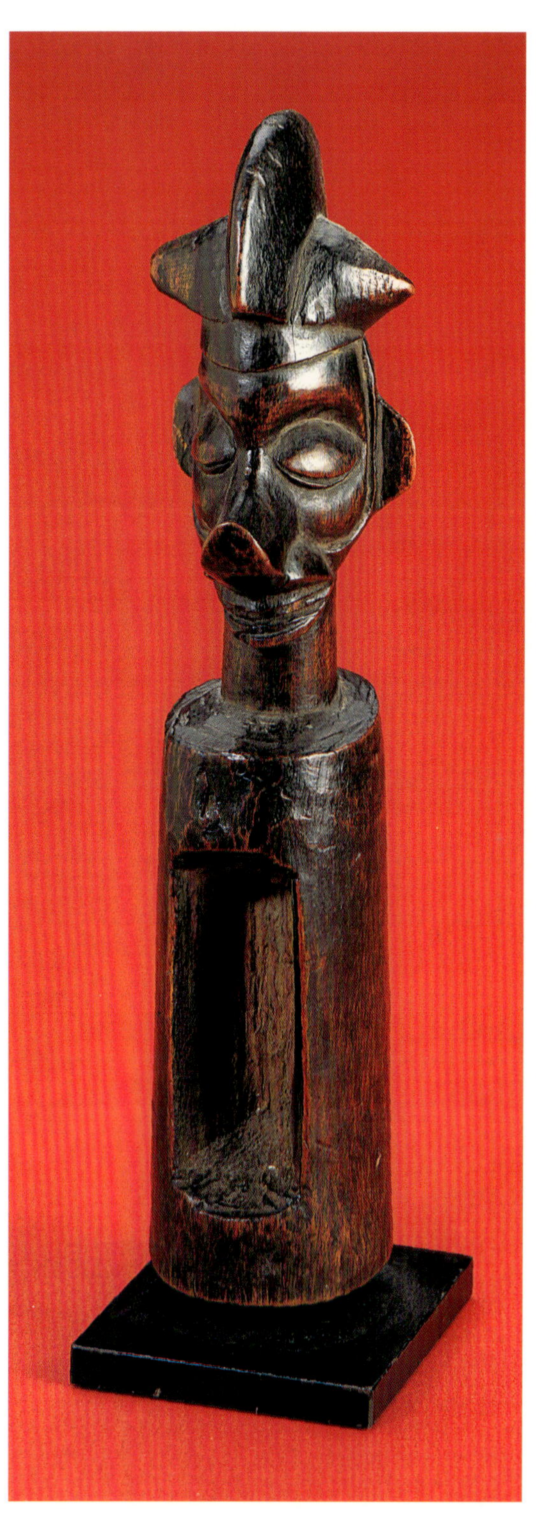

▼▲▼
68
CHARM CONTAINER
Yaka, Zaire
Wood
H. 14 cm.
FMCH 88.1025

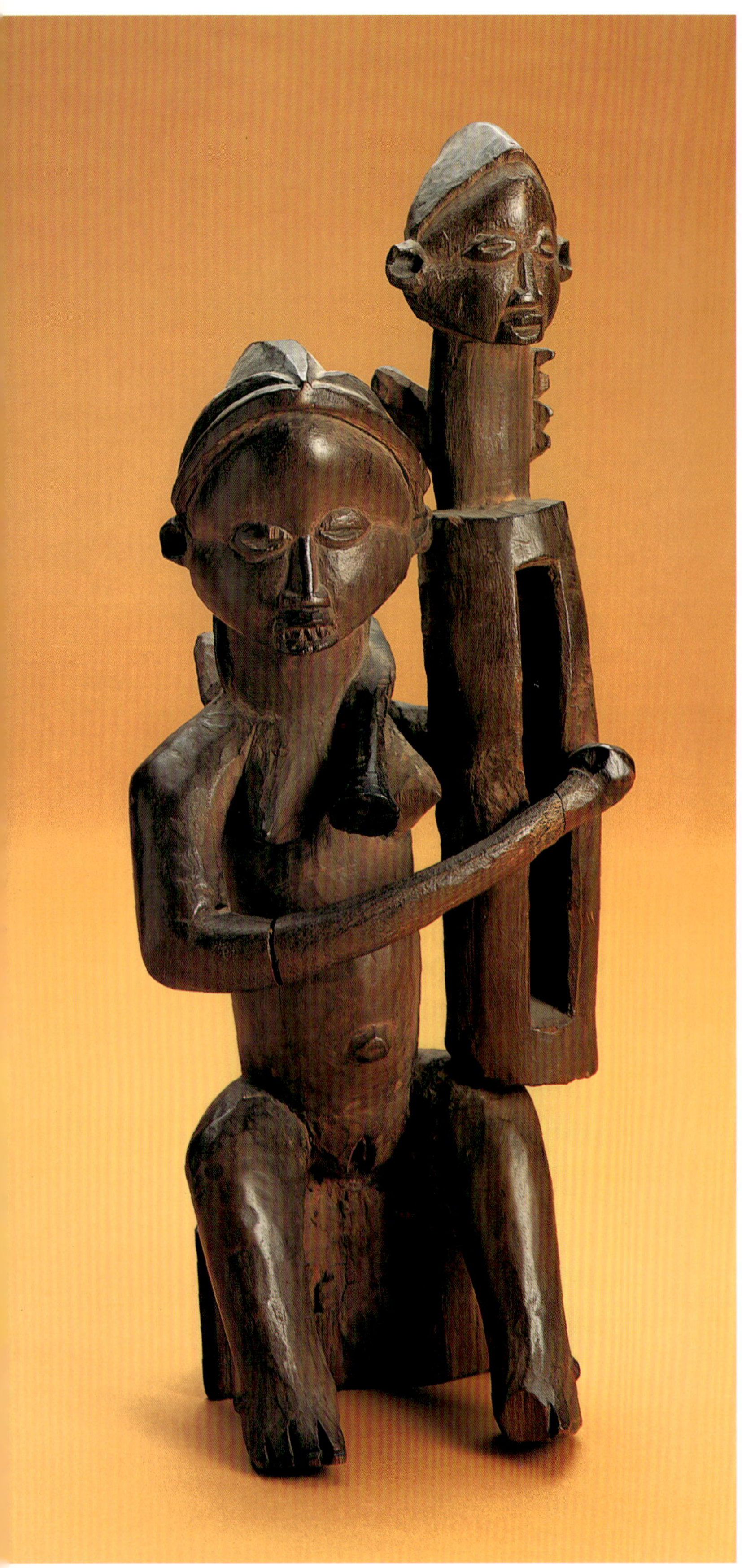

69. Charm Figure, Mbala, Zaire

Mbala wooden statuary selectively reproduced daily habits and social customs, likely as a means of symbolically concentrating and condensing Mbala life and life processes. These statues found their meaning amid the sacred regalia of the landed Mbala lineage chief, where both malevolent and protective influences were contained for collective survival and prosperity. The authority of the lineage chief embodied vital force; his justice was sought together with that of his *mukongo* tribunal, and his influence in both life and death was both feared and revered.

This figure is one of a pair of *pindi* charms invoked by a lineage chief as an official act in the event of war, great disputes, bad harvest, epidemics, lack of game or natural disaster. *Pindi* charms were also used in the performance of rites of the ascension to leadership and were associated with the bracelet of rulership. *Pindi* charms commonly were created as pairs, featuring the figure of a woman with child and the figure of a drummer.

The Joss *pindi* charm depicts a seated *ngoombu* diviner sounding a *n'koku* drum and carrying a *gaandu* adz on her left shoulder. Diviners were often called to settle disputes over succession. On the day following the death of a chief, the diviner would designate the person responsible for the death, to whom would be administered the poison oracle on the edge of the deceased chief's burial pit.

The charm figure bears an affinity to a number of well-known *pindi*. A figure of a woman with child in the Museum für Völkerkunde, Hamburg; a maternity figure formerly in the Raoul Blondiau collection; a male figure in the Jesuit Collection, Heverlee,

▼▲▼
———
69

CHARM FIGURE

(pindi)

Mbala, Zaire

Wood and

camwood powder

H. 30.5 cm.

FMCH 85.974

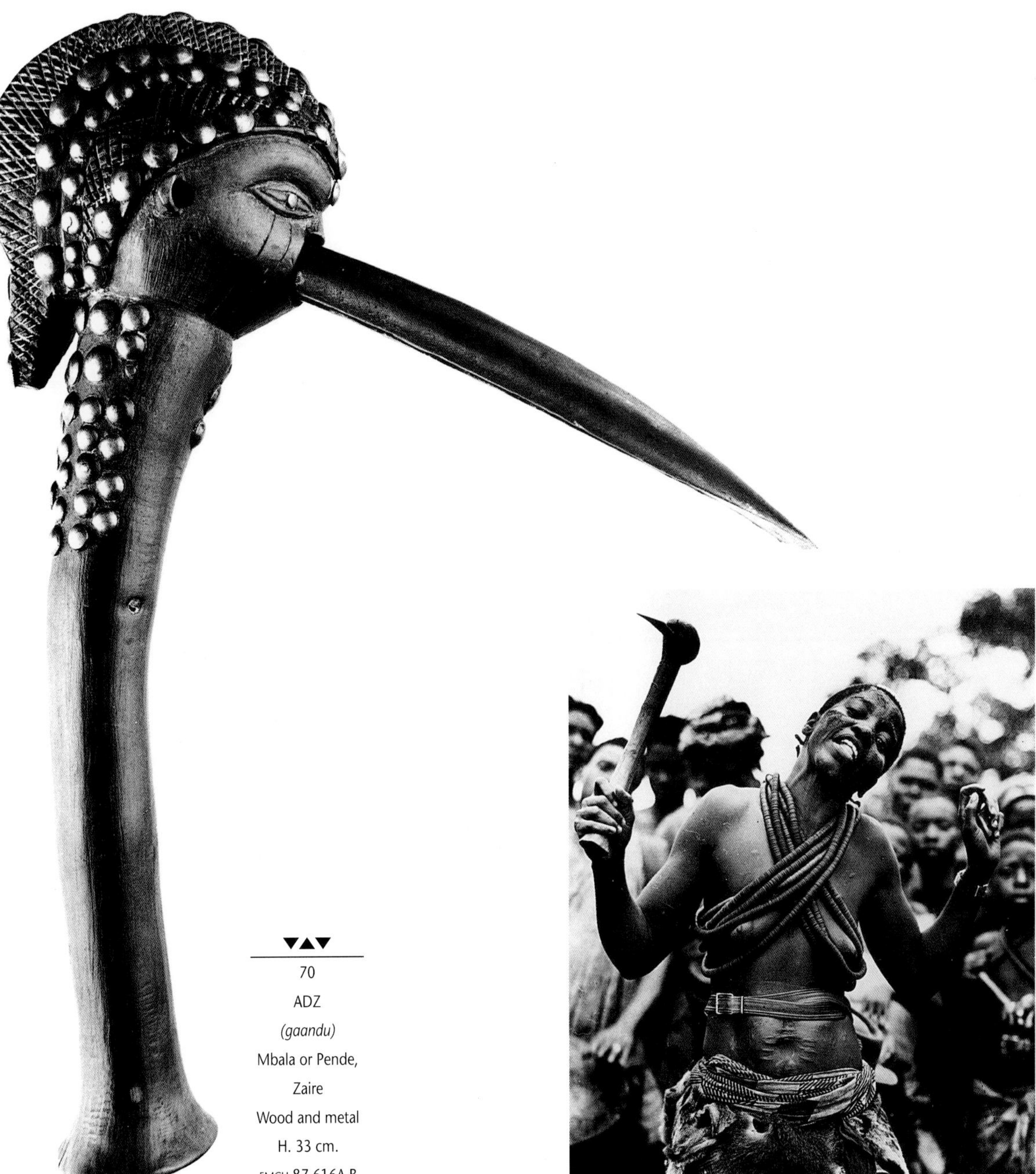

▼▲▼

70

ADZ

(gaandu)

Mbala or Pende,
Zaire

Wood and metal

H. 33 cm.

FMCH 87.616A,B

FIG. 41

Woman dancing
with adz.
Kwango, Zaire.
Photo: J. Mulders.
© Africa-Museum,
Tervuren (Belgium).

Belgium; and another at Tervuren demonstrate similarities in body stance, treatment of the stool, feet, extended eye cavity and coiffure. The stylistic uniformity of this group of *pindi* suggests that they all were carved well before 1933 in the workshop located on the Kwilu River between the towns of Lusanga and Bulungu, where the Heverlee object is known to have originated. APB

70. ADZ, MBALA OR PENDE, ZAIRE

The ensign of authority, the *gaandu* adz was carried on the left shoulder of a lineage chief or of a diviner when he visited his charges or clients. The adz, which is modeled on a standard woodworking tool used in carving mortars, drums, and statuettes, could also be used as a weapon. As an authority symbol, it refers to the diligence and determination necessary to affect future generations. In its cutting aspect, the *gaandu* is said to cut the vines needed to hold together a people. At the extremity of the handle is a carved head, from the mouth of which emerges the blade as if an extended tongue. Throughout the Kwango region this feature refers to the directives of elders and ancestors. APB

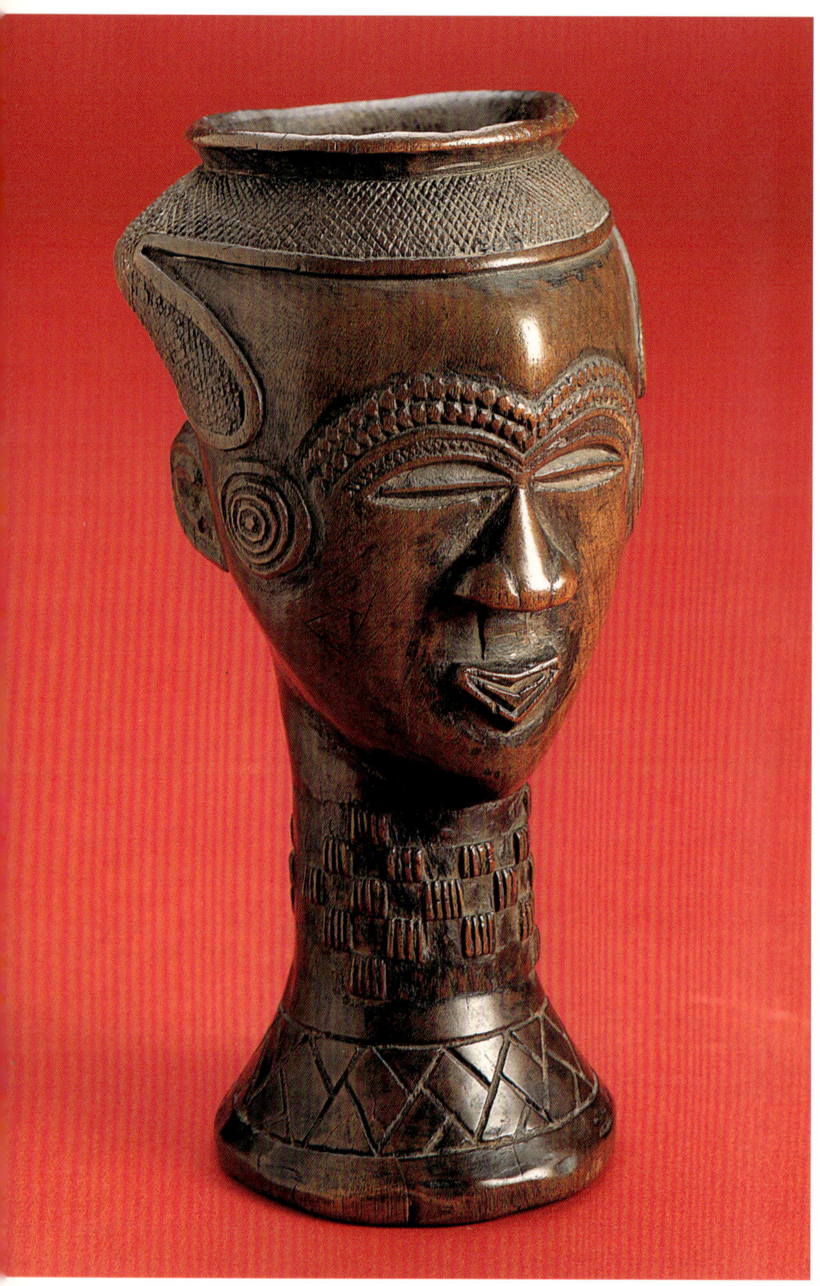

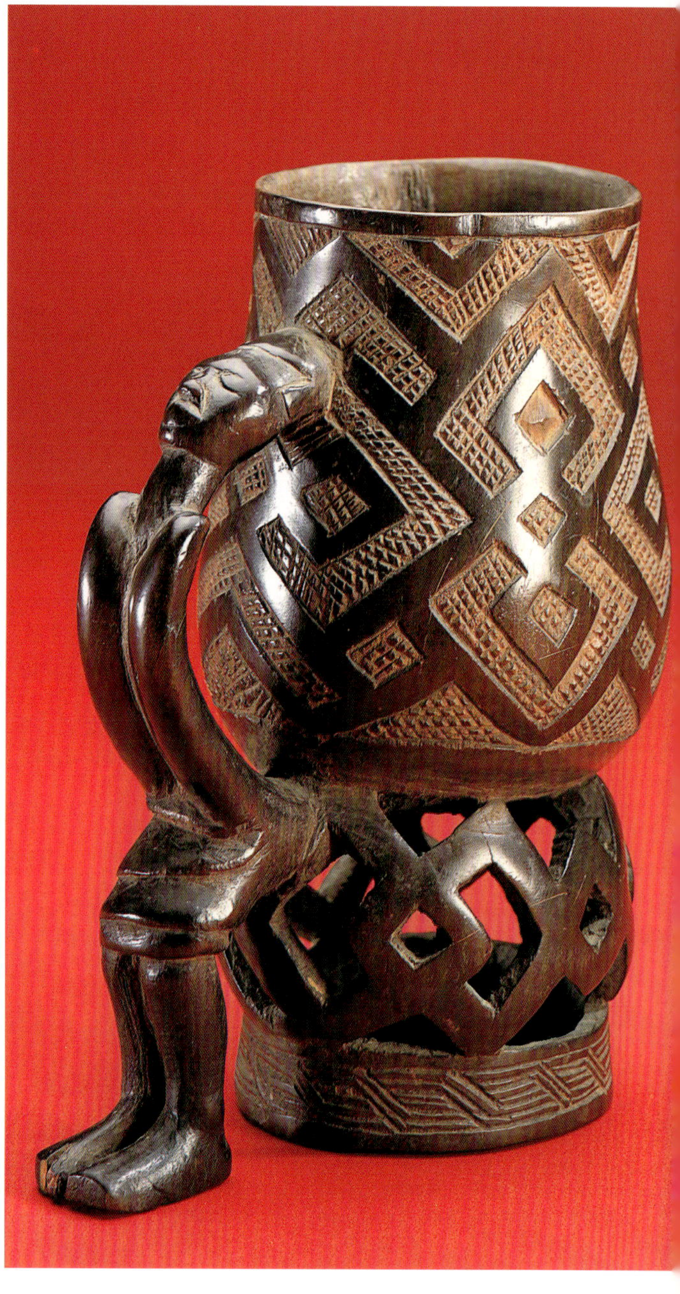

▼▲▼
71
PALM WINE CUP
Kuba, Zaire
Wood and encrustation
H. 19 cm.
FMCH 87.1435

▼▲▼
72
PALM WINE CUP
Kuba, Zaire
Wood
H. 18.5 cm.
FMCH 87.617

71, 72. Palm Wine Cups, 73. Mortar, Kuba, Zaire

Among the Kuba of south-central Zaire, utilitarian objects such as this pepper and spice mortar and palm wine cups are elaborately decorated with geometric designs, faces and human figures. Anthropomorphic designs are considered the most prestigious. This display brings personal prestige and status to the owners, suggesting their exceptional wealth and power. Among the Kuba, an individual's status is based on two factors: clan affiliation and possession of title. Being born into a powerful or royal clan can be a distinct advantage, giving an individual the ability to draw on shared clan resources and influence to buy an important title and to advance his own reputation and thus the reputation of his clan. Most titles are bought, although they are also given by the king as a reward. The title, in return, becomes a source of income (Vansina 1968:15). Each man or woman can only hold one title, so that once a title is obtained, elevation of status is achieved by increasing the importance of the title (Mack 1980:171).

The cups and mortar are individually designed and the decorations include human faces and figures. The faces on the cups may be stylized portraits of the owners, who may be identified through status symbols such as the neck collar (FMCH 87.1435) and medicinal scarification on the cheek (Vansina 1981:232). The motif on the mortar of a head going directly into a single leg and foot is well known among the Kuba as a pun on the "foot of the palm wine cup" (Vansina 1981:231).

The two carved cups are for drinking palm wine. Old stories tell how there was a lake filled with palm wine out of which everyone drank. A woman polluted it, and when people refused to drink, the lake dried up and palm trees grew in the lake bed. A pygmy tasted the sap of the tree, discovered the palm wine and became drunk (Torday 1925:125-27; Torday and Joyce 1910:235-36). Since then, palm wine is never to be drunk alone (de Heusch 1982:178). Rather, it is shared among friends, usually from a common cup such as these, which is supplied by the host. The host displays his carved cup and passes it; each man in turn holds the cup, drinks, and passes it

along. In this way the status of the host is reinforced as each guest handles the elaborate cup. Carved cups have been replaced in modern Zaire by plastic ones as old cups are sold and new status symbols such as bicycles flourish.

ELISABETH L. CAMERON

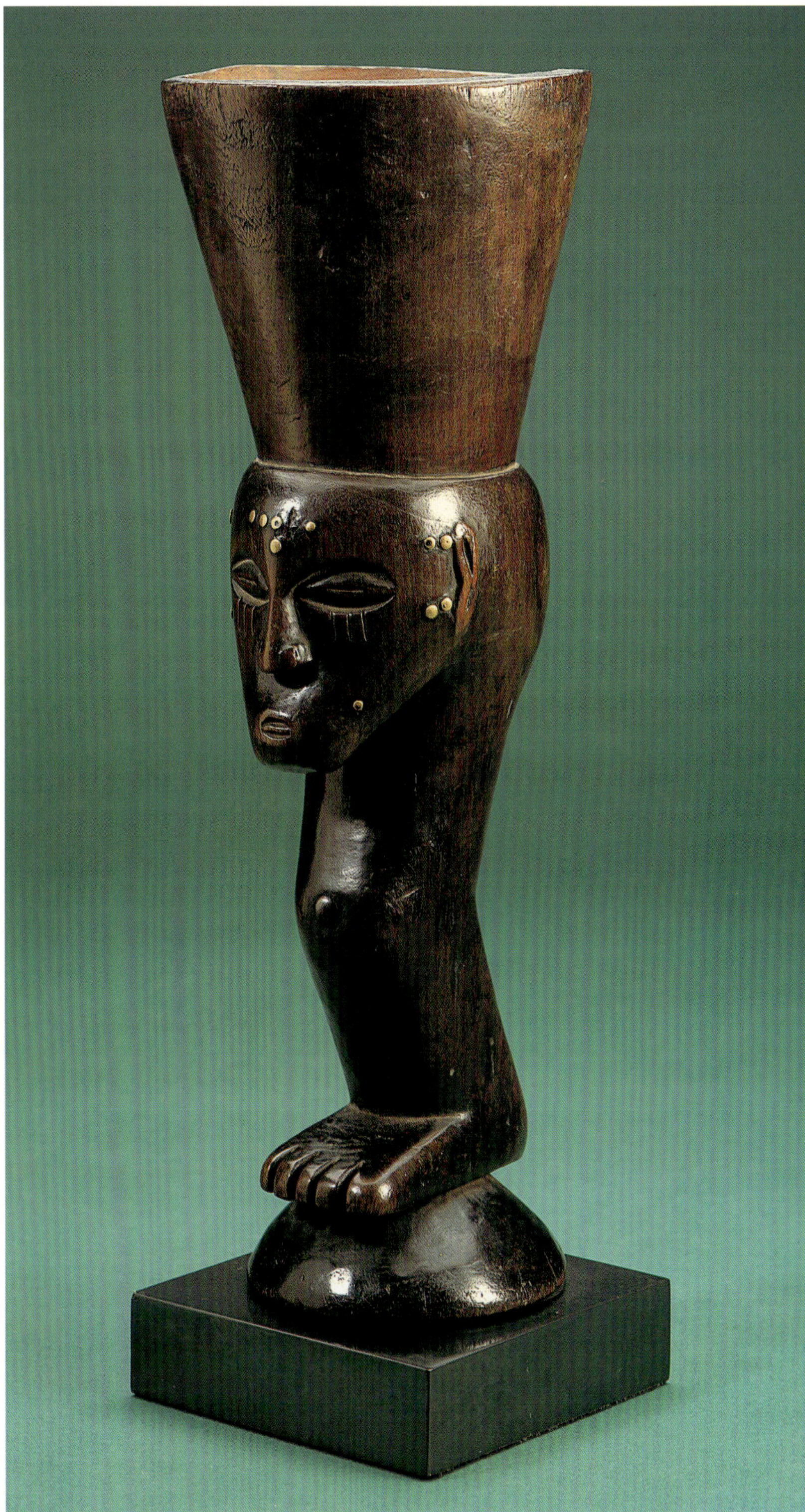

▾▲▾

73
MORTAR
Kuba, Zaire
Wood and tacks
H. 31 cm.
FMCH 92.9

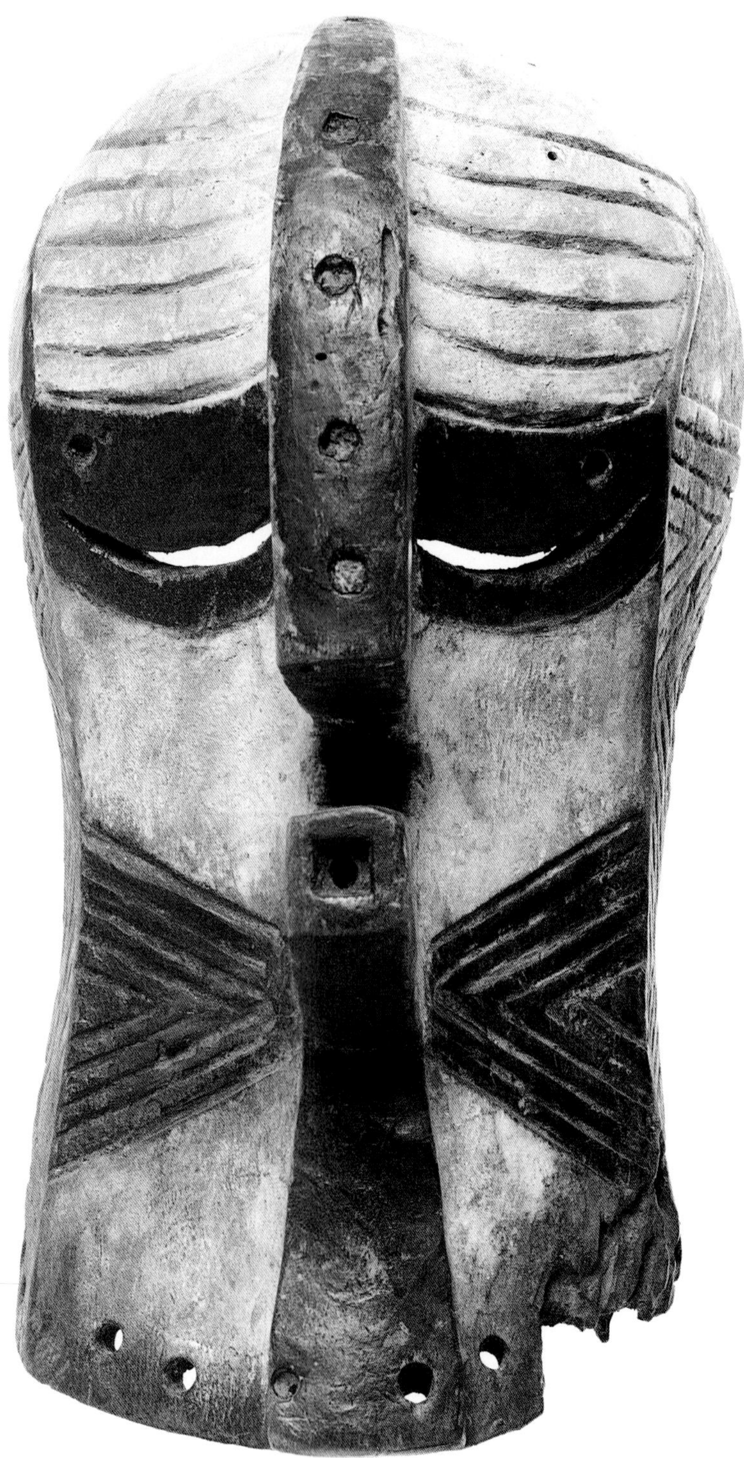

▼▲▼

74

MASK

(kifwebe)

Luba,

Shaba Province,

Zaire

Wood, fiber,

pigment

and kaolin

H. 35 cm.

fmch 87.1413

74. MASK, LUBA, SHABA PROVINCE, ZAIRE

Bifwebe (singular, *kifwebe*) have been used since at least the early twentieth century by initiatory associations of the Songye and Luba peoples of Zaire. This example is clearly Luba, resembling works collected during the early 1970s in the area of Kabalo (Shaba Province) by the Institut des Musées Nationaux, Kinshasa. The facial planes of these masks are flatter, and the crest, eyes and mouth are far less voluminous and protuberant than those of the highly geometric Songye pieces.

Each *kifwebe* society of the Songye and Luba is comprised of two types of maskers: one female and numerous males (Hersak 1986:38; Wenga-Mulayi 1974:77). The Songye traditionally use color to distinguish sex; female masks are predominantly white and male masks, which are similar in form, have red, white and black striations and salient crests. The Luba, however, do not distinguish sex with color. Most Luba masks, both male and female, are black and white, although recently the details of some have been highlighted by red and even orange and green (Wenga-Mulayi 1974:71). Black, which is often used for the nose-forehead extension and for the vertical strip below the mouth, has an active, protective function appropriate for power objects. White is associated with the spirits of the dead who are incarnated by the masker (Wenga-Mulayi 1974:110). In the past, Luba differentiated gender by facial form rather than color. Female masks were round and substantially larger in size; male masks tended to resemble those of the Songye (Colle 1913:440; Wenga-Mulaye 1974:76). Oblong shapes have recently come into use for both genders, and scarification markings (geometric and figurative) placed directly under the eyes have begun to be used as the main indicators

distinguishing female masks from their male counterparts (Wenga-Mulayi 1974:75).

The absence of facial markings on this mask provides the most convincing evidence that it is male. Another feature in support of this identification is the presence of broadly spaced incisions confined only to the forehead. Although the Luba claim that all *bifwebe* must be entirely covered by grooved, linear striations (*mpongo*), which represent the underworld abode of the founding spirits of the society (Wenga-Mulayi 1974:109-110), there are numerous examples like this one on which the lines appear only on parts of the face. Wenga-Mulayi associated the broadly spaced lines incised on the forehead of a male mask known as Matembo (wasp) with its ferocity (Wenga-Mulayi 1974:53).

Kifwebe masking probably originated in an area of admixture between the Songye and Luba, although both peoples claim that the *bifwebe* originated among the neighboring group and that they speak Kisongye or Kiluba respectively. With the diffusion of the society, substantial differences in iconography, symbolism and contextual use of masks developed among the Songye and Luba (Hersak 1986:42). Yet both groups maintain that the masker's source of power is *masende/majende*, or malevolent magical practice (Hersak 1986:37, 38; Wenga-Mulayi 1974:147). Among the Songye the use of this potent magic is more pronounced in the political power play and regulatory function of the maskers. Among the Luba it seems to be veiled by an association with the world of the ancestors and with cults such as *bukasanji* and *kyeusi*, which are concerned with the expulsion of evil spirits and sorcerers and, in the latter case, also with therapeutic matters (Wenga-Mulayi 1974:32, 34).

DUNJA HERSAK

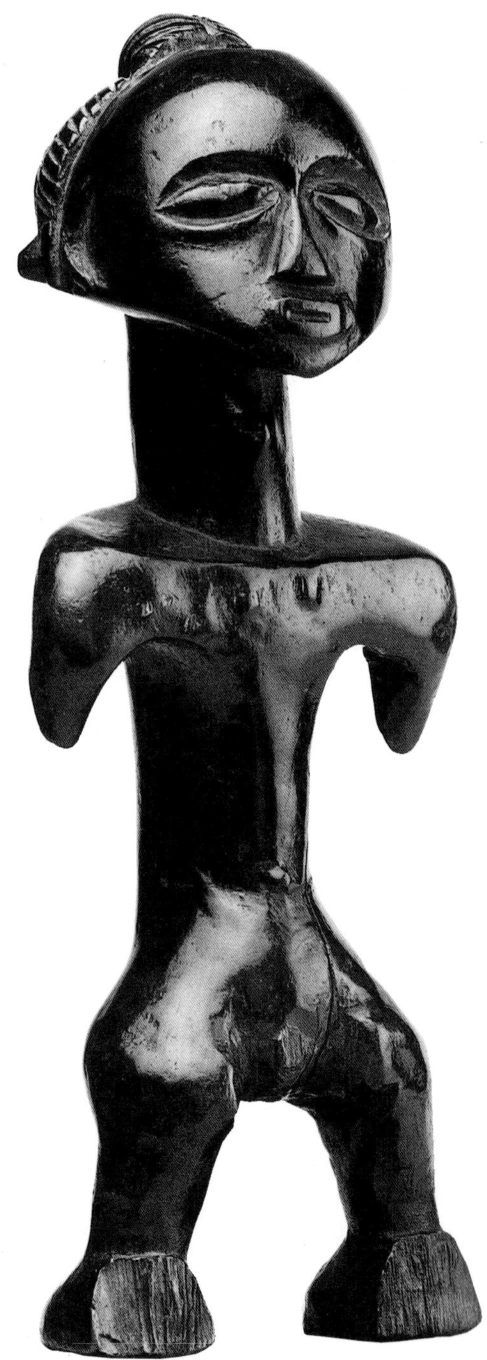

75. STANDING MALE FIGURE, LUBA, ZAIRE

This standing male figure, which was collected without documentation, is most certainly from the Luba world, although beyond the heartland, in a stylistic niche bordering the Luba-Shaba and the Luba-Kasai. The Luba of Kasai emigrated west from the Luba heartland in progressive waves during the eighteenth century, when the Luba kingdom was at the height of its expansion and certain chiefs either fled or were expelled from the kingdom. Sculptures emanating from this zone of cultural movement and resettlement reflect a complex superimposition of styles and influences on a recognizable Luba foundation (Felix 1987:82).

The coiffure of this figure recalls sculptures from Kabongo, the former royal capital of the Luba-Shaba kingdom. Yet, its male gender, lack of scarification, and ready stance indicate a provenance further west than Kabongo. The mouth has the rectangular precision of figures from the north-west Luba and southern Songye. The shelf-like plane of the shoulders, the long trunk-like neck, and the articulated Adam's apple occur in sculpture from the western Luba sector. The figure's small scale, quiet demeanor, and smooth, polished surface suggest that the figure might have been used for the remembrance and loving worship of a family ancestor.   MARY H. NOOTER

76. IVORY PENDANT, LUBA, ZAIRE

Luba ivory pendants represent ancestral spirits. As such, they belong to a broad category of Luba sculpture called *mikisi mihasi* (Colle 1913:435). The miniature figures are portraits, or at least likenesses, and are named and honored in the memory of certain revered ancestors. Sculpted from ivory, as well as

from bone and horn, these delicate diminutive figures are suspended from bandoliers together with
other objects, including amulets, beads and horns.
The bandoliers are worn diagonally across the torso
or may be attached to the arm. Devotees anoint the
figures with oil in homage to the ancestors. Such
treatments, together with regular handling and con-
tact with the human body, give the figures a smooth,
lustrous surface and a rich, caramel color ranging
from yellowish-brown to auburn. The figures also are
sometimes attached to the top of scepters carried by
chiefs.

Luba ivories were widely collected during the
nineteenth century and are now represented in large
numbers in museum and private collections.
Although each figure is slightly different in details of
form and iconography, all share a minimalist conception of the human form. The Joss pendant empha-
sizes head and torso to the total exclusion of the legs.
The gesture of the hands on the breasts signifies
devotion, respect, and according to some Luba
spokespersons, the containment of royal secrets
(Nooter 1990:43). Large, demure eyes dominate the
head, which inclines along the natural curve of the
ivory. The artist's careful attention to detail is evident
in the description of the coiffure and scarification.
The scarifications have been rendered generically as
incised circles, except for two sets of large, raised
swellings on the figure's abdomen, identifiable as
milalo. All Luba scarifications are named and each
serves a particular purpose. *Milalo* are considered to
be particularly erotic and beautiful, and in the past
all women were expected to have these marks of fem-
ininity and Luba social identity (Nooter 1991:244-
247).   MHN

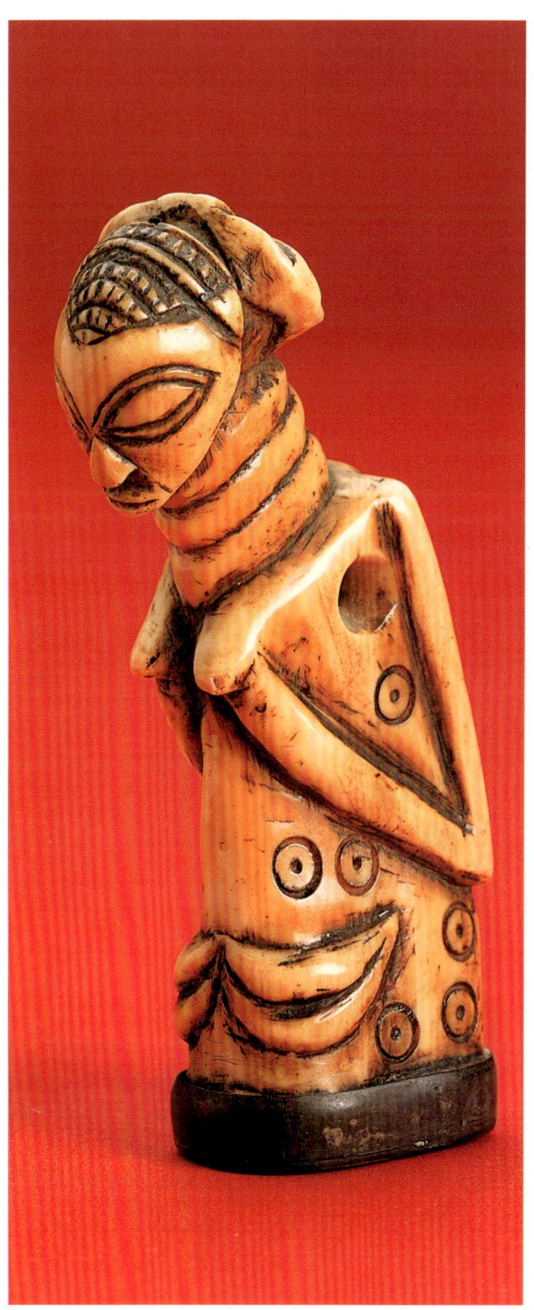

76
IVORY PENDANT
(mikisi mihasi)
Luba, Zaire
Hippopotamus tooth
L. 10 cm.
FMCH 87.1321

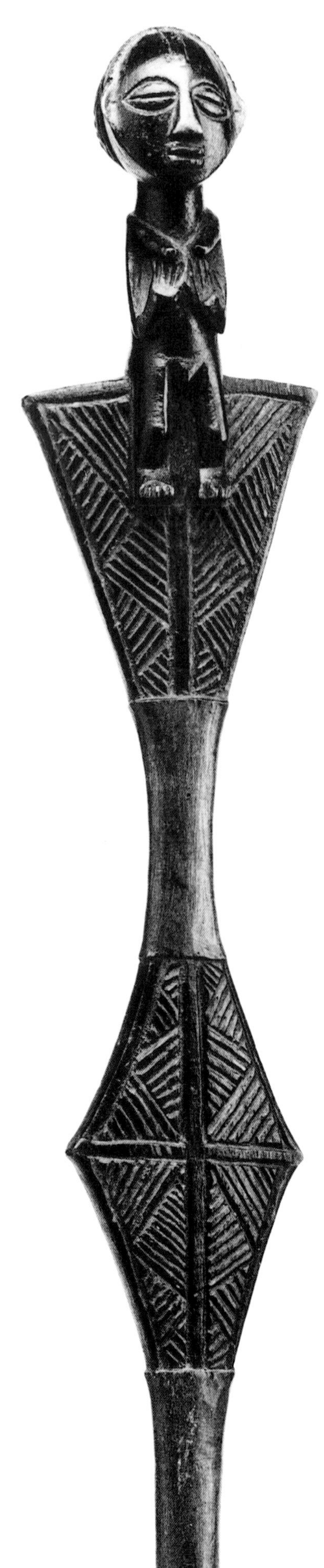

77. STAFF OF OFFICE, LUBA, ZAIRE

A small figure seated aloft the top of the staff quietly affirms the power of its owner. Staffs are among the key items associated with Luba chieftaincy, although they may also belong to titleholders and territorial governors. In addition to enhancing and extending the visual presence of a ruler (Fraser and Cole 1972:concluding chapter), the staff is a multi-purpose object. As a historical document, in the past staffs were planted in battlefields to signify victory. Staffs were also offered as payment to the ferrymen who controlled important river crossings and brought as gifts by emissaries from the Luba kingdom to cement alliances with foreign chiefdoms (Reefe 1981). Staffs that contained medicinal substances were used to cure illness.

Luba staffs also function as memory devices (Nooter 1991:162-173). Through their forms and designs, staffs help their owners to remember historical and geographical facts. Staffs delineate the lands under their owners' jurisdiction and the natural resources of those lands; they record how particular chieftaincies were incorporated into the Luba kingdom and the genealogical histories of royal families; and finally, they help to recall the various tutelary spirits associated with prominent chiefdoms and the locales of those spirits. The ability to elicit so much information makes Luba staffs effective tools for transmitting knowledge from chiefs to their successors, generation after generation. Staffs were still being made for use in the late 1980s and were used by chiefs and some dignitaries. The iconography of these sculptures has, however, been modified to accommodate changing ideologies.

The carving style suggests that this staff was probably created in the early to mid-twentieth-century. While following the canon of nineteenth-century examples, the staff is distinguished from these by the omission of copper around the central shaft and the uninterrupted curving silhouette that joins the two broad sections of the staff. The long, bare shaft of a staff generally represents the savanna, while the broad, patterned sections depict centers of

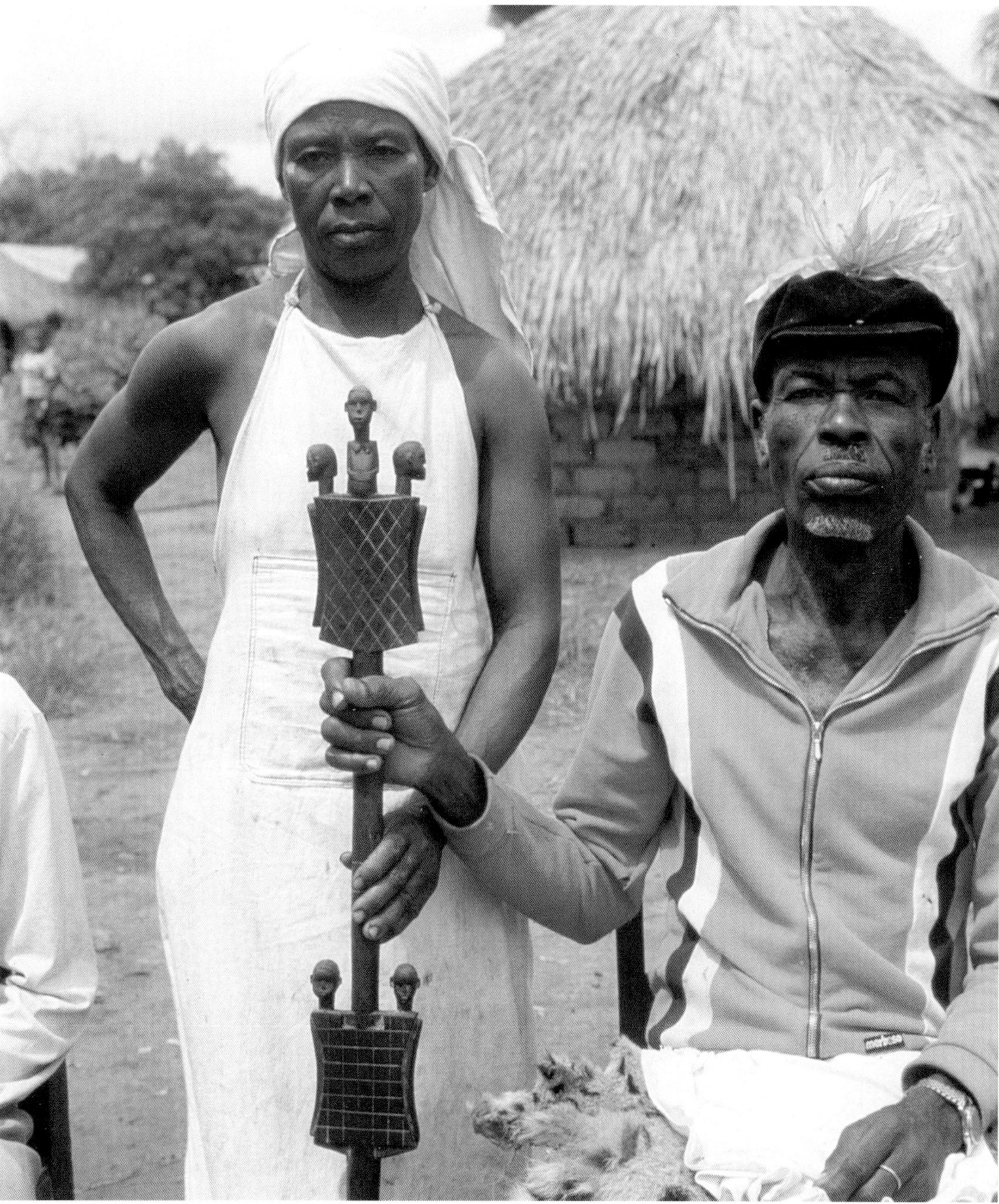

political organization and social order. Incised geometric patterns adorn the broad sections of staffs. Referred to as "scarification patterns," they both beautify the staff and contain the *bizila*, or secret taboos associated with Luba royalty. It is these more concealed dimensions of Luba power, encoded in the staff's abstract designs, that empower the owners of such emblems and enable them to perform supernatural feats.

The sculpted human figures adorning Luba staffs are less essential than the geometric patterns. In one case, a staff owner described the female figure atop his staff as a symbolic representation of the king himself (Nooter 1990:42). Seemingly female, but partially male, the figure bespeaks the ambiguous gendering of the authority of Luba kings. For, although kings are men, they derive much of their power from their mothers, wives, and sisters, and when they die, Luba kings are reincarnated as female priestesses.   MHN

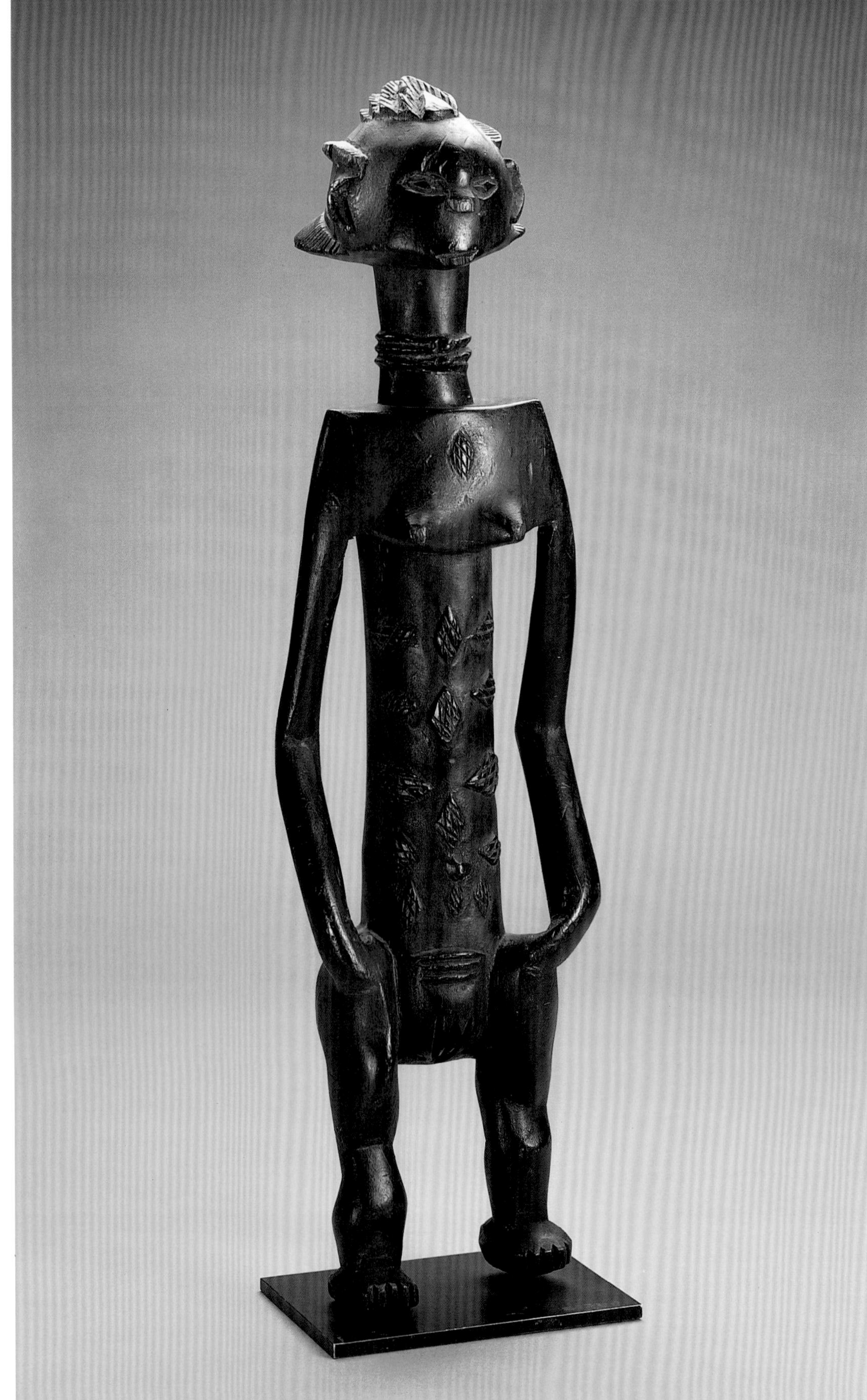

78
STANDING
FEMALE FIGURE
Luba, Zaire
Wood
H. 55 cm.
FMCH 87.1412

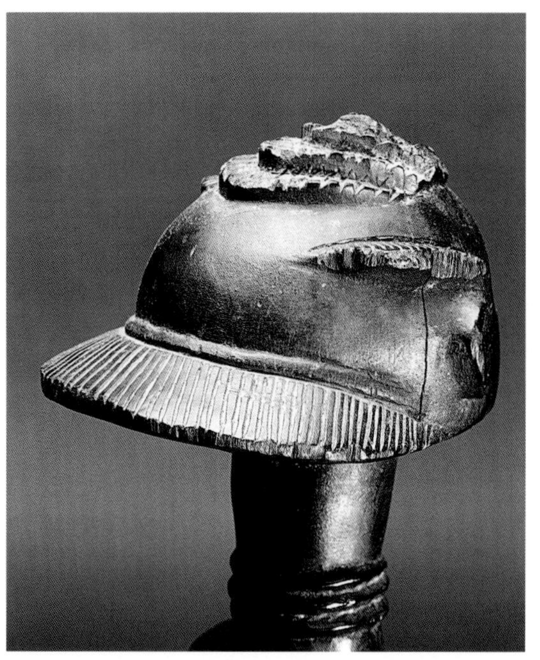

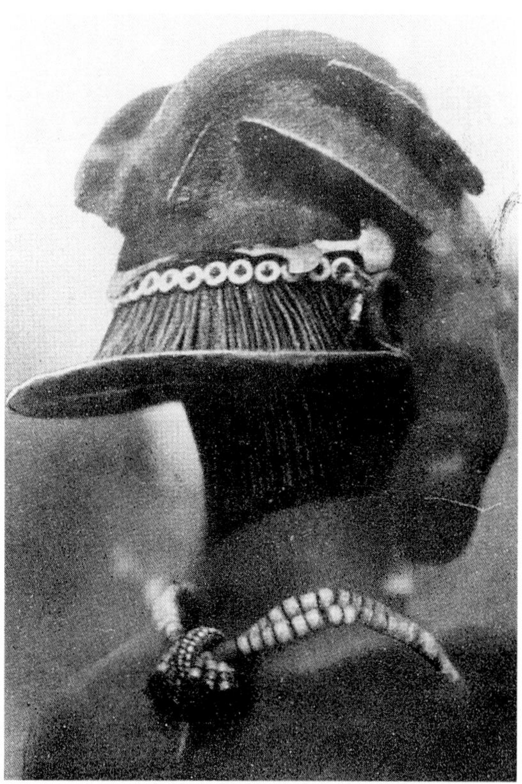

78. STANDING FEMALE FIGURE, LUBA, ZAIRE

The angular, attenuated limbs, cascading fan-shaped coiffure, and small, pinched features of this standing female figure are hallmarks of a Luba art style attributed to towns and villages along the shore of Lake Kisale in the collective of Kinkondja. Sometimes called "Shankadi" by historians of African art (de Maret et al. 1977), this stylized approach to the human form is distinguished from the more fully rounded and naturalistic approach of Luba communities to the east.

The precise context in which this figure was used is impossible to ascertain, since free-standing figures are not restricted to any single domain. They may be used for divination, or as part of a chief's royal treasury, or for religious veneration and invocation. The absence of additions to the figure in the form of medicinal substances and other powerful ingredients suggests that the figure may have been used for ancestral commemoration or as a protective guardian.

The arms of most Luba female figures gesture to their breasts, but the arms of this figure hang astride the long torso, hands meeting the angular hips in an inverted configuration. Shankadi figures are carved from a single piece of wood, but often portray the head, neck, chest, torso, and limbs as discrete volumes. Here, the long, columnar neck is coquettishly ringed by a three-stranded necklace, and the torso displays the widely-spaced, diamond-shaped scarification (*ntapo*) characteristic of this style of Luba sculpture and intended to beautify as well as to affirm social identity. According to Albert Maesen (pers. comm. 1988), the type of hairstyle depicted on this sculpture is called *mikanda*, meaning "steps" or "cascade". The regional origins of this coiffure are unknown. However, a number of late nineteenth- and early twentieth-century photographs show Luba women wearing variations of this style, which appears on many Luba figures.   MHN

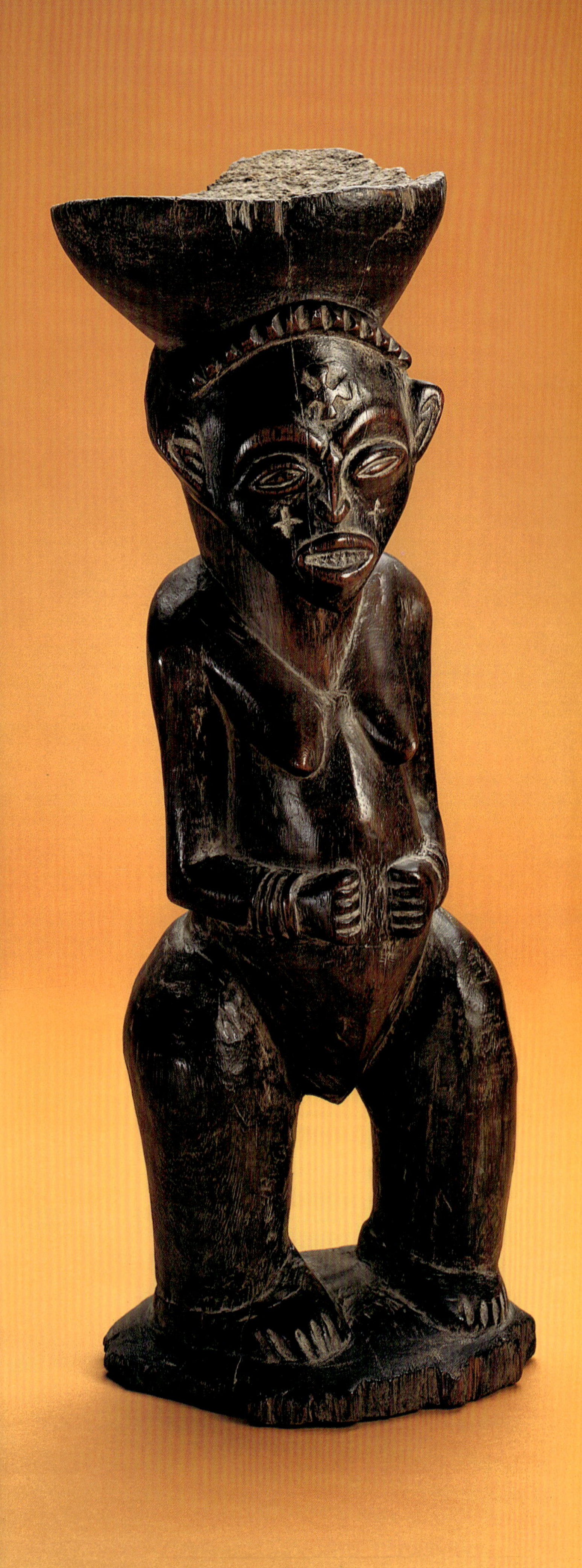

79
MORTAR WITH
FEMALE FIGURE
Kanyok (?), Zaire
Wood
H. 44 cm.
FMCH 87.1449

79. MORTAR WITH FEMALE FIGURE, KANYOK (?), ZAIRE

Certain stylistic characteristics of the female figure of this unique caryatid mortar suggest an attribution to the Kanyok. The Kanyok, who are related to the Luba, live between the Kalundwe and the Mbuji-mayi Rivers, and the Southern Kete. The cruciform scarification represented in relief on the forehead of the figure is borrowed from the Chokwe but is also used by other peoples of the Kasai: the Southern Kete and the Nsapo Nsapo, a group of Songye origin living among the central Lulua.

Kanyok sculpture has not yet been studied in depth, but Frans M. Olbrechts (1946, 1959:78-79) has classified it as part of the great Luba stylistic complex. He has observed a resemblance in the motifs and style of the objects, an influence which could have come from the Chokwe, because of the predilection for the representation of genre subjects. The most remarkable characteristics for Olbrechts were the lengthening of limbs, the oval face with lowered eyes and the hairstyle composed of two small spherical buns at the nape of the neck. Benefiting from Albert Maesen's unpublished information, Joseph Cornet (1972:236-237) subsequently reported that Olbrechts' definition applies overall to the manner of a specific master and his workshop who worked during the end of the nineteenth century in the Kanda Kanda region; but he noted that a more traditional manner of plastic expression also existed among the Kanyok. The opulence of the feminine forms and the vivacious look of the large, open eyes of the caryatid stool preserved in Tervuren (MRAC RG. 23478 [1919]; Gillon 1979:figs. 164 and 165) support the presumed attribution of this mortar to the Kanyok. MARIE-LOUISE BASTIN

80. MASK, TUKONGO (KONGO-DINGA)

The style of this copper covered wooden mask suggests that it was collected among the Kongo-Dinga, a people who call themselves Tukongo (Ceyssens 1984:33,34) and are closely related to the Lwalwa (Neyt 1981:201). Both groups live in the Western Kasai Province of Zaire: the Kongo-Dinga occupy high grasslands on the western bank of the upper Kasai or Kasai-Luka River in Angola as well as Zaire; and the Lwalwa live on similar terrain directly opposite them on the eastern bank of the river. The Chokwe are their southern neighbors, while the Lunda Kingdom is to the southeast.

For an unspecified period of time, the upper Kasai has attracted small, extremely independent groups like the Tukongo, who have resisted any type of centralized authority. Although the Tukongo slowly succumbed to domination by the more tightly organized Lunda and European powers between 1875 and 1925 (Ceyssens 1984:23), individual communities maintained objects and rituals emphasizing their indigenous ownership of the land.

Copper, a rare and bright metal mined throughout much of central Africa, was reserved among the Lunda for those who possessed political authority. It was rare, expensive and very difficult for small communities to obtain. Yet, the Kongo-Dinga fashioned extremely important masks known as *Ngongo Munene* from pure, beaten copper, symbolizing autocthonic powers that could never be transferred to outsiders (Bastin 1961:figs. 3-7; Neyt 1981:202-207, fig. X3). Copper masks of various types have also been used by the Tukongo at the installations and funerals of chiefs and have been considered essential to counter droughts, epidemics and other calamities. The significance of copper-covered wooden masks like this example may be linked to this Tukongo concept of indigenous ownership and ancestral protection (see Neyt 1981:204, 207, fig. X3).

BARBARA W. BLACKMUN

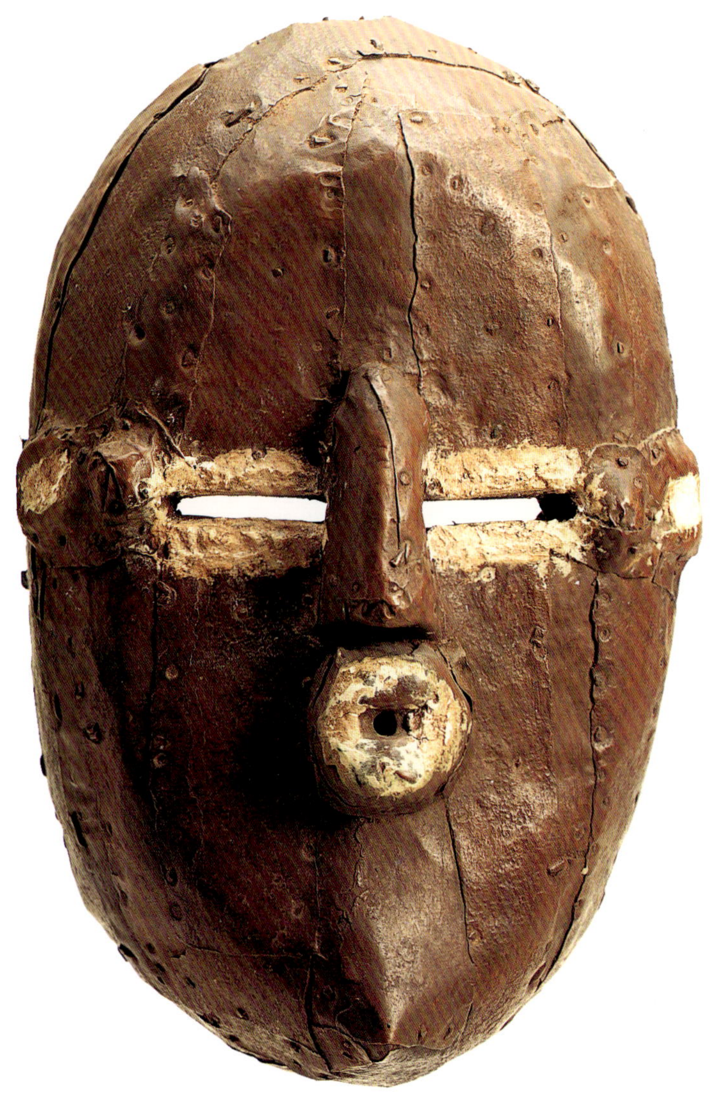

▼▲▼
80
MASK
Tukongo (Kongo-Dinga)
Wood, copper, cord,
pigment and nails
H. 30.5
FMCH 88.965

81. STAFF WITH FEMALE FIGURE, CHOKWE, ANGOLA

The finesse with which the female figure decorating the top of this Chokwe staff was sculpted and the particularity with which the eyes were represented with an encrustation of metal are rarely observed on this type of object but are common in ancient statuary. This seems to suggest that the origin of this piece was Angola, as early as the end of the nineteenth century. No collected example shows the use of this technique on objects executed after this time, when the Chokwe expanded into today's southern Zaire.

According to the Chokwe, the *mbweci* staff was commonly used by men during their journeys, giving them at once both countenance and prestige. The staff is frequently decorated by a female image, evoking the owner's ancestor, who was responsible for protection. The figure of this staff is represented seated, the elbows at the knees, the hands carried to the breasts, a gesture connoting fecundity. In the art of the Chokwe, this pose is rare. The sculpture of the face is particularly carefully done and the physiognomical details are rendered along the traditional stylistic canon. The signs of ethnic membership are represented by the minute reproduction of scarification on the forehead and cheeks; the half-open mouth reveals teeth filed to a point. The imposing

hairstyle is in reality built up of multiple small plaits of hair coated with a mixture of red clay and castor oil. Here it is characteristically parted in the middle and stylistically represented by interlaced curved lines. Metal wires ornament the neck, the wrists and the ankles. Some brass nails, originally introduced to Chokwe country by the commercial European caravans during the middle of the eighteenth century, add sparkle to this exquisitely original object.

MARIE-LOUISE BASTIN

82. CEREMONIAL AX WITH MALE AND FEMALE FIGURES, UPPER ZAMBEZI REGION, ANGOLA OR ZAMBIA

The long, curved spur of the ax head, etched with fine, geometric designs and crossing through the top of the handle, identifies the origin of this ax as the upper Zambezi region, a meeting place of Zambian and Angolan peoples. The head of the ax is similar to those of two axes preserved in the Museum Municipal Santos Rocha in Figueira da Foz, Portugal (nos. 3190 and 3191) since at least the beginning of this century. The 1905 catalogue of that museum identified no. 3190 with "Zambezia." The handles of both the Santos Rocha axes ornamented with fine, brass wire braid, a greatly honored technique in this cultural region. A similar decorative ax with a spurred head of sinuous form and a handle with finely braided brass wire has been identified as Shona (Zirngibl 1983:fig. 159). The zigzag motives used to decorate the tip of the handle of this ax are also occasionally observed on certain headrests of the Shona, but are more frequently found in the ornamentation of complexly stylized Chokwe objects.

Identification of this ax with the Shona is doubtful primarily because they do not represent humans in their work. A unique feature of the ax is the two small figures sculpted in high relief to represent a male and female standing back to back under the ax head. The masculine figure appears to represent a soldier giving a military salute with his right hand,

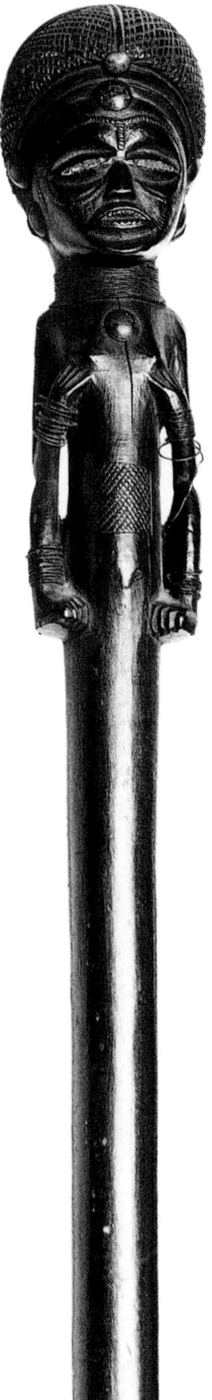

81

STAFF WITH

FEMALE FIGURE

(mbweci)

Chokwe, Angola

Wood and metal

H. 81.3 cm.

FMCH 87.1501

which is raised to a cylindrical headdress decorated
with the inverted image of a bird with spread wings.
A rectangular cartridge pouch appears in front of a
belt, and what appears to be a powder bulb hangs
from a shoulder strap on the right side. The eyes and
ears are masked by the edge of the headdress. A
pointed nose and a slit mouth are accompanied on
each cheek by oblique linear scarifications. The same
economy of resources also presides in the representation of physiognomic traits in the female figure,
whose two ears are represented by curiously circular
rims, well disengaged from the hairstyle, which is
composed of vertical plaits. The most remarkable
characteristic of the female sculpture is her ample
bosom.   MLB

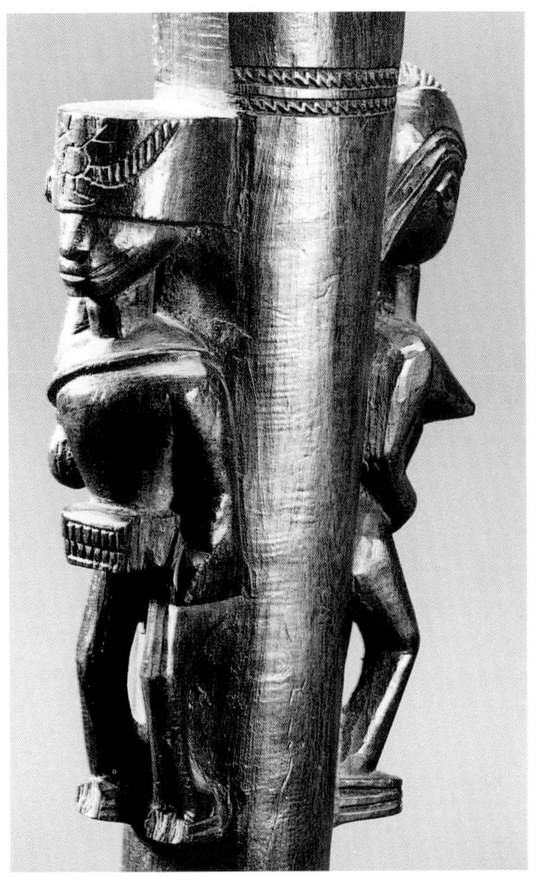

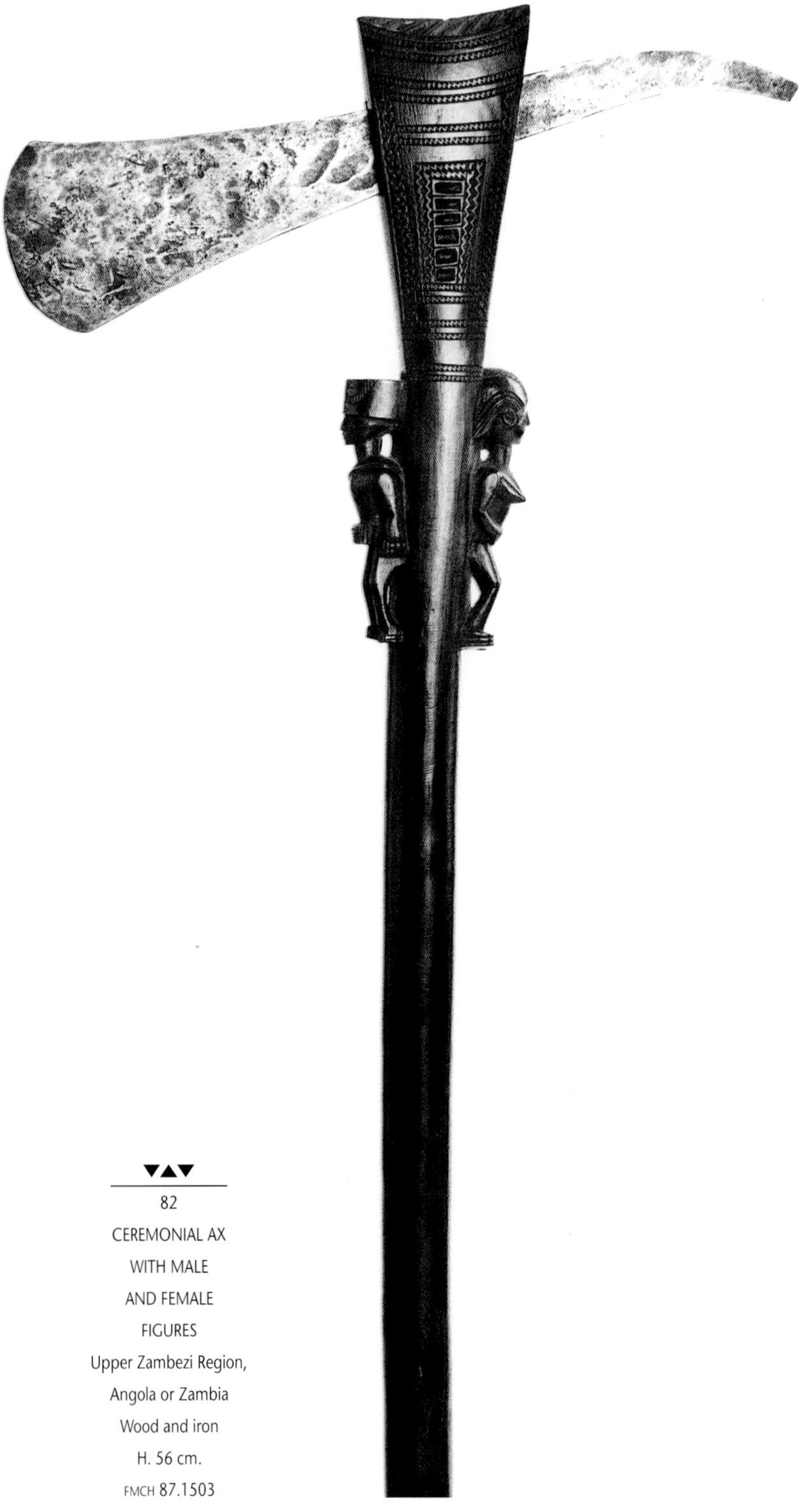

▼▲▼
82
CEREMONIAL AX
WITH MALE
AND FEMALE
FIGURES
Upper Zambezi Region,
Angola or Zambia
Wood and iron
H. 56 cm.
FMCH 87.1503

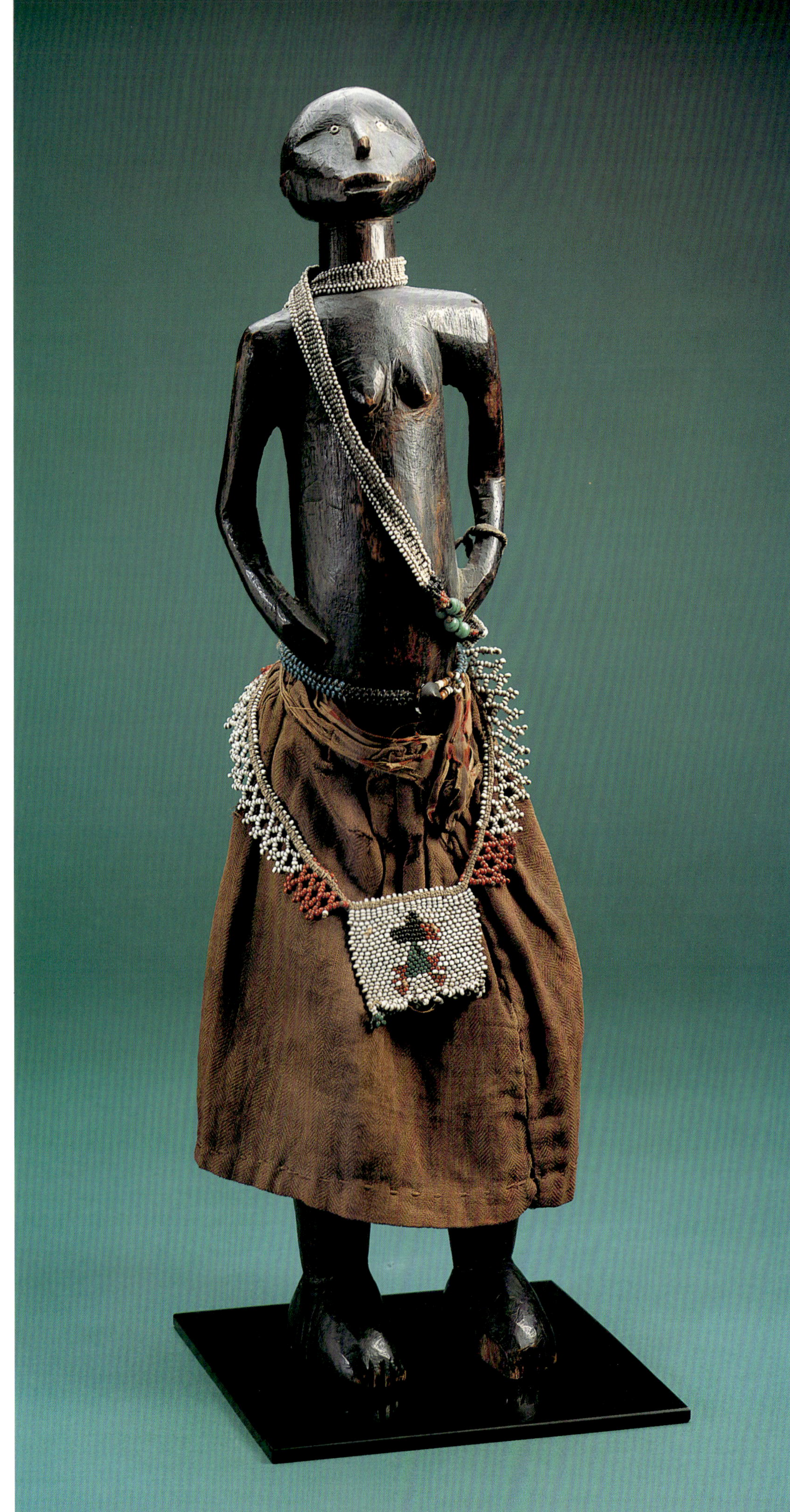

83
STANDING
FEMALE FIGURE
Maravi (?), Malawi,
southeast Africa
Wood, beads,
cotton cloth,
buttons, thread
and leather
H. 48 cm.
FMCH 86.1738

83. STANDING FEMALE FIGURE
MARAVI (?), MALAWI, SOUTHEAST AFRICA

The provenance of this clothed wooden figure of a standing female is uncertain. In 1989 the figure was published as a Zulu carving (Robbins and Nooter 1989:fig. 1368) on the basis of the beadwork patterns that cross the body, encircle the waist, and decorate the rectangular pouch or purse. This ornamental beadwork, however, is typical not only of the South African Zulu women but also of Ngoni women of Malawi in southeast Africa. Led by the Zulu warrior hero Zwangendaba and his successors, the Ngoni migrated northward between 1822 and 1848, invaded the lands immediately to the north and west of Lake Malawi, and eventually settled southwest of the lake during the second half of the century (Pachai 1973:22-40). Their women's traditional beadwork is still in indigenous use, and women from neighboring Yao and Maravi groups also make similar geometric beaded patterns.

Recognizing that Zulu-inspired beadwork was also produced by others in southern Africa, one must consider the possibility that the provenance of the Joss figure was other than the Zulu area.[1] The figure itself does not resemble any known Zulu carving, and on formal grounds it should be associated with the Lake Malawi region. The compact, rounded head rests upon a long tubular neck and occupies approximately one tenth of the figure's height. The prominent lips overshadow an insignificant chin. The eyes are represented by tiny beads or pierced cylinders of bone, which are placed high in the face under a slight suggestion of lifted brows. Small conical breasts emerge from the upper part of the elongated torso, and the hands are placed on the sides of the abdomen. The figure's dynamic stance is created by the backward tilt of the head, which balances the sharp protrusion of the buttocks. The widely spaced knees are flexed forward, and the legs are anchored by exceptionally heavy feet shaped like inverted bowls. Parallel, vertical grooves indicate toes. This combination of features is characteristic only of carvings originating near Lake Malawi.[2] This figure is, for

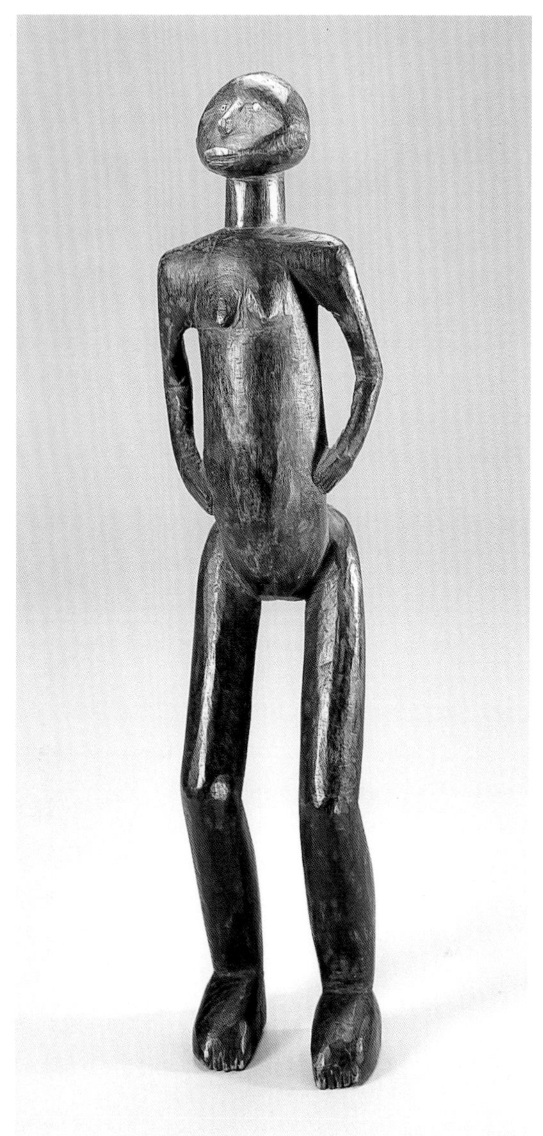

example, remarkably similar to a figure in the Museum für Völkerkunde, Berlin, which was collected by Carl Wiese in 1904 among the Maravi people (Krieger 1990:73, fig. 528).[3]

Very few figural carvings have been associated with the Maravi,[4] most of whom live southwest of the lake, between the Shire, Luangwa, and Zambezi Rivers, and near the Zambezi in coastal Mozambique. In the past this group, led by hereditary paramount chiefs, regulated a network of trade routes reaching from the Congo to the Indian Ocean (Barretto 1899:463-4,480). The Maravi share a number of customs, stories of origin, clan names, and masking traditions with some of the Makonde groups

(Dias and Dias 1964:70-71, 74; Blackmun and Schoffeleers 1972:38).

In addition to the carving in Berlin, there are two other well-known figural sculptures the idiosyncratic style of which relates to this example in proposition, dynamism and pose. Acquired from the town of Blantyre in the central Maravi area during the first decade of this century, these figures are now in the British Museum (Holy 1967:figs. 110, 112). One figure portrays a standing male, while the other (apparently by the same hand) represents a woman carrying a large child on her back. As with the Berlin example, little collection data was recorded. Since its inception as a mission and trading center in the 1870s, Blantyre has been a crossroads where the Yao from the eastern shores of Lake Malawi (Rangeley 1963), the Sena and Chikunda from southern Mozambique (Tew 1950:31; Rangeley 1964:50,51), and many other groups have intermingled with the Maravi. The original source of the Blantyre pair of figural sculptures was therefore problematic until Maria Kecskesi, in her recent work on the "pickaback motif," suggested that the pose of the woman carrying the adolescent child referred to the practice among the Yao and Makonde of lifting young initiates to the shoulders of adult sponsors during coming-of-age ceremonies (Kecskesi 1982:54,55). This information, plus stylistic comparison with simpler Yao figural carvings in the Berlin museum (IIIE 305, IIIE 306), suggests that this Blantyre figural group should be attributed to the Yao.

Unfortunately, even if the provenance of the Joss and Berlin figures were proven to be either Ngoni or Maravi, the absence of a documented figural carving tradition in either group would still make their function obscure. If they were created by the Maravi, however, speculation suggests that they might have been used for instruction during initiation of boys into the men's Nyau Society, or during ChiNamwali, the preparation of girls for adulthood. Corresponding initiatory sessions and ceremonies were once mandatory for Makonde youth, and have been carefully researched. In discussing numerous examples of carved Makonde female figures, Jorge Dias explains that "some of these statues appear to have been used during puberty rites, together with those of males, for educational purposes" (Dias 1961:51). Wembah-Rashid explicitly describes the pairing of carved male and female figures in Makonde performances miming sexual intercourse (Wembah-Rashid 1971:41). The usual indigenous age-grade instruction throughout the Lake Region impressed upon the young people their adult obligations and warned them severely of corresponding prohibitions and sanctions. While traditional education of the Maravi sought to teach responsible behavior through the use of tangible objects such as clay figurines of humans and animals, these were customarily destroyed after use. Wooden figurines could have been disposed of in a similar way.

The evidence for the provenance of the Joss figure is, thus, rather thin. Both the Ngoni/Zulu beadwork and the style of the carving suggest a link with the region of Lake Malawi. This link is strengthened by the collection at an early date of a similar figure among the Maravi. While the Ngoni are an intrusive group in the lake region, there are correspondences between Maravi and northern Makonde arts, masks, history and customs. Makonde figures and their functions have been documented and a Makonde provenance cannot be ruled out. Unless additional research documents the use of wooden figures in Maravi traditional instruction, the origin of the Joss example may remain problematic.[5]

Barbara W. Blackmun

[1] Michael Conner, who is making a thorough study of Ngoni beadwork, confirms that the beaded patterns on the Joss figure are "classic Zulu/Ngoni of an early (1900s) type" (pers. comm. 1990). Nevertheless, the shape and material of the cloth skirt are not typically Ngoni, and he is inclined to believe that even though their scale is so closely adjusted to the figure, the beaded articles may have been collected separately.

[2] While the cylindrical torso, widely spaced legs, rounded head, and eyes made of inlaid beads can be found among Zaramo and Nyamwezi carvings in Tanzania (see Krieger 1990:figs. 242, 251; Robbins 1989:fig. 1350), these examples are less dynamic than either the Joss figure. Although the Bemba of nearby Zambia carve elongated figures in similar proportions and poses (see Holy 1967:fig. 107), inlaid beads are not typically used to repre-

sent the eyes. Nearer the lake, there are Makonde figural sculptures with inlaid eyes and elongated bodies that display a hint of movement (Holy 1967:fig. 84; Krieger 1990:fig 400).

[3] The Maravi are known in modern Malawi by the name of their dominant northern subgroup, the Chewa. Other Maravi peoples are the Chipeta, Nyasa, Nsenga, Nyanja, Zimba, Ntumba, Mbo, and the Mang'anja.

[4] Only one ethnographic reference to figurines among the Maravi has come to my attention. In 1906 Alice Werner wrote that the Chewa subgroup made small wooden figures of "a few short pieces of wood the size of one's forefinger [are] bound together with a cloth into the figure of a child's doll. Inside the calico is concealed a tiny box made of the handle of a gourd cup, supposed to contain the spirit of a dead ancestor" (1906:68-69). However, this account has not been corroborated elsewhere and no illustrations accompanied her description.

[5] Kenji Yoshida has recently published a thorough study of initiation rites among the western Chewa, a subgroup of the Maravi residing in Zambia. While Yoshida's wife, Mariko, was able to document the tutelary use of moist clay figures of various animals (*vilengo*) during ChiNamwali (Yoshida 1992:248-250, pl. 14), they observed no wooden figures used during the instruction of either the boys or the girls. It should be noted, however, that wherever carved figures have been documented throughout the entire Lake Malawi region, their existence has been a very closely guarded secret.

84. CARVED FIGURE, AZANDE, SOUTHERN SUDAN

The segmented form of the limbs and the rigid frontal pose of this figure are typical of the carving of the Azande, who live in both the southern Sudan and northeastern Zaire. The detailed description of the hairstyle and scarification marks suggests an affinity with the figurative pottery of the Azande and the Mangbetu. A number of related figures are in collections dating from the late nineteenth century up to the 1920s. The earliest dated example of a similar figure is one collected by Romolo Gessi in the White Nile region of the southern Sudan in 1883 and now in the Museo preistorico ed etnografico "Luigi Pigorini," Rome (Schildkrout and Keim 1990:240, fig. 12.7).

Zande figures like this are usually either male or female, although sometimes they are hermaphroditic. Their original use is not documented, but there is some indication that in the Sudan carved figures were sometimes placed on graves along with other offerings. If this is so, this figure could have been a representation of an ancestor. ENID SCHILDKROUT

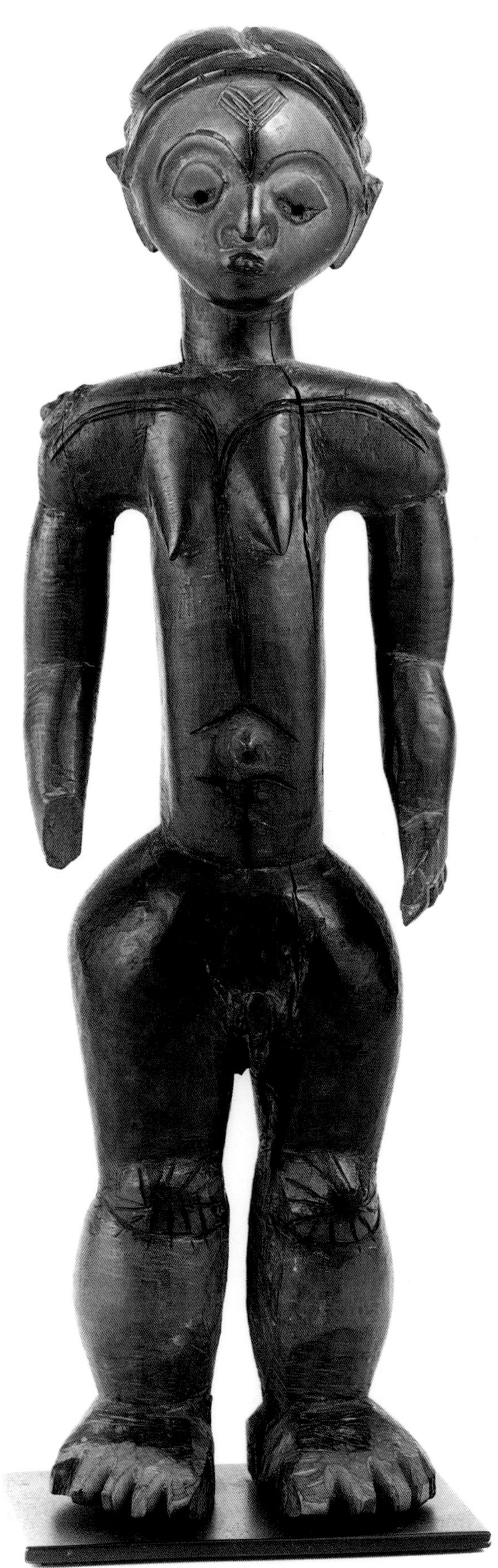

▼▲▼

84
CARVED FIGURE
Azande,
southern Sudan
Wood
L. 48 cm.
FMCH 86.1731

85. BLACKWARE POT, AZANDE, NORTHWESTERN ZAIRE

This beautifully formed blackware pot represents a
female figure, whose torso forms the bowl of the pot.
The details of the hairstyle and the geometric incisions on the body of the pot suggest that the pot
comes from the Azande who live just north of the
Mangbetu. The shape of the pot is reminiscent of
figurative Mangbetu pottery, most of which was
made during the first two decades of the twentieth
century. Wilhelm Junker and Georg Schweinfurth,
nineteenth-century German travelers to the region
described similar hairstyles of the Azande (Schildkrout and Keim 1990:84, fig. 4.17) Zande men were
fine potters in the nineteenth century and well into
this century. They may have inspired Mangbetu male
carvers, who traditionally worked in wood and ivory,
to begin working in clay.

The burnished black surface of this pot is found
on some of the finest examples of Zande utilitarian
pottery, but the fine sculpting of the neck suggests
that this piece was made as a prestige object. Such
objects were given as gifts or used on special occasions for drinking wine.   ES

86. CERAMIC VESSEL, MANGBETU, NORTHEASTERN ZAIRE

The Mangbetu of northeastern Zaire are well known
for finely shaped ceramic vessels. This jar is a classic
example of a style of pottery that became popular in
the first decade of the twentieth century. The neck of
the jar depicts a Mangbetu woman with an elongated
head and a wrapped, fan-like coiffure, a naturalistic
depiction of the cranial reshaping and hairstyle that
were popular among the Mangbetu from the later
nineteenth century. The elongation was achieved by
periodically binding the heads of infants with finely
braided raffia thread.

Among the Mangbetu, women made most
domestic pottery, whereas among the Azande, their
neighbors to the north, men were potters. Mangbetu
men, traditionally wood and ivory carvers, began to
work in clay when figurative ceramics became popular in the area. Many of the pots representing the
Mangbetu were made by Zande male potters or by
Mangbetu men. In some cases, women made the

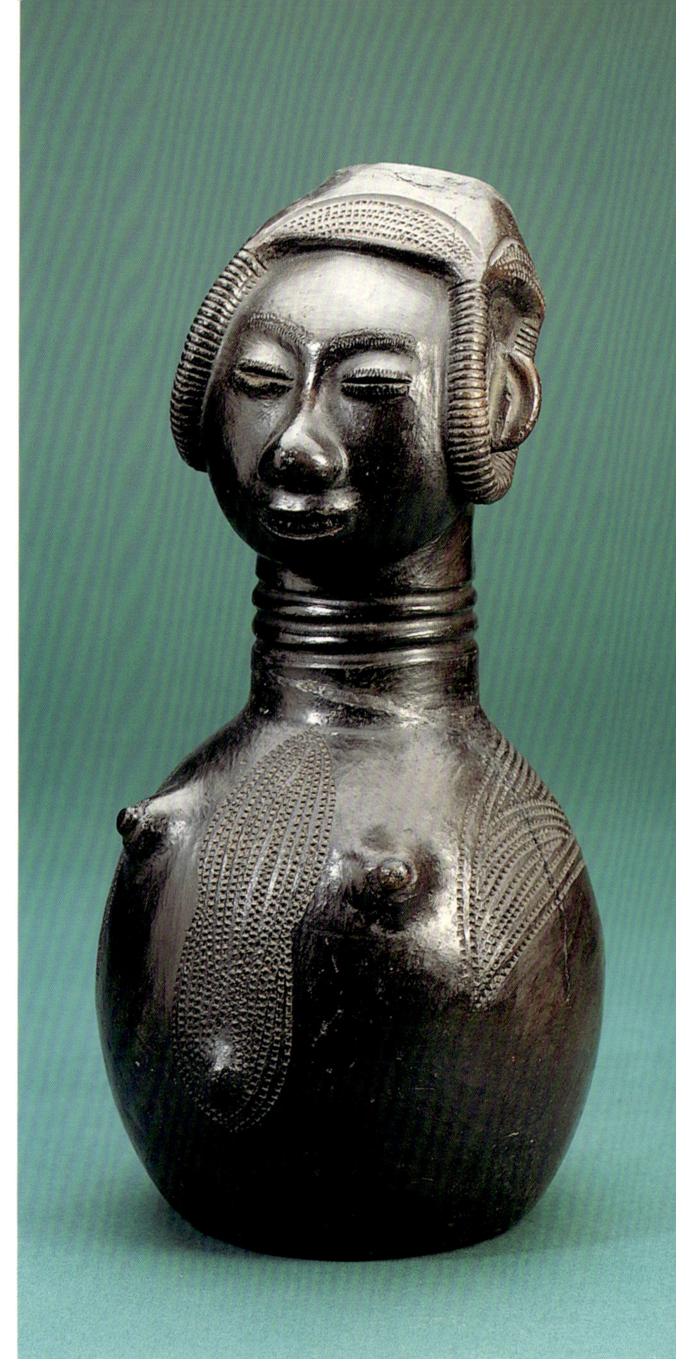

85
BLACKWARE POT
Azande,
northwestern Zaire
Ceramic
H. 26.5 cm.
FMCH 87.57

bases of the pots, applying traditional incised geometric designs, as on this example, while men sculpted the heads.

Many of these pots were made as prestige items. They were used by chiefs at large palm wine drinking parties, when a bamboo straw would be used for drinking wine from the pots. The pots were also given as gifts to visiting dignitaries, both African and European. The pottery very quickly became popular with European administrators and travelers in the area, who purchased numerous examples, which they took back to Europe. By the late 1930s, however, the art form began to disappear, either because the artists died out or because the market for the pottery decreased. ES

87. Side-blown Trumpet, Mangbetu, northeastern Zaire

Ivory, side-blown trumpets like this one have been made and used by Mangbetu court musicians in northeastern Zaire since pre-colonial times. In the nineteenth century, rulers commissioned court musicians to hollow out ivory tusks and carve them into trumpets for use in court orchestras. The ivory trumpets form part of musical ensembles that include several types of slit gongs, also known as "talking" drums, as well as iron bells and rattles. Among the Mangbetu, there is a special repertory of court music that celebrates the status of traditional rulers. As the court musicians play, Mangbetu chiefs dance before large audiences; their skill at dancing is regarded as an indication of their ability to rule. The musicians and dancers are accompanied by groups of women sitting on stools, rhythmically clapping and singing along with the court orchestra.

The Mangbetu decorated their ivory trumpets with both incised geometric designs and carved heads. This example is typical of late nineteenth- and early twentieth-century carving. It features a stylized face and an elongated skull, portraying the fashion of head binding popular at that time. A similar elongation of heads appears on Mangbetu pottery and on wood carvings of the same period. ES

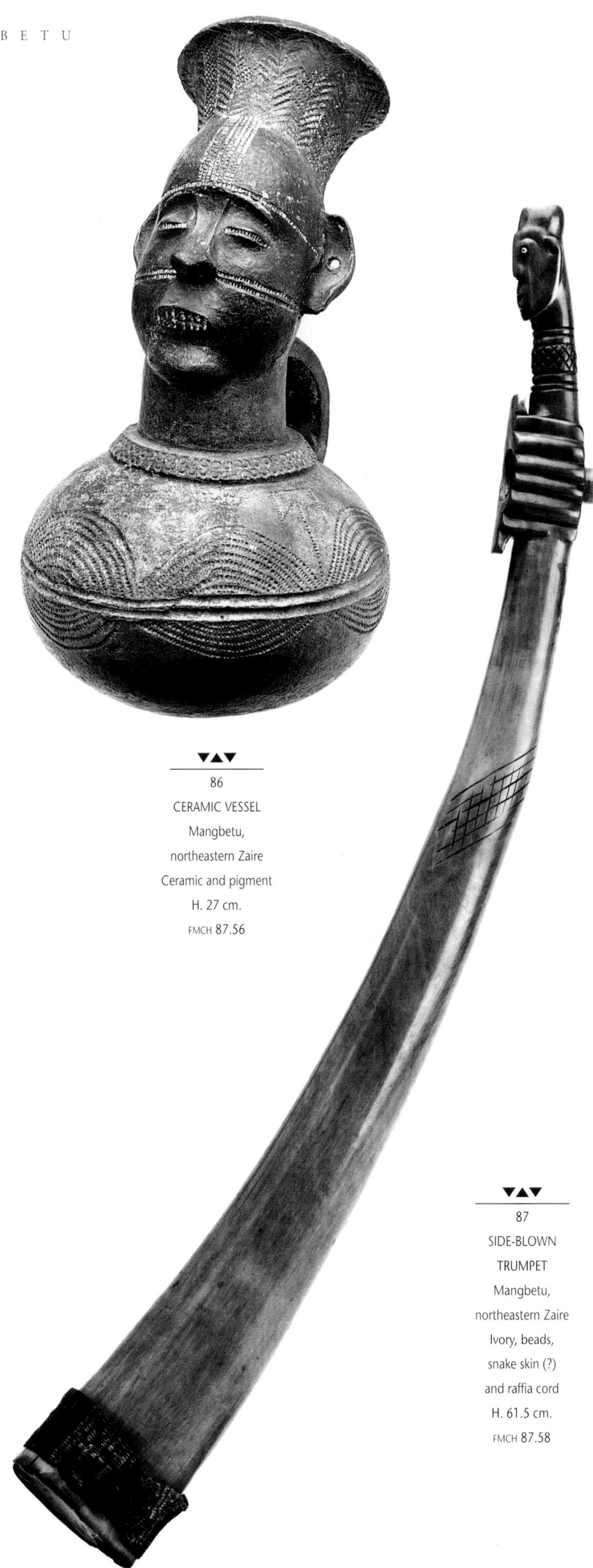

▼▲▼
86
CERAMIC VESSEL
Mangbetu,
northeastern Zaire
Ceramic and pigment
H. 27 cm.
FMCH 87.56

▼▲▼
87
SIDE-BLOWN
TRUMPET
Mangbetu,
northeastern Zaire
Ivory, beads,
snake skin (?)
and raffia cord
H. 61.5 cm.
FMCH 87.58

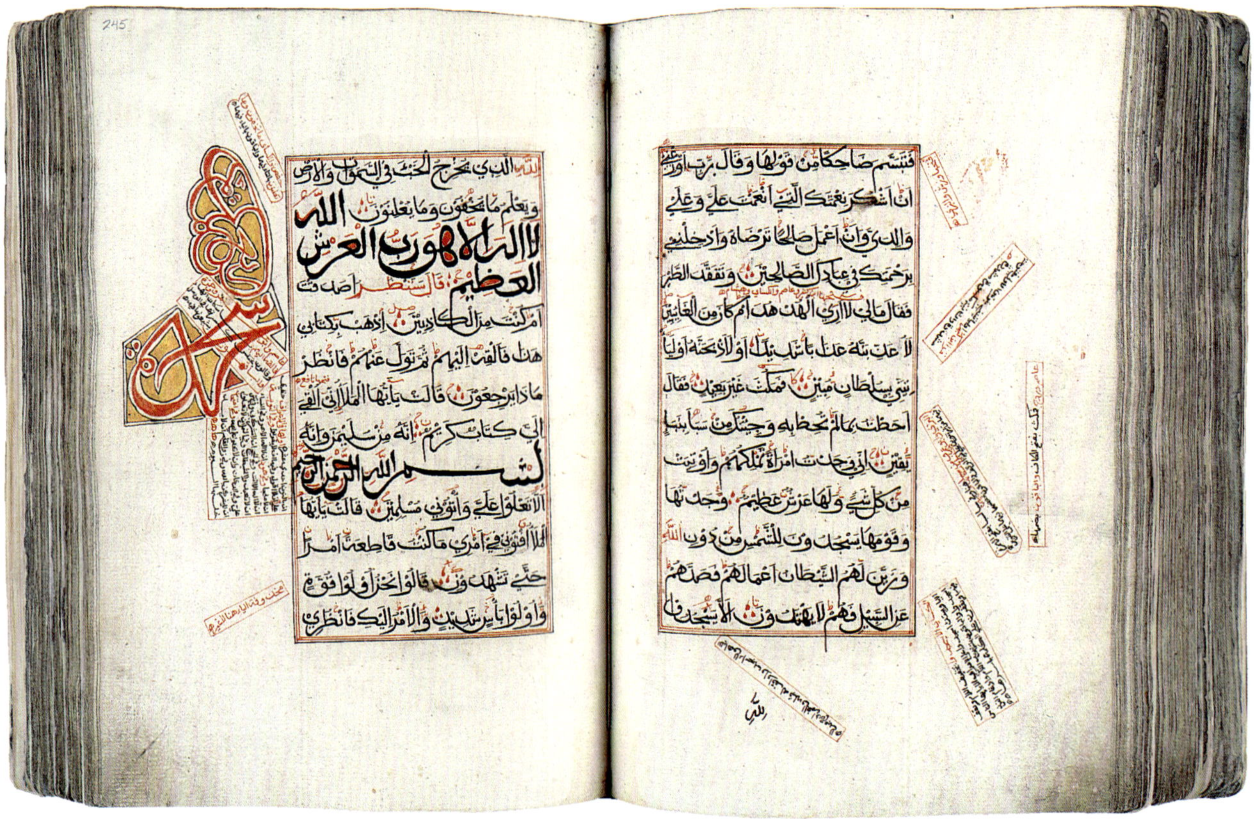

88. Koran, Swahili, Siyu, Kenya

88
KORAN
Swahili, Siyu, Kenya
Leather and paper
H. 26.5 cm.
FMCH 90.184A,B

This complete volume of the Koran from the early nineteenth century consists of 417 folios bound in a contemporary black leather binding with stamped designs. The Koranic text begins on folio 3b and ends on folio 402b. Folios 403a-404b explain the Koran's content, and folios 405a-413a record short prayers. On the very last text folio (413b), the *shahādah*, the Muslim profession of faith, is repeated in both a large central medallion and its flanking cartouches.

The text is written in an elegant, cursive script that resembles *thuluth*. The formation of certain letters, however, recalls the North African *maghribi* script.[1] The same fluid calligraphy, but smaller in scale, is also found in the carefully outlined commentaries in the text margins . These annotations are contemporary with the text and must have been written by the same scribe.

Both the text and the commentary are primarily written in black ink, whereas the diacritical marks, the punctuation at the end of each verse (*āyah*), and the word "Allah" always appear in red. Red ink is also reserved for certain phrases and others are written in large black letters; both thus stand out from the rest of the text.

One of the most striking features of this Koran is its lavish illumination: the first two chapters (*sūrah*s) the "Opening" (*al-Fātihah*) and the "Cow" (*al-Baqarah*), for instance, are set in an elaborately decorated double-page frontispiece (folios 3b and 4a). The chapter headings appear in black reverse painting, and the text area is surrounded by decorative borders painted in black, red, and yellow. The widest border is embellished with a continuous floral scroll, typical of Swahili designs (de Vere Allen 1973:pl. 1). Reverse painting and floral borders are used for three other chapter headings.[2]

Illumination designs also mark the text divisions of the Koran. Each of the thirty sections (*ajzā'*) is indicated by one or several inscribed and brightly colored medallion(s). Finally, at the points where ritual prostration is required, the word *sajdah* (prostrate)—often transformed into an imaginative, almost abstract design—is written in the margins.

The extensive decorative program served not only to enhance the Koran's aesthetic quality but also to highlight certain aspects of the text, helping the reader to maintain the correct rhythm, pause where necessary, and stress the right phrases. The Koran's well-worn folios confirm that it was, in fact, used for teaching and recitation in local mosques. Moreover, an inscription on folio 3a claims:

In the name of God the Merciful, the Compassionate. May God's prayer / and blessings be upon the Prophet, his family, and his companions. This is a *waqf* fixed by the descendants of the daughter of Shaykh Dumayl bin Mu'izz bin 'Umar / and his descendants. It is not to be sold or given away as gift or inherited / until God inherits the world and all that is in it. And He [i.e., God] is the best of heirs./ He who does otherwise after he hears this, commits a sin. Those who do otherwise, God is the all-hearing and the all-knowing.

An abbreviated version of this inscription appears on folio 413a. Both notations, which were written in a different hand than the text, were probably added when the Koran was endowed to the mosque.

Although the exact identity of the patron and the location of the mosque await further research, the quality of this Koran suggests that it is one of the finest examples of Siyu's prolific manuscript production (de Vere Allen 1979:20-24; Brown 1985:180-84). It confirms the high degree of religious scholarship and artistic sophistication that characterized this East African Muslim community.

MASSUMEH FARHAD

[1] These characteristics were first noted by Simon Digby (1975:51) in reference to another Swahili Koran.
[2] Similar illumination designs appear in the Koran discussed by Simon Digby (1975:52, fig. 2).

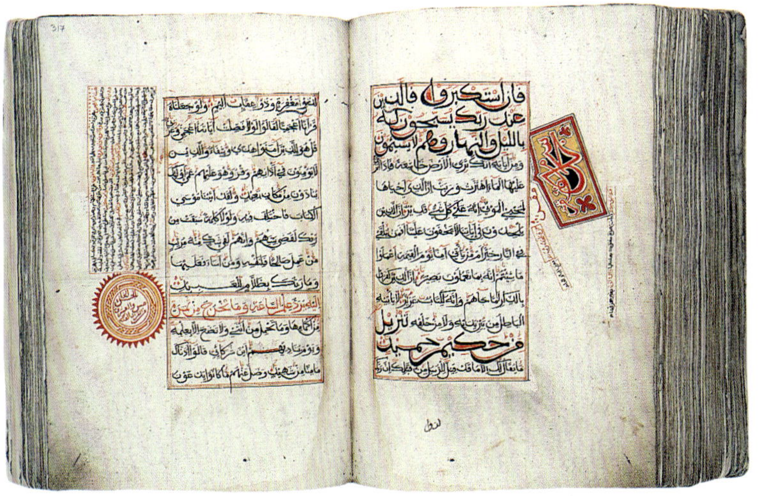

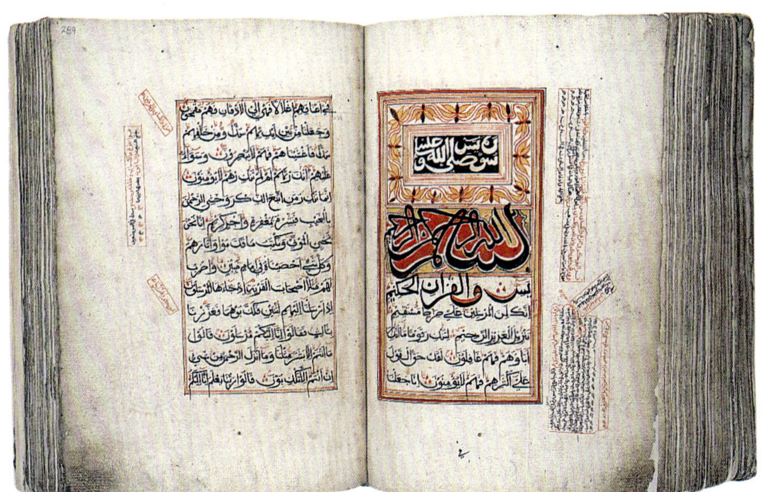

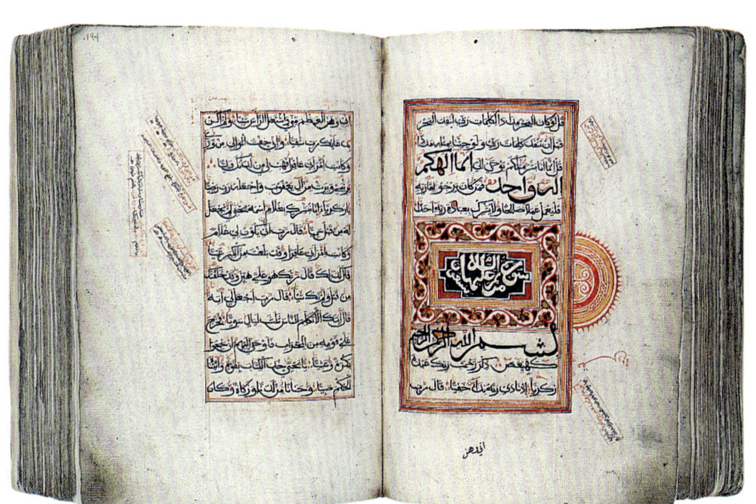

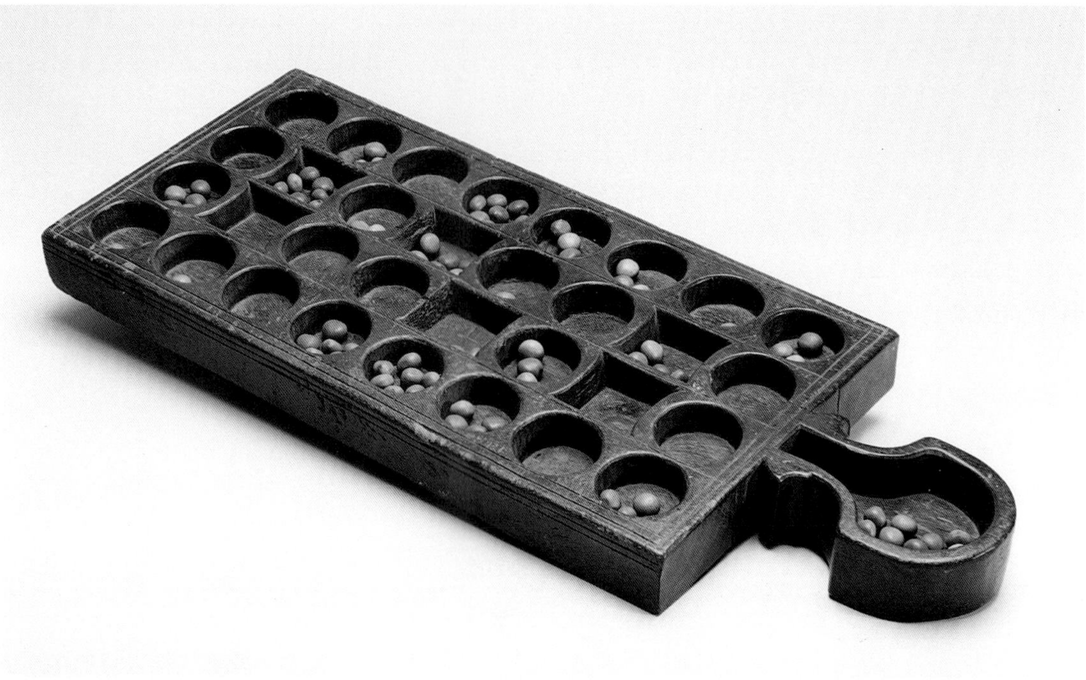

89
GAME BOARD
(bao)
Swahili, Tanzania
Wood
L. 77.3 cm.
FMCH 90.179

89. GAME BOARD, SWAHILI, TANZANIA

This cupulate board is used for playing *mankala*, a board game involving calculative strategies. *Mankala* is believed to be the oldest and most widely distributed game in the world. The oldest extant game board, dating from ca. 5000 B.C., was found in the Middle East, where the game is still commonly played. *Mankala* is also played in central, southern and southeastern Asia, and throughout Africa and the Americas. The routes of transmission are not precisely known, except to the Americas: African slaves brought *mankala* to Guyana, Surinam, Brazil, many Caribbean islands, and the United States.

Mankala is played with a predetermined number of identical pieces on boards containing two, three, or four parallel rows of holes. The board is divided between two individuals, or rarely two teams. Alternating turns, each player removes the entire contents from a hole on his side of the board and, moving counterclockwise, drops them one-by-one in successive holes around the board or, in the case of a four-row board, around his half of the board. The goal is to capture the majority of the pieces or immobilize the opponent under established rules.

Two-row games are the most widely distributed in the world, while three-row games are rarely found outside Ethiopia, and four-row games are found only in central, eastern and southern Africa. Only in Africa, where *mankala* is known under hundreds of local names, are all three board types found.

The most common boards are holes scooped out of the ground or holes cut into the exposed roots of trees. Non-edible seeds or pebbles serve as pieces. Portable boards formed from clay, cast in precious metal, or carved out of fine wood and furnished with large storage cups or decorated with incised or carved

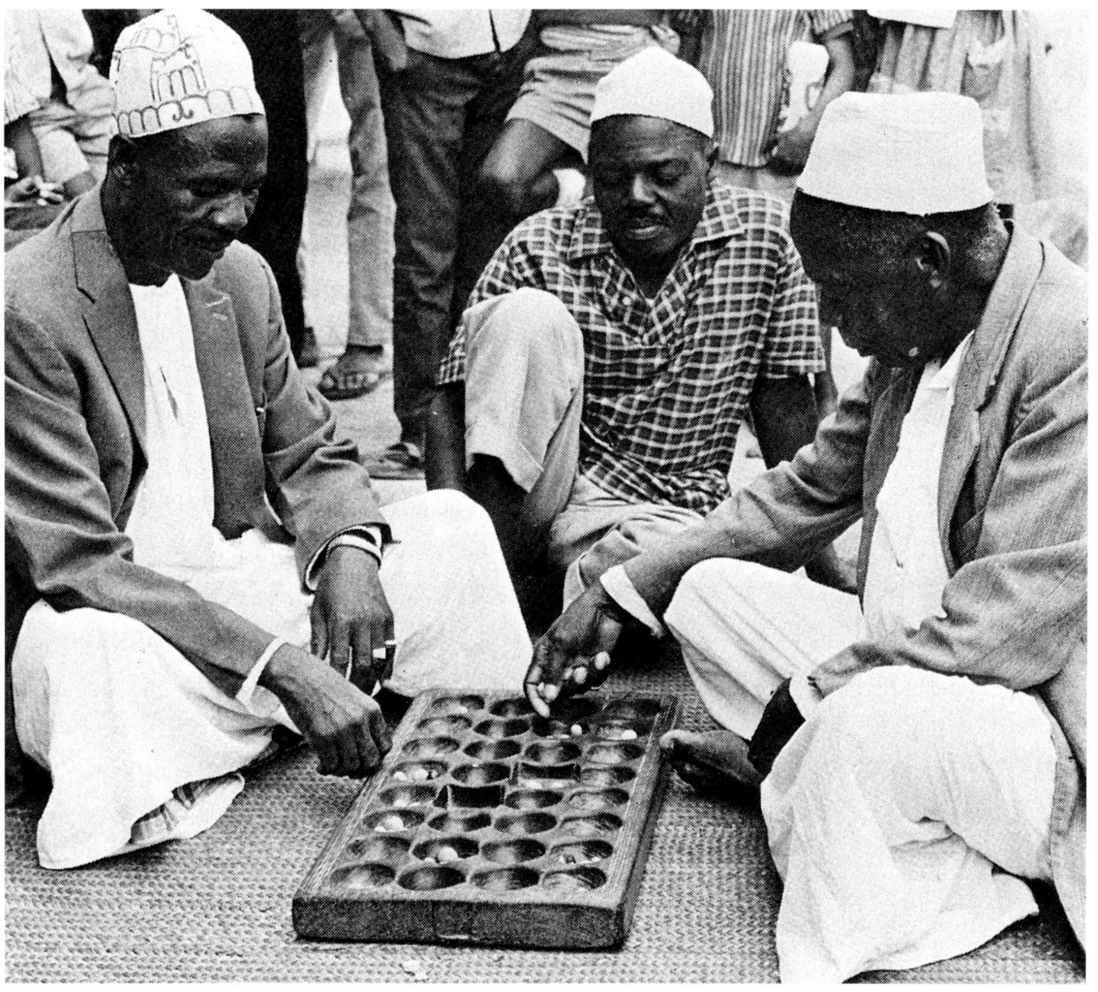

A *bao* game in progress.
Courtesy of
National Development
Corporation, Tanzania.

relief decoration rank as prestige objects. Imported cowry shells, coral beads, forged iron forms and carved ivory balls are used as playing pieces for these more refined game boards.

Holes are identical on all types of mankala game boards except those for *bao kiswahili*, a very complicated version of *mankala*, which is played in Kenya, Tanzania, Zanzibar, Mozambique and Malawi. On *bao kiswahili* boards, the shape of the fourth hole from the right in each player's inner row is distinct from the others. Called *kuu*, meaning "principal" in Kiswahili, these holes are used under special rules during the early stages of the game. However, the different shape may also serve as a reminder to accumulate pieces in the hole or lose the game. The extraordinary number of holes in the inner rows makes this game board an unusual instrument for playing *bao kiswahili*. It was probably designed by the owner to test new game strategies.

ROSLYN A. WALKER

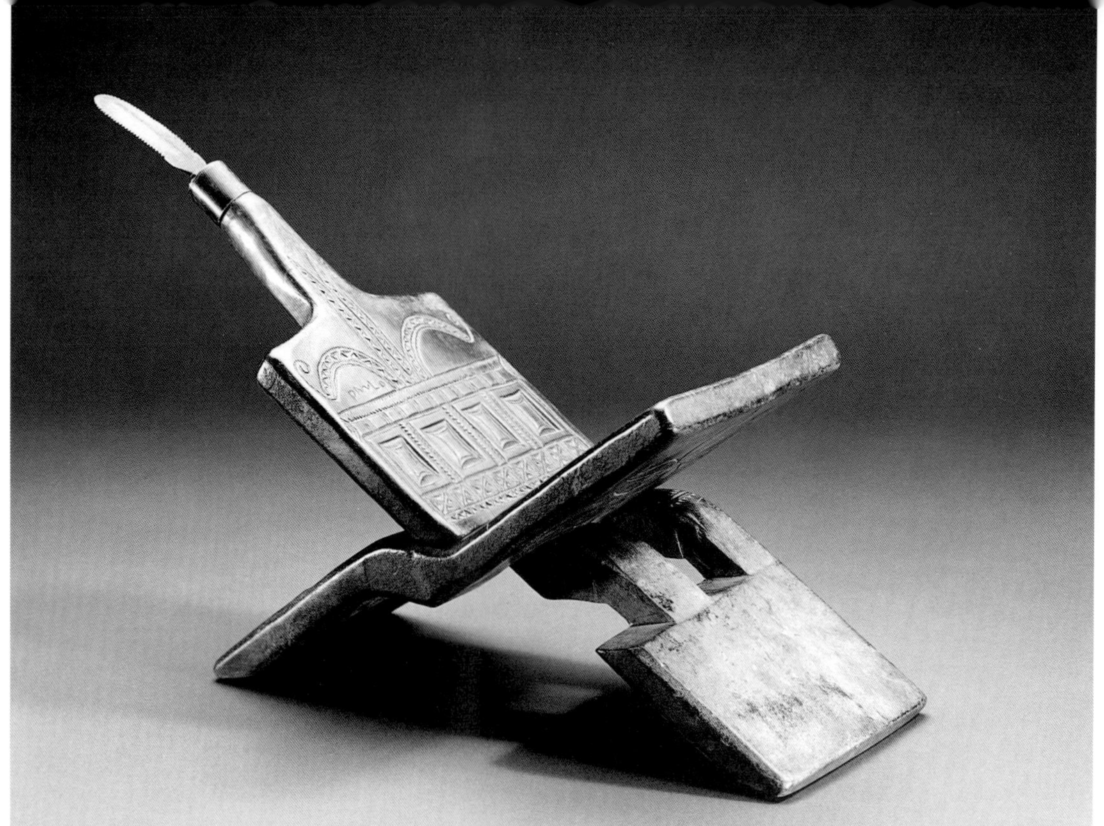

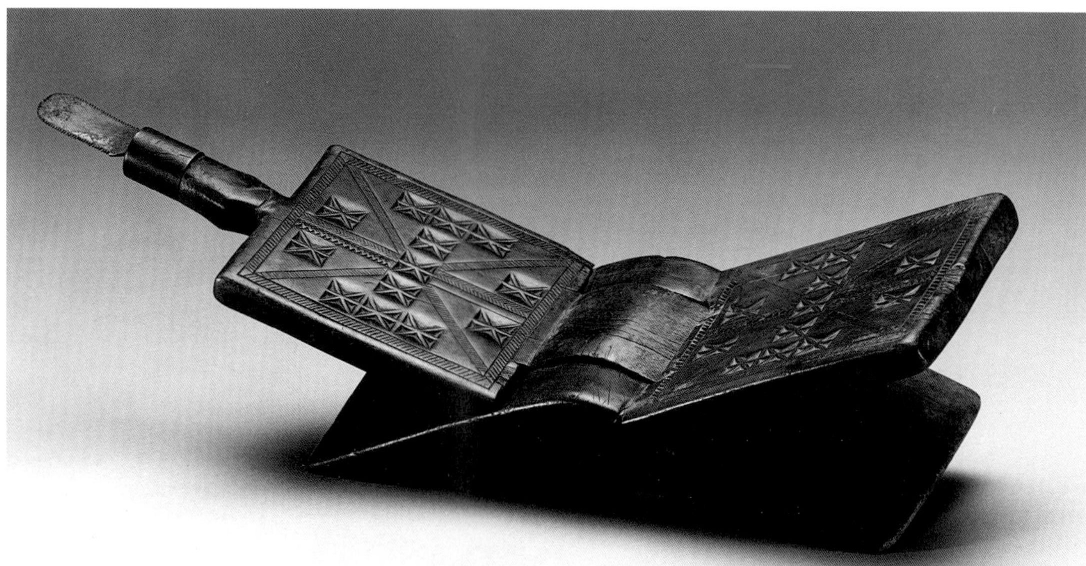

90-93. COCONUT GRATERS, SWAHILI, BAGAMOYO, TANZANIA

Since the nineteenth century, the Swahili have produced a coconut grater (*mbuzi*) that resembles a Koran stand. Carved from one piece of wood, the interlocked pieces are hinged and fold open in an x-shape. The coconut is scraped on a protruding metal blade, the grated by-product is then pushed through a basketry sieve to produce milk, a staple ingredient for East African stews (De Vere Allen nd:16).

PAULETTE PARKER

▼▲▼	▼▲▼
(top)	*(bottom)*
90	91
COCONUT GRATER	COCONUT GRATER
(mbuzi)	*(mbuzi)*
Swahili,	Swahili,
Bagamoyo,	Bagamoyo,
Tanzania	Tanzania
Wood	Wood
W. 55.6 cm.	W. 81 cm.
FMCH 91.315	FMCH 91.316

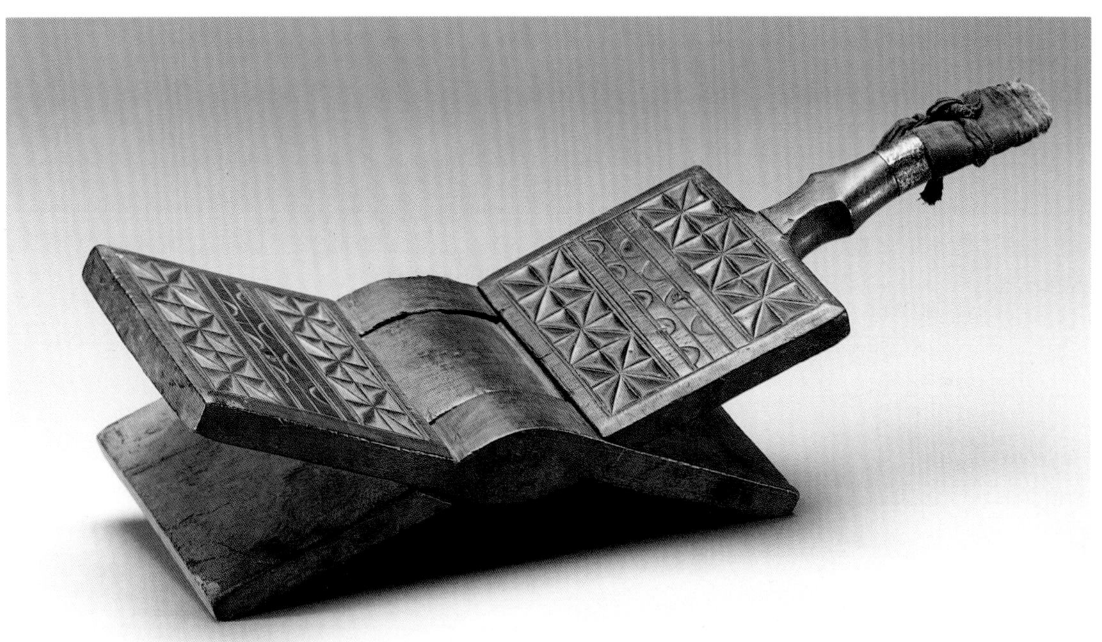

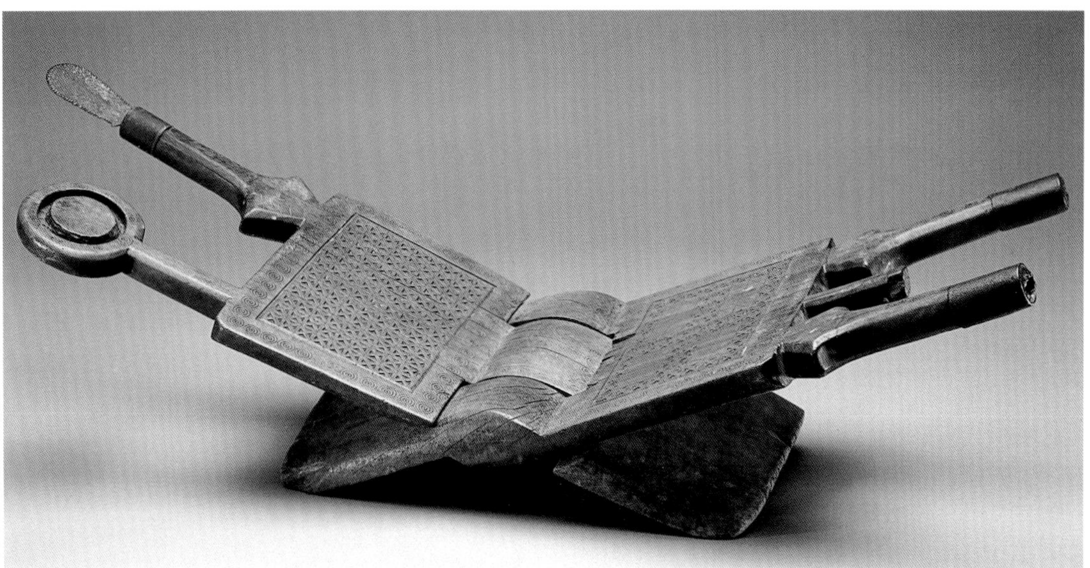

▼▲▼

(top)

92

COCONUT GRATER

(mbuzi)

Swahili,

Bagamoyo,

Tanzania

Wood

W. 42.8 cm.

FMCH 91.317

▼▲▼

(bottom)

93

COCONUT GRATER

(mbuzi)

Swahili,

Bagamoyo,

Tanzania

Wood

W. 48.?

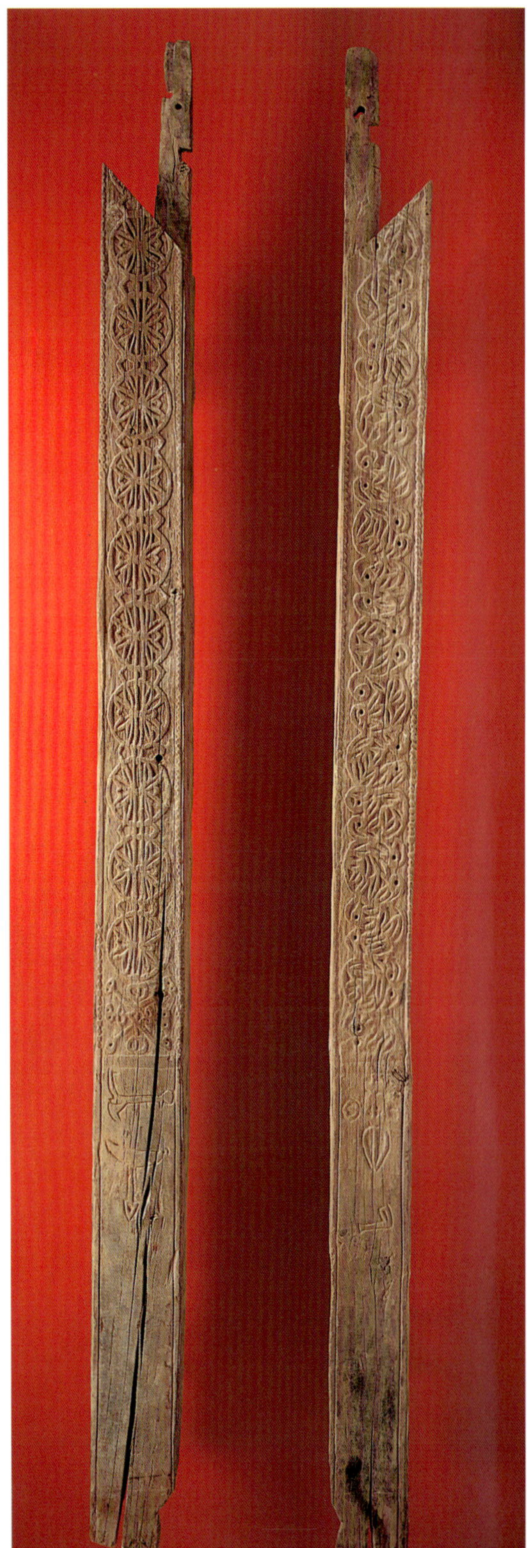

94. DOOR POSTS, SWAHILI, SIYU, PATE ISLAND, KENYA

Although they frame a single door, these eighteenth century door posts have totally asymmetrical patterns. The axes, bow and arrow and broad-bladed spear carved on the bottom of the posts were meant to warn people against carrying actual weapons inside the home or using them with evil intent.   PP

95. DOOR LINTEL, SWAHILI, LAMU ISLAND, KENYA

During the post-1780 period, an elaborate, deeply carved curvilinear floral design known as the "Zanzibar" style swept the Swahili Coast. This style appeared on furniture and household objects, as well as doors and door frames. With Lamu Island's narrow streets and high, windowless stone walls, these elaborately carved wooden doors were used not only to give a house a unique identity, but also to indicate the wealth and status of the owner (de vere Allen nd:7)   PP

96. WOODEN INSCRIPTION, SWAHILI, TANZANIA

English translation:

> and drinks. So will they not be thankful? But they take gods other than God (Allah) hoping to be helped. They are not able to help them even if they had soldiers made ready. So let their speech not sadden you, for verily We know what they keep secret and what they make public. Does man not see that verily We created him from a sperm-drop?

Text is from the Koran constituting the Yurat Ya Sin (The Chapter of Ya Sin), from verse 73 through 77.   PP

▼▲▼
95
DOOR LINTEL
Swahili,
Lamu, Kenya
Wood
L. 144 cm.
FMCH 90.182

▼▲▼
96
WOODEN
INSCRIPTION
Swahili,
Tanzania
Wood
H. 312 cm.
FMCH 90.178A-C

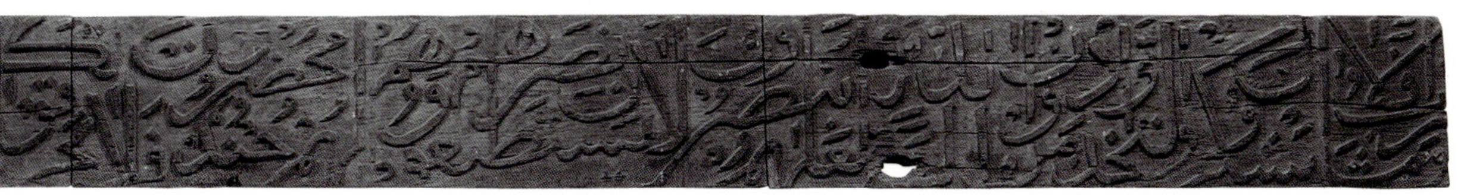

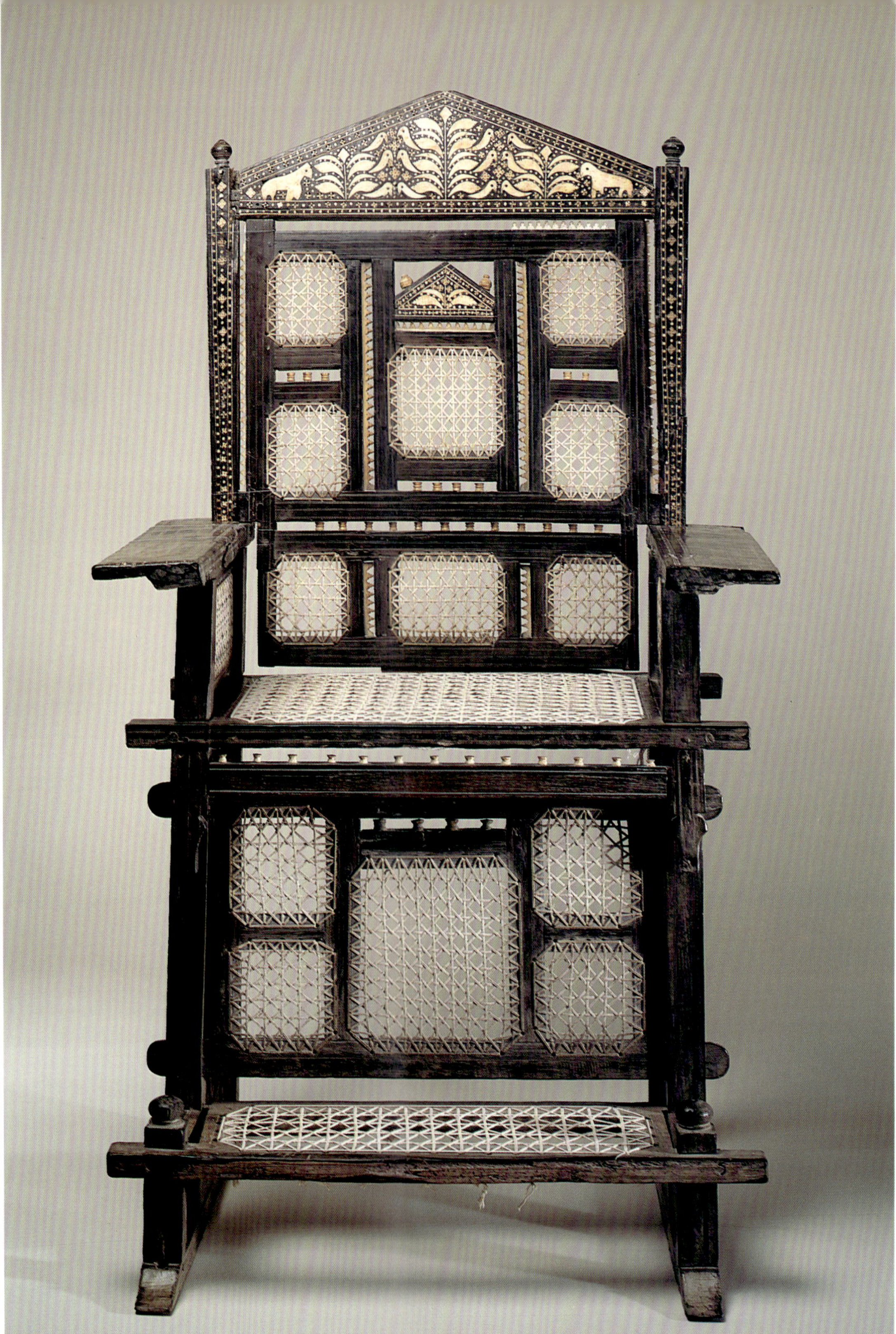

97. CHAIR, SWAHILI, LAMU ISLAND, KENYA

The *kiti cha enzi*, "Grandee's Chair" or "Chair of Power," was derived from an Egyptian Mamluk prototype and used throughout the royal courts of the Swahili world. During the golden age of Swahili culture, from the fourteenth to the nineteenth centuries, this elaborately carved ebony and ivory inlaid chair was a symbol of status, rank, and power and was offered to visiting dignitaries as a sign of prestige and as a gesture of respect. The ivory inlay and bird and animal figures portrayed on the triangular back panel distinguish this chair (de Vere Allen nd:12; 1989:54-63)

PP

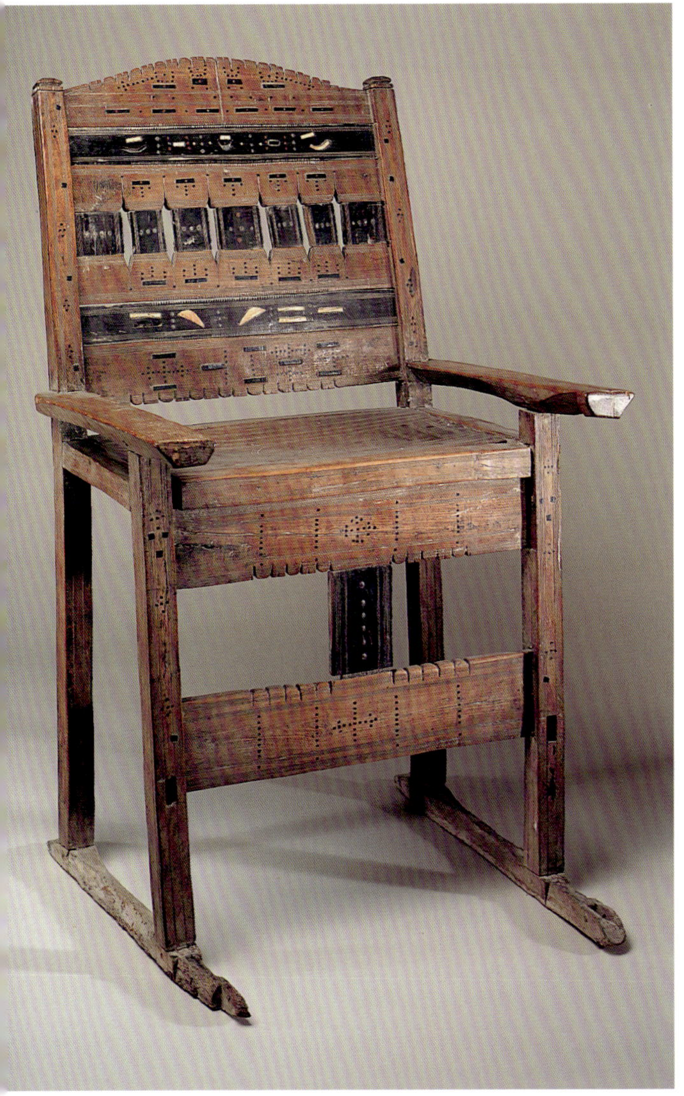

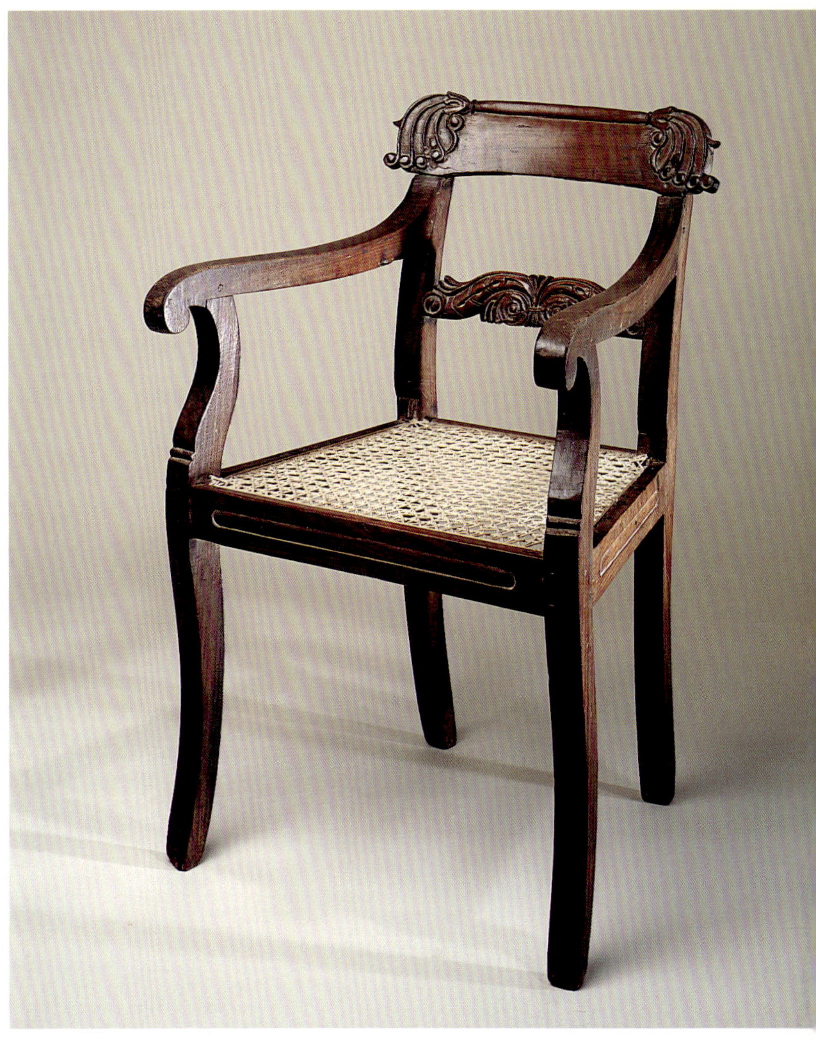

98. Chair, Swahili, Siyu, Pate Island, Kenya

This traditional Swahili grille-work chair is indicative of the political and cultural conservatism of Siyu Town during a period in which European and Indian styles were being whole-heartedly embraced by the rest of the Swahili world. Siyu, known in the nineteenth century as a "town of craftsmen," remained fiercely anti-Zanzibari. Until the 1880s, when its population was decimated by smallpox, Siyu continued to produce a great quantity of chairs in the traditional Swahili grille-work style chairs (de vere Allen 1989:62)

PP

99. Chair, Swahili, Lamu Island, East Africa

From the beginning of the nineteenth century, the people of Lamu Island abandoned traditional Swahili notions of architecture and material culture in favor of "the latest thing" from overseas, usually India. By the late nineteenth century, they were producing a Swahili variation of the Indian interpretation of the English Regency elbow chair. This carved fiber-strung chair was typical of the furnishings innovative Swahili craftsmen produce and Swahili households adopted in support of their cosmopolitan lifestyle (de vere Allen 1989:61).

PP

▼▲▼
(left)
98
CHAIR
(kiti cha mtaawanda)
Swahili, Siyu,
Pate Island,
Kenya
H. 111 cm.
FMCH 90.171

▼▲▼
(right)
99
CHAIR
Swahili,
Lamu Island,
Kenya
H. 82.6 cm.
FMCH 90.175

BIBLIOGRAPHY

Abimbola, 'Wande
1976   *Ifa: An Exposition of Ifa Literary Corpus.* Ibadan: Oxford University Press Nigeria.

Abiodun, Rowland A.
1975   "Ifa Art Objects: An Interpretation based on Oral Tradition." In 'Wande Abimbola, ed., *Yoruba Oral Tradition,* 421–69. Ile-Ife, Nigeria: Department of African Languages and Literatures, University of Ife.
1989   "The Kingdom of Owo." In Henry Drewal, et al., eds., *Yoruba: Nine Centuries of African Art and Thought,* 91–115. New York: Center for African Art and H.N. Abrams.

Abiodun, Rowland, Henry John Drewal and John Pemberton
1991   *Yoruba: Art and Aesthetics.* Zurich: The Center for African Art and Rietberg Museum.

Abraham, Roy Clive
1958   *Dictionary of Modern Yoruba.* London: University of London Press.

Adams, Marie Jeanne
1982   *Designs for Living: Symbolic Communication in African Art.* Cambridge: Carpenter Center for the Visual Arts.

Akinnaso, F. N.
1981   "Names and Naming Principles in Cross-Cultural Perspectives." *Names: The Journal of the American Name Society* 29, 1:37–63.
1983   "Yoruba Traditional Names and the Transmission of Cultural Knowledge." *Names: The Journal of the American Name Society* 31, 3:39–58.

Allison, Philip A.
1959–62   Unpublished documents, National Museum, Lagos.

Barber, Karin
1991   *I Could Speak Until Tomorrow: Oriki, Women and the Past in a Yoruba Town.* Washington, D.C.: Smithsonian Institution Press.

Barretto, Manoel
1899   "Report Upon the State and Conquest of the Rivers of Cuama." In George McCall Theal, ed., *Records of South-Eastern Africa: Collected in Various Libraries and Archive Departments in Europe,* 3. Cape Colony: Government Press.

Bascom, William R.
1969   *Ifa Divination: Communication Between Gods and Men in West Africa.* Bloomington: Indiana University Press.

Bassing, A.
1973   "Grave Monuments of the Dakakari." *African Arts* 6, 4:36–39.

Bastian, Adolf
1875   *Die deutsche Expedition an der Loango-Küste, nebst älteren Nachrichten über die zu erforschenden Länder.* Jena: Hermann Costenoble.

Bastin, Marie-Louise
1961   "Un masque en cuivre martele des Kongo du nord-est de Angola." *Africa-Tervuren* 7, 2:29–40.
1979   "Art songo. Oeuvres anciennes de l'art des Songo d'Angola." *Art d'Afrique Noire* 30:30–43.
1982   *La Sculpture Tshokwe.* Meudon: A. and F. Chaffin.

Bedaux, R.
1977   *Tellem: een bijdrage tot de geschiedenis van de Republiek Mali.* Berg en Dal: Afrika Museum.

Beier, Uili H.
1963   "A Note on the Woodcarvings of the Obi of Agbor, Odu." *Journal of Yoruba, Edo and Related Studies* 9:24–25.

Beier, Ulli H., comp.
1970   *Yoruba Poetry: an anothology of traditional poems.* Cambridge: Cambridge University Press.

Ben-Amos, Paula
1976   "Men and Animals in Benin Art." *Man* 2:243–52.
1980   *The Art of Benin.* New York: Thames and Hudson.

Bentor, Eli
1988   "Life as an Artistic Process: Igbo Ikenga and Ofo." *African Arts* 21, 2:66–71, 94.

Bernatzik, Hugo Adolf
1933   *Äthiopen des Westens: Forschungsreisen in Portugiesisch-Guinea.* 2 vols. Vienna: L.W. Seidel und Sohn.

Berns, Marla C.
1993   "Art, History, and Gender: Women and Clay in Africa." *African Archaeological Review* 11:133–53.

Beyioku, A. Fagbenro
1946   "Historical and Moral Facts about the Gelede Cult." mss., Archives, National Museum, Lagos, Nigeria.

Biebuyck, Daniel
1977   "Sculpture from the Eastern Zaire Forest Regions: Metoko, Lengola and Komo." *African Arts* 10, 2:52–58.

Blackmun, Barbara and Matthew Schoffeleers
1972   "Masks of Malawi." *African Arts* 5, 4:36–41, 69, 88.

Bowald, Fred
1939   *In den Sümpfen des Rio Nunez.* Zürich: Büchergilde Gutenberg.

Bradbury, R.E.
1957   *The Benin Kingdom and the Edo-Speaking Peoples of South-Western Nigeria.* Ethnographic survey of Africa: Western Africa, pt. 13. London: International African Institute.

Bravmann, René A.
1974   *Islam and Tribal Art in West Africa.* London: Cambridge University Press.

Brink, James T.
1981   "Antelope Headdress (*Chi Wara*)." In Susan Vogel, ed., *For Spirits and Kings: African Art from the Paul and Ruth Tishman Collection*, 24–25. New York: Metropolitan Museum of Art.

Brown, Howard W.
1985   "History of Siyu: The Development and Decline of a Swahili Town on the Northern Kenya Coast." Ph.D. dissertation, Indiana University.

Burton, Richard Frances, Sir
1876   *Two Trips to Gorilla-land and the Cataracts of the Congo*. 2 vols. London: S. Low, Marston, Low, and Searle.

Burton, William F. P.
1927   "The Country of the Baluba in Central Katanga." *Geographical Journal* 70, 4:321–42.
1961   *Luba Religion and Magic in Custom and Belief*. Sciences Humaines, 35. Tervuren: Annales. Musée Royal de l'Afrique Centrale.

Calvocoressi, David
1978   *Rescue Excavation of the First Otunba Suna*. Ibadan: Department of Archeology.

Capello, Hermenegildo and Robert Ivens
1969/1882   *From the Benguella to the Territory of Yacca. Description of a Journey into Central and West Africa*. Alfred Elwes, trans., 2 vols. New York: Negro University Press.

Carroll, Kevin
1966   *Yoruba Religious Carving: Pagan and Christian Sculpture in Nigeria and Dahomey*. New York: Praeger.

Ceyssens, Joseph Henry Cecil
1984   "Pouvoir et parente chez les Kongo-Dinga du Zaire." Ph.D. dissertation, Catholic University of Nijmegen.

Chaffin, Alain and Francoise Chaffin
1979   *L'art Kota: les figures de reliquaire*. Meudon: A. and F. Chaffin.

Christie's
1978   *African Art from the Collection of the Late Josef Mueller*. Catalogue of sale held June 13, 1978, London.
1989   *Tribal Art*. Catalogue of sale held July 4–5, 1989, London.
1992   *Important Tribal Art and Antiquities from the Collection of William A. McCarty-Cooper*. Catalogue of sale held May 19, 1992, New York.

Cincinnati Art Museum
1889   *Congo: Notes Taken from a Conversation with Carl Steckelmann, June 18, 1889*. Unpublished manuscript.

Cole, Herbert M. and Chike C. Aniakor
1984   *Igbo Arts: Community and Cosmos*. Los Angeles: UCLA Museum of Cultural History.

Cole, Herbert M. and Doran H. Ross
1977   *The Arts of Ghana*. Los Angeles: UCLA Museum of Cultural History.

Colle, Pierre
1913   *Les Baluba (Congo Belge)*. Brussels: Albert Dewit.

Conradt, L.
1902   "Die Ngumba in Sudkamerun." *Globus* 81:333–37, 350–72.

Cornet, Joseph
1972   *Art de l'Afrique noire au pays du fleuve Zaïre*. Brussels: Arcade.

Crowther, Samuel A.
1852   *A Vocabulary of the Yoruba Language*. London: Seeleys.

Dark, Philip J. C.
1982   *An Illustrated Catalogue of Benin Art*. Boston: G.K. Hall.

de Ganay, Solange
1947   "Un jardin d'essay et son autel chez les Bambara." *Journal de la Société des Africanistes* 17:57–63.
1949   "Aspects de mythologie et de symbolique Bambara." *Journal de psychologie normale et pathologie* 41, 2:181–201.

de Heusch, Luc
1982   *The Drunken King, or, The Origin of the State*. Roy Willis, trans. Bloomington: Indiana University Press.

de Maret, Pierre, Nicole Dery and Cathy Murdoch
1977   "The Luba-Shankadi Style." *African Arts* 7, 1:8–15, 88.

Denyer, Susan
1978   *African Traditional Architecture, A Historical and Geographical Perspective*. New York: Africana Publishing Co.

de Oliveira, Eresto Veiga
1972   *Peoples and Cultures*. Lisbon: Overseas Museum of Ethnology.

Deschamps, H.
1962   *Traditions orales et archives au Gabon: Contribution a l'ethno-histoire*. Paris: Berger-Levrault.

de Sousberghe, Leon
1959   *L'art Pende*. Brussels: Palais des academies.

Detavernier, H.
1990   "Terres cuites Koma du Nord-Ghana." *Arts d'Afrique Noire* 74:17–27.

de Vere Allen, James
1973   "A Further Note on Swahili Ornament." *Art and Archeology Papers* 4:pl. 1.
1979   "Siyu in the 18th and 19th Centuries." *Transafrican Journal of History* 1–2:20–24.

Dias, Antonio Jorge
1961   *Portuguese Contribution to Cultural Anthropology*. Johannesburg: Witwatersrand University Press.

Dias, Antonio Jorge and Margot Dias1
964   *Os Macondes de Mocambique*, 2 vols. Lisbon: Junta de Investigacões do Ultramar, Centro de Estudos de Anthropologia Cultural.

Digby, Simon
1975   "A Qur'an from the East African Coast." *Art and Archeology Research Papers* 7:51.

Dozon, Jean-Pierre
1985   *La société bété: Histoires d'une "Ethnie" de Cote-d'Ivoire*. Paris: ORSTOM/Karthala.

Drewal, Henry J.
1977   *Traditional Art of the Nigerian Peoples: The Milton D. Ratner Family Collection*. Washington, D.C.: Museum of African Art.
1987   "Art and Divination among the Yoruba: Design and Myth." *Africana Journal* 14, 2–3:139–56.
1988   "Beauty and Being: Aesthetics and Ontology in Yoruba Body Art." In A. Rubin, ed., *Marks of Civilization: Artistic Transformations of the Human Body*, 83–96. Los Angeles: UCLA Museum of Cultural History.
1989   "Art and Ethos of the Ijebu." In Drewal et al., eds., *Yoruba: Nine Centuries of African Art and Thought*, 117–45. New York: Center for African Art and H.N. Abrams.
1990   "African Art Studies Today," *African Art Studies: The State of the Discipline*, 29–62. Washington, D.C.: Smithsonian Institution Press.

Drewal, Henry J., J. Pemberton III, with R. Abiodun
1989   *Yoruba: Nine Centuries of African Art and Thought*. New York: Center for African Art and H. N. Abrams.

Drewal, Margaret T.
1992   *Yoruba Ritual: Performers, Play, Agency*. Bloomington: Indiana University Press.

Drewal, Margaret T. and Henry J. Drewal
1987   "Composing Time and Space in Yoruba Art." *Word and Image: A Journal of Verbal/Visual Enquiry* 3, 3:225–51.
1983   "An Ifa Diviner's Shrine in Ijebuland." *African Arts* 16, 2:60–67, 99–100.

Du Chaillu, Paul Belloni
1861   *Explorations and Adventures in Equatorial Africa*. New York: J. Murray.
1867   *A Journey to Ashango-land: and further penetration into Equatorial Africa*. London: J. Murray.

Ezra, Kate and Mary Jo Arnoldi
1992   "Sama Ba: The Elephant in Bamana Art." In Doran H. Ross, ed., *Elephant: The Animal and Its Ivory in African Culture*, 99–111. Los Angeles: UCLA Fowler Museum of Cultural History.

Fagg, William
1964   *Afrique: cent tribus - cent chefs-d'oeuvre*. Paris: Louvre.
1971   *African Sculpture from the Tara Collection*. Terre Haute: Art Gallery, University of Notre Dame.
1979   *Tribal Art*. Catalogue of sale held at Christies, April 3, 1979, London.

Fagg, William and Margaret Plass
1964   *African Sculpture: An Anthology*. London: Dutton.
1966   *African Sculpture: An Anthology*. Revised ed. London: Studio Vista.

Felix, Marc L.
1987   *100 Peoples of Zaire and Their Sculpture: The Handbook*. Brussels: Zaire Basin Art History Research Foundation.

Fernandez, J. and R.
1975   "Fang Reliquary Art: Its Quantities and Qualities." *Cahiers d'Etudes Africaines* 60, 15, 4:723–46.

Fitzgerald, R.T.D.
1942   "The Dakarkari Peoples of Sokoto Province, Nigeria: Notes on their Material Culture." *Man* 42:25–36.
1944   "Dakakari Grave Pottery." *Journal of the Royal Anthropological Institute* 74:43–57.

Fraser, Douglas and Herbert M. Cole, eds.
1972   *African Art and Leadership*. Madison: University of Wisconsin Press.

Freeman, Thomas Birch
1968/1844   *Journals of Various Visits to the Kingdoms of Ashanti, Aku, and Dahomi in Western Africa*. London: Cass.

Galhano, Fernando
1971   *Esculturas e objectos decorados da Guiné Portuguesa no Museu de Ethnologia Ultramar*. Lisbon: Junta de Investigaçes do Ultramar.

Gallois-Duquette, Danielle
1979   "Woman Power and Initiation in the Bissagos Islands." *African Arts* 12, 3:31–34, 93.
1983   *Dynamique de l'art Bidjogo (Guinée Bissau): Contribution à une anthropologie de l'art des Sociétés Africaines*. Lisbon: Instituto de Investigaço Cientifica Tropical.

Garrard, Timothy F.
1984   "Akan Silver." *African Arts* 17, 2:48–53.

Gillon, Werner
1979   *Collecting African Art*. New York: Rizzoli.

Gollnhofer, Otto, Pierre Sallée and Roger Sillans
1975   *Art et artisanat Tsogho*. Paris: Office de la recherche scientifique et technique outre-mer.

Green, Kathryn L.
1987   "Art and Ethnic Boundaries: Shared Masking Traditions in Northeastern Ivory Coast." *African Arts* 20, 4:62–69, 92.

Harris, P. G.
1938   "Notes on the Dakakari People." *Journal of the Royal Anthropological Institute* 68:113–52.

Herold, Erich
1985   "Traditional sculpture of the Bete tribe, Ivory Coast." *Annals of the Näprstek Museum* 13:81-166.

Hersak, Dunja
1986   *Songye Masks and Figure Sculpture.* London: Ethnographica.

Holy, Ladislav
1967   *Masks and Figures from Eastern and Southern Africa.* London: Paul Hamlyn.

Imperato, Pascal James
1970   "Dance of the Tyi Wara." *African Arts* 4, 1:8–13, 71–80.

Jeffreys, M. D. W.
1956a   "Anam Ofo: A Cult Object Among the Ibo." *South African Journal of Science* 52, 10:227–33.
1956b   "The Degeneration of the Ofo Anam." *Nigerian Field* 21, 4:173–77.

Johnson, Mark
1987   *The Body in the Mind: The Bodily Basis of Meaning, Imagination, and Reason.* Chicago: University of Chicago Press.

Kecskesi, Maria
1982   "The Pickaback Motif in the Art and Initiation of the Rovuma Area." *African Arts* 16, 1:52–55, 94–95.

Krieger, Kurt
1969   *Westafrikanische Plastik.* 3 vols. Berlin: Museum für Völkerkunde.
1990   *Ostafrikanische Plastik.* Berlin: Veröffentlichungen des Museums für Völkerkunde, N.F. 50.

Labouret, Henri
1931   *Les tribus du Rameau Lobi.* Travaux et Mémoires de l'Institute d'Ethnologie, 15. Paris: Insitute d'Ethnologie.

Laburthe-Tolra, Philippe
1985   *Initiations et sociétés secrètes au Cameroun: les mysteres de la nuit.* Paris: Karthala.

Laburthe-Tolra, Philippe and Christiane Falgayrettes-Leveau
1991   *Fang.* Paris: Musee Dapper.

Lawal, Babatunde A.
1970   "Yoruba Sango Sculpture in Historical Retrospect." Ph.D. dissertation, Indiana University.

Loudmer-Poulain
1979   *Arts primitifs. A divers amateurs, collection de M.X.* Catalogue of sale held November 22, 1979, Paris.

MacGaffey, Wyatt
1986   *Religion and Society in Central Africa: The BaKongo of Lower Zaire.* Chicago: University of Chicago Press.

Mack, John
1980   "Kuba Embroidery Patterns: A Commentary on their Social and Political Implications." In K.G. Ponting and S.S. Chapman, eds., *Textile History,* vol. 2, 163–74. Bath: Pasold Research Fund, Ltd.

McKesson, J.
1987   "Réflexions sur l'évolution de la sculpture des reliquaires Fang." *Arts d'Afrique Noire* 63:7–21.

Maeson, Albert
1956   "Les Holo du Kwango." *Reflets du monde* 9:31–44.

Meyer, Piet
1981   *Kunst und Religion der Lobi.* Zurich: Museum Rietberg.

Murray K. C.
1927-57 Unpublished archive material, National Museum, Lagos, Nigeria.

Neyt, Francois
1981   *Traditional Arts and History of Zaire: Forest Cultures and Kingdoms of the Savannah.* Brussels: Societe d'Arts Primitifs.
1985   "Tabwa Sculpture and the Great Traditions of East Central Africa." In Evan M. Maurer and Allen F. Roberts, eds., *Tabwa: The Rising of a New Moon: A Century of Tabwa Art,* 65–89. Ann Arbor: University of Michigan Museum of Art.

Nooter, Mary H.
1990   "Secret Signs in Luba Sculptural Narrative: A Discourse on Power." In Christopher D. Roy, ed., *Iowa Studies in African Art: The Stanley Conferences at The University of Iowa,* vol. 3. Iowa City: University of Iowa Press.
1991   "Luba Art and Statecraft: Creating Power in a Central African Kingdom." Ph.D. dissertation, Columbia University, New York.

Obayemi A.
1976   "The Yoruba and Edo-speaking Peoples and Their Neighbors Before 1600." In J.F. Ade Ajayi Ade and Michael Crowder, eds., *History of West Africa,* 2nd ed., vol. 1. London: Longman, Harlow.

Okae, Samuel Okoh
1971   "Body Decorations and Ornaments of the People of Mampong Ashanti." Senior thesis, University of Science and Technology, Kumasi.

Okediji, Moyo
1992   *Principles of 'Traditional' African Art.* Ibadan: Bard Book.

Olbrechts, Frans M.
1946   *Plastiek von Kongo.* Antwerp: Staandaard Boekhandel.
1959   *Les Arts Plastiques du Congo Belge.* Brussels: Editions Erasme.

Pachai, Bridglal
1973   *Malawi: The History of the Nation.* London: Longman.

Perrois, L.
1979   *Arts du Gabon: Les Arts Plastiques du Bassin de l'Ogooué.* Arnouville-les-Gonesse: Arts d'Afrique Noire.
1985   *Ancestral Art of Gabon: From the Collection of the Barbier-Mueller Museum.* Geneva: The Museum.

Picton, John
1991   "On Artifact and Identity at the Niger-Benue Confluence." *African Arts* 24, 3:34–49, 93–94.

Prouteaux, Maurice
1925   "Divertissements de Kong." *Bulletin du Comité études historiques et scientifiques de l'Afrique occidentale française* 8, 4:606–50.

Rangeley, W. H. J.
1963   "The Ayao." *Nyasaland Journal* 13, 1:7–27.
1964   "The Portuguese." *Nyasaland Journal* 17, 1:42–71.

Ravenhill, Philip
1980   *Baule Statuary Art: Meaning and Modernization.* Working Papers in the Traditional Arts, #5. Philadelphia: Institute for the Study of Human Issues.
1988   "An African Triptych: On the Intrepretation of Three Parts and the Whole." *Art Journal* 47, 2:88-94.

Reefe, Thomas Q.
1981   *The Rainbow and the Kings: A History of the Luba Empire to 1891.* Berkeley: University of California Press.

Robbins, Warren M. & Nancy Ingram Nooter
1989   *African Art in American Collections.* Washington: Smithsonian Institution Press.

Ross, Doran H.
1977   "The Iconography of Asante Sword Ornaments." *African Arts* 11, 1:16–25.
1982   "The Heraldic Lion in Akan Art: A Study of Motif Assimilation in Southern Ghana." *The Metropolitan Museum of Art Journal* 16:165–80.

Ross, Doran H. and Timothy Garrard, eds.
1983   *Akan Transformations: Problems in Ghanaian Art History.* Los Angeles: UCLA Museum of Cultural History.

Roy, Christopher D.
1985   *Art and Life in Africa: Selections from the Stanley Collection.* Iowa City: University of Iowa Museum of Art.

Rubin, William, ed.
1984   *"Primitivism" in 20th Century Art: Affinity of the Tribal and the Modern.* New York: Museum of Modern Art.

Ryder, Alan Frederick Charles
1969   *Benin and the Europeans, 1485-1897.* New York: Humanities Press, Inc.

Sarpong, Peter
1977   *Girl's Nubility Rites in Ashanti.* Tema, Ghana: Ghana Publishing Corporation.

Scantamburlo, Luigi
1978   "The Ethnography of the Bijagos People of the Island of Bubaque, Guinea-Bissau." M.A. thesis, Wayne State University.

Schaefer, Stacy
1983   "Benin Commemorative Heads." In Paula Ben-Amos and Arnold Rubin, eds., *The Art of Power, The Power of Art: Studies in Benin Iconography,* 71-78. Los Angeles: UCLA Museum of Cultural History.

Schildkrout, Enid and Curtis A. Keim
1990   *African Reflections: Art from Northeastern Zaire.* New York: American Museum of Natural History.

Sieber, Roy
1961   *Sculpture of Northern Nigeria.* New York: Museum of Primitive Art.

Siegmann, William C. with Cynthia E. Schmidt
1977   *Rock of the Ancestors: Liberian Art and Material Culture from the Collections of the Africana Museum.* Suakoko, Liberia: Cuttington University College.

Silverman, Raymond A.
Forthcoming   "Some Comments on the *Do* Traditions of the Bondoukou Region (Côte d'Ivoire)." In Patrick McNaughton, ed., *Exploring the Lands of Do.*

Siroto, Leon
1968   "The Face of the Bwiiti." *African Arts* 1, 3:22–27, 86–89, 96.

Soyinka, Wole
1987/1975   *Death and the King's Horseman.* New York: Hill and Wang.

Steckelmann, Carl
1889   *Descriptive Catalogue of the Collection of African Curiosities.* Indianapolis: Gilmore and Miller.

Temple, Olive Susan Miranda Macleod
1922   *Notes on the Tribes, Provinces, Emirates, and States of the Northern Provinces of Nigeria.* Lagos, Nigeria: C. M. S. Bookshop.

Tessmann, Günter
1912   "Die Kinderspiele der Pangwe." *Baessler-Archiv,* old series, 2:250–80.
1913   *Die Pangwe: völkerkundliche Monographie eines westafrikanischen Negerstammes; Ergebnisse der Lübecker Pangwe-expedition 1907–1909 und früherer Forschugen 1904–1907.* 2 vols. Berlin: E. Wasmuth.

Tew, Mary
1950 *Peoples of the Lake Nyasa Region*. London: Oxford University Press.

Thompson, Robert Farris and Joseph Cornet
1981 *The Four Moments of the Sun: Kongo Art in Two Worlds*. Washington, D.C.: National Gallery of Art.

Timmermans, Paul
1962 "Les Sapo Sapo pres de Luluabourg." *Africa-Tervuren* 8, 1/2:29–53.

Torday, Emil
1925 *On the Trail of the Bushongo: An Account of a Remarkable & Hitherto Unknown African People, Their Origin, Art, High Social & Political Organization & Other Culture*. London: Seeley, Service & Co., Ltd.

Torday, Emil and T.A. Joyce
1910 *Notes ethnographiques sur les peuples communément appelés Bakuba, ainsi que sur les peuplades apparentées. Les Bushongo*. Brussels: Musee Royal de l'Afrique Centrale.

Tuckey, James Hingston
1818 *Narrative of an Expedition to Explore the River Zaire, Usually Called the Congo, in South Africa, in 1816, under the Direction of Captain J. K. Tuckey*. London: J. Murray.

Underwood, Leon
1948 *Masks of West Africa*. London: Alec Tiranti, Ltd.

Vansina, Jan
1978 *The Children of Woot: A History of the Kuba Peoples*. Madison: University of Wisconsin Press.
1981 "Palm Wine Cups." In Susan Vogel, ed., *For Spirits and Kings: African Art from the Paul and Ruth Tishman Collection*, 231–32. New York: The Metropolitan Museum of Art.

Varnedoe, Kirk
1992 *Ideas and Objects: Towards a definition of Museum Scholarship*. Report of a joint meeting of The Smithsonian Forum on Material Culture and The Smithsonian History Roundtable.

Vogel, Susan M.
1977 *Baule Art as the Expression of a World View*. Ph.D. dissertation, New York University.
1980 *Beauty in the Eyes of the Baule: Aesthetics and Cultural Values*. Working Papers in the Traditional Arts, #6. Philadelphia: Institute for the Study of Human Issues.
1988 "Baule Scarification: The mark of Civilization." In Arnold Rubin, ed., *Marks of Civilization: Artistic Transformations of the Human Body*, 97-105. Los Angeles: UCLA Museum of Cultural History.

Wardwell, Allen
1986 *African Sculpture from the University Museum, University of Pennslyvania*. Philadelphia: Philadelphia Museum of Art.

Wembah-Rashid, J. A. R.
1971 "Isinyago and Midimu." *African Arts* 4, 2:38–44.

Wenga-Mulayi, M.
1974 "Etude socio-morphologique des masques blancs Luba ou *bifwebe*." Mémoire de licence, Université Nationale du Zaire, Lubumbashi.

Werner, Alice
1906 *The Natives of British Central Africa*. London: Archibald Constable & Co., Ltd.

Westerdijk, Peter
1984 *African Metal Implements: Weapons, Tools, and Regalia*. Greenvale, N.Y.: Hillwood Art Gallery, School of the Arts, Long Island University.

Weston, Bonnie E.
1984 "Northeastern Region," In Herbert M. Cole and Chike C. Aniakor, eds., *Igbo Arts: Community and Cosmos*, 145–61. Los Angeles: UCLA Museum of Cultural History.

Williams, Jeri Bernadette
1992 "Power and Survival: Form and Function of Bidjogo Shrine Sculpture." M.A. thesis, University of California, Los Angeles.

Yoshida, Kenji
1992 "Masks and Transformations Among the Chewa of Eastern Zambia." In Shohei Wada and Paul K. Eguchi, eds., *Africa 4*, 203-274. Senri Ethnological Studies No. 31. Osaka, Japan: National Museum of Ethnology.

Zahan, Dominique
1960 *Sociétés d'initiation Bambara: le N'domo, le Korè*. Paris: Mouton and Co.
1974 *The Bambara*. Leiden: E.J. Brill.
1978 "Kore Hyena Mask." In Jacqueline Fry, ed., *Twenty-Five African Sculptures*, 44–48. Ottawa: National Gallery of Canada.
1980 *Antilopes du soleil: arts et rites agraires d'Afrique noire*. Vienna: Edition A. Schendl.
1981 "Antelope Headdress: Female (*Chi Wara*)." In Susan Vogel, ed., *For Spirits and Kings: African Art from the Tishman Collection*, 22–24. New York: Metropolitan Museum of Art.

Zirngibl, Manfred A.
1983 *Seltene Afrikanische Kurzwaffen. Rare African Short Weapons. Rares armes courtes africaines*. Grafenau: Morsak-Verlag.

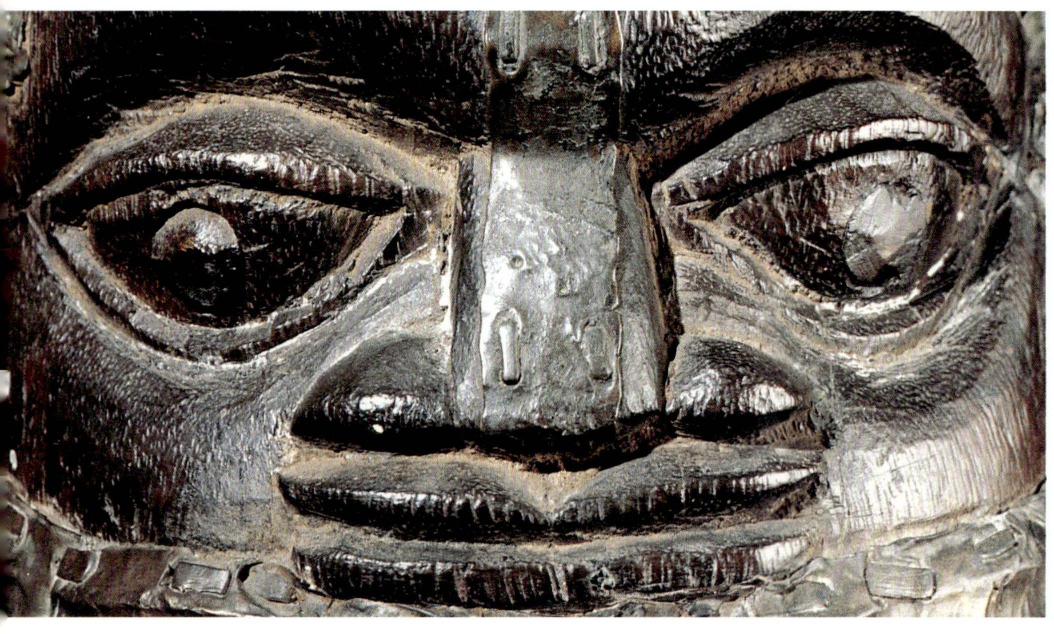

▾▲▾

PUBLICATION PRESENTATION

UCLA PUBLICATION DESIGN SERVICES

JUDY HALE   Production Coordination

BARBARA KELLY   Publication Design

FOWLER MUSEUM OF CULTURAL HISTORY

DANIEL R. BRAUER   Director of Publications

ELISABETH L. CAMERON   Research Assistant

ANTHONY A.G. KLUCK   Assistant Director of Publications

DENIS J. NERVIG   Photography (unless otherwise noted)

AMY WALSH   Editing

The following photograhs are by Richard Todd. Figures 12 and 32.
Catalogue 3, 4, 5 (detail), 8, 11, 13, 25, 25 (detail), 28, 30, 38, 42a,
42b, 44, 48, 51, 55, 60, 62, 67 (detail), 70, 74, 75, 77, 81, 82, 84 and 87.

*Editing and layout were accomplished on Macintosh computers using
QuarkXPress and Adobe Garamond and Stone font software.*

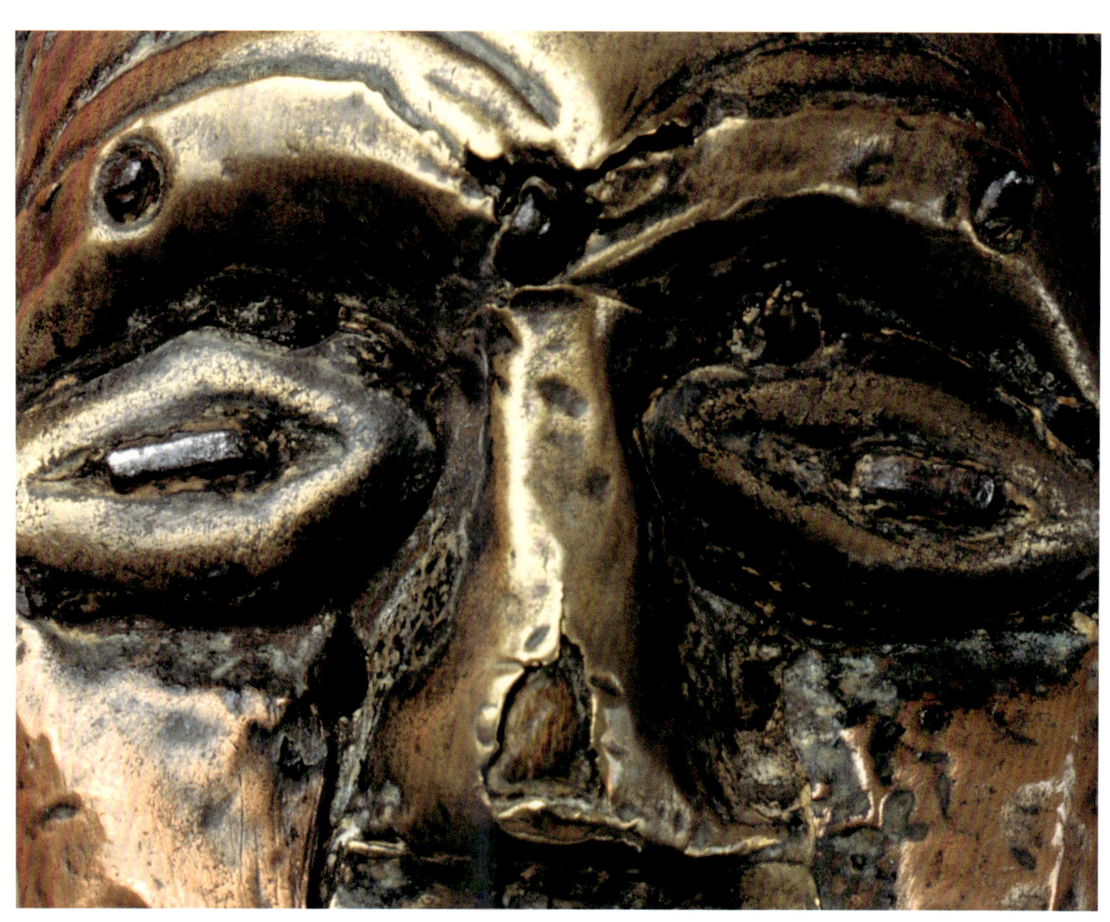

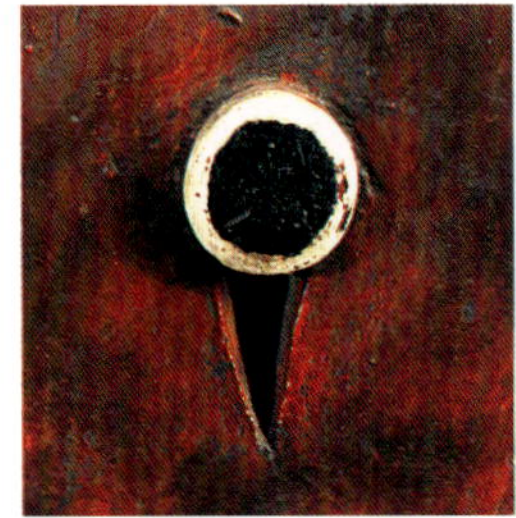